ADMINISTRATIVE AND MANAGEMENT THINKERS

Relevance in New Millennium

BOOKS BY THE SAME AUTHOR

1. Advanced Public Administration
2. Public Administration: Theory and Practice
3. Public Financial Administration
4. Public Health Policy and Administration
5. Public Personnel Administration: Theory and Practice
6. Administration and Management of NGOs: Text and Case Studies
7. Panchayati Raj in India: Theory and Practice
8. Urban Development and Management
9. Management Techniques: Principles and Practices
10. Encyclopaedia of Disaster Management (Set in 3 Vols.)
11. Management of Hospitals: Hospital Administration in the 21st Century (Set in 4 Vols.)
12. Hospital Core Services
13. Hospital Managerial Services
14. Hospital Preventive and Promotive Services
15. Hospital Supportive Services
16. Health Care System and Management (Set in 4 Vols.)
17. Health Care Management and Administration
18. Primary Health Care Management
19. Health Care Organisation and Structure
20. Health Care, Policies and Programmes
21. Nursing Services: Management and Administration
22. Distance Education in 21st Century
23. Encyclopaedia of Higher Education in 21st Century
24. Human Values and Education
25. Stress Management
26. Population Policy and Family Welfare Administration
27. International Administration
28. International Civil Service : Principles, Practice and Prospects
29. Social Welfare Administration (2 Volumes)
30. Family Planning Programme and Beyond
31. Education Policy and Administration
32. Human Resource Development in 21st Century
33. Disaster Management
34. Slum Improvement through Participatory Urban Based Community Structures
35. Development Planning and Administration
36. Public Health Administration
37. Hospital Administration: Theory and Practice
38. Principles, Problems and Prospects of Co-operative Administration
39. Personnel Administration in Co-operatives
40. Public Personnel Administration and Management
41. Right to Information and Good Governance
42. Health Education: Theory and Practice
43. School Health Education
44. Good Governance: An Integral Approach
45. Disaster Administration and Management

IN PRESS

46. Education of Lifestyle and Lifetime Diseases
47. Health Education of Communicable and Non-Communicable Disease
48. Health Education Administration : From International Level to Village Level
49. Education for Healthy Urban Cities
50. Environment and Value Education
51. Women Health Education
52. Rural Health Education

ADMINISTRATIVE AND MANAGEMENT THINKERS

Relevance in New Millennium

DR. S.L. GOEL
Editor, The Indian Journal of Public Administration, New Delhi
Former Vice-President, Executive Council,
Indian Institute of Public Administration, New Delhi
Professor of Public Administration (Retd.)
Panjab University, Chandigarh
Emeritus Fellow, University Grants Commission
Director, State Bank of India (Local Board), Chandigarh
Director, National Horticulture Board, Ministry of Horticulture,
Government of India, New Delhi
Formerly Member UGC, Member Distance Education Council
and Member All India Board of Management, AICTE

DEEP & DEEP PUBLICATIONS PVT. LTD.
F-159, Rajouri Garden, New Delhi-110027

ADMINISTRATIVE AND MANAGEMENT THINKERS
Relevance in New Millennium

ISBN 978-81-8450-077-6

Typeset by S.S. COMPOSERS,
3190, Mohindra Park, Shakur Basti, Delhi-110034.

Printed in India at MAYUR ENTERPRISES,
WZ Plot No. 3, Gujjar Market, Tihar Village, New Delhi - 110 018.

Published by DEEP & DEEP PUBLICATIONS PVT. LTD.
F-159, Rajouri Garden, New Delhi-110027.
Phones: 25435369, 25440916
E-mail: ddpbooks@yahoo.co.in • ddpubs@gmail.com
Showroom:
2/13, Ansari Road, Daryaganj, New Delhi-110002 • Telefax: 23245122

Contents

Preface

The evolution of Public Administration and Management is as essential or rather more significant than the development of science and technology as the benefits of science and technology can be harnessed through Public Administration and Management.

"If our civilization fails" declared Prof. W.B. Donhm of Harvard, "it will be mainly because of a breakdown of administration." "There is no subject", says Charles A. Beard, "more important . . . . Than this subject of administration. The future of civilized government, and even, I think, of civilization itself rests upon our ability to develop a science, a philosophy and a practice of administration, competent to discharge the functions of civilized society."

"Good Public Administration", writes Leif H. Share, Director of the Government Institution of Organization and Management, Oslo, Norway, "could serve as a major instrument for promoting economic and social development and for introducing needed advances in science and technology; but major reforms in the organizations and operations of government and in the knowledge, skills and attitudes of public employees at all levels were often necessary for it to do so; deficiencies in administration had been a major reason for past failures in the implementation of national development plans."

The existing knowledge of Public Administration and Management is not a sudden development but it took thousands of years to develop this knowledge to ensure decent life to the people.

Public Administration and Management are not independent disciplines as the knowledge of social sciences, physical sciences, natural sciences have their bearing on them. All the thinkers have taken care of other disciplines as far as they impinge on the theory and practice of Public Administration and Management.

It was not possible to include all the Administrative thinkers as their number is vast. A great effort has to be made by many thinkers till the Administrative thought is fructified. It is being developed as the ecology, particular knowledge of science and technology goes on changing.

We have included 23 Administrative Thinkers in this book. The first two have been included with a purpose, i.e. Srimad Bhagavad Geeta and Ramayana by Lord Krishna and Lord Rama respectively. These two thinkers have elaborated their thought in ancient times in India. Their thoughts are relevant for all times and especially in the present context. These two philosophers exclusively talk on how to manage life in order to get bliss on this earth. Thus, their approach is to provide thoughts to make this universe worth-living. Other thinkers have developed their theories according to their perception and need of that time. All of them have done excellent work and through their readings we can improve the administration and management at all levels.

Though many of the thinkers have been criticized later on but most of us forget that they had written at a given point when circumstances were different. However, they remain relevant, for example, we are making use of Taylor's theory in disaster management (Incident Command System) in USA and India.

All the chapters have been supplemented with case studies, charts and specifically their relevance for the present administration and management thought. We are highly indebted to all those thinkers in the book and not included in the book for giving their creative and innovative thoughts to the development of the discipline and profession.

It is hoped that the book "Administrative and Management Thinkers: Relevance in 21st Century" would be of great use to students of Public Administration and Business Management as well as to those who are working in administration whether in government, private sector, public enterprises, etc.

S.L. GOEL

PART A

1

Lord Krishna: Geeta

Bhagavad Gita which is called the Gospel of Humanity deals with metaphysics, religious outlook and ethical codes recommends a strenuous life but does not give any room for selfish impulses. Gita is the philosophy of karma (action) based on jnana (knowledge) and supported by Bhakti (devotion). Gita implies that the self-effort is the keynote for success. It gives advice to be self-reliant, be bold, be manly and cheerful, do one's duty with a sense of devotion, develop a balanced mind, humility, purity, self-control and service to others. It gives the message that, to fight against the evil is the duty of man, Nishkama Karma or selfless devotion to duty is the advocated value for everyone in the present time. Dharma is the universal guiding force to attain self-perfection and social harmony. Ancient Indian Education was mostly value based and aimed at the cultivation of such virtues like truth, goodness, beauty, non-violence sincerity honesty, respect, altruism, compassion, love and duty. Certain virtues or ethical modes sustain the glory of the earth.[1]

Today, the world as a whole is passing through a terrible crisis. The old world with its thoughts, opinions, and institutions is in a state of rapid dissolution; none can yet see clearly the shape of things to come. Deeply imbedded in the modern consciousness is a desire for the creation of a stable

FIG. 1.1

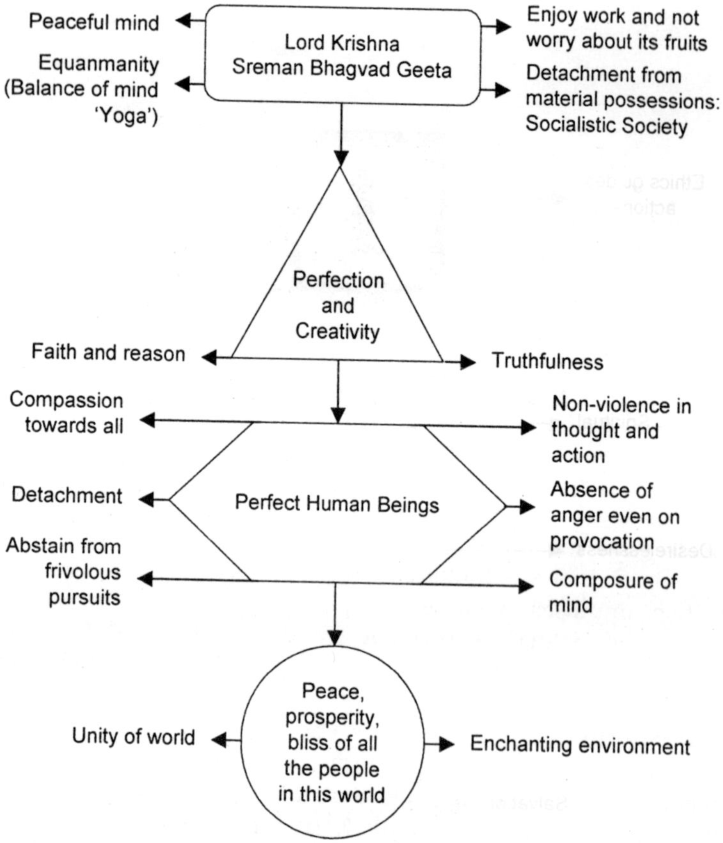

civilization. Thinkers in the East and the West give expression to this urge when they speak of the future world order. If the future is to witness the emergence of world civilization, the collective wisdom of mankind has to be utilized for its realization, the greatest contribution shall come not from sects and creeds or parties and leaders, but from the spiritual benefactors of humanity, like Krsna, Rama, Buddha, Jesus, and Mohammad. The present world context, with its gushing passions and high aspirations, somewhat resembles the conditions that obtained in India in the age of the Mahabharata war when the message of the Gita was

FIG 1.2

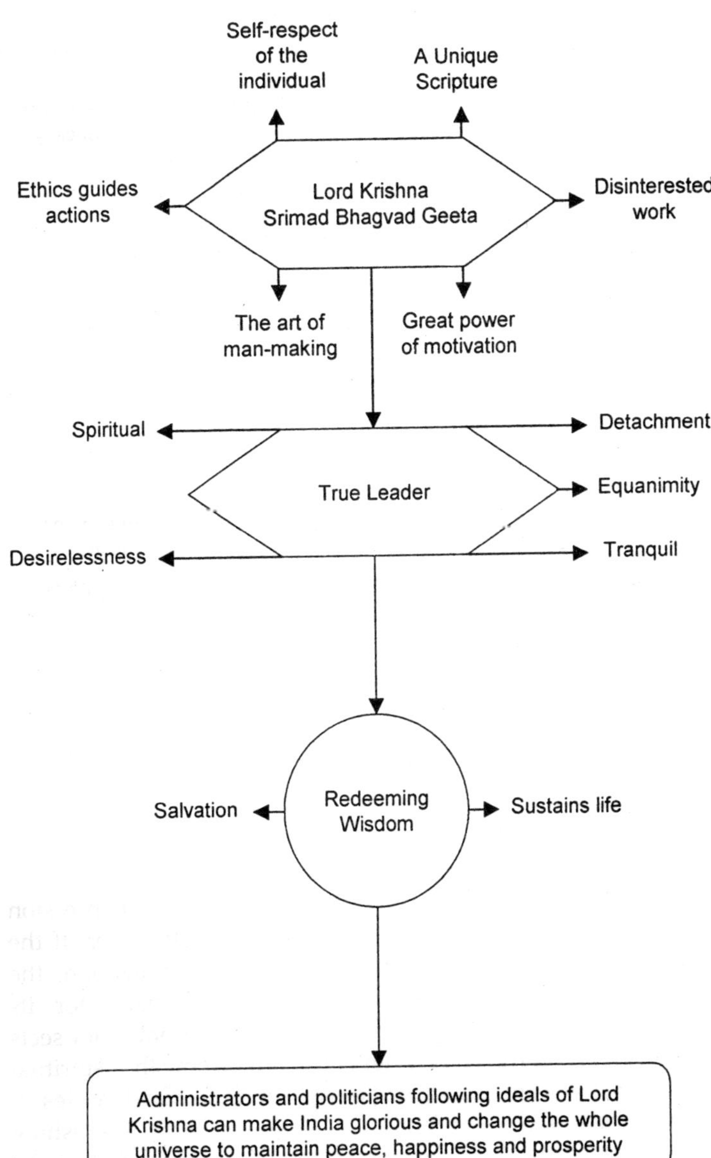
Self-respect of the individual
A Unique Scripture
Ethics guides actions
Lord Krishna Srimad Bhagvad Geeta
Disinterested work
The art of man-making
Great power of motivation
Spiritual
Detachment
True Leader
Equanimity
Desirelessness
Tranquil
Salvation
Redeeming Wisdom
Sustains life
Administrators and politicians following ideals of Lord Krishna can make India glorious and change the whole universe to maintain peace, happiness and prosperity

delivered. In these days of conflict, struggle, and confusion, we can have no better guide to show us the path to freedom and peace than the message of the rational, universal, and comprehensive spirituality which Krsna taught in the Gita over 3000 years ago. It is God's message to man—eternal, ancient, and ageless. Momentous problems are there before us which stagger the wisdom of the earth's bravest and the best. Let us hope and pray that the new interest that is evident in many quarters in the 'song cesteial', as Edwin Arnold called the Gita may be productive of real and lasting benefit to humanity at large.[2]

Among the leaders of thought and action who have appeared on the Indian horizon, none stands so unique for nobility of thought and versataility of character as Bhagavan Sri Krsna, the great teacher of the Bhagavad Gita. With the increasing popularity of the Gita in modern times, a growing appreciation of the personality of Sri Krsna is becoming evident. In the West, Carlyle, Walt Whitman, and Emerson were the first to respond to the spiritual beauty and philosophic depth of the Gita. Burnouf, the French translator of the Gita, wrote that 'no greater book has ever come from the hands of man'?[3]

The Gita is not an original work in the sense in which we usually understand the term, though it is supremely original statement of what Aldous Huxley calls 'The Perennial Philosophy'. It is a continuation of the ancient philosophy that you find in the Upanisads. The Gita summarizes the essential teachings of Vedanta and presents them in a popular manner. That is why it has become the scripture of the vast masses in this country. When we study the Gita, we are not merely studying the Upanisadic philosophy, but also the ethical implications of that philosophy. We want ethical guidance, and the Gita provides it. A metaphysics which speaks of the highest Reality without reference to everyday life will not be of much use to us. Therefore, the sublime ethical implications of the Vedanta are elaborated in the Gita.

From all these considerations the Gita has assumed an importance in our life, and that importance is increasing day-by-day. In his preface to the English edition of the Gita by Charles Wilkins, Warren Hastings, the first British Governor General of India, declared that 'the writers of the Indian philosophies will survive, when the British dominion shall have long ceased to exist and the sources which it yielded of wealth and power are lost to remembrance'. Since these lines were written, the Gita has been establishing an ever-widening empire in the hearts of men and women both in the East and the West. Its appeal to the thinking minds of India in the past, is in sharp contrast to the indifference and often hostility displayed by the modern mind to the scriptures and prophets of the world. The source of this power lies in the two important features of its message — its rationality and its universality.[4]

Duty: The First Stage of Ethical Discipline

To this end, the Gita gives a two-fold advice. Firstly, all work, whether pleasant or unpleasant, should be performed in the sense of duty. What does this imply? That work by itself is neither high nor low, but the preferences of the ego evaluate all work according to its whims. It is at this stage that man seeks for a comfortable life and a comfortable religion. The sense of duty teaches us to disregard the false values which the ego has attached to 'life and work'. This negation of the ego and its values is also the transcendence of the ego itself. This helps us to realize the second characteristics of the saksin, namely, freedom from limited vision or, what amounts to the same thing, getting universality of outlook. Secondly, by not caring for the fruits of our actions or by being unattached to them, we are asked to realize the first characteristic of the saksin, namely, detachment. The only condemnation of the Gita makes of those who work with various selfish motives is that they are men of small understanding: krpanah phalahetavah, and defines karma-yoga as dexterity in action: yogah karmasu kausalam. It extols this attitude in these words. (Gita II, 51) The Wise, possessed of this evenness of minds abandoning the fruits of their actions, freed for ever from the fetters of life, attain that state which is beyond all evil.

In its comprehensive vision of the drama of human life on earth, the Gita ever seeks to impart to man a sense of purpose and direction, which is spiritual freedom and perfection; prevents him from getting stuck up in a static sect or system, by exhorting him to move on and grow and develop; and inspires him with a spirit of active tolerance and fellowship, by gently pointing out to him that the goal is one, though the paths are many. The modern world, with its prevailing confusion of values and ends, has need to capture this vision of the Gita and turn its course, in the beautiful language of the Vedic hymn (Brhadaranyaka Upanisad, I, 3.28), from the unreal to the real, from darkness to light, and from death to immortality:

Asato ma sat gamaya;
Tamaso majyotir gamaya;
Mrtyor ma amrtam gamaya

From the unreal lead me to the real, from darkness lead me to light, from death lead me to immortality.

The Upanisadic vibrations of truth and beauty, goodness and love, became caught in a later stage in a mighty condenser of personality, who shook up India spiritually and politically during his earthly career round about 1400 B.C. and whose voice continues to shake up even today. Sri Krsna, the author of the Gita, has affected Indian thought and life in such a profound way that has no parallel in India or elsewhere; his influence is both intensive and extensive.

True knowledge must therefore be made the basis of all that we do in society; and the mark of true knowledge, we read, in humility rather than arrogance; candour in lieu of hypocrisy, peace and purity instead of restlessness; and passion, and earnest self-control taking the place of egoistic attachment to things of sense. The knowledge needed can be acquired, normally, through the gateways of sense; but another and a surer way, we learn, is that of patience inward contemplation and Yogic concentration. The proper object of such contemplation has to be, naturally, what we have been taught to learn and honour as the highest Ideal. Such Ideals can conceivably be different, and different also can be the methods of acquiring and realizing them.[5]

The Gita is a bottomless sea containing endless strata of meaning. Just as a diver diving deep into the sea lays his hands on precious gems, even so, diving deeper and deeper into the secrets of the Gita, the seeker goes on discovering ever new piles of extraordinary gems of ideas. But the king of birds, Garuda, as well as the tiny mosquito both take their flight in the air, each according to his or its capacity. In the same way each and every student of the Gita makes something out of it according to his or her comprehension.

There is a world of difference between the cult of equanimity preached by the Gita and the doctrine of the so called equality preached by modern socialism. Modern socialism is anti-theistic in its outlook, whereas the cult of equanimity preached by the Gita sees God everywhere and in everything. One uproots Religion, while the other upholds Religion at every step; one is violent in its conception, while the other establishes the principle of non-violence; one is based on self-interest, while the other has no room for selfishness. One, though abolishing all distinctions in the matter of interdining and social intercourse, etc., maintains disunion in spirit; while the other, though maintaining due discrimination in the matter of interdining and social intercourse according to the bounds prescribed in the Sastras, does not admit any disparity in spirit and exhorts us to perceive the Supreme Spirit as the same in all. The goal of one is mammon-worship, while that of the other is God-Realization. In one there is identification with one's party and disrespect for others; while in the other there is complete absence of pride, and respect for all which comes from a sense of the immanence of God. In one, there is emphasis on external behaviour, while in the other it is the spirit which matters; in one it is material happiness which is of primary importance, while in other it is spiritual happiness that counts; in one there is want of tolerance for others' wealth and others' views, in the other there is equal respect for all; one is dominated by partiality and prejudice, while the other prescribes conduct which is free from partiality and prejudice.[6]

There is hardly any room for doubt that there was a great personality named Krsna, who was a Ksatriya king and a householder, though the details of his life remain mostly legendary. He lived in the world, but was not of the world. Having attained a great spiritual height, he attempted to preach Brahma-jnana to the then existing society. He realized in his life the ancient truth of the Rg.Veda that 'Existence is One, which the sages call by various names', and tried to reconcile contradictory philosophical and religious views of people.[7]

Let us discuss the important administrative concepts in Srimad Bhagavad Geeta which are more advanced than the existing one. Their understanding would help the people to lead a life of bliss.

1. The Art of Man-making

When a determined nation elaborately plans for its own development and progress apart from its political plans and economic schemes, it must necessarily look for its own cultural genius in order to impart, mould and polish the character of the individuals. The nation-building work starts with the discovery of a mental poise and a physical dynamism in the young intelligent citizens. All the great thinkers through their varied philosophical flights have in their final conclusions realised the need for programmes to evolve the individual. By disciplining and thereby improving the individual even culture tries to raise the tempo of quality and beauty of the total national life. A world ordered for progress through improved individuals constituting the community is the direction in which all philosophers and scriptural prophets preach and work. Bhagawad Geeta is a scripture which tries to integrate the personality of the individual student and make him capable of facing dynamically all his challenges in life. In short, when the modern world in its materialistic viewpoint strives to bring about a higher standard of living by improving the world around man, the deep thinkers of the scriptures and the rational philosophers conclusively indicate that the happiness and glory of the world depend upon the standard of life that the individuals come to live.

Every nation must determine its own political institution and economic system and work out diligently the schemes that they evolve. So too. philosophers of the world have their exhaustive theories and detailed schemes for the development of the human personality. The Bhagawad Geeta reveals certain definite schemes by which every individual can work out his own self-improvement. The nation is constituted of individual citizens. If the citizens are strong, efficient, industrious, self-sacrificing then nation becomes great; if the individuals are selfish, immoral, idle and corrupt, it would be a sad nation indeed. In individual redemption lies national redemption and progress. In the Bhagawad Geeta philosophical theories are couched in a language of least confusion and she suggests schemes for self-improvement which are unique in their variety and effectiveness. They are most acceptable to the intelligent modern youth—as they are direct, simple and easy-to-do-exercises for the unfoldment of personality.[8]

2. Good Governance

The test of Good Governance is to promote the physical, social and spiritual development of the people. In Mahabharata in addition to various places where duties of King and his officials are described, an entire book, Shanti Parva, has been devoted to the art of governance. After the Great War, King Yudhishthira approached his grandfather Bhishma who was lying on a bed of arrows and requested him to give a discourse on the duties and morality of King, state officials, and of the public. Some of these Elements and Essentials of Good Governance are listed below:

1. The eternal duties of kings are to make their subjects happy, to observe truth, and to act sincerely.

   (Shanti Parva, Chapter LVIII, Verse 11)

2. One becomes a king for protecting Dharma and enhancing virtuous acts, and not for acting capriciously. (The same is applicable to his ministers and servants.)

   (Shanti Parva, Chapter XC, Verse 3)

3. Righteousness is called Dharma. It is Dharma that restrains and limits all evil act of men, therefore, a king should follow the dictates of Dharma.

(Shanti Parva, Chapter XC, Verses 18, 19)

Our scriptures have laid emphasis on implementing policy as ordained in Dharma. To quote:

Tasmacchastram pramanam te karyakaryavyavasthitau
Snatva sastra vidhanoktam karma kartum iharhasi

(One ought to understand what is duty, and what is forbidden in the commands laid down by the scriptures (Shastras). Knowing such rules and regulations, one should behave as ordained by scriptures]

(Gita, Chapter XVI, Verse 24)

Lord Krishna further says:

Pravrittim cha nivrittim cha karyakarye bhayabhaye

[O Partha ! that understanding by which one knows what ought to be done and what ought not to be done, what is to be feared and what is not, what is obligatory and what is permitted, leads to the righteous path (Sattviki Pravritti).

To quote Yajurveda:

O virtuous and prosperous king, be knowledgeable about your conduct as protector of the learned, and impeller towards our progress and prosperity. Be in control of your passions, and conduct yourself in a righteous manner. Be a friend to us. Know the conduct as laid down by all sages.

(Yajurveda, Chapter VIII, Verse 50)

To quote Shanti Parva:

The foundation of good governance is Dharma (righteousness). The King, his ministers and state employees who have taken the oath of their offices to uphold Dharma and to act in accordance with the common good, must not act unjustly or unethically so as to secure their private good through selfishness. If they don't behave appropriately, they all will surely go to hell along with destroying the moral basis of governance.

[Shanti Parva, Chapter LXXXV, Verses 16-17]

To quote Manusmriti:

1. Brahma has created the King to be the protector of the Varna and public order [common good) so that they discharge their several duties according to their Dharma and rank.

   (Manusmriti, Book VII, Verse 35)

2. Thus conducting himself (and) ever intent on (discharging) his [prescribed) royal duties, a King shall order all his officials (to work) for the good of his subjects.[9]

   (Manusmriti, Book IX, Verse 324)

Vidura advises Dhrtarastra to engage in the welfare of the people

यथा यथा हि पुरुषः कल्याणें कुरुते मनः ।
तथा तथास्य सर्वार्थाः सिद्धयन्ते नात्र संशय ।।

Vidura-Niti-Udyoga Parva

Dharma for a king is to look after the welfare of the people.

मानसं सर्वभूतानां धर्ममाहुर्मनीषिणः ।
तस्मात् सर्वेषु भूतेषु मनसा शिवमाचेरत् ।।

शान्ति 183 - 31

अद्रोहेणैव भूतानां यः स धर्मः सतां मतः।

शान्ति 21-11-12
Udyoga-Parva

Bhisma Pitamaha advised Yudhisthira that truth and right conduct are essential for a king. Besides, he should follow the path shown by noble people.

न हि सत्यादृते किंचिद् राज्ञां वै सिद्धिकारकम् ।
सत्ये हि राजा निरतः प्रेत्य चेह च नन्दति ।।

शान्ति 56-17

Through these and various other verses, moral tone has been set for the conduct of a King, and good governance of the kingdom."[10]

3. Acquire Complete Knowledge about Good Governance

तद्विद्धि प्रणिपातेन परिप्रश्नेन सेवया ।
उपदेक्ष्यन्ति ते ज्ञानं ज्ञानिनस्तत्त्वदर्शिनः ।। 4/34

Bhagavad Gita

Understand the true nature of that Knowledge by approaching illumined soul. If you prostrate at their feet, render them service, and question them with an open and guiltless heart, those wise seers of Truth will instruct you in that Knowledge

For the attainment of Knowledge, faith, reverence and guiltlessness of heart are of primary importance. The intention is to make it clear that spiritual instruction given to a man devoid of faith and reverence cannot be properly received and retained by him. Illumined souls need no prostrations, personal services, respect and homage for themselves. But they do not feel inclined to discuss the higher truths when someone asks them impertinent questions with a heart full of pride and mischief and with a view to testing their knowledge. Therefore, he who desires to attain Knowledge should in the first instance approach the preceptor with faith and reverence in his heart, and surrendering himself to serve him to the best of his ability. Just as water flows from a higher to a lower level, so too, knowledge can flow only to lower level. It is, therefore, essential for a student to be desirous of getting such knowledge which can make him perfect.

The object of true knowledge is the integral Brahma or God, who is Truth, Consciousness and Bliss solidified for it is He who is realized through such knowledge. Constantly visualizing that transcendent reality as equally present everywhere is what is meant by "seeing that object of true knowledge."

The opposites of virtues, viz., lust for honour and glory, hypocrisy, violence, anger, duplicity, crookedness, malice, impurity, fickleness, covetousness, attachment, egotism, the sense of mineness, differentiation, impiety, association with evil man and other such evil propensities are conducive to the growth of ignorance, which is the cause of birth and death and degrade the soul. Hence they are the same as ignorance and as such should be totally abandoned.

True, that spiritual illumination shines of itself in a pure heart, and, as such, it is not something acquired from without; but to attain this purity of heart means long struggle and constant practice. It has also been found, on careful enquiry in the sphere of material knowledge, that those higher truths which have now and then been discovered by great scientific men, have flashed like sudden floods of light in their mental atmosphere, which they had only to catch and formulate. But such truths never appear in the mind of an uncultured and wild savage. All these go to prove that hard Tapasya, or practice of austerities, in the shape of devout contemplation and constant study of a subject, is at the root of all illumination, in its respective spheres.[11]

Knowledge is powerful and without this public officials cannot discharge their duties. In this context, it may be of interest to note that without the expert trainers and desirous trainees, there can be no knowledge. Knowledge depends both on the teacher and taught.

Men should act according to buddhi or understanding. If we are victims of our impulses, our life is as aimless and devoid of intelligence as that of the animals. If we do not interfere, attachments and aversions will determine our acts. So long as we act in certain ways because we like them and abstain from others because we dislike them, we will be bound by our actions. But if we overcome these impulses and act from a sense of duty, we are not victims of the play of prakrti. The exercise of human freedom is conditioned and not cancelled by the necessities of nature.[12]

न हि ज्ञानेन सदृशं पवित्रमिह विद्यते ।
तत्स्वयं योगसंसिद्धः कालेनात्मनि विन्दति ।।

4/38 Bhagavad Gita

There is no purifier as great as Knowledge, as knowledge is power, he who has attained purity of heart through a prolonged practice of Karmayoga automatically sees the light to Truth in the self in course of time.

4. Dedication and Devotion to Work

मयि सर्वाणि कर्माणि संन्यस्याध्यात्मचेतसा ।
निराशीर्निर्ममो भूत्वा युध्यस्व विगतज्वरः।।

3/30 Bhagavad Gita

Therefore, so long as while performing action or enjoying their fruit a participant is found to have the feeling of possession and desire with regard to those actions and their fruit, or so long as his mind is subject of morbid feelings such as attraction and repulsion, joy and grief, etc., it should be clearly understood that all his actions have not been dedicated to god or public good.

Pt. Jawaharlal Nehru, while addressing the Fourth Annual General Body Meeting of the Indian Institute of Public Administration, appropriately remarked that:

> "In a period of dynamic growth, however, we want as civil servants—persons who are not, if I may use the word without any disrespect, merely head clerks but people with minds, people with vision, people with

desire to achieve, who have some initiative for doing a job and who can think how to do it. But, the person who is to be completely neutral is a head clerk and no more. He would do his work efficiently as a head clerk, no doubt but nothing more. Can a person be neutral, I ask you, about basic things which we stand for, our state stands for, our plan stands for e.g. a socialist pattern of society."[13]

तस्मादसक्त: सततं कार्यं कर्म समाचर ।
असक्तो ह्याचरन् कर्म परमाप्नोति पूरुष: ।।

3/19 Bhagavad Gita

We should go on efficiently doing our duty without attachment. Doing work without attachment man attains the Supreme, i.e. excellence.

Renunciation of attachment involves renunciation of desire as well; for it is from attachment that desire springs up (II. 62). Desire will cease when renunciation is followed. It is, therefore, that renunciation of the desire for fruit has not been separately mentioned.

Public officials who become attached to senses, they cannot achieve excellence. They become slaves of their senses. They should work without having any personal interest as it causes diversion leading to blockage of mind.

ध्यायतो विषयान् पुंस: सङ्गस्तेषूपजायते ।
सङ्गात्संजायते काम: कामात्क्रोधोऽभिजायते ।।

2/62 Bhagavad Gita

The man relying on sense objects develops attachment for them; from attachment comes up desire, and from desire (unfulfilled) springs anger. Anger disturbs the equilibrium of mind causing imbalance.

Sri Krishna explains Yoga as 'balance of mind' (Chap. II.48). When an action is motivated by desire, anxiety as to whether the desired result is going to be obtained or not will surely disturb the peace of mind of the doer. Again, when an action is inspired by self-interest, the doer is likely to lose sight of what is right or what is wrong. Even when he has chosen to do the right thing. undue eagerness for obtaining the result is likely to make him swerve .from the path of rectitude; whereas a doer, if he is detached towards the result, is saved from all anxiety. There is nothing to divert him from the righteous path. This teaching that we ought to discharge our obligations, social or otherwise, with a sense of responsibility, at the same time banishing from our minds all thought of obtaining personal benefit there from and in a spirit dedication to the Lord is what is meant by Karma-Yoga.[14]

मा वाऽकर्ता भव प्राज्ञ किमकत्तर्ण्तयेहिते ।
साध्यं साध्यमुपादेयं तस्मात्स्वस्थो भवानघ ।।

|| 7 || (Utpatti Pakasna Book 3)

Neither think yourself as actor, because no actor can manage to do anything. Conduct whatever is your duty, and remain at your ease with having done your part. (Yoga Vasistha-Utpatti-Prakarana, Book 3) If you want to secure real happiness, then renounce all and secure happiness infinitely greater than what you could have had through your personal property.

The essential nature of true penance is not only to possess anything but nothing. Even a single thing will bring back the desire of property.

Only those who have completely renounced will reach the highest goal of life, Moksha; the others still with the delusion get entangled in personal matters.

The object of Gita is to discover a golden mean between the two ideals of action and of contemplation, preserving the merits of both. Karma-yoga is that golden mean in which the merits of both the ideals are happily integrated. It advocates a life of activity with detachment as the guiding spirit and one's spiritual unfoldment as the goal of one's activities. Thus, it discards neither ideal but integrating the spirit of renunciation of the one and the activism of the other, it purifies and elevates man. This fusion of the two ideals in Karma-yoga gives due regard to social welfare on the one hand and on the other leads an individual to the fulfilment of his spiritual aspirations. Thus the Gita ignores neither the society nor the individual. It does not advocate a life of inaction but instead recommends a life of intense action in which self is effaced in all its aspects.[15]

5. Detached Action

The secret right action in reality is not a secret. It does not lie in any formula that we repeat. There is no magic by means of which we can follow the path of idleness and yet make our life productive. No! The secret lies in our own motives, in our power of application. It is not the strong physical vehicle which makes the productive human being; it is skillfulness in action, knowing how to adjust ourselves quickly, how to perform a task with the least expenditure of energy. This is what gives immediate success. We should take action in time to solve problems of employees before they become violent and result in strikes, destruction and unpleasant atmosphere.

Gita has given us some thoughts which if followed can remove tension and stress among the employees.

कर्मण्येवाधिकारस्ते मा फलेषु कदाचन् ।
म कर्मफलहेतुर्भुमा ते सङ्गोऽस्त्वकर्माणि ॥
|| 2/47 || Bhagavad Gita

Man has a right to action alone, not to the renunciation of action. If out of egoism he forcibly tries to renounce all action, he will not succeed in the attempt (111.5); for his nature will compel him to act (III.33; XVIII.59, 60). In this way he will be abusing his authority, and by refusing to perform an obligatory duty he will also have to bear the evil consequences of violating the commands of the scriptures.

योगस्थ: कुरु कर्माणि सङ्ग त्यक्त्वां धनंजय
सिद्धयसिद्धयो: समो भूत्वा समत्वं योग उच्यते
|| 2/48 || Bhagavad Gita

Lord Krishna tells Arjuna, to perform his duties established in Yoga, renouncing attachment, and even-tempered in success and failure; evenness of temper is called Yoga (48). The word 'Yoga' bears a peculiar meaning in the Gita and the Lord conveys that peculiar meaning by defining it as equanimity. The Lord thus establishes identity between Yoga and equanimity, and shows that one can become a Yogi by attaining equanimity through any discipline whatsoever.

दुरेण ह्यंवर कर्म बुद्धियोगाद्धनंजय ।
बुद्धौ शरणामन्विच्छ कृपणाः फलेहृतवः ॥
|| 2/49 || Bhagavad Gita

By declaring action with a selfish motive is far inferior to the Yoga of equanimity. The Lord has shown that the fruit of actions prompted by desire is the attainment of fleeting and momentary pleasure whereas the fruit of Karmayoga is realization of God. Thus there is no comparison whatsoever between the two. The word 'Karma' in this verse cannot be interpreted in the sense of prohibited action, for such action is altogether worth renouncing and its fruit is nothing but untold misery and suffering. Therefore, it cannot be cited as a fit subject of comparison to bring out the glory of the Yoga of Equanimity.

बुद्धियुक्तो जहातीह उभे सुकण्तदुष्कृते ।
तस्माद्योगाय युज्यस्व योगः कर्मसु कौशलम्
|| 2/50 || Bhagavad Gita

Endowed with equanimity, one sheds in this life both good and evil. Therefore, strive for the practice of this Yoga of equanimity. Skill in action lies in (the practice of this) Yoga. We should avoid favouring some employees at the cost of others. Our actions should be fair and impartial.

6. Control over Senses

योगयुक्तो विशुद्धात्मा विजितात्मा जितेन्द्रियः ।
सर्वभूतात्मभूतात्मा कुर्वन्नपि न लिप्यते ॥
|| 5/7 || Bhagavad Gita

The Karmayogi, who has fully conquered his mind and mastered his senses, whose heart is pure, and who has identified himself with the Self of all beings, remains untainted, even though performing action.

So long as one's mind and senses are not controlled, they naturally run after sense enjoyments; and so long as impurities in the form of likes and dislikes exist in the mind it is difficult to remain equipoised in success and failure. Hence, until the mind and senses are fully controlled and perfect purity of heart is attained a practicant, cannot be called a real Karmayogi.

7. No Temptation to take Credit for Action/Results

Public officials should not be tempted to personify them for results to come into lime-light. This would add to the impurities in mind to make him proud.

युक्तः कर्मफलं त्यक्त्वा शान्तिमाप्नोति नैष्ठिकीम् ।
अयुक्तः कामकारेण फले सक्तो निबध्यते ॥

|| 5/12 || Bhagavad Gita

Offering the fruit of action to God, the Karmayogi attains everlasting peace in the shape of God-Realization; whereas he who works with a selfish motive, being attached to the fruit of actions through desire, gets tied down.

सन्तुष्टिपरतश्प्तस्थ महतः पूर्णचेतसः ।
क्षीराब्धेरिव शुद्धस्य मुखे लक्ष्मीर्विराजते ॥

Yoga Vasistha, Mumuksu-Prakarana,
Book 2, Saloka 13.

There is a beauty shining in the face of one, whose mind has the satisfaction of contentment, the fullness of magnanimity and the purity of thoughts likes that of the milky ocean in it.

8. Avoidance of Lust and Anger

Everybody in the world seeks happiness. But very few know what is real happiness and how to attain it. Due to this ignorance they run away with the wrong idea that happiness consists only in enjoying the objects of senses. That is why they hanker after them and strive to attain them. And when they find themselves balked in their efforts, they are seized with anger. But as a rule one who is habitually under the sway of lust and anger can never be happy.

He alone is a real 'Nara' or man, who having thus subdued his evil propensities like lust and anger and developed dispassion and quietism attains God, the embodiment of Truth, Knowledge and Bliss. The word 'Narah' signifies such a person, no matter to which sex he belongs.

शक्नोतीहैव यः सोढुं प्राक् शरीरविमोक्षणात् ।
कामक्रोधोद्भवं वेगं स युक्तः स सुखी नरः ॥

|| 5/23 || Bhagavad Gita

He alone who is able to stand in this very life the urges of lust and anger is a yogi and he alone is a happy man. He who lives a holy life with his gentle and peaceful conduct, is said to be truly living in this world and no other.

9. Selfless Service

The great secret of true success or true happiness, then, is this; the man who asks for no return, the perfectly unselfish man, is the most successful. It seems to be a paradox. Do we not know that every man who is unselfish in life gets cheated, gets hurt? Apparently, Yes, "Christ was unselfish, and yet he was crucified." True, but we know that his unselfishness is the reason, the cause of a great victory—the crowning of millions upon millions of lives with the blessings of true success.

Ask nothing; want nothing in return. Give what you have to give; it will come back to you—but do not think of that now. It will come back multiplied a thousand fold—but the attention must not be on that. Yet have the power to give; give, and there it ends.[16]

"Man is born to give not to grab" grabber pays the penalty in the form of misery; the giver reaps the reward in the form of joy."

The resources, the bodily effort and the mental disposition becomes multiplied in the man of yajna. Such a man is never in want, always in affluence. His bounteous mind is the real Kamdhenu. Becaue of his frame of mind he is ever in prosperity. This is the plan and purpose of cosmos.

इष्टान् भोगान् हि वो देवा दास्यन्ते यज्ञभाविता: ।
तैर्दत्तानप्रदायैभ्यो यो भुङ्क्ते स्तेन एव स: ।।
|| 3/12 || Bhagavad Gita

The essence of the spirit of service is contained in the following words of Vivekananda: "This is the gist of all worship—to be pure and to do good to others. He who sees Shiva in the poor, in the weak, and in the diseased, really worships Shiva; and if he sees Shiva only in the image, his worship is but preliminary. He who has served and helped one poor man seeing Shiva in him, without thinking of his caste, or creed, or race, or anything, with him Shiva is more pleased than with the man who sees Him only in the temples. He who wants to serve the father must serve the children first. He who wants to serve Shiva must serve His children, must serve all creatures in the world first."[17]

10. Developing Perfection

In the right view both of life and of yoga all life is either consciously or sub-consciously a yoga. For we mean by this term a methodized effort towards self-perfection by the expression of the potentialities latent in the being and a union of the human individual with the universal and transcendent existence we see partially expressed in man and in the cosmos. When a man casts away, all the desires of his mind, ever satisfied in himself, by himself, then he is a man of steady wisdom:

प्रजहाति यदा कामान्सर्वान्पार्थ मनोगतान् ।
आत्मत्येवात्मना तुष्ट: स्थितप्रज्ञस्तदोच्यते ।।

|| (2&55) || Bhagavad Gita

He is unshaken in adversity, completely unattached to pleasures, free from attachment, fear, anger. Such a one is indeed a seer of steady wisdom.

दुःखेष्वनुद्विग्नमनाः सुखेषु विगतस्पृहः ।
वीतरागभयक्रोधः स्थितधीर्मुनिरुच्यते ॥

|| (2&56) || Bhagavad Gita

He who is everywhere unattached, neither rejoices at the good nor is vexed by the evil, he is a master of perfect wisdom. Perfection is very important to impart quality To attain success in life and to reach the desired goal one must have a positive attitude. Faith in oneself and in God, courage, strength and fearlessness are the characteristics of a positive intellect. For a man of intense faith nothing is impossible in this world.

11. Motivation

We now discuss the definition of motivation as contained in Ancient Sanskrit literature. Bhagavad Geeta presents an excellent example of motivation. In ancient Sanskrit literature, motivation is not dependent upon external factors but internal. Arjun, who is an expert in the knowledge of war feels totally depressed and does not want to fight. Lord Krishna, first understands his state of mind which is the first essential step in motivation and then incite him to overcome his weakness. Here, Lord Krishna incites Arjuna based upon reasoning and right means. The purpose is not to achieve the goal only but to achieve goal based on Dharma (righteousness). Thus the means of motivation are perfect and not transitory and are valid for all times to come. Lord Krishna advises Arjuna the path of righteousness to achieve results which Arjuna achieves. The foreign literature emphasizes any means to incite the individual to increase productivity and that is why, there is unhealthy competition. The means of motivation are permanent and once mastered would be self-sustaining and self-stimulant.

Thus the Bhagavad Gita suggests the following to motivate a person.

(a) Understanding the potentialities of the person—his strength and weakness.
(b) Analysis of the problem affecting his behaviour.
(c) Imparting knowledge based on fact to remove his weakness.
(d) Constant hammering the suggested knowledge in different styles.
(e) Assessment of the visible impact on his motivation and effort to keep it alive.

Let us first depict the state of Mind of Arjuna before the war as laid down in Gita Sloka 32, Chapter I.

न काङ्क्षे विजयं कृष्ण न च राज्यं सुखानि च ।
किं नो राज्येन गोविन्द किं भोगैर्जीवितेन वा ॥
|| 1/32 || Bhagavad Gita

Krishna, I do not covet victory, nor kingdom nor pleasures. Govinda, of what use will kingdom, or luxuries, or even life be to us!

Drawing a faithful picture of the state of his mind, Arjuna said that victory, kingdom and earthly pleasures which he would gain by killing those near and dear ones were not at all wanted by him. He clearly visualized that the slaughter of those relations would bring him in this world as well as in the next nothing but mental agony and torture. Then, what for should he fight, why should he put them to death? What should he do with a kingdom and pleasures obtained by such dreadful means? He puts it as his definite opinion that after killing them, life would be of no use to him whatsoever.

Arjuna now gives his reasons for not coveting a kingdom and other pleasures obtained by wading through the blood of his kith and kin as laid down in Slokas 33 and 34, Chapter-I.

येषामर्थे काङ्क्षितं नो राज्यं भोगाः सुखानि च ।
ते इमेऽवस्थिता युद्धे प्राणांस्त्यक्त्वा धनानि च ॥
|| 1/33 || Bhagavad Gita

आचार्यः पितरः पुत्रास्तथैव च पितामहाः ।
मातुलाः श्वसुराः पौत्राः श्यालाः सम्बन्धिनस्तथा ॥

|| 34 || Bhagavad Gita

Here Arjuna says that rulership of a kingdom and all the pleasures and enjoyments which follow in the wake of the possession of such authority, were not necessary for his own use at all. He knew it well that such pleasures were neither permanent, nor the possessions themselves everlasting. If he had craved for a kingdom, it was only for those brothers, friends and relations; but now he observed that they had all assembled on the battlefield ready to sacrifice their lives. Of what use would be the kingdom, luxuries and pleasures, if they all departed from the earth by mutual slaughter? Therefore, from any point of view whatsoever, it was undesirable to start the War.

Lord Krishna in Sloka of Chapter II questions Arjuna and give sermons to motivate him to do his duty—to fight war irrespective of the fact whether there is victory or defeat.

कुतस्त्वां कश्मलमिदं विषमे समुपस्थितम् ।
अनार्यजुष्टमस्वर्ग्यमकीर्तिकरमर्जुन ॥

|| 2/2 || Bhagavad Gita

Lord Krishna said: Arjuna, how has this infatuation overtaken you at this odd hour? It is shunned by noble souls; neither will it bring heaven, nor fame, to you.

Calling this dejection and faint-heartedness of Arjuna as unworthy of noble souls and calculated neither to lead to heaven, nor to bring fame, the Lord gives His reasons for expressing amazement and wonder. The intention was that the sentiment with which Arjuna was now overpowered was not entertained by men possessed of nobility of character, and was not likely to lift Arjuna to heaven or contribute to his fame. Out of the four objects of life it would lead to the fulfilment of none-neither of Moksa (salvation), nor of Dharma (virtue), nor of Artha (wealth), nor of Kama (enjoyment). Therefore, possessed of a strong intellect as he was, how could Arjuna be subjected to such a depression of spirits at that odd hour on the battle-field, faced with the imminent danger of a clash of arms with very powerful adversaries?

क्लैब्यं मा स्म गमः पार्थ नैतत्त्वय्युपपद्यते ।
क्षुद्रं हृदयदौर्बल्यं त्यक्त्वोत्तिष्ठ परंतप ॥ 2/3 ॥

Lord Krishna in Slokas 11, 22, 23 of Chapter 2 makes Arjuna understand that your attachment is not real as these physical bodies are not real.

Yield not to unmanliness, Arjuna; it does not behove you. Shaking off this paltry faint-heartedness stand up, o scorcher of enemies.

अशोच्यानन्वशोचस्त्वं प्रज्ञावादांश्च भाषसे ।
गतासूनगतासूंश्च नानुशोचन्ति पण्डिताः ॥
|| 2/11 || Bhagavad Gita

Lord Krishna said: Arjuna, you grieve over those who should not be grieved for, and yet speak like the learned; wise men do not sorrow over the dead or the living.

वासांसि जीर्णानि यथा विहाय नवानि गृह्णति नरोऽपराणि ।
तथा शरीराणि विहाय जीर्णान्यन्यानि संयाति नवानि देही ॥
|| 2/22 || Bhagavad Gita

As a man shedding worn-out garments, takes other new ones, likewise the embodied soul, casting-off worn-out bodies, enters into others which are new.

नैनं छिन्दन्ति शस्त्राणि नैनं दहति पावकः ।
न चैनं क्लेदयन्त्यापो न शोणयति मारुतः ॥

|| 2/23 || Bhagavad Gita

Weapons cannot cut it nor can fire burn it; water cannot wet it nor can wind dry it. In this way, Lord Krishna motivates Arjuna who is fully motivated to do his duty. An important factor to remember here is the art of communication by Lord Krishna. This is called in modern management as Transactional Analysis or Inter-personal relations. Until and Unless, this rapport is developed, motivation becomes difficult. Managerial effectiveness depends to a great extent upon the human factor, as we know that human rather than capital is key to development. If we can diagnose the causative factors affecting human behaviour, we would be able to sublimate those factors and put them to constructive use. This technique can even help the manager to diagnose his own behaviour. This understanding can provide him kinetic energy to influence, direct and therefore condition the behaviour of the people in his organization.

12. Leadership

Lord Krishna made following observations which are essential for good leadership.[18] Without performing action, man does not attain actionlessness, or perfection in Karmayoga (III.4):

(1) Merely by renouncing action, man does not attain perfection in Jnanayoga (III.4).
(2) Man cannot remain totally inactive even for a moment (III.5).
(3) Outwardly renouncing action and mentally dwelling on the objects of senses, is hypocrisy (III.6).
(4) He who performs action disinterestedly, controlling the mind and senses, is the best of men (III.7).
(5) Action is superior to inaction (III.8).
(6) Desisting from action, one cannot even maintain the body (III.8).
(7) Action performed for the sake of sacrifice causes no bondage, but leads to salvation (III.9).
(8) Action has been enjoined upon man by the Creator, Brahma, and disinterested performance of action leads to the highest good (III.10, 11).
(9) He who enjoys objects without performing his duty is a thief (III.12).

(10) He who derives his sustenance from what is left after sacrifice, just for the sake of keeping up his body, gets absolved of all the sins (III.13).

(11) He who, without performing sacrifices, cooks food only for nourishing his body is a sinner (III.13).

(12) He who, abandoning his duties, hinders the operations of the wheel of creations, leads a sinful life and lives in vain (III.16).

(13) Doing work without attachment, man attains God (III.19).

(14) It was through action that Janaka and others reached perfection in ancient times (III.21).

(15) Other men imitate what a great man does; therefore, a great man should perform action (III.21).

(16) God has no duty, and yet He works with a view to maintaining the world order (III.22).

(17) The wise man has no duty, and yet he should work in the interest of the world order (III.25).

(18) A wise man should in no way deter men from the performance of their duty by renouncing action himself or by instructing men to do so, but should perform duties himself and get others to do the same (III.26).

(19) The man of perfect knowledge should not unsettle the minds of men attached to action by instructing them to renounce their prescribed duties (III.29).

Gita in Sloka 7 Chapter XIII and in Slokas 2, 3 and 4, Chapter 16, mentions the qualities of true leader.

अमानित्वमदम्भित्वमहिंसा क्षान्तिरार्जवम् ।
आचार्योपासनं शौचं स्थैर्यमात्मविनिग्रहः ॥ 13/7 ॥

Absence of pride, freedom from hypocrisy, non-violence, forbearance, straightness of body, speech and mind, devout service of the preceptor, internal and external purity, steadfastness of mind and control of body, mind and the senses.

अहिंसा सत्यमक्रोधस्त्यागः शान्तिरपैशुनम् ।
दया भूतेष्वलोलुप्त्वं मार्दवं ह्रीरचापलम् ।। 16/2 ।।

Non-violence in thought, word and deed, truthfulness and softness of speech, absence of anger ever on provocation, disclaiming doership in respect of actions, quietude or composure of mind, abstaining from malicious gossip, compassion towards all creatures, absence of attachment to the objects of senses even during their contact with the senses, mildness, a sense of shame in transgressing against the scriptures of usage, and abstaining from frivolous pursuits.

तेजः क्षमा धृतिः शौचमद्रोहो नातिमानिता ।
भवन्ति सम्पदं दैवीमभिजातस्य भारत ।। 16/3 ।।

Sublimity, forbearance, fortitude, external purity, bearing enmity to none and absence of self esteem—these are the marks of him, who is born with the divine gifts.

दम्भो दर्पोऽभिमानश्च क्रोधः पारुष्यमेव च ।
अज्ञांन चाभिजातस्य पार्थ सम्पदमासुरीम् ।। 16/4 ।।

Hypocrisy, arrogance and pride, and anger, sternness and ignorance too, these are the marks of him, who is born with demoniac properties.[22]

13. Sustainable Development: A Real Approach

Gita's model of development is based on mutual help and cooperation with ultimate goal on spirituality and not materialism as propounded by western model of development. Advanced countries are exploiting the nature to provide luxuries of life to their people. They make gadgets which people enjoy to lead a higher standard of living but in turn there are many disturbances in the environment resulting into in ecosystem-cosmos dis-equilibrium. The population living in developed world is enjoying 80% of the wealth of the world which is politically unstable morally untenable and psychologically unsound. In Chapter 3 and slokas 10, 11, 12, 13, Lord Krishna preaches:

सहयज्ञाः प्रजाः सृष्ट्वा पुरोवाच प्रजापतिः ।
अनेन प्रसविष्यध्वमेष वोऽस्त्विष्टकामधुक् ।। 3/10 ।।

देवान् भावयतानेन ते देवा भावयन्तु वः ।
परस्परं भावयन्तः श्रेयः परमवाप्स्यथ ।। 3/11 ।।

इष्टान् भोगान् हि वा देवा दास्यन्ते यज्ञभाविताः ।
तैर्दत्तान्प्रदायैभ्यो यो भुङ्क्ते स्तेन एव सः ।। 12 ।।

यज्ञशिष्टाणिनः सन्तो मुच्यन्ते सर्वकिल्बिषैः ।
भुन्जते ते त्वघं पापा ये पचन्त्यात्मकारणात् ।। 3/13 ।।

Sloka 10 specifies that God created mankind to perform their duty in the shape of offerings to Gods, charities, austerities, personal service, in the form of svadharma. Besides, performance of ones duty would continue to fulfil ones earthly requirements as well. Thus, for success the entire team must have one single inspiring ideal at the altar of which everyone must readily surrender his personal greed and vanity. A large number of people coming together to act in union at the same altar of grace, for the total glory of all is the real yajna. This yajna spirit is a gift received from the creator by man-as a community, not as an individual.[19]

Swami Chinmayananda explains the Yajna Spirit as propounded by Lord Krishna, "Every where around us, from the twinkling stars to flowing rivers, nature, serves the world in the Yajna Spirit. The sun shines but demands no appreciation from anyone. Rains fall, rivers flow, plants, flower; trees bear fruits; towering mountains stand. . . all serve the world to make it what it is, and none of them seem to demand even a passing recognition from the people benefited by it. They all do their duties discovering a joyous fulfilment in the very performance."[20]

Sloka 11 suggests that the demigods being pleased by sacrifices will also bestow blessings on you and thus by co-operation between men and demi-gods, prosperity will attain the highest good. When men in a community strive co-operatively, without ego and ego-centric desires, the cosmic forces that constitute the environment, shall cherish them in turn. In short, when man works in the yajna spirit, the outer circumstances must miraculously change their pattern to be conducive to the common will of the selfless community striving for the good of all.[21]

In Sloka 12, it has been mentioned that Gods bestow all desired enjoyments without asking for them provided the human beings give these enjoyments in return. According to the Hindus, the entire universe is home and all creatures belong to it. In brotherly love, striving together, gather the profits and distribute them equally to all—not according to needs, it is blind and ready equity in distribution. . . together produce together enjoyment.[22]

In sloka 13 it has been said that the virtuous who enjoy of what is leftover after sacrifice are absolved of all sins. Others who prepare food for personal sense enjoyment, verily eat only sin.

Each is to strive hard sincerely, producing as much as he can for the welfare of all and himself, to receive from the society only his humble share. He who thus gives and enjoys is free to enjoy his share. This is the Hindu Socialism. . . based upon the guidance for the evolution of man of godhood.[23]

Thus, the development is based on mutual cooperation and not individualism thereby protecting environment safety and avoids its degradation.

R.B. Lal in his book, The Gita in the light of modern Science (Somaiya Publications, Bombay, 1970) rightly observes that according to the Gita all things animate or inanimate have existence in God, as such they are all like cells or the members of the vast body of God, interconnected and interdependent. As a logical corollary to this theory of creation, the Gita has laid down for all creatures a principle of service, of cooperation, of mutual help and organized collective effort which is at once the law of their life and growth and happiness. To designate this universal principle, the Gita has used three words, namely, yajna, lok sangrah and karmaphala tyaga. Yajna is any action, specially, organised action, performed for the good of the society. Lok-Sangraha means working for the maintenance of the world or in order to set an example to others. Karmaphala, tyaga or the renunciation of the fruit of one's labour, sharing with those less fortunate or using for their benefit whatever one has earned by the sweat of one's brow-knowledge, wealth, power, position or piety.[24]

In Chapter VI slokas 9 and 10 Lord Krishna says that he who looks upon all irrespective of foes, relatives, well wishers affectionate benefactors, the neutrals, the mediators, the envious, the pious and the sinners, etc. is supreme. He also neither seeks nor needs in the least degree any object of enjoyment. All wealth belongs to the divine and those who hold it are trustees, not possessors. Therefore, saving for one's self is discarded. These views can make this world and its environment just, based on equity and social justice.

सुहृयन्मित्रार्युदासीनमधयस्थद्वेष्यबन्धुषु ।
साधुष्वपि च पापेषु समबुद्धिर्विषिष्यते ॥

|| (6/5) || Bhagavad Gita

He who looks upon well-wishers and neutrals as well as mediators, friends and foes, relatives and objects of hatred, the virtuous and the sinful with the same eye, stands supreme.

Self-realisation is not mere awakening to a higher plane of consciousness, but the kindling of a fresh light to illuminate the world around us. Our entire view of life becomes transformed. No more is there an egocentric view of life. There is a universal sense of belonging and oneness—an expense on within, sufficient to embrace the whole cosmos and wrap it with love. This discovery of oneness is the cathedral of joy, the dome of peace, the temple of contentment.[25]

योगी युन्जीत सततमात्मांनं रहसि स्थित: ।
एकाकी यतचित्तात्मा निराशीरपरग्रह: ॥ (6/10) ॥

Living in seclusion all by himself, the Yogi who has controlled his mind and body, and is free from desires and void of possessions, should constantly engage his mind in benedication.

Bhagavad Gita enunciates clear, definite and scientific interconnection and interdependence of the whole cosmos which is the essence of this universe in toto. All the life in this world is made of five elements panchbhutas—earth, water, fire, sky and wind.

As stated in Chapter 4 Sloka 22 human beings must lead a simple life based on contentment and self control. Greed is lust for wealth, prompted by which man is ever busy devising means of multiplying his possessions, refuses to part with them, seeks even to usurp the rights of others minding not what is right and what is wrong. His mind becomes restless.

Such a person—who has disciplined his physical personality, mental nature and intellectual attitude, he finds an undiluted peace in himself under all circumstances—both positive and negative. Lord Krishna in Chapter XI of Bhagavad Gita manifests his cosmic form, i.e.

(i) The existence of the entire cosmos (past, present and future) with all its animate and inanimate objects in it (B.G. 11.7).
(ii) Enduced with innumerable forms extended on all sides encompassing entire cosmos (B.G. 11.16).
(iii) Supreme, indestructible, upholder of the eternal dharma (B.G. 11.18).
(iv) Terrible splendors filling the cosmos with your radiance (B.G. 11.30).
(v) All the beings including deries, sages, semi-divine beings from a part of me (B.G. 11.15).

If we adjust ourselves to the divine life as manifested by lord himself, we are bound to be in tune with the cosmos. Gita believes in holistic view of development, interconnection among all the creatures, mutual cooperation, contentment, self-control, lack of greed. All these, if put into practice, can lead sustainable development and this world would become the best place to live.

Agreeing to the above view of Gita Julian Huxley, distinguished biologist had stated in his book 'Religion without Revelation', "Science has gone a long way towards proving the essential unity of all phenomena. She has at least a very strong basis for reasonable belief in this unity and continuity. There seems no escape from the belief that all reality has both a material and mental side, however, rudimentary and below the level of anything like our consciousness that mental side may be the one ultimate world substance as two of its aspects. . . they can not be separated and it is false philosophy to try to think them apart."

The devoted person ceases to have any trace of selfishness or egotism and he does not claim anything in the world as personal. He views everything as belonging to God and he carries out his duty in a disinterested spirit with reverence and love.

Thus Gita has the answer to serious environmental problems facing the globe today. The need is to change the attitude of the people in both developed and developing countries. Gita confirms the living entity to be only one of the multi-energies and when this energy is freed from material contamination, it becomes fully conscious and liberated.

However, leaders, in both the spheres political and administrative, should be pure in thought, and actions. They have let down the nation since their pursuit of materialism is unlimited and beyond satisfaction.

To quote Gandhiji; "Civilization in the real sense of the term consists not in the multiplication but in deliberate and voluntary reduction of wants. This alone promotes real happiness and contentment and increase the capacity to service."

God never stores for the morrow. He never creates more than what is strictly needed for the moment. If therefore we repose faith in this providence, we should rest assured that He will give us our daily bread, meaning every thing that we require . . . our ignorance of negligence of the divine law, . . . has given rise to inequalities with all the series attendant upon them. The rich have a superfluous store of things which they do not need, and which are therefore neglected and wasted, while millions are starved to death for want to sustenance. If each retained possession only of what he needed, no one would be in want, and all would live in contentment.

"The world will live in peace only when the individual composing it make up their mind to do so.

I do not believe that multiplication of wants and machinery contrived to supply them in taking the world a single step nearer its goal. I whole heartedly detest this mad desire to destroy distance and time, to increase animal appetites and go to the ends of the earth in search of their satisfaction.

I value individual freedom, but you must not forget that man is essentially a social being. He has risen to his present status by adjusting his individualism to the requirements of social progress. Unrestricted individualism is a law of the beasts of the jungle. We have to learn to strike the balance between freedom and social restraint. Willing submission to social restraint for the sake of the well-being of the whole society, enriches both the individual and the society of which one is a member."

The teachings contained in Bhagavad Gita are a rich source of knowledge about self and the environment in which the self operates.

VALUES IN SRIMAD BHAGAVAD GITA

Selected Slokas

Given below are the five verses from Bhagavad Gita (Chapter XIII, from 7th to 11th enumerating the important values. The original Sanskrit test is followed by the transliteration in and the meaning:

अमानित्वमदम्भित्वमहिंसा क्षान्तिरार्जवम् ।
आचार्योपासंनं शौचं स्थैर्यमात्मविनिग्रहः ॥

13/7 (Srimad Bhagavad Gita)

Amanitvamadambhitvamahimsa ksantirarjavan
Acaryopasanam saucam sthairyamatmavinigrahah.

Absence of pride, freedom from hypocricy, non-violence, forbearance, straightness of body, speech and mind, devout service of the preceptor, internal and external purity, steadfastness of mind and control of body, mind and the senses.

इन्द्रियार्थेषु वैराग्यमनहंकार एव च ।
जन्ममृत्युजराव्याधिदुःखदोषानुदर्शनम् ।।
|| 13/8 ||(Srimad Bhagavad Gita)

Indriyarthesu vairagyamanahankara eva ca,
Janmamrtyujaravyadhidukhadosanudarsanam

Dispassion towards the objects of enjoyment of this world and the next, and also absence of egotism, pondering again and again on the pain and evils inherent in birth, death, old age and disease.

असक्तिरनभिष्वङंगः पुत्रदारगृहादिषु ।
नित्य च समचित्तत्वमिष्टानिशटोपपत्तिषु ।।
|| 13/9 || (Srimad Bhagavad Gita)

Asaktiranabhisvangah putradaragrhadisu
Nityam ca samacittatvamistanistopapattisu

Absence of attachment and the feeling of mineness in respect of son, wife, home, etc. and constant equipoise of mind both in favourable and unfavourable circumstances.

मयि चानन्ययोगेन भक्तिरव्यभिचारिणी ।
विविक्तदेशसेवित्मरतिर्जनसंसदि ।।
|| 13/10 || (Srimad Bhagavad Gita)

Mayi cananyayogena bhaktiravyabhicarini
Viviktadesasevitvamaratrijanasamasadi

Unflinching devotion to Me through exclusive attachment, living in secluded and holy places, and finding no enjoyment in the company of men.

अध्यात्मज्ञाननित्वं तत्त्वज्ञानार्थदर्शनम् ।
एतज्ज्ञानमिति प्रोक्तमज्ञांन यदतोऽन्यथा ।।
|| 13/11 ||(Srimad Bhagavad Gita)

Adhyatmajnananityatvam tattvajnanarthadarsanam
Etajjnanamiti proktamajnanam yadatonatha.

Fixity in self-knowledge and seeing God as the object of true knowledge and what is other than this called ignorance.

CONCLUSION

Bhagavad Gita has plainly given sermons to people through Arjun that this world is one, having interconnections among the entire fabric of world—both animate and inanimate. Even among the animate objects. Human beings, plants, animals, there are deep relations. In addition, this world is to enjoy for a limited period as here everything is transitory. Thus, the human beings must understand this unity and euphermal nature and not indulge in destruction through greed, lust for power/authority as these would recoil on them. It is the duty of everyone on this earth to maintain the beauty of nature and not disturb its equilibrium. Material progress is not to be mistaken for inner progress. When technology outstrips moral development, the prospect is not that of a millennium but of extinction. Our ancient heritage is a potent antidote to the current status to standardise soul and seek salvation, i.e. moksha.

If we abstract the Krsna element from the Indian heritage, it will be reduced to almost elementary proportions. He has entered into our religion and philosophy, mysticism and poetry, painting and sculpture; music and dancing, into all that pertains to the varied life of a people advanced in culture and civilization. His personality has a charm for all varieties and levels of people. He has been and continues to be the perennial 'pied piper' of the Indian heart and intellect, drawing all to him, our girls and our boys, our saints and our sages, our intellectuals and our artists, our stateman and our diplomats. The Bhagavata Purana of a later age, gave expression to the wonder of generations when it stated that Sri Krsna is God Himself, unlike other avataras who were merely aspects and parts of Him (1.3.28). Where shall we seek for this mesmerism of Sri Krsna, for this focusing of affections and loyalties of a whole people, except in the character of that person and the character of his people?

The great epic, The Mahabharata, illumines the India of a heroic and creative age. The galaxy of its heroes belongs to a wide range of the lovable and the hateful, the righteous and the wicked, the gentle and the ferocious, the admirable and the detestable. The one character that dominates this galaxy, alike by its force and charm as by its loftiness and brilliance, is Sri Krsna. Respected by the sages and loved by the people, feared by the wicked and sought after by the good, full of tender solicitude for the welfare of women and the masses, and honouring those to whom honour is due, the Mahabharata depicts Sri Krsna as a rare hero, at once human and divine, engaged in shaping the mind and face of the India of his time, through a long life characterized by ceaseless activity on the one hand and calm detachment on the other. The Mahabharata describes the tumultuous scenes of national welcome which the citizens of Indraprastha and Hastinapura used to accord to Sri Krsna, their leader, during his rare visits to India's capital.[26]

Relevance

Srimad Bhagavat Geeta is a philosophy which encompasses social, political, ethical and eternal truths and thus would remain valid in all periods of human life. It contains all the essence of four Vedas. The Geeta is a bottomless sea which contains Jewels at all its levels. Jayadayal Goyandha beautifully explains the everlasting philosophy of Gita.

Swami Ranganathananda beautifully says: "There is a world of difference between the cult of equanimity preached by the Gita and the doctrine of the so-called equality preached by modern socialism. Modern socialism is anti-theistic in its outlook, whereas the cult of equanimity preached by the Gita sees God everywhere and in everything. One uproots Religion, while the other upholds Religion at every step; one is violent in its conception, while the other establishes the principle of non-violence; one is based on self-interest, while the other has no room for selfishness. One, though abolishing all distinctions in the matter of inter-dining and social intercourse, etc. maintains disunion in spirit; while the other, though maintaining due discrimination in the matter of interdining and social intercourse according to the bounds prescribed in the Sastras, does not admit any disparity in spirit and exhorts us to perceive the Supreme Spirit as the same in all. The goal of one is mammon-worship, while that of the other is God-Realization. In one there is identification with one's party and disrespect for others; while in the other there is complete absence of pride; and respect for all which comes from a sense of the immanence of God. In one, there is emphasis on external behaviour, while in the other it is the spirit which matters; in one it is material happiness which is of primary importance, while in the other it is spiritual happiness that counts; in one there is want of tolerance for others, wealth and others' views, in the other there is equal respect for all; one is dominated by partiality and prejudice, while the other prescribes conduct which is free from partiality and prejudice.

The Gita has a simplicity which we very often miss. We are accustomed to complicate things. We cannot appreciate simple things. The human mind wants, in the name of the philosophy and religion, something striking in the form of books, dress, rituals, etc. Simple character or simple ethical beauty is not much appreciated. Simple beauty is not understood by ordinary men. Truth which is simple is clothed in a variety of ways, and we get, not the naked truth but a dressed up truth. When you come to the Gita, you have the presentation of truth in all its simplicity which helps to take us through life's probems. It frees us from all attachments to joys and sorrows, etc. so that we may be attached to truth only. It gives us absolute calm, and a freedom from all conditionings—external and internal. We want this independence and freedom of the individual to be maintained at all costs. This is what philosophy seeks to confer on life. If we have this, what else do we require? One who attains this remains fresh, in spite of life's aging, and retains the freshness of a new-born babe even unto death. He has philosophy to guide him. This is the true test of philosophy—a philosophy which helps us to pass through life's struggles without getting scorched, which helps us to remain as fresh at the end of the journey as at the beginning.

The Gita lights the lamps of wisdom in the hearts of men and leaves them to solve their own problems. In the Gita, in all its eighteen chapters, we are face to face with a philosophy which seeks to impart redeeming wisdom by which men may work out their own salvation. This is its dynamic feature. On our own endeavours depends the taking hold of this wisdom and making something out of it. Philosophy, understood in the Vedantic sense, should not be mere academic study and discussion, but should be closely related to life and its problems, sustained by life and helping to sustain life in turn. That is the philosophy which is revealed in the succeeding verses of the Gita.[27]

Notes and References

1. H.C. Hemamalini, Values of Sustainability in the Traditions of Indigenous Indian Knowledge and their Implications in *University News*, January 30 Feb. 06, 2006, p. 64.
2. Speech delivered by Swami Ranganathananda at the Gita Jayanti Celebrations Observed under the auspices of the Rama Krishna Ashrama, Mysore, Dec. 1934, quoted in Swami Ranganathananda, *External Values for a Changing Society*, Vol. I, Bombay, Bhartiya Vidya Bhawan, 1994, p. 113.
3. *Ibid.*
4. Swami Ranganathananda, The Charm and Power of The Geeta, Kolkata, Advaita Ashrama, 2004, pp. 9-10.
5. S.K. Belvalkar, The Bhagavad Gita, A General Review of its History and Character in the *Cultural Heritage of India*, Vol. II, Calcutta, The Rama Krishna Mission Institute of Culture, 2001, p. 155.
6. Jayadayal Gayandka, Bhagavad Gita, Gita Press, Gorakhpur, pp. 5-17.
7. Swami Sudhananda, The Teachings of the Bhagavad Gita in the *Cultural Heritage of India*, Vol. II, Calcutta, The Rama Krishna Mission Institute of Culture, 2001, p.160.
8. Swami Chinmayananda, The Art of Man-Making, Mumbai, 2002, CMT, pp. 1-2.
9. Quoted in O.P. Dwivedi, Common Good and Good Governance, in *IJPA*, July to Sept. 1998, pp. 253-64.
10. *Ibid.*

11. Swami Harshananda, Attainment of Yoga, Maladies and Remedies, in *Yoga—Its Various Aspects*, Ramkrishna Math, pp. 203-04.
12. Swami Jagadananda, *Learn to Live*, Vol. I, Chennai, Rama Krishna Math, p. 28.
13. V. Jaganadhanan, Jawaharlal Nehru and Public Administration, *IJPA*, New Delhi, 1975.
14. Radha Krishna, The Bhagavad Geeta, Harper Collins, New Delhi, 1996, p. 746.
15. Swami Vijayananda, Gita on Karam Yoga, in *Yoga: Its Various Aspects*, Sri Rama Krishna Math, Madras, pp. 25-26.
16. Swami, Harshananda, Attainment of Yoga, *op. cit.*, pp. 203-04.
17. Swami Jagdananda, *Learn to Live*, Vol. I, Chennai, Shri Rama Krishna Math, p. 256.
18. Bhagavad Gita, Chapter III, Jayadayal Goyandka, Gita Press, Gorakhpur.
19. Swami Chinmayananda, The Art of Man Making, Talk of Bhagavad Geeta. Mumbai, Central Chinmaya Trust, 2002, p. 184.
20. *Ibid.*, p. 105.
21. *Ibid.*, p. 106.
22. *Ibid.*, p. 107.
23. *Ibid.*, p. 109.
24. R.B. Lall, The Gita in the Light of Modern Science, Bombay, Somaiya Publications, 1970.
25. Swami Chinmayananda, The Art of Man Making, *op. cit.*, 251.
26. Swami Ranganathananda, "Eternal Values for A Changing Society", Vol. I, Bharatiya Vidya Bhavan, Mumbai, 400 007, pp. 101, 110, 142, 131.
27. Swami Ranganathananda, "Eternal Values for a Changing Society" Vol. I, pp. 84, 98.

2

Lord Rama: Ramayana

Rama is presented in every context as the ideal man. There were occasions on which the great rsis, or the celestials, stood before him with joined palms and urged him to remember that he was the supreme Being Himself. But he seldom moved from the position that he was a mere man, Rama, son of Dasaratha. No doubt, he is described as the possessor of all the virtues a man can inherit or acquire, but there is not the least suggestion that he obtained them just because he was divine and not because he underwent the necessary discipline laid down for ordinary men. If he developed subtle intelligence, or philosophic wisdom, and could excel in military feats, or in answering controversialists, or even in singing, it was only because he diligently engaged himself in the study of the respective subjects and in serving his seniors and preceptors.[1]

The Ramayana, along with the Mahabharata and the Puranas, constitute the epic literature of India, comprising the Itihasa and the Puranas, the study of which has been rightly stressed as necessary for the correct interpretation of the Vedas. For over two thousands years, the Ramayana, like Mahabharata, has been influencing deeply the religious and moral thought as well as the literary production of India. In fact the Ramayana and the Mahabharata are, declared Swami

CHART 2.1

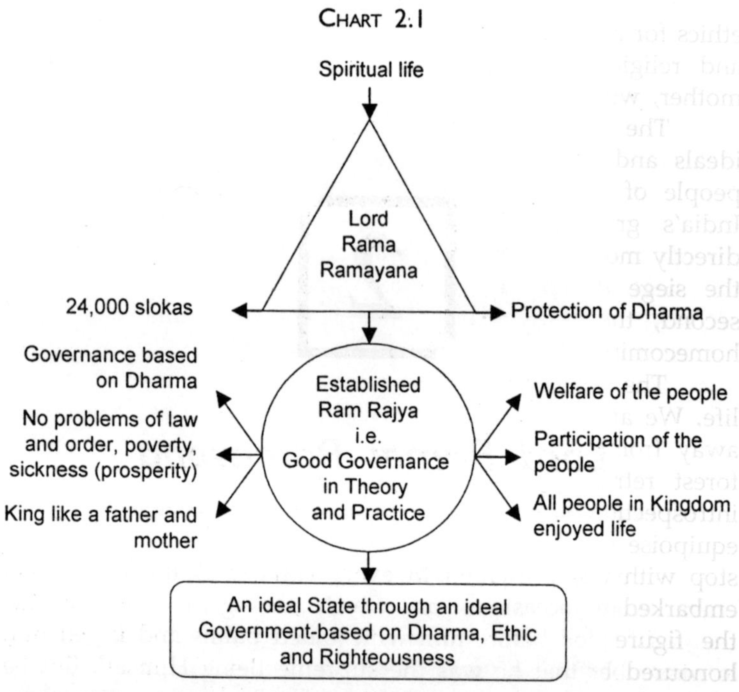

Vivekananda, 'the two encyclopedias of the ancient Aryan life and wisdom portraying an ideal civilization, which humanity has yet to aspire after. According to Macdowell, Probably no work of world literature, secular in its origin, has ever produced so profound an influence on the life and thought of the people as the Ramayana.[2]

Universally regarded as one of the world's most important literary and religious works, Ramayana has had a profound influence on the art, culture, social life, family relations, gender, politics and nationalism in the Indian sub-continent. The everlasting and moral value of this epic has been extolled through the centuries, and it has helped in moulding the national character largely.

Long ago the Ramayana became popular in South-east Asia and manifested itself in text, temple architecture and performance, particularly in Java, Sumatra, Borneo, Indonesia, Thailand, Cambodia and Malaysia. Today, it belongs to the whole humanity because it is capable of serving as a code of ethics for all human beings, irrespective of caste, creed, colour and religion. All roles whether of a king, brother, father, mother, wife, etc. are ideal.

The characters and incidents in Ramayana provide the ideals and wisdom of common life, and help to bind the people of India, regardless of caste and language. Two of India's greatest festive events—Dusshera and Diwali are directly motivated by the Ramayana. The first commemorates the siege of Lanka and Rama's victory over Ravana; the second, the festival of lights, celebrates Rama and Sita's homecoming to their kingdom in Ayodhya.

The Ramayana gives a many-sided picture of perfect life. We are accustomed to regard such a life as one led far away from the turmoils of the work a day world in some forest retreat and characterized by an unbroken cause of introspection or meditation leading up to a state of mental equipoise or illumination. The Ramayana, however, does not stop with this partial view. For along with the ascetics who embarked upon such severe discipline, we are always shown the figure of Rama himself, towering above them all the honoured by these very ascetics as the special manifestation of the Lord for the protection of dharma. We are brought face to face with a series of difficult, baffling, and tragic situations, and shown how Rama and the other principal characters react to them and ultimately tide over them without swerving in the least from the highest principles of spiritual life laid down in the scriptures. Inner perfection issues out in virtuous action which overcomes evil and transforms the evil-doer is thus Valmiki's main theme.[3]

The Valmiki Ramayana contains 24,000 slokas (verses), narrating in Sanskrit the tale of Rama and his consort Sita. The Valmiki Ramayana consists of seven parts called Khandas. Historically the date of the epic is a matter of considerable controversy and is nearly impossible to fix with certainty. Extensive scholarly work on the linguistic, stylistic, sociological, geographical and political data narrows down the possible dates of the epic to the period between 750 B.C. and 500 B.C. The Valmiki Ramayana is a treasure of moral principles and ethical precepts appreciable to personal and national life.

From the floating mass of the Rama story current in his time, Valmiki composed an ornate poem, which was subjected to additions of various kinds in subsequent times. The Ramayana (the world literally means the history of Rama) of Valmiki, to which normally the term "Ramayana" is applied, comprises, in its present form, seven Books containing about 24,000 stanzas. Before dealing with the problems of the transmission of the text of the Ramayana, let us consider the origin and development of the Rama story. In order to understand the origin of the Rama story in its proper perspective, it is necessary that we should know the story as presented by Valmiki.

Bereft of the additional matter, the story of the Ramayana may be told in brief outline as follows: As a result of the palace intrigue, Rama, the eldest son of Dasaratha, the king of Ayodhya, is banished into the forest to the south in exile for fourteen years, after the arrangements for his installation as heir apparent were made complete; and Bharta, a younger son of Dasaratha who was with his maternal uncle at that time, is declared heir apparent instead. Rama's father broken-hearted at the separation from his beloved son, Rama, Dasaratha dies. Bharata, on his return from his maternal uncle's residence, refuses kingship, follows Rama to the forest, and entreats him to return and accept his rightful position; he is persuaded to go back to Ayodhya as Rama's regent only after the latter promised to rule as the king, after completing the period of his exile. Some times passes, and Ravana, the king of Lanka, abducts Sita from forest, in the course of his search for Sita, Rama enters into an alliance with Sugriva, whom he places on the throne of Kiskindha after killing his brother Valin. After crossing the waters, Rama invades Lanka with the aid of Sugriva's army. Bibhisana, the younger brother of Ravana, deserts the latter, and joins Rama. After a fierce battle, Ravana is killed along with his sons, other relatives, and army. Rama recovers Sita and returns to Ayodhya. After an ideal rule for a period. Rama abandons Sita on hearing a scandal about her spreading among his subjects on account of her stay in Lanka. Two sons are born to Sita. Rama later performs the horse sacrifice. After crowning Kusa, who had his headquarters at Kusasthali, and Lava, who had his capital at Sravasti, Rama departs to heaven along with Bharata, Satrughna and the citizens of Ayodhya, Laksmana having died earlier.

MAIN ADMINISTRATIVE THOUGHTS OF RAMAYANA

Welfare of the People by the State

A focal point and theme—When the reins of government are grasped by the hands of kings possessed of such heroic and noble outlook, there is bound to be progress in every department of the country's activities. The development of the state including the welfare of the people depends upon the caliber and values of the kings or Chief Executive in modern times. The descendants of Iksvaku were all without exception noted for their piety reign in particular, Ayodhya and the provinces attained a high level of prosperity; and it is again and again pointed out by Valmiki that people had then a plentiful supply of the good things of life, of horses and cattle and corn and wealth.[4] Under his efficient administration the various orders of society discharged their proper responsibilities; and the high virtues practiced by the king and his principal officers led smoothly and inevitably to the raising of the cultural level of the subjects. What better tribute can be paid to any ruler and his ministers than what Valmiki, for example, repeats in the case of Dasaratha, namely that there was none during his reign who was atheistic or untruthful or slenderly read or illiterate.[5] Valmiki Ramayana explains the philosophy of the state by describing the main duty of the king and now chief executive and the administrators who rule the kingdom. The following statements from the Valmiki Ramayana describe this philosophy:

The king is for the welfare of people (2.67.34) and strives for excellence for the kingdom. He is to ensure through his administration righteous life for the people. He is to ensure that administration of the kingdom is based on Dharma. The present Government of India must look to its learned literature like Ramayana and improve upon it. The existing situation in India has been described by former President of India K.R. Narayanan, while delivering his address, on the eve of Independence Day, on 14th August, 2000, was critical of the nexus between politicians and criminals, who are, in the process polluting the environment of the country. The malpractices in every sphere have become cancerous and are engulfing the entire system geared to provide good standard of living to people. T.N. Chaturvedi in his Editorial on the Special Number on Ethics in Public life of the Indian Journal of Public Administration (July-Sept., 1995) has rightly remarked:

The potential damage and threat to the political fabric of a system is not dependent on the character of government, i.e. whether it is an activist or limited in scope. History shows that neither a capitalist nor a socialist nor a welfare State is immune to the corrosive evil of corruption. The standards of conduct and behaviour of people in political authority have their malignant influence in other walks of life in society. The ethical dimensions of how influential and powerful people conduct themselves in private life and the public domain set a precedent for the lesser human beings and groups in society to follow or to seek justification for their own self-seeking or even scandalous conduct. The perniciousness ripple-effect encompasses all segments of society. It is not only the public systems that are under attack. The people harbour grievances against trade, industry, business, academia, medical and other professional groups and organizations. The evil within and outside the government circle, is thus, not limited to any narrow confines. Similarly, the influence of ethical conduct in positive terms is also not contained or concerned with only some specific sections and select groups but is relevant to the entirety of society and its wider network of relationships. As is often said, the moral basis for the unity and stability of society demands that ethical restraints must operate not only in respect of individuals but also organized groups—be they industrial, business and trade associations, labour unions, political parties, military and civil services, judiciary, non-governmental organizations, academic or professional associations, agriculturists organisations, etc.—apart from government itself. The all-pervading and inter-locking nature of ethics in public life is to be comprehended in all its manifestations and dimensions. This is borne out by history in different times and ages and also by the prowess of civilization today

In the scriptures, it is ordained that the king would look after the welfare of the people just like one looks after his family. Such a conductive atmosphere is essential for moral and spiritual growth of the people. There are hardly any problem in such a kingdom. Even Kautilaya has written:

In the happiness of the king,
Lies the happiness of people,
In the happiness of people,
Lies the happiness of the king.

We must learn from Ramayana and look after the welfare of the people which has become the last priority in the present times. We must improve our present Governance based upon Ramayana values. Administration is never something apart from people and their needs; rather it is the means by which these needs are met and the administrator who thinks of his organization as something apart from the community will fail to recognize significant problems of the citizens and the administration and will not be in a position to deliver the goods.

Time has come for a strong message to be conveyed that administration is for the people and not for the public servants themselves. There has to be a change of attitudes, and public servants should realize that efficiency will be measured not in terms of what the services purport to offer, but in terms of public satisfaction. Simultaneously, there has also to be a cleansing of the services and codification of the ethics, value systems and the interface with the politicians.

2. Leadership value of Lord Rama

Lord Rama believed in Participative type of leadership. The leader of the participative or helping style wants his staff to participate in setting objectives for their work. He uses them for decisions, team planning and the team cooperation in getting work done. Consequently the staff take responsibility for the work and is committed to the work.

The participative leader trusts his staff's abilities. He listens to their opinions and encourages them to contribute their ideas as to how to provide better services. He always helps them improve their skills. He gives them more responsibility as their skills improve. He spends much of his time with his staff. He works with them to solve problems in the community.

Characteristics of Democratic Leaders which Existed in Lord Rama

- share information with his colleagues;
- prevent dominant personalities from having disproportionate influence;
- solicit opinions, facts, and feelings from participants;
- assist participants in communicating with one another;
- minimize blame-oriented statements;
- redirect in focused discussion back to the problem at hand;
- encourage the generation of alternative solutions;
- delay evaluation of alternatives until all have been presented; and
- guide the process of screening alternatives and selecting the solution.

Lord Rama possessed all qualities of leadership, i.e. Spiritual, moral, ethical, sense control, mind control, good character. Leadership traits mostly require:

- Intelligence
- Emotional stability
- Energy and enthusiasm
- Accommodation and adaptability
- Human Engineering
- Co-existence with subordinates
- Objectivity
- Willingness to make personal sacrifices to assist subordinates
- Develops team spirit.

The attributes that are required in leadership may be briefly summarized as: technical competence, missionary zeal, the capacity to motivate others, the ability to get along with people, cultural adaptability, the capacity to organize and manage, the capacity to inspire confidence in others, patience and dignity. Besides, a leader must believe in the ideas of the organization, be willing to accept hardships and be prepared to work in a spirit of service. His ambition and enthusiasm should not be dampened by local conditions which may not provide him with the necessary facilities. All these qualities were available in Lord Rama.

When King Dasaratha intends to appoint Rama as the crown prince he describes Rama's qualities as follows:

- Detachment,
- Tranquility,
- Gentleness in Speech, and
- Equamanity.

3. Adequate Services

Adequate services both in quantity and quality were made available to the people. The capital itself was in every way a source of attraction. Its roads were spacious, well laid out, and regularly watered to keep down the dust. Everything was clean: the food eaten was pure, and the water available was 'sweet as the juice of the sugarcane'. Agriculturists and traders received special attention and protection. From various countries merchants naturally flocked to take advantage of the conveniences offered by Ayodhya, and its streets looked beautiful with well-arranged rows of shops. Undue competition and oppression being thus removed through the vigilance of the king and his ministers, it became possible for all classes of society to breathe freely and strive successfully for full self-expression.[6]

4. Defence Administration

This state of affairs was maintained partly with the help of a thoroughly trained and equipped army. It was stationed in the various forts which were carefully provided with enough wealth, corn, water, arms, machines and artisans. The capital itself was the abode of mighty warriors of straight-forward ways, of great learning and culture. There were great car-warriors by thousands, whose arrows sped with irresistible force, but who would never degrade themselves by striking the fugitive or in any other manner violating the rules of chivalry. Faithful and loyal because of their own sense of duty and honour, they were doubly attached to their king and country owing to the kind and dignified treatment given to them.[7]

5. People's Participation

The king's personality was no doubt the mainspring of the progress which country made; but it was by no means a case of a one-man show. The east is often described as having known and relished only despotic monarchy. The Ramayana, however, presents an entirely different picture. For at every turn we find the ministers, learned men, and the principal officers of the army consulting together and shaping the policy of the State. On important occasions people from different parts of the land assembled and took part in the discussions. Free expression of opinion was to take place before any one spoke out his views. In the matter of Rama's installation as heir apparent, for example, there was an exceptionally large gathering. Then in a mighty voice, solemn and resonant, Dasaratha announced his intention of retiring from the heavy duties of administration and giving his aged frame its much-needed rest. 'If what I have proposed is proper', said he 'by way of conclusion', and is it to your liking, do you accord approval to it, and advise me as to what else I am to do and in what manner.

This principle of ascertaining the opinion and seeking the advice of the people on all important occasions was observed by ancient kings.

Valmiki has wisely upheld the ideal of dharma which has a comprehensive sweep and which enables its votaries, irrespective of their vocation or status in society, to enjoy inner perfection and freedom while dedicating their virtues to the welfare of others. If this ideal, exemplified by the sage in the motives and activities of his numerous characters is grasped and put into practice, all the creeds may survive the present crisis, work side by side without the feeling of hostility, and make people intelligent, efficient, and self-sacrificing enough to solve the problems of the family, country, or even of the world as a whole.[8]

6. Education is an Important Ingredient of Development

Constitutional methods and military efficiency, however, were not the sole factors connected with the welfare of the people. Rather, one might put it the other way about: the king and his ministers remained constitutional, and the soldiers and other sections of the subjects discharged their functions conscientiously and without mutual encroachment, as a result of the high standard of education common in those days. Governmental methods and the cultural level became so interdependent that it was difficult to say which was the cause and which the result. Education was so organized that each section of the society knew not merely the details of fulfilling its own special function, but also the relative place of its contribution in the general scheme. It was also a part of the training to create the mental attitude needed to keep competition within specified and healthy limits.[9]

7. Training of King

The work of the ruler and the leaders was thus to see that the proper kind of education was given to the different sections of society, and also to help all individually and collectively to blossom forth and spread their fragrance from within their own particular spheres. To the Brahmana, the king's question, for example, always ran: Do your disciples regularly wait upon you during their period of study? To the ksatriya it was modified into: 'Do your disciples always remain mailed?'. And so also questions were put to each of the other sections with the necessary variation. The king's training had to be all-comprehensive; for he was the chief executive officer and had to know the art of bringing out the best from the varied temperaments that constituted his country's real wealth. He had to be a patron in every department of its activities and to arrange festivities and demonstrations calculated to stimulate the powers of originality and invention.[10]

8. Dharma to Guide the People

Dharma was then the chief factor that shaped men's lives. As the artistic sense colours the entire outlook of the artist and gives a touch of individuality and beauty not merely to his painting or music but also to his writings and discourses, nay, even his walking, eating, and sitting, so also dharma was meant to give a holy, blissful, loving, and heroic turn to the outlook of its votary and introduce its distinctive fragrance and sweetness into all the activities of his daily life. Through his thoughts and manifold contacts each individual was to evolve steadily and dedicate his virtues to the service of society.

Valmiki has wisely upheld the ideal of dharma which has a comprehensive sweep and which enables its votaries, irrespective of their vocation or status in society, to enjoy inner perfection and freedom while dedicating their virtues to the welfare of others. If this ideal, exemplified by the sage in the motives and activities of his numerous characters, is grasped and put into practice, all the creeds may survive the present crisis, work side by side without the feeling of hostility, and make people intelligent, efficient and self-sacrificing enough to solve the problems of the family, country, or even of the world as a whole.

Ramayan is an ideal scripture which suggests as to how family, social and national values can create an ideal state popularly known as Ram Rajya. In such a state there is no scope of any problem—law and order poverty, social conflicts and justice. We shall discuss briefly some values enshrined in Ramayana which can be a source of solace to the present day world engulfed in crisis of all types. Ramayana's approach to all problems were based on ethical and moral values which are a product of worth mentioning. When Lord Rama was asked to go to priests for fourteen years, his brothers, mothers got annoyed and wanted him to disobey the king and get control of the whole kingdom. On hearing the views of his family members Lord Rama remakred.[11]

If this kingdom and all that we experience, including our bodies, were true in the ultimate sense, then it would have been proper for you to make an effort on the lines proposed by you. He observed:

- Enjoyments are momentary like streaks of lightning appearing in the clouds. So also is life—it is like a small drop of water sprinkled on a red hot piece of iron.
- For men in the grip of the serpent of Time, to long for these extremely temporary enjoyments is like what it is for a frog to cry for food when it is already in the mouth of a serpent.
- Man struggles day and night in various kinds of work for securing objects of enjoyment for his body. But, the truth is that the body is different from the true Self.
- For all creatures, extremely temporary is the association with their kith and kin like father, mother, sons, brother, wife and others. It is only like the association that the traveller has in a way side inn or even like pieces of wood floating down a river.
- Fortune is unstable like a shadow. So is youth, like a wave in a water receptacle. Sexual enjoyments are dream-like and unsubstantial. Life, after all, is of very short duration. Yet, strangely enough all living beings run after these values as the be-all and end-all of life.
- This transmigratory life resembles a dream. It is full of suffering arising from diseases. It is as evanescent as a castle in the air, but yet foolish man goes after it.
- Sunset and sunrise mark the ebbing away of life. We see all around others succumbing to old age and death. But still man does not realise that this is his fate also.
- Without realising that every day and every night that he is now enjoying, mark the termination of those that have gone before, the foolish and unreflective man blindly runs after enjoyments. He does not realise the rapidity with which time rolls on.

- The contents of our life-span are like water kept in an unbaked pot. It leaks out and is exhausted every moment. Like enemies, many kinds of diseases are ever ready to attack and destroy the body.
- Old age and disease are ever assailing the body, and in their wake death too is watching for the opportune moment to pounce upon man like a tigress.
- In this world you find that man thinks of his own body as 'I'—of this body which is only a synonym for worms, dirt and ashes. With reference to such a despicable thing like this body, he feels that he is a world-renowned king.
- How can this body be the spirit (Atman)—this body which is nothing but a combination of skin, bones excreta, blood, etc.? It is extremely changeful also. How can such a body be identified with the Atman?
- Lakshmana! This body for the love of which you say you are going to destroy the world—this identification with the body is the cause of all evil.
- The conviction that 'I am the body' is what is called Avidya (ignorance). The conviction that 'I am not the body but the light of Consciousness', is called Vidya (knowledge).
- Avidya is the cause of transmigratory life, and the eradication of it is accomplished by Vidya. Therefore, all who aspire for liberation should cultivate Vidya. In the cultivation of Vidya, the chief obstructing factors are passions like lust and anger.
- Of all these, anger is the greatest obstruction. For, overcome by anger, man murders even his father, brother, well-wishers and friends.
- From anger arises distress in mind. Anger keeps on tightly ties to the transmigratory life. Anger effaces a man's righteous tendencies. Therefore, anger is to be abandoned by all means.

- Anger is man's most terrible enemy. Desires and longings of the heart constitute the Vaitarani—the river of hell difficult to cross. Contentment is Nandanavana, the forest of Nandana—the garden of heaven. Peace at heart is verily Kamadhenu—the heavenly cow of plenty.[12]

Control over Mind

- Lord Rama has control over his mind. Therefore, Lord Rama advised practise of calmness of mind. Thereby you can avoid having enemies. The Atman is distinct from the senses, mind, Prana, Buddhi and other categories. Pure and changeless, the Atman is the universal self-conscious intelligence shining without the help of any other entity (svayamjyoti). As long as one does not realise the distinctiveness of the Atman from the body, the senses and the Prana, so long will one be subject to the sufferings of transmigratory life, including death. Therefore, ever think of the Atman as residing in the heart in complete separation from the body-mind complex. While knowing the Atman thus, follow the ways of the world at the same time. Do not feel distressed. Enjoyments and sufferings befall man according to his operative Karma (prarabdha).
- Though coursing along the flow of worldly life and appearing to be the agent of various actions, one who knows the real Self is never bound by the good and evil fruits of actions.
- Being pure and unaffected within, one is not affected by Karmas. Always remember these instructions.
- Thus you will never fall a victim to the sufferings of Samsara; and you, too, O mother, keep in your mind all these truths that I have spoken to Lakshmana.
- You wait for my return. Your sorrows will not last very long. Living beings who are subject to their

Karma cannot always live in the same situation, as different environments are required for the experience of the fruits of their Karmas. So it is not given to them to live always with the same people in the same place. They have to part according to the quanta of Karma coming to fruition.

- Men subject to Karma are like boats caught in a current of water. They go in different directions according to the speed and direction of the water. And after all, fourteen years will pass away like a moment.
- Mother! Abandon grief and permit me to go. If you do so, I shall be able to live in the forest in peace.

Ethical Values

Rama ruled following ethical values. Today, we are not running the country based on values. B. Rattan Reddy opines that there is no doubt that Indian Administration needs a strong core of dynamic values to transform its ethos at all levels. Laws can be enacted and rules framed to this end. Enforcement agencies can prosecute and the system can punish. This will have an impact. Nonetheless, enforcement of morality through law will largely remains an external process that can at best delineate a framework for public behaviour that should not be transgressed. But beyond that, laws or rules have inherent limitations in addressing the question of societal and individual change. As such, lasting public morality and ethics cannot be forced from outside. These must take roots and grow within the system itself. People have to understand and accept it so that change becomes organic. Lord Rama selected and promoted his employees based on merit and belief in Ethical values.

HRD in brief is transformation of Potential Human Resources into Kinetic Human Resources for optimization of the potential capacity of employees. It has been rightly said in a study of the Capacity of United Nations Development System that "Human rather than capital is the key to development." Development is not a mechanical process. It is a human enterprise and its success will depend ultimately on the skill, quality and motivation of the persons associated with it. As Professor Iris Claude has commented:

> "In a very significant sense, the identify of every organization. . . . Is lodged in its professional staff. Members, stockholders, or citizens may control the organization but they can do it, the staff is the organization."

It is therefore, by increasing the efficiency, integrity and the intelligence of its personnel that the organization will give itself the real means for advancing towards growth and productivity. The constant improvement of the efficiency of an employee is as much the responsibility of the employee himself as of the organization.

Family Life

His elder brother Bharata came to Rama and requested again and again to return to Ayodhya and sit on its throne. This was asserted by all the family members. At this, Lord Rama replied which need be followed by people today to lead a happy life.

Our father ordered me to spend fourteen years in the Dandaka forest and then only return to the city; and for that period, he has assigned the kingdom to you, Bharata. So it is clear that the kingdom has been given to you by our father himself. And to me likewise has been assigned the kingdom of Dandaka forest by our father. It is therefore the duty of us both to obey strictly the command of our father. One who disobeys his father and goes about doing things according to his own sweet will, is as good as dead even while living. He is sure to be consigned to hell after death. Therefore, you rule over the kingdom, and we shall look after the forest.[13]

Public Life

Lord Rama returned to Ayodhya after 14 years and ruled over the state. In Chapter 18 it has been mentioned that—

- Rama, who was the object of everyone's love, now ruled the kingdom, and Lakshmana, though he never desired it, was installed as the heir apparent. He continued to serve Rama devotedly.
- Rama in reality is the Supreme Being, the witness of all activities, free from all blemishes, devoid of agency and similar limitations, ever unchanging, and always immersed in his inherent Bliss. Still having taken up a human form and the role of a teacher, he performed innumerable Yagas including Aswamedha, in which he distributed an enormous quantity of wealth as Dakshina.
- During Rama's rule, women were never widowed and had not to mourn for that reason. There was no fear from serpents nor from diseases.
- The Kingdom never suffered from the depredations of thieves and no disaster overtook the people. There was never the unfortunate situation of old men surviving, while the young and the children died. All were devoted to the thought and worship of Rama.
- The clouds rained in season and according to necessity. The subjects were all devoted to Dharma and to the rules and regulations of Varna and Ashrama.
- Rama looked upon his subjects as his own children and they considered him as their father. They were all devoted to Dharma. In this way Rama ruled over the country for ten thousand years.

Today, we are seeming around the world large number of problems facing the people because of poor governance. Let us take the example of India.[14]

The country is passing through a terrible crisis these days. The aggravation of material greed has, as a reaction, set ablaze the fire of corruption at all levels. Through the dominant influence of the present material civilization and the ideal of enjoyment fostered by it, even the basic framework and moral fibre of the country has been affected by an internal demoralization. The heart trembles at the sight of the moral degradation practiced today in the field of public administration. There is no limit to the fraud and hypocrisy that are being practiced in the name of politics.

Good Governance is the essential ingredient for delivering economic development and social upliftment. Administrative culture mediates among individuals, groups and communities and needs to be strengthened, if the new millennium is to be made meaningful and socially-productive.

Good governance is not an alien or new concept for India. Even today "Ram Rajya" connotes the highest achievable level of good governance. The need of the hour is to look back, rediscover our cultural heritage, customs, practices, beliefs and values, painstakingly enunciated by the Great Rishis of India. Since the days of Great King Bharata, from whose name is derived the name of our motherland, the essence of governance by rulers (Raj Dharma) has been a strict code of conduct, a sense of duty and service to subjects, willingness to sacrifice for the sake of upholding moral values and fair play and justice above all.

We have to follow the teachings of Ramayana for good governance and welfare of people.

It is to the credit of India's constitutional framers and freedom fighters that they left a solid foundation for good governance and liberal democratic tradition which although wakened, can be made resurgent. In this task, both the secular and spiritual institutions must work together rather than fencing out, in the name of secularism, the spiritual domain from contributing to good governance. There is a need to bring both together for sustaining the common good. Although they have different perspectives and objectives (one dealing with the welfare and care of life here and now, while the other striving for the life hereafter), nevertheless, both are needed to serve the common good of the Loka and the fight for good governance.[15]

The Test of Good Governance is to promote the physical, social and spiritual development of the people. God has created the universe will all facilities essential for people. It is a place to enjoy bliss as well as necessary material comforts. Human beings are expected to conduct their affairs in such a way, especially through good governance, so as to achieve the full benefits of job of living.

Diffusing glory with your rays,
You have scaled the shining realm of heaven.
By you are supported all things that are,
O God All Creator, essence all-divine,
(RV X, 170, 4)

CONCLUSION

Valmiki's is not the only Ramayana now available to us. In Sanskrit itself there is the Adhyatma Ramayana which reminds the reader at every turn that Rama was conscious of his divinity at all times although he continued to behave like an ordinary man, suffering patiently the sorrows that fell to his lot. Many a poet of later years has drawn inspiration from the glorious history of Rama and has either translated these two Ramayanas into the regional languages, or produced original compositions giving elaborate treatment to particular episodes. Painters and sculptors have also been drawing their best subjects from this sacred theme; and in different parts of the country one may see mighty temples erected in honour of Rama, containing his image in a heroic pose within the shrine, or his story depicted in colours all over the walls. In the afternoons or at nights, when work is over and leisure is available, here and there might also be seen groups of devotees, including women and children, listening eagerly to the exposition of the Ramayana and imbibing the principles of dharma as the ancients conceived it. The story-tellers are specially trained in the art, though there may not be much in common between their modern performances and those given by the original chanters, Kusa and Lava, the disciples of Valmiki. In all these ways and many more, the ideals presented by the sage have spread to every corner of the country. There is no doubt that Rama's character as a hero and as a man of virtuous action and that of Sita as a model heroine have been instrumental in shaping the lives of many who genuinely aspire after dharma.

Valmiki has wisely upheld the ideal of dharma which has a comprehensive sweep and which enables its votaries, irrespective of their vocation or status in society, to enjoy inner perfection and freedom while dedicating their virtues to the welfare of others. If this ideal, exemplified by the sage in the motives and activities of his numerous characters, is grasped and put into practice, all the creeds may survive the present crisis, work side by side without the feeling of hostility, and make people intelligent, efficient, and self-sacrificing enough to solve the problems of the family, country, or even of the world as a whole.

Relevance

Besides being a fine specimen of the poetic art and also history, the Ramayana is also a Dharmasastra, a sacred text teaching righteousness. It expounds the principles of eternal law (Sanatana Dharma), and presents the ideals of good conduct (sadacara), which is one of the bases of dharma. According to the Smrtis the epic draws attention to other topics of the Dharmasastra, such as nitya, naimittika, and kamya varieties of Karma-regular, occasional, and optional duties.

The Ramayana also deals with polity, administration, diplomacy, war and other topics, which fall within the domain of the Arthasastra. The benefits of good government and democracy are exemplified in the Ramarajya, while the contrary is shown under Ravana. Many precepts relating to Kama (legitimate enjoyment) can be found at several places in the Ramayana. The Ramayana is Nitisastra expounding lofty ethical ideals. The importance of moral virtues—simple living, modesty, restraint, obedience to elders, charity, and humanity—is fully stressed. It is easy to collect from the Ramayana a string of ethical thoughts that have become proverbs.

The Ramayana brings out the strength and weakness of the Aryan character. The superiority of the Aryans lay in the sternness of their character, their spirit of sacrifice, supreme regard for truth, love of adventure, and perseverance. Rama is the embodiment of the high ideals of Aryan Life. In him is presented the strange combination of a faithful and dutiful son, an affectionate brother, a loving husband, a stern, relentless hero, and an ideal king. Lakshmana and Bharata represent ideal brothers, while Sita a dutiful wife. In Dasaratha is brought out the weakness of the male for feminine grace, which resulted in great disaster not only to him but also to the kingdom. Prevalence of polygamy, some forms of superstitious practices, and evil effects of the caste system, are among the weak spots of the Aryan life hinted at in the Ramayana.[16]

Rama's Kingdom was full of happiness both physical and ethical. The rule which Lord Rama had over his kingdom was known as Ram Rajya which has become synonymous with Good Governance. Ram Rajya would remain an ideal form of Government to be cherished where there would be no corruption, but would promote happiness and welfare of the people. There was no problem of law and order. Thus Ram Rajya would guide the rulers and leaders in all times to come.

Notes and References

1. Swami Nishsreyananda, The Culture of Ramayana, in *Culture Heritage of India*, Vol. II, The Rama Krishna Mission, Institute of Culture, Calcutta, 2001, p. 46.
2. A.D. Pusaker, The Ramayana, Its History and Character, *Ibid.*, p. 14.
3. Swami Nishsreyananda, *op. cit.*, p. 32.
4. Ram, I. 6.7
5. *Ibid.*
6. Swami Nishreyananda, *op. cit.*, p. 32-33.
7. *Ibid.*, p. 33.
8. *Ibid.*, p. 34, 39.
9. *Ibid.*, pp. 35-36.
10. *Ibid.*, p. 36.
11. *Ibid.*, p. 39.
12. Swami Tapsyananda, Adhytma Ramayana, Sri Ramakrishna Math, Madras.
13. *Ibid.*, p. 109.
14. *Ibid.*, pp. 366-67.
15. O.P. Dwivedi, Common Good and Good Governance, in *IJPA*, July to Sept., 1998, pp. 263-64.
16. A.D. Pusaker, The Ramayana: Its History and Culture, in the *Cultural Heritage of India*, Vol. II, pp. 27-28.

3

Kautilya

INTRODUCTION

Kautilya is the most popular name in Indian Administration. His great work, the Arthasastra, is the oldest text on Public Administration and was written sometimes between 521 and 300 BC.

Kautilya known by the name of Chanakya was an eminent and outstanding personality in Indian Ancient history. He was the Prime Minister of the Mauryan ruler Chandergupta. The Arthasastra which has been accepted as a treatise in the Governance of State had gone out of circulation for centuries. It was rediscovered by the great scholar Shamastry in 1909 A.D. The authorship of Arthasastra is ascribed to Visnugupta which is believed to be the real name of Kautilya.

The Arathasatra has been divided into fifteen adhikarnas or books—Five deal with internal administration of the state, the next eight with relations of other states while the last two are miscellaneous in Character. Each book is divided into seven chapters.

CHART 3.1

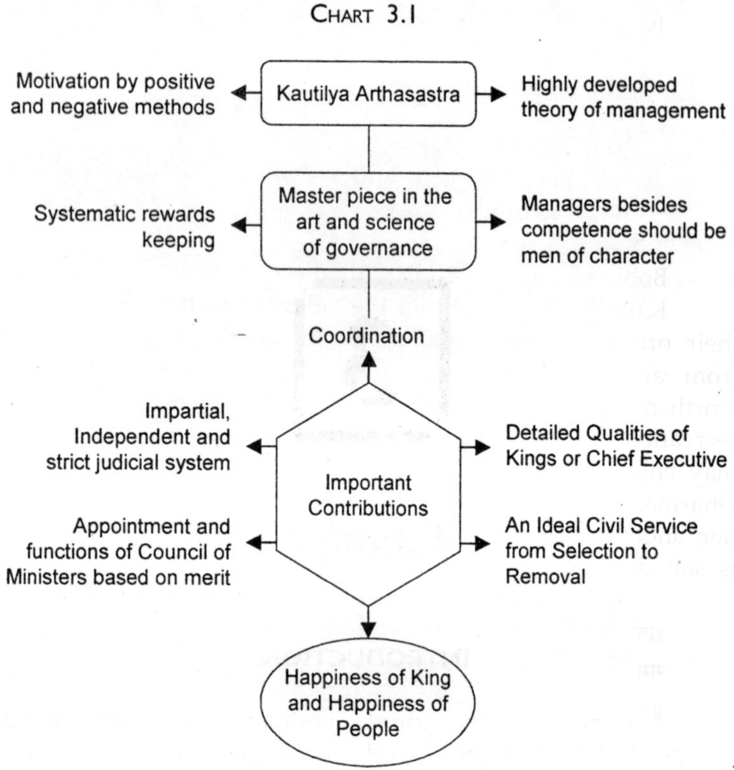

IMPORTANT CONTRIBUTIONS TO ADMINISTRATIVE THOUGHT

I. Qualities of the King

Chief Executive—The success or failure of administrative system depends upon the quality of Chief Executive, i.e. kings in the old times. Kautilya mentions the following qualities: (Book 1.5)

(a) Adequate education and disciplined in science.
(b) Good Governance for his subjects.
(c) Welfare of the people.
(d) Righteousness and Good relationships with the people.

(e) Avoidance of negative qualities—
  (i) Lust,
  (ii) Anger,
  (iii Greed,
  (iv) Vanity,
  (v) Haughtiness, and
  (vi) Excessive joy.

Book 1.7 clearly asserts all these as follows:

Kautilya enjoins on all the rulers that they should keep their organs of sense under perfect control and keep away from all unrighteous and uneconomical transactions. It is worth mentioning that he does not advocate a life devoid of recreations and enjoyments. It is even mentioned that a ruler may enjoy in an equal degree all the three pursuits of life - Dharma, Artha and Kama which are interdependent upon one another. If anyone of the three is enjoyed to an excess, it is self defeating and hurts the other two also.

धर्मार्थाविरोधेन कांम सेवेत न निस्सुखः स्यात् ।
समं वा त्रिवर्गमन्योन्यानुबन्धम् ।
एको ह्यत्यासेवितो धर्मार्थकामानात्मानमितरौ च पीडयति ।

(Book I.7)

Arthasastra is defined by the author as 'the science which treats of the means of acquiring and ruling the earth'. This is followed by an explanation of thirty-two technical terms used by him in his work. In the concluding verses he says that the sastra establishes and maintains the triad, viz. virtue, wealth, and pleasure (dharma, artha, and kama), and sets down unrighteous acts detrimental to wealth (artha).

The king's functions are described in the Dharma-Sutras as comprising the protection of the person and property of his subjects (which involves as its corollary the guardianship of the property of minors and others, the custody of lost and ownerless property, and compensation for property stolen and not recovered for its owner), and the administration of justice, the guardianship of the law of the social order, the regulation of trade and commerce, and so forth. These functions are highly developed in the Arthasastra of Kautilya, a work of maturity achieved, no doubt, on the basis of its predecessors.[1]

The Dharma-Sutras lay down a high standard for the King's duties. These were not only required to provide for an extensive system of state relief to the indigent, the helpless, and the learned, but also enjoined to keep before him the objective of securing for his subjects freedom from want and fear. The early Buddhist texts likewise hold before us the examples of good kings who observed what are called the ten royal virtues and, more specifically, the duties of the pious Buddhist jayman. On the other hand, we have highly realistic pictures in the Jatakas of tyrannical kings endangering the lives and properties of their subjects.[2]

The king as head of the state must attend to immediately all urgent matters. To quote U.N. Ghoshal again king must at once attend to all urgent calls of business and not put them off; for, when postponed, they may prove too difficult or even impossible to accomplish. Readiness for action is described as a religious vow for a king, and the root of all royal business is his enterprise.[3]

(1) The king should have control over the senses which is motivated by training in the sciences, secured by giving up lust, anger, greed, pride, arrogance and fool hardiness. (6.1)

(2) Absence of improper indulgence in the pleasure of sound, touch, colour, and smell by the sense of hearing, touch and sight, the tongue and the sense of smell, means control over the senses; or the practice of (this) science gives such control. (6.2)

(3) For the whole of this science means control over the senses. (6.3)

(4) Therefore, by casting out the group of six enemies he should acquire control over the senses, cultivate his intellect by association with elders, keep a watchful eye by means of spies, bring about security and well-being by energetic activity, maintain the observance of their special duties (by the subjects) by carrying out his own duties,

> acquire discipline by receiving instruction in the sciences, attain popularity by association with what is of material advantage and maintain proper behaviour by doing what is beneficial. (1.7.1.)

The above description must be taken seriously as in today's administrative system, the Chief Executive, Prime Ministers do not follow the above mentioned qualities and indulge in corrupt practices resulting in loss to the prestige of the Chief Executive as well as the country. Most of the Chief Executives in India have lost their positions because of poor qualities. We need to learn from Kautilya's description and make our country free of corrupt practices which is eating away the country like cancer.

2. Selection of King's Officials

Kautilya mentioned that the appointment of officials should be chosen from among those who have both theoretical knowledge and practical experience. In addition they should be born in high family and possessed of wisdom, bravery, sincerity and loyalty. Much importance is attached to integrity and character of persons to be appointed. They are tried by offering allurements: those who withstand these are to be selected, others dropped. The tests are to correspond to jobs. Thus those whose purity has been tested under the monetary allurement may be employed revenue collectors, in civil and criminal courts and so on.

The function of offering allurements is to be performed by spies who collect information about content or discontent prevalent among the officials to be appointed.

Kautilya's Arthasastra has written in detail about the selection, salary structure, duties and responsibilities, code of conduct, disciplinary actions, etc. for the personnel engaged by the kings. Let us mention them briefly and compare them with our present system.

Selection of Top Personnel

As per Chanakya: The duties of Public Officials assigned were that they shall always be at the side of the

King, neither too close nor too far away, and:

- not talk slyly against other advisers;
- not say things which are not carefully thought out and which are untrue, uncultured, or outside his knowledge;
- not laugh loudly when there is nothing to laugh about; when there is cause, he may laugh but not too loudly;
- avoid [uncouth behaviour like] spitting and breaking wind;
- neither talk in secret with another [adviser] not become quarrelsome in public debate;
- not dress [above his station] like royalty nor in a gaudy or clownish fashion;
- not openly ask for gems or special favours;
- not indulge in [unseemly gestures like] winking, biting the lips and frowning;
- not interrupt while another is speaking;
- not antagonize the powerful;
- not associate with [disreputable] women, pimps, envoys of neighbouring kings, those supporting the enemy, dismissed officers, wicked people, those who form a group for a single objective nor with specialized lobbies. (5.4.8-10, 14).7

अमात्यसम्पदोपेताः सर्वाध्यक्षाः शक्तितः कर्मसु नियोज्यम् ।
कर्मसु चैषां नित्यं परीक्षां कारयेत् ।।
चित्तानित्यत्वान्मनुष्याणाम् ।
अश्वसधर्माणो हि मनुष्या नियुक्ताः कर्मसु निकुर्वते ।।

(Book 11-9)

These duties are not similar to the existing civil services. The servants of the kings were totally committed to him and must be loyal to him. A servant could be removed or eliminated at the behest of the king if he finds him useless for him.

Service under a King has been compared to living in a fire [but is, in fact, worse]. A fire may burn a part of one's body and, at its worst, all of it; but a King [goes from one extreme to another]. He may either confer prosperity or may have the whole family, including wives and children, killed. [therefore,] a wise man makes self-protection his first and constant concern. (5.4.16.17).8 There were no safeguards for the servants of the king like the civil service of today which enjoys many immunities as in India (Article 311 of the constitution).

Kautilya realised the importance of providing fringe benefits to the employees in the service of the state and has described a number of such fringe benefits in his arthashastra, e.g. if a Government servant dies while on duty, his sons and wives shall be entitled to his salary and good allowance. Minor children and old or sick relatives shall be [suitably] assisted. On occasions such as funerals, births or illnesses, the families [of the deceased government servant] shall be given presents of money and shown honour [as a mark of gratitude to one who died in the King's service] (5.3.28-30).

ACTION AGAINST GOVERNMENT SERVANTS COMMITTING FINANCIAL IRREGULARITIES

All superintendents endowed with the excellence of a minister should be appointed to works according to their capacity, (2) and he should constantly hold on inspection of their works, men being inconsistent in their minds, and (3) for, men being of a nature similar to that of horse change when employed in works. (2.9.16)

He who causes loss of revenue consumes the property of the king. If he causes loss through ignorance and other causes, he should make him pay that suitably multiplied. He who procures double the normal revenue, consumes the countryside. (2.9.17)

We should learn from these abstracts from Kautilya's Arthasastra. Our civil servants are causing a great loss in the sense that the people receive only ten paisa out of a rupee spent by the government. We may follow the spirit of Kautilya's Arthasastra and take action so that we can make the best use of money and usher in an era of socio-economic development.

Kautilya mentions 40 ways of causing financial impropriety. These are tabulated on the next page. These are of great relevance for us as corruption has reached its peak in most of the countries of the world especially India. We should learn a lesson and take a cue from Kautilya to improve our system to stop cancerous corruption.

The remaining twelve are:

29.30 Fraud in periods of payments:

(i) discrepancy in months in a year.
(ii) Discrepancy in days in a month.

(in both cases, not recording receipts or payments to the advantage of the fraudulent officials and the disadvantage of the public)—

- Personally supervised work
- Heads of Accounts
- Labour accounts
- Measurement of work
- Totalling
- Quality
- Price
- Weighing
- Measuring
- Containers for goods (2.8.20,21).26

Watchfulness of the conduct of Government officials through the institution of informers was also recommended. They were rewarded if correct information was supplied while they got punishment for wrong information. (2.829, 30, 31, 32)

It is deplorable that people who have the opportunity to serve the nation in high capacities should use it to line their own pockets and indulge in ostentious living. While we are crying for foreign capital, some, including ministers, invest their wealth overseas. Far from setting the much needed good example, some politicians take the lead in activities that are not to the best interest of the nation. Prof. Smith notes that for development of Nigerian industry, agriculture, communications, etc., large scale complicated plans were devised. But when we get down to putting these plans into operation we find that the implementation of the great development programs rapidly creates facilities not so much for the development intended but for social corruption of all sorts.

No drive against corruption can succeed unless and until the government itself is firmly committed to the task of weeding out dishonest and corrupt officials, irrespective of rank and status. All government employees, irrespective of rank, whose integrity and honesty are even slightly in doubt, should be dealt with severely. Punishment for corruption should be exemplary, the least being dismissal from service. The government should also ensure that anti-corruption agencies are manned by personnel whose integrity and spirit of dedication can never be questioned.[4]

Cheating the Government

The remaining twelve are: 7-18 and 29-30 fraud in period of payments:

(i) discrepancy in months in a year.
(ii) discrepancy in days in a month.

31-40 Discrepancies in the following:

- Personally supervised work.
- Heads of Accounts.
- Labour accounts.
- Measurement of work.
- Totalling.

King selected persons in his service who possessed highest personal qualities of leadership, intellect, energy and other personal attributes as described in [{6.1.2-6}] and the [best] attributes of a state with the help of courtiers and other friends of the king. We have today established independent and impartial Public Service Commissions at the Union and State Levels but their creditability is under cloud as has been reported about these bodies from time to time. There is a need to learn from Kautilya's Arthasastra to ensure right selections.

3. Qualities Essential in Subjects

The success of Kingdom or a country does not depend only on the head of the State but also upon the quality of people. Kautilya describes the following qualities essential among the people. A Kingdom or a country will become prosperous when the people are happy and prosperous. The stability of a kingdom is co-terminus with the happiness of the subjects.

दुर्दशना हि राजानः प्रजां नाशयन्ति

The rulers who are not accessible to the subjects will only ruin them. The kings employee would be punished if they cheat the people.

Type	*Details*	*Punishment*
Obstruction	Failure to carry out (orders or) a task (or to collect due taxes) Failure to realize the profit from an undertaking.	A fine of one-tenth of the amount involved.
	Failure to delivery the profit to the Treasury	
Using government property for personal profits	Lending government property at interest	Double at (personal) profit made
	Trading in government goods	
Falsification of the date	Showing a later date than the one on which income was received.	One-fifth of the amount involved.
	Showing money incurred on an earlier date (in both cases using the money for personal benefits for a period)	
Causing loss to Govt.	Collecting less than the fixed amount of revenue or exceeding the sanctioned amount of expenditure	Four times the amount lost.

Misuse of Govt. property: (i) by the official himself, (ii) by allowing himself, (iii) by substituting one article (of higher value) by another	If gems and jewelry If high valued articles All others Not delivering revenue to the Treasury	Death Middle SP Restitution plus equal amount as fine
Misappropriation	Not paying authorized expenditure (such as not handing over the gifts, as ordered by the king)	Twelve times the amount

A king who is in contact with his people will be able to understand their problems and work for their welfare. On the other hand, if he lives within a shell he will not be able to identify the problems and work for their solution. Pt. Jawaharlal Nehru has said that civil servants should retire in their homes but should mix with all binds and conditions of people, from them, they would learn that is not in their files.

Stealing in Transactions with the Public
(Twenty-eight of the forty ways of stealing)

Favour shown for a bribe	1. Revenue due on a given date is allowed to be paid later	11. Making payment to a favourite earlier than due	19. Goods bought (wholesale but shown as bought retails and a higher price paid)
Public exploited	2. Revneue not due till later is collected earlier (by force) to compensate for above	12. Delaying a payment due on a given date	20. Goods sold at retail prices but shown as sold wholesale (at a lower price).
Favour shown	3. Revenue due (from a bribe giver) is suppressed	13. Making payment not due to someone	21. Suppressing a sale by giving away the goods

Public Exploited and revenue embezzled	4. Revenue not due is made to be paid	14. Not paying the due amount to someone	22. Suppressing a purchase
Corruption	5. Revneue not paid is shown as paid		23. In a supposed purchase) goods not received but payment made.
Public exploited	6. Revenue paid is shown as not paid (but misappropriated)		24. In a (supposed sale) price received but goods not delivered.
Corruption	7. Small amount of revenue paid is made out of paid in full	15. Large payment misrepresented as a small one	25. Selling a high priced item but charging a lower price.
Public exploited	8. Though paid in full, only small amount shown as received.	16. Small payment made, shown as large amount	26. Buying a high price item but paying a lower price.
Corruption	9. Revenue paid in by one shown as paid by another (a bribe giver)	17. Payment due to one person paid to another for a cut	27. Lowering the price
Public exploited	10. Revenue paid in one kind (of higher value) shown as another (of lower value)	18. Payment made in one kind (of lower value) shown as another (for higher value)	28. Raising the price (to someone who does not give a bribe.

न्याययुक्तं राजांन मातरं मन्यन्ते प्रजाः ।

To a ruler who is just, the subjects are attached as to their own mother.

तादृशः स राजा इह सुखः ततः स्वर्गमाप्नोति ।

Such a ruler will be happy in this world and will attain heaven thereafter

A ruler who looks after his subjects will be loved by them. The kingdom will progress along with the subjects and everyone will be happy. His good deeds will also ensure for him an exalted place in heaven.

Kautilya rightly feels:

In the happiness of the King,
Lies the happiness of people,
In the happiness of the people,
Lies the happiness of the King.

4. Appointment and Functions of Council of Ministers

A king cannot function without. competent ministers. Just as a single wheel cannot move a vehicle, a king cannot function without assistance. Therefore, he must have good counsellors in the form of ministers.

सहायसाध्यं राजत्वं
चक्रमेकं न वर्तते ।
कुर्वीत सचिवांस्तस्मात्
तेषां च श्रृणुयान्मतम्

(Book 1-7)

A lot of thought has been given by Kautilya in Book 1-7 to the acquisition of dependable and competent ministers. A good minister should have a multitude of accomplishments and be free from such failings as are enumerated in the relevant chapter. On the positive side it has been mentioned that he should be a native of the same territory, born in a high family, influential, well trained in arts, gifted with foresight, wise, of strong memory, bold, eloquent, skilful, intelligent, possessed of enthusiasm, dignity and endurance, pure in character, affable, firm in loyal devotion, endowed with excellent conduct, strength, wealth and bravery. On the other side, he has to be free from procrastination and fickle-mindedness, should not be subject to excessive hatred and enmity. One may not be able to get a perfect minister from that point of view but an attempt should be made to acquire one with a high percentage of these attributes.

Just out of affection, a person should not be made or retained as a Minister if he is found to be arrogant or lacking in modesty.

From the above statements, we find that Kautilya was more advanced than the present day government. For example, in India, Ministers are criminals, corrupt and have all vices but still they continue causing a great harm to the development of the country. Criminalization of politics is a common phenomenon today.

K.P.A. Menon in his book 'Kautilya on Rajniti' mention the role of ministers, a ruler cannot and should not act on his own in important matters. He has to be advised by his ministers and other counsellors. Ministers should be chosen with great care. In the Arthasastra, Kautilya has discussed even the size of the ministry and come to his own conclusion that there should not be any rigidity about the number. Every precaution should be taken to ensure that no information leaks out from the council chamber. There are certain types of vital information that should be known only to two persons. Modern concepts of administration like maintenance of secrecy, sancity of decisions taken in the council chamber, etc. seem to have been known to the ancient rulers and law-givers.

मन्त्रमूलाः सर्वारम्भाः ।

Proper counsel should be taken before starting on any venture.

Even where an intelligent ruler is quite clear in his mind about the objectives and the methods to be employed he is not expected to embark on any venture without taking proper counsel. In ancient India, a ruler used to spend a lot of his time in the council chamber consulting his ministers on all important matters of public interest including even matrimonial alliances of the members of the royal family.

कार्यान्धस्य प्रदीपो मन्त्रः ।

A person who is blind to (ignorant about) his task gets enlightenment from counsels.

All by himself a ruler may be in a confused state, unsure of how to proceed in his tasks. He gets enlightenment from the council chamber when he discusses the matter with his ministers who are both learned and trustworthy.

मन्त्रप्रमादाद्द्विषतां वशमुपयाति

By wrong counsel the king becomes subdued by his enemies.

After mentioning that a king should consult his cousellors before starting on any important venture, it is being made clear that he should be guided by wise and mature cousellors. Wrong advice leading to wrong action will weaken the state and the enemies who are waiting for such opportunities are bound to take advantage of such a situation.

5. Administrative System

Kautilya lays emphasis on monarchical concentration, Administrative and decision-making powers were regarded as finally resting in the king.

So far as the departmental structure is concerned, the director or the head of the administrative department has under him the following five officers:

(1)	Lekhaka	Clerk
(2)	Rupadarsaka	Inspector of coins
(3)	Sankhyayaka	Accountant
(4)	Nivigrahaka	In-charge of the balance
(5)	Uttaradhyaksha	Supervisor

Public administration of the day enumerated by Kautilya comprised:

(1) The central executive machinery
(2) Mantri-parishad or the consultative body
(3) The civil service
(4) The provincial and local government

The central executive machinery comprised the king, his trusted advisers and the departmental heads having their offices in the capital. The chief officials of the state were:

(1) Mantris
(2) Purohita
(3) Senapati
(4) Yuvaraj
(5) Duwarika
(6) Antaravamsika
(7) Prasastri
(8) Samaharta
(9) Sannidhata
(10) Pradcsta,
(11) Nayaka
(12) Paura
(13) Vyavaharika
(14) Karmantika
(15) Mantriparishadadhyaksha
(16) Adhyaksak
(17) Dandapalas
(18) Antapalas
(19) Atavikas

The king occupied the central position in the administration. He delegated powers to senior officers under whom worked junior officers. The administrative machinery was well-knit; the mantris, amatyas and mahamatras (departmental heads) constituted the core of the central executive.

The administrative hierarchy of the departmental head (mahamatra) was as follows:

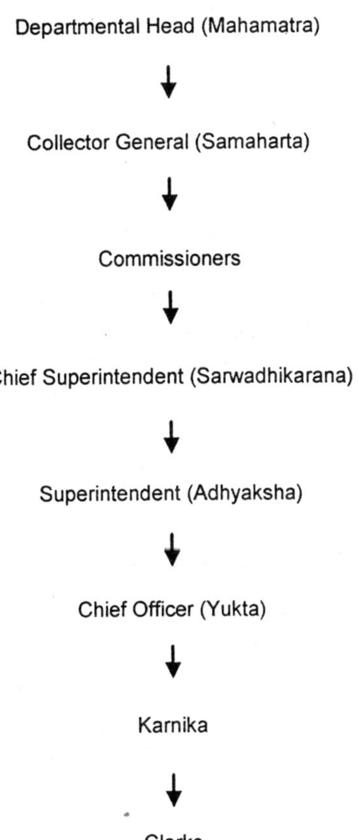

Motivation

Arthasastra identifies four different methods of motivation, viz., sama, dama, danda and bheda. As a group they can be referred to as 'motivation means' and their various combinations as 'means-mix'. Sama is the persuasion method of motivation, dama is the 'incentive system' or the reward method of motivation, bheda is the 'internal competition' method of motivation, and danda is punishment method of motivation by use of power/authority/force or to use the current terminology from management literature, the Theory X method of motivation. Arthasastra also suggests the sequencing of the use of the above stated means. The 'natural method' is to use the sama (persuasion) and the dama (incentives) first, creating internal competition comes next and the use of force comes as the last method. Arthasastra also suggests that different situations require different types of motivation means-mix.

6. Dandaniti: Judicial System

After quoting his predecessors Kautilya makes his own 'comments on the degree of punishment'. Kautilya asserts that while imposing severe punishment the ruler becomes repulsive to the people, one who awards mild punishment becomes contemptible. Whoever imposes punishment as deserved becomes respectable. If justice is well administered people devote themselves to righteousness and undertake Productive ventures thereby ensuring prosperity to themselves and the nation.

The word itself should not however, be interrelated in a narrow sense of the science of punishment. In a sense it is the administration of justice and it should also be understood for dispensing justice, there has to be a machinery for administration.

Kautilya says that the lawful application of danda ensures the complete happiness of the individual, its unlawful or vicious application causes universal disaffection, and its non-application produces anarchy symbolized by the law of the jungle.

According to Kautilya, Dandaniti is a means to make acquisitions, to keep them secure, to improve them and to distribute among the deserved the profits of improvement. This is being emphasised in a number of aphorisms in this section. A ruler should not be lax in enforcing justice and punishing those who deserve punishment, whether they are his enemies who have been subdued or the offenders within the kingdom. At the same time, the punishment should not be either too severe or mild. It should be related to the magnitude of the offence. Protection of one's own self should be considered as one's vital objective.

दण्डः सर्वसम्पदा योजयति ।

Alround prosperity is attained through proper administration of justice.

This is no exaggeration. If the evil doers are properly punished the country will be at peace. People carry on their vocations without any hindrance and there will be alround prosperity. They will work hard when they know they can retain their earnings.

Administration of justice is the most important task of the ruler. If he fails in that primary responsibility the subjects will be helpless. Maintenance of law and order is considered to be. the most important responsibility of the state in the modern age. It was so in ancient days also in a better form.

न दण्डादकार्यणि कुर्वन्ति ।

If there is no proper administration of justice wickedness will thrive.

It has been mentioned in Chapter III of Arthasastra that if Danda is not enforced it will lead to what is known as Matsyanyaya—the bigger fish eating the small fish, the strong harassing the weak.

दण्डो हि विज्ञानेन प्रणीयते ।

It is through the knowledge of the Sastras one gets a proper idea of matters relating to administration of justice.

In administering justice and awarding punishments one should not be guided by one's personal ideas on the subject. He should master the subject through careful studies. The word used is knowledge (*fokku*) which means true wisdom and it is acquired through the study of Sastras on the subject.

Book Three deals with the administration of justice. Judges *(dhamasthas)* have the status of high officials *(amatyas)*. There is no reference to gradation among judges: perhaps appeals lay only to the king. Judges are to look into cases arising out of transactions, trespass, scuffles and so on, ordinarily after a complaint has been lodged. The clerk of the court keeps the record. In the discussion, there are terms which appear to stand for evidence (desa *karana)* and witness *(srota)*.

Sacred law *(dharma)*, evidence *(vyavahara)*, history *(charitra)* and edicts of king *(rajasasana)* are said to be the four basis of law. Edicts of kings are to override the other bases in case of conflict among them.

The code of law is set forth under seventeen heads including marriage, property, slaves and labourers, forcible seizure of an object and verbal or physical injury.

The code is cruel; there is also no conception of equality before the law. Thus for eliciting confessions and punishing crimes eighteen kinds of torture are mentioned. These include whipping, suspension with the head downwards, heating the body, exposure to a cold wintry night on coarse green grass, burning the joint of a finger, and so on (3.8). In case of abuse, defamation and assault, the punishment for a crime varies with the case of the offender.

Under the law, slavery is legitimate—a whole chapter (3.13) deals with slaves and labourers. Poverty may also lead to slavery; a person may voluntarily enslave himself. A person's life may be mortgaged by others also. The ransom necessary for a slave to regain his freedom is equal to what he has been sold for. However, a slave who tries to run away may not regain his freedom.

7. Meticulous Attention to Financial Administration

It is an obvious fact that one cannot achieve anything unless he has got wealth—whether it is the pursuit of love, earning name and fame or facing one's enemies.

> All (State) activities depend first on the Treasury. Therefore, a King shall devote his best attention to it. A King with a depleted Treasury eats into the very vitality of the citizens and the country.
>
> Kautilya, *The Arthasastra* (2.81.2 and 2.1.6)

The following means of increasing the wealth of the state have been suggested by Kautilya, in his Arthasastra, which are relevant even today:

- ensuring the prosperity of state activities (and enterprises);

- continuing well tried (and successful) policies;
- eliminating theft;
- keeping strict control over government emplolyees;
- increasing agricultural production;
- promoting trade;
- avoiding troubles and calamities;
- reducing (tax) exemptions and remissions; and
- Increasing cash income. (2.8.3)

For collecting the money from people, the king should be judicious.

A wise and experienced ruler will carefully look after his subjects. He should be like a wreath-maker who goes from tree to tree in the garden collecting flowers without uprooting them, not like the charcoal burner who burns up the whole tree. One consumes milk by milking the cow not by selling it. A monarch should also follow the same principle and enjoy the wealth of the kingdom. A king should not be oppressive and ruin his subjects through heavy taxes and other levies. Plants yield flowers to the wreath-maker without any damage to themselves and the wreath-maker, in turn nurtures the plants.

Kautilya advises the king to keep an eye on his money against its being pilferaged by employee.

Kautilya has prescribed strict conduct rules and strict disciplinary action. He made the following statements to enforce strict discipline.

"Just as it is impossible not to taste honey or poison that one may find at the tip of one's tongue, so it is impossible for one dealing with government funds not to taste, at least a little bit, of the King's wealth." (2.9.82)

"Just as it is impossible to know when a fish moving in water is drinking it, so it is impossible to find out when government servants in charge of undertakings misappropriate money." (2.9.83)

"It is possible to know even the path of birds flying in the sky, but not the ways of officers moving with their intentions concealed." (2.9.84)

"Those officials who do not eat up the king's wealth but increase it in just ways and are loyally devoted to him shall be made permanent in service." (2.9.86)

"He who causes loss of revenue consumes the property of the king, and he who procures double the normal revenue consumes the country side, eats the King's wealth." (2.9, 13,15)

यथा ह्यनास्वादयितुं नशक्यं
जिह्वातलस्थं मधुं वा विषं वा ।
अर्थस्तथा ह्यर्थचरेण राज्ञः
स्वल्पोऽप्यानास्वादयितुं न शक्य : ।।
मत्स्या यथान्तस्सलिले चरन्तो
ज्ञातुं न शक्याः सलिलं पिबन्तः
युक्तास्तथा कार्यविधौ नियुक्ता
ज्ञातुं न शक्याः धनमाददानाः
अपि शक्या गतिर्ज्ञातुः
पततः खे पतत्रिणां ।
न तु प्रच्छन्नभावानां
युक्तानां चरतां गतिः ।।

(Kautilya Book II-9)

Kautilya even recommended that illegal earnings may be confiscated. He wrote that strict action may be taken against dishonest people while loyal and devoted servants may be made permanent and rewarded:

न भक्षयन्ति येत्वर्थान् ।
न्यायतो वर्धयन्ति च ।
नित्यधिकाराः कार्यास्ते ।
राज्ञः प्रियहिते रताः ।।

Kautilya advised to be strict on those who work against the interest of the state and its people. He recommended strict action against anti-social elements.[5] Book Four named Kantaka-sodhana (removal of thorns or anti-social elements), deals with a number of miscellaneous topics, those relate to;

public protection against deceitful and fraudulent artisans and merchants; penalty for manufacturing counterfeit coins and for disturbing the currency; fraud in respect of weights and measures; remedies against providential calamities, e.g. fire, flood, epidemics, and famine; protection from the acts of evil-doers living by secret and foul ways; seizure of criminals on suspicion, along with the stolen property, or in the act of theft, post-mortem examination in the case of sudden deaths; eliciting confession from suspects by questionings or physical tortures; protection of the people from the oppressions of government servants; ransom or fine in lieu of mutilation of limbs of criminals, when ordered by the court; death-penalty with or without torture; outrage on girls; and punishment for transgression of social obligation.

8. Department for Substantive Functions

The *Arthasastra* discuss in detail the functions of about 30 departments for the performance of substantive state functions. We may classify them under six heads as follows:

(1) Production,
(2) Trade,
(3) Measurement,
(4) Tax collection,
(5) Defence, and
(6) Foreign Alliances.

Production

The departments in this category are those of Agriculture, Pasture Lands, Forest Produce, Weaving, Mining and Gold. Thus, officials dealing with agriculture are to grow the kings crops; they are to be possessed of knowledge about the raising different crops, forecasting of rainfall, and methods of irrigation. Mining operations are discussed for the production of copper, lead, tin and mercury in the king's mines. The scientific knowledge and technology displayed in the course of discussion are obviously are of primitive character. Thus the use of honey, sheep's milk, oil and ghee is mentioned for metallurgical operations.

Trade

Departments dealing with trade are those of Commerce Cows, Liquor, Slaughter House. Department of commerce deals mainly with the sale of the liquor, to sell the king's liquor and also regulate its trade. The department of prostitutes (qanikas) is to employ them for the king's court and is also to regulate their private business.

Measurements

The departments in this category are those dealing with: (1) weights and measures, and (2) the measurement of space and time, They are to have measuring instruments manufactured. Various units of measurements have also been mentioned. It is interesting to note that one of the small units of weight *(masha)* mentioned here, is still in use by some jewellers in India.

Tax Collection

Some taxes and fees are to be collected by almost every department. However, there is a department of taxes which is to collect these from traders who are selling goods in or out of the capital city. Goods intended for export must bear the seal, otherwise fines are levied.

Defence

Departments dealing with defence are those of Armoury, Boats, Horses, Elephants, Chariots and infantry. The armoury is to manufacture bows, arrows, swords, razor like "weapons and armour." The other departments are similarly to manufacture or raise, and maintain, their boats, chariots, animals and men. The good qualities and training of animals have been discussed in detail.

It is notable that the *Arthasastra* does not mention any departments for health, education or welfare; nor is there provision for extension or promotional services.

Each department is to have a head *(adhyaksa)*. He is to be assisted by accountants, writers, coin examiners, treasurers, and policemen.

D. Mackenzie Brown appreciates Kautilya's superb administrative competence. He writes that, "The extraordinary thoroughness of Kautilya's work, its imminent inductiveness and practical character, its influencing logic and heedlessness of adventitious moral or religious standards and its wide range of subjects and interests—which give it a unique combination of features that in European literature, we find only separately in an Aristotle, a Machiavelli and a Bacon—must have cooperated with the rise of a well-knit empire of unprecendented dimensions under the Mauryan and succeeding dynasties to depress creative political thought in the centuries after Kautilya.[6]

Relevance

Kautilya has not written for the then existing governments. He is relevant today and would remain so in 21st century. His ideas are based on research and personal observation. His writings, if studied and implemented can change the quality of governance in India. The most important point he mentioned was the state. He does not allow even to king, the Chief Executive all powers. He makes him function under certain principles so that he can get the co-operation of the people, Council of Ministers and Civil Service. It must be made a compulsory reading for M.A. students of Political Science and Public Administration. The present Governments must learn about the collection, increase and protection of money from Kautilya. Kautilya believes in analysis and experience as the yardsticks for decision-making Kautilya has identified basic elements of management and administration which should be followed by modern organizations to achieve efficiency and economy.

1. The means of starting undertakings and assignments.
2. Excellence of men and material.
3. Suitable apportionment palace.
4. Provision against failure. (Planning for problems)
5. Accomplishment of results.[7]

Training system in India is not helping in promoting excellence. He wanted the training to be professional, intelligence, mental framework, behaviour and most important character. We must introduce a great position of development of human beings for management. Arthasastra gives a great importance of record keeping. The information was collected for the following:

1. The activity of each state department
2. The working of state factories and conditions governing production in them.
3. Prices, Samples, standards of measuring instruments for various kinds of goods.
4. Laws, transactions, customs and regulations in force in different regions, villages, castes, families and corporations.
5. Salaries and other pre-requisites of state servants.[8]

Since Right to Information Act 2005 is in operation GOI and State Governments must learn, from Arthasastra about records keeping. The Arthasastra should be conducted a foundation/basic book for managers so that the managers can run administration based on efficiency, character building, mental balance and welfare of the people, i.e. social responsibility of managers. He suggested the following to improve governance:

1. The persons at the top level should be men of integrity and their main function should be the welfare of the people. There is no place of criminals or corrupt persons at the top level. To maintain the development of the country, it is essential to have right type of people who function according to righteousness.
2. Treasury should be well maintained. Corruption among officials should be curbed through secret information against officials.
3. There should be perfect relationships among the Government and Governed.
4. Meticulous approach should be done to select the personnel to run administration. Their work should be followed secretly to ensure their integrity.

5. The entire machinery of government rested on Dharma or righteousness probity.

Kautilya would always remain relevant for providing the Art and science of Governance in all types of Government—Soicialist, Communist, Capitalist, monarches.

Kautilya's Arthashastra is a political treatise and what is more a work of practical and useful advice to the king on how best to govern his kingdom and build up his power and authority. A proper well developed administration is *sine-qua-non* for ensuring prosperity and human welfare.

Notes and References

1. CVi, (Kautilya Arthasastra).
2. U.N. Ghoshal, The Monarchial States in Cultural Heritage in India, Vol. II, 2001, pp. 468, 469-70.
3. U.N. Ghosal, *op. cit.*, p. 454.
4. S.L. Goel, Public Financial Administration, *op. cit.*, pp. 473-75.
5. U.N. Ghosal, *op. cit.*, p. 456.
6. Mackenzie Brown, D., Indian Political Thought: From Manu to Gandhi, 1958, p. 52.
7. R.P. Kangla, Book 1, Chapter 15, Sutra 42, p. 35.
8. R.P. Kangla, Book 2, Chapter 7.

4

Swami Vivekananda (1863-1902)

INTRODUCTION

It is seldom that an eminent luminary and practical saint like Swami Vivekananda appears amongst mankind. His was a multi-faceted personality whose emotions, words and deeds exhibited profound harmony. Endowed with sharp intellect, noble heart, and a powerful mind, his whole being was ever centered on the amelioration of the suffering humanity and building India.

Swami Vivekananda, the great soul loved and revered in East and West alike as the rejuvenator of Hinduism in India and the preacher of its eternal truths abroad, was born at 6:33, a few minutes before sunrise, on Monday, January 12, 1863. It was the day of the great Hindu festival Makarasamkranti, when special worship is offered to the Ganga by millions of devotees. Thus the future Vivekananda first drew breath when the air above the sacred river not far from the house was reverberating with the prayers, worship, and religious music of thousands of Hindu men and women.

The Datta family of Calcutta, into which Narendranath had been born, was well known for its affluence, philanthropy, scholarship, and independent spirit. The grand

CHART 4.1

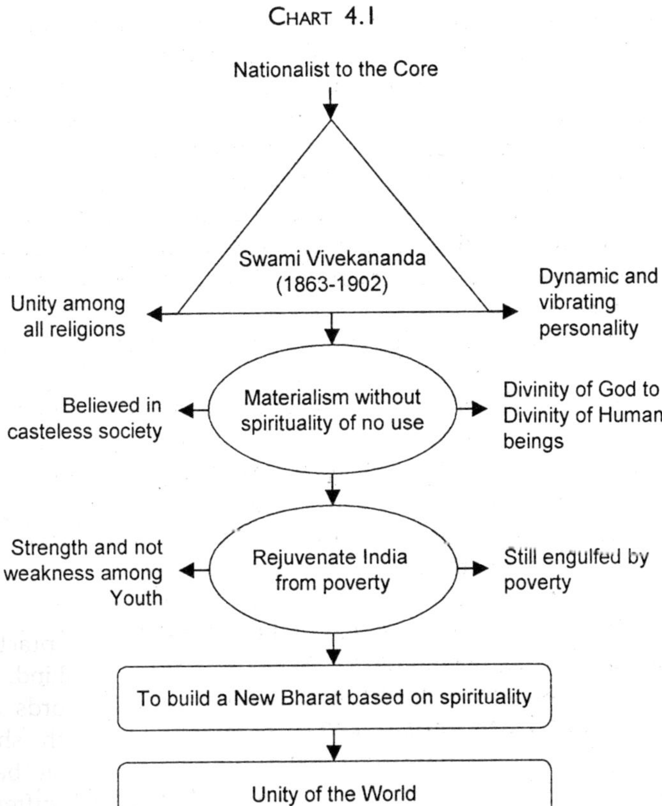

father, Durgacharan, after the birth of his first son, had renounced the world in search of God. The father, Viswanath, an attorney-at-law of the High Court of Calcutta, was well versed in English and Persian literature and often entertained himself and his friends by reciting from the Bible and the poetry of Hafiz, both of which, he believed contained truths unmatched by human thinking elsewhere. He was particularly attracted to the Islamic culture, with the educated Moslems of North-Western India. Moreover, he derived a large income from his law practice and, unlike his father, thoroughly enjoyed the worldly life.

Bhuvaneswari Devi, the mother, was cast in a different mould. Regal in appearance and gracious in conduct, she belonged to the old tradition of Hindu womanhood. As mistress of a large household, she devoted her spare time to sewing and singing, being particularly fond of the great Indian epics, the Ramayana and the Mahabharata, large portions of which she had memorized. She became the special refuge of the poor, and commanded universal respect because of her dignified detachment in the midst of her many arduous duties. Two sons were born to her besides Narendranath, and four daughters, two of whom died at an early age.

At the age of six he was sent to a primary school. One day, however, he repeated at home some of the vulgar words that he had learnt from his classmates, whereupon his disgusted parents took him out of the school and appointed a private tutor, who conducted classes for him and some other children of the neighbourhood in the worship hall of the house. Naren soon showed a precocious mind and developed a keen memory.

Soon the excitement of his boyhood days was over, and in 1879 Narendranath entered the Presidency college of Calcutta for higher studies. After a year he joined the General Assembly's Institution, founded by the Scottish General Missionary Board and later known as the Scottish Church College. It was from Hastie, the principal of the college and the professor of English literature, that he first heard the name Sri Ramakrishna. Paramhansa Narendra met Ramakrishna for the first time in November 1881 at the house of the Master's devotee Surendranath Mitra, young man having been invited there to entertain the visitors with his melodious music. The Ramakrishna Paramahamsa was much impressed by his sincerity and devotion, and after a few inquiries asked him to visit him at Dakshineswar. Narendra accepted. He wished to learn if Ramakrishna was the man to help him in his spiritual quest.[1]

In 1881, however, he happened to meet Swami Ramakrishna and that proved to be a turning point in his life. He was initially skeptical towards the teaching of his master, but after a brief period of doubt and resistance, he surrendered and accepted Swami Ramakrishna as his friend, philosopher and guide.

After the death of Ramakrishna in 1886, he undertook an extensive travel of almost the whole of India, and thereby acquainted himself with the social and economic conditions of the country. He came to feel that India, in spite of its rich spiritual heritage and very strong cultural history, had not been able to root out poverty, weakness and social evils. He strongly felt the need of bringing about a spiritual revolution, which, he also realized, required a very strong spiritual leadership.[2] He died on July 4, 1902 at a young age of 39.

HIS ADMINISTRATIVE THOUGHTS

I. World Peace and Brotherhood

He loved humanity and wanted the world leaders to promote peace which is vital for the humanity. All the nations of the world are spending huge amounts on defence services and nuclear power which can destroy this world. Administration in different countries is spending a great deal of their resources in unnecessary activities. We must create oneness in the world. If the Nations of the World follow the principles of Swami Vivekananda, there can be peace all around. To quote Swami Vivekananda—Why take a single instrument from the great religious orchestras of the earth? Let the grand symphony go on. Be pure, give up superstitions and see the wonderful harmony of nature. Each man should have the perfect exercise of his individuality but these individualities form a perfect whole.

Each creed has something to add to the wonderful structure. Man has an idea that there can be. only one religion, that there can be only one Prophet, and that there can be only one Incarnation; but that idea is not true. By studying the lives of all these great messengers, we find that each, as it were, was destined to play a part, and a part only; that the harmony consists in the sum total, and not in one note. As in the life of races—no race is born to alone enjoy the world. None dare say no. Each race has a part to play in this divine harmony of nations. Each race has its mission to perform its duty to fulfil. The sum total is the great harmony.

No civilization can grow unless fanaticism, bloodshed, and brutality stop. No civilization can begin to lift up its head until we look charitably upon one another; and the first step towards that much-needed charity is to look charitably upon the religious convictions of others. Nay more, to understand that not only should we be charitable, but positively helpful to each other, however different our religious ideas and convictions may be.[3]

To Swami Vivekananda, a Universal religion must balance the aspects of religion. He elaborates as "And this religion is attained by what we, in India, call Yoga—union. To the worker, it is union between men and the whole of humanity, to the mystic, between his lower and Higher Self, to the lover, union between himself and the God of Love, and to the philosopher, it is the union of all existence. This is what is meant by Yoga[4], and the aim of yoga is union, realization of oneness. Vivekananda says, "Religion is realization, not talk, nor doctrine, nor theories. . . . it is being and becoming, not hearing or acknowledging; it is the whole soul becoming changed into what it believes.[5]

2. Education and Training Promote Man-making, i.e. Creating Excellence

In public administration today we are giving emphasis on Human Resources Development as we know that Human rather than capital is the key to development. Swami Vivekananda has beautifully put it as: Education is the manifestation of the perfection already in man. Education is not the amount of information that is put into your brain and run riot there, undigested, all your life. We must have life-building, man-making, character building assimilation of ideas. The education that does not help the common mass of people to equip themselves for the struggle for life, which does not bring out strength of character, a spirit of philanthropy, and the courage of a lion—is it worth the name? The end of all education, all training, should be man-making. The end and aim of all training is to make the man grow. The training, by which the current and expression of will are brought under control and become fruitful, is called education. What our country now wants are muscles of iron and nerves of steel, gigantic wills which nothing can resist, which can penetrate into the mysteries and secrets of the universe and will accomplish their purpose in any fashion, even if it meant going down to the bottom of the ocean and meeting death face to face. It is man-making religion that we want. It is man-making theories that we want. It is man-making education all round that we want.[6] He further adds, "We want that Education by which character is formed, strength of mind is increased, the intellect is expanded, and by which one can stand on one's feet.[7]

3. Education of the Masses

Even after 60 years of Independence we have not been able to provide 100 percent literacy to masses. To quote Swami Vivekananda—My heart aches to think of the condition of the poor and low in India. They sink lower and lower every day. They feel the blow showered upon them by a cruel society, but they do not know whence the blow comes. They have forgotten that they too are men. My heart is too full to express my feelings. So long as the millions live in hunger and ignorance, I hold every man a traitor who, having been educated at their expense, pays not the least heed to them. Our great national sin is the neglect of the masses and that is the cause of our downfall. No amount of politics would be of any avail until the masses in India are once more well-educated, well-fed and well-cared for.

A nation is advanced in proportion as education and intelligence spread among the masses. The chief cause of India's ruin has been the monopolizing of the whole education and intelligence of the land among a handful of men. If we are to rise again, we shall have to do it by spreading education among the masses. The only service to be done for our lower classes is to give them education to develop their individuality. They are to be given ideas. Their eyes are to be opened to what is going on in the world around them, and then they will work out their own salvation. Every nation, every man and every woman must work out their own salvation. Give them ideas—that is the only help they require and then the rest must follow as effect. Ours is to put the chemicals together, the crystallization comes in the law of nature.

Remember that the nation lives in the cottage. Your

duty at present is to go from one part of the country to another, from village to village, and make the people understand that mere sitting about idly won't do any more, make them understand their real condition and say, "O Ye Brothers, all arise! How much longer would you remain asleep!' Go and advise them how to improve their own condition and make them comprehend the sublime truths of the shastras, by presenting them in a lucid and popular way. Impress upon their minds that they have the same right to religion as the Brahmans. Initiate, even down to the Chandalas, in these fiery mantras. Also instruct them in simple words about the necessities of life, and in trade, commerce, agriculture, etc.[8]

4. Emphasis on Means and not the End can Improve the Functioning of Government

In government, we want to achieve the result by any means causing inefficiency, corruption and instability. Swami Vivekananda beautifully puts it as: Our great defect in life is that we are so much drawn to the ideal, the goal is so much more enchanting, so much more alluring, so much bigger in our mental horizon, that we lose sight of the details altogether.

But whenever failure comes, if we analyse it critically, in ninety-nine percent of cases we shall find that it was because we did not pay attention to the means. Proper attention to the finishing, strengthening, of the means, is what we need. With the means all right, the end must come. We forget that it is the cause that produces the effect; the effect cannot come by itself; and unless the causes are exact, proper and powerful, the effect will not be produced. Once the ideal is chosen and the means determined, we may almost let go the ideal, because we are sure it will be there, when the means are perfected. When the cause is there, there is no more difficulty about the effect, the effect is bound to come. If we take care of the cause, the effect will take care of itself. The realization of the ideal is the effect. The means are the cause: attention to the means, therefore, is the great secret of life. We also read this in the Gita and learn that we have to work, constantly work, with all our power, to put our whole mind in the work, whatever it be, that we are doing. At the same time, we must not be attached. That is to say, we must not be drawn away from the work by anything else, but still we must be able to quit the work whenever we like. We are to take care of ourselves—that much we can do—and give up attending to others, for a time. Let us perfect the means; the end will take care of itself. For the world can be good and pure, only if our lives are good and pure. It is an effect, and we are the means. Therefore, let us purify ourselves. Let us make ourselves perfect.[9]

5. Women Empowerment through Education

We see that there is a great discrimination in Government to women. Swami Vivekananda feels hurt about this. To quote him: It is very difficult to understand why in this country so much difference is made between men and women, whereas the Vedanta declares that one and the same Self is present in all beings. Writing down Smritis, etc. and binding them by hard rules, the men have turned the women into mere manufacturing machines. In the period of degradation, when the priests made the other castes incompetent to study the Vedas, they deprived the women also of all their rights. You will find in the Vedic and Upanisadic age Maitreyi, Gargi and other ladies of revered memory have taken the place of Rishis. In an assembly of a thousand Brahmanas who were all erudite in the Vedas, Gargi boldly challenged Yajnavalkaya in a discussion about Brahman.

All nations have attained greatness by paying proper respect to women. That country and that nation which do not respect women have never become great, nor will ever be in future. The real Shakti worshipper is he who knows that God is the Omnipresent force in the universe, and sees in women the manifestation of that force. In America men look upon their women in this light and treat their women as well as can be desired, and hence they are so prosperous, so learned, so free and so energetic. The principal reason why our race has so degenerated is that we had no respect for these living images of Shakti, Manu says, 'Where women are respected, there the Gods delight, and where they are not, there all work and effort come to naught.' There is no hope of rise for that family or country where they live in sadness. Women have many and grave problems, but none that cannot be solved by that magic work education.

In trying to define the national ideal and suggesting remedies for social evils, Swami Vivekananda's attention was naturally drawn to the plight of women. He wanted their progress, for the progress of a nation depends upon the progress of its women. He wrote about the imperative need of women's progress in the following way: "All nations have attained greatness, by paying proper respect to the women. That country and that nation which do not respect the women have never become great, nor will ever be in future. The principal reason why your race has so much degenerated is that you had no respect for these living images of Sakti. Manu says, "where women are respected there the gods delight; and where they are not, there are works and efforts come to naught. There is no hope of rise for that family or country where there is no estimation of women, where they live in sadness."[10]

6. Science of Yoga

Yoga is a holistic approach to life. Yoga in administration can bring perfection and responsiveness. To quote Swami Vivekananda: "The science of Yoga claims that it has discovered the laws which develop this personality, and by proper attention to those laws and methods, each one can grow and strengthen his personality. This is one of the great practical things and this is the secret of all education. This has a universal application. In the life of the householder, in the life of the poor, the rich, the man of business, the spiritual man, in everyone's life, it is a great thing, the strengthening of this personality. They are laws, very fine, which are behind the physical laws, as we know. That is to say, there are no such realities as a physical world, a mental world, a spiritual world. Whatever is, is one. Let us say, it is a sort of tapering existence, the thickest part is here, it tapers and becomes finer and finer; the finest is what we call spirit; the grossest, the body. And just as it is here, in the microcosm, it is exactly the same in the macrocosm. This universe of ours is exactly like that; it is the gross external thickness, and it tapers into something finer and finer until it becomes God.[11]

Swami Vivekananda harmonized the conflict among the different attitudes. So says he: "Every man must develop according to his own nature. As every science has its methods so has every religion. The methods of attaining the end of religion are called Yoga by us, and the different forms of Yoga we teach, are adapted to the different natures and temperaments of man. We classify them in the following way, under four heads:

1. *Karma-Yoga*: The manner in which a man realizes his own divinity through works and duty.
2. *Bhakti-Yoga*: The realization of the divinity through devotion to, and love of, a Personal God.
3. *Raja-Yoga*: The realization of the divinity through the control of mind.
4. *Jnana-Yoga*: The realization of a man's own divinity through knowledge.

7. Scientific Approach to Religion

The last note that Vivekananda struck in the inspiring music of his Parliament of Religious speeches from 11th to 12th September, 1893, was the world-wide proclamation of this very age-old Indian wisdom.[12]

"If the Parliament of Religions has shown anything to the world, it is this: It has proved to the world that holiness, purity, and charity are not the exclusive possession of any church in the world, and that every system has produced men and women of the most exalted character. In the face of this evidence, if anybody dreams of the exclusive survival of his own religion and the destruction of others. I pity him from the bottom of my heart, and point out to him that upon the banner of every religion will soon be written, in spite of resistance: 'Help and not Fight', 'Assimilation and not Destruction', 'Harmony and Peace and not Dissension'.

8. Deep Sympathy to all Genuine Service to Poor People

He told his brother disciples at the Abu Road Station,

just prior to his leaving for the West, the following passionate words:

"I have now traveled all over India, and lately in the Maharashtra area and the Western Coasts. But alas! It was an agony to me, my brothers, to see with my own eyes the terrible poverty and misery of the masses, and I could not restrain my tears! It is not my firm conviction that it is futile to preach religion amongst them without first trying to remove their poverty and their sufferings. It is for this reason—to first find some means for the salvation of the poor of India—that I am not going to America."[13]

9. Pride in Natural Heritage

In regenerating India, Swami Vivekananda often spoke of going back to the past cultural heritage. Why did he glorify the past so much? Swami Vivekananda's idea was that to create enthusiasm in a huge nation it was necessary to arouse the national pride. And what have Indians to be proud of except this cultural heritage? He said: "Now-a-days, everybody blames those who constantly look back is the cause of all India's woes. To me, on the contrary it seems that opposite is true. So long as they forget the past, the Hindu Nations remained in a state of Stupor, and as soon as they begun to look into their past, there is on every side fresh manifestation of life."[14]

10. Casteless Society

In trying to remove the evils of social differences, Swami Vivekananda was against all strife, for that will weaken the nation. So he said: "Therefore, it is no use fighting among the castes. What good will it do? It will divide us all the more, weaken us all the more, degrade us all the more. The solution is not by bringing down the higher, but by raising the lower up to the level of the higher. And that is the line of work that is found in all our books, inspite of what you" may hear from some people whose knowledge of their own scriptures and whose capacity to understand the mighty plans of the ancients are only zero. What is the plan? The ideal at one end is the Brahmana and the ideal at the other end is the Chandala, and the whole work is to raise the

Chandala up to the Brahmana. Slowly and slowly you find more and more privileges granted to them.[15]

CONCLUSION

Speaking about Swami Vivekananda, C. Rajagopalachari said, "But for him we would not have gained our freedom. We, therefore, owe everything to Swami Vivekananda. May his faith, his courage and wisdom inspire us so that we may keep safe the treasure received from him."

In praise of Swami Vivekananda, Romain Rolland said: "He was less than 40 years of age when he lay stretched upon the pyre. But the flame of that pyre is still alight today. From his ashes, like those of the phoenix of old, has sprung a new the conscience of India—the magic bird faith in her unity and in the Great message, brooded over from Vedic times by the drawing spirit of his ancient race—the message for which it must render account to the rest of mankind."

It will be interesting to you to know about the impact of Vivekananda on India. He powerfully influenced India's Independence struggle and many progressive social reform movements, like the one for removal of untouchability, and others for the uplift of women and the weaker sections. His influence is deepening decade after decade. And something very significant has happened in a very humble way recently. The Government of India has presented Vivekananda before the youth of India, by its recent circular D.O. No. F.6/1/84 dated 17 Oct. 1984: 'that the birthday of Swami Vivekananda is to be observed as National Youth Day every year from 1985 onwards as it was felt that the philosophy of Swamiji, and the ideals for which he lived and worked, could be a great source of inspiration for the Indian youth.

The President of India and the Prime Minister of India both addressed the youth on this year's January 12th Observance. It was a significant step toward educating youth in human excellence. "I cannot conclude this speech than by sharing with you a famous passage from Swamiji's lecture on *The Mission of the Vedanata* in which he sends out to everyone this inspiring message of the means of achieving total human excellence."

Teach yourselves, teach everyone, his real nature; call upon the sleeping soul and see how it awakes. Power will come, glory will come, goodness will come, purity will come, and everything that is excellent will come, when this sleeping soul is roused to self-conscious activity.[16]

What a Life?

We must know what Swami Vivekananda says about the nature of India's Unique influence on the world.[17]

We never preached our thoughts with fire and sword. If there is one word in the English language to represent the gift of India to the world, if there is one word in the English language to express the effect which the literature of India produces upon mankind, it is the one word, 'fascination'. It is the opposite of anything that takes you suddenly; it throws on you, as it were, a charm imperceptibility. To many, Indian thought, Indian manners, Indian customs, Indian philosophy, Indian literature are repulsive at the first sight; but let them persevere, let them read, let them become familiar with the great principles underlying these ideas, and it is ninety-nine to one that the charm will come over them, and fascination will be the result.

'Slow and silent, as the gentle dew that falls in the morning, unseen and unheard, yet producing a most marvelous result (the flowers), has been the work of the calm, patient, all-suffering spiritual race upon the world of thought'. If you want to know India, study Vivekananda. In his everything is positive and nothing negative.

—Rabindranath Tagore

A Yogi of the highest spiritual level in direct communion with the truth who had for the time being consecrated his whole life to the moral and spiritual uplift of his nation and of humanity, that is how ! I would describe him. If he had been alive, I would have been at his feet.

—Subash Chandra Bose

Relevance

His ideas both spiritual and national would remain relevant for the generations to come. These ideas are based on Vedantic philosophy which is based on thousands years of research of rishis in India.

It is rightly stated by Dr. R.C. Majumdar and R.G. Pradhan that, "The nascent nationalism in India received a great momentum from the life and activities of modern Indian Nationalism; he largely created it and also embodied in his own life its highest and noblest elements." He dealt with all the main problems of modern India and pointed out their solutions in his 'Lectures from Colombo to Almore'. In 1897 he said, "Let the country be your only God for the coming fifty years." He was not a politician but his ideas and patriotism inspired many to serve the country, combining spirituality with intense activity in their own lives; we may recall the names of the heroes of the revolutionary movements, Mahatmaji and Netaji, whose contributions are on the top in making India politically free in just five years after Swamiji gave his first clarion call.

Swami Vivekananda is well-known throughout the cultured world as a powerful Hindu missionary who vindicated the spiritual glory of India even in lands other than his own.[18] Glorious has been his spiritual mission to the peoples of other climes, but equally glorious has been his message to his own people for working out a constructive programme to build the nation from within. He has placed the ideal of spirituality not only as a means of individual liberation or Moksa, but also as a fundamental principle through which the collective thoughts and activities of the land are to be organized. To him religion is the national activities. He has laid down that the political, social and economic reconstruction in India must be made along a line altogether different from that in other countries of the world. He has interpreted our past history with a rare insight and vision drawing our attention to the wonderful principles of nation-building in Indian civilization and culture, and showing the practical bearing of those principles on the solution of the vital problems agitating our mind today. The fundamental principle of national reconstruction in India has been indicated by the Swami in one of his lectures as follows:

> "National union in India must be the gathering up of the scattered spiritual forces. A nation in India must be the union of those whose hearts beat to the same spiritual tune."

He discovered that the life-blood of the Indian nation is spirituality and consequently delivered his message to modern India as follows:

> "When the blood is strong and pure, no disease germs can live in that body. Our life-blood is spirituality. If it flows clear, if it flows strong and pure and vigorous, everything is right; political, social, any other material defects, even the poverty of the land will all be cured if that blood is pure. For if the disease-germ is thrown out, nothing will be able to enter into the blood."

The Swami clearly explained this in these words:

> "I see that each nation, like each individual, his one theme in this life which is its centre, the principal note round which every other note comes to form the harmony. In one nation political power is its vitality as in England, artistic life in another, and so on. In India religious life forms the centre, the key note of the whole music of national life; and if any nation attempts to throw off its national vitality, the direction which has become its own through the transmission of centuries—that nation dies. And therefore, if you succeed in the attempt to throw off religion and take up either politics or society or any other thing as your centre, as the vitality of your national life, the result will be that you will be extinct."

Indian scriptures are full of treasures which Swami Vivekananda wanted Indians to be proud of. He will always remain relevant. In a brief period, the whole of India has set-up thousands of institutions named after Vivekananda and Lord Rama Krishna Parmhansa which are engaged in the promotion of knowledge enshrined in our ancient literature to make India strong based on spirituality.

Notes and References

1. Swami Nikhilananda Vivekānanda, A Bigraphy, Kolkata, Advaita Ashrama, Seventeenth Edition, June 2006, pp. 1-25.

2. Basant Kumar Lal, Contemporary India Philosophy, New Delhi, Motilal Banarsi Das, 2002, p. 1
3. Swami Vivekananda, Bold Message for World Peace, Belgaum, 2003, Sri Chamundeshwari Printers, Bangalore, pp. 38-47.
4. Swami Vivekananda, Complete Works, III, p. 419.
5. *Ibid.*, p. 432.
6. Swami Ranganathananda, Swami Vivekananda and Human Excellence, Kolkata, Advaite Ashram, 2004, p. 45.
7. Swami Vivekananda, Education, Sri Ramakrishnan Math, Madras, 2006, p. 86.
8. Swami Vivekananda, Education, Madras, Sri Ramakrishna Math, 2006, pp. 61-64.
9. *Ibid.*, pp. 47-48, 55.
10. Manu Samhita, III, pp. 56-96.
11. Swami Vivekananda, Education, *op. cit.*, pp. 26-27.
12. The Complete Works, Vol. I, p. 24.
13. The Life of Swami Vivekananda: By His Eastern and Western Disciples, 1915, Vol. III, p. 14.
14. The Complete Works, Vol. IV, p. 324.
15. Swami Vivekananda, India and Her Problems, *op. cit.*, p. 84.
16. The Complete Works of Swami Vivekananda, Vol. 3, III, p. 193.
17. *Ibid.*, p. 110.
18. "The paragon of all monistic system is the Vedanta philosophy of Hindostan and the paragon of Vedantist missionaries was the late Swami Vivekananda who visited our land some year ago." (William James: Pragmatism, p. 151).

5

Mahatma Gandhi: An Outstanding Personality (1869-1948)

Mohandas Karam Chand Gandhi, the Father of the Nation, who got independence for India from a foreign rule by bloodless revolution was born on 2nd October, 1869 at Porbandar and died on 30th January, 1948. Mahatma Gandhi may be said to be the greatest administrative, social and political thinker. His thinkings have influenced a vast number of people and a large number of institutions—Government, voluntary, private which came into existence to preach the philosophy of Mahatma Gandhi. His ideas were not limited to a particular area but influenced the entire world. Gandhism became a philosophy based on spirituality, socialism and economics.

Mahatma Gandhi, who was man of high character and great courage of conviction, and who lived more for others than for himself, whose greatness was intrinsic, and not extrinsic as derived from power of position of society. He gives us an experience of human excellence, of the true glory of the human spirit. He teaches us that to be selfish, to be self-centred, to exploit others, and die away one day, does not constitute human excellence, does not express the true

CHART 5.1

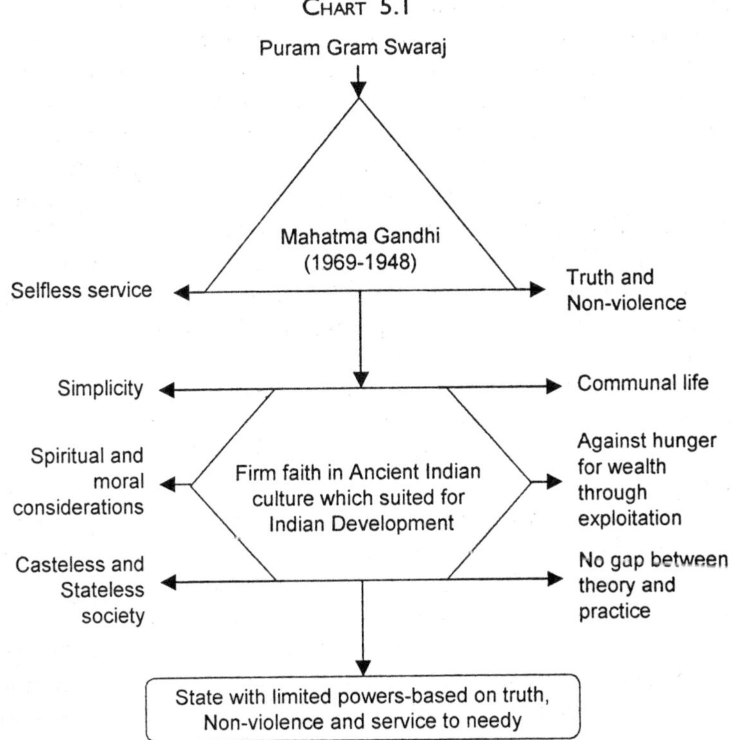

glory of the human spirit. He preaches to us in silence that to be manly and to stand on one's own feet, to extend the hand of fellowship to others, to use every ounce of surplus energy to bring happiness and cheer to millions of one's fellowmen—this is the true glory of man. As expressed by Vivekananda in a letter written from Chicago in 1894 to the then Maharaja of Mysore (Letters of Swami Vivekananda, 10th Edition complete works of Swami Vivekananda, p. 119)

In essence, Gandhi's life and work were based on loyalty to a few simple but eternal principles—humanism as expressed in non-violence and truth, the exaltation of means over ends, and the stress on duty rather than rights. Justice to him was devotion to the cause of the oppressed, and liberty connoted duty more than rights. These principles provided the key to his conception of the art of life, which derived its strength and sustenance from a strong moral foundation. Gandhi's philosophy covered nearly everything under the sun and his literary output is breath-taking. On a rough count, during the fifty years of his public life, he ground out some ten million words. These consist chiefly of his profuse journalistic writings, report of his speeches and conversations, letters and memoranda, and other fragments, besides of course the few, very few books that he wrote.[1]

His ideas were not based on theory, he worked with ideas and proved their worthwhileness. His Ideas on Administrative thoughts were entirely different from British as well as the existing models in other countries. His model of administration was mixed with spiritualism, socialism and economics. In his own words, "You cannot divide social, economic, political and purely religious work into watertight compartments."

Non-violence, naked truth, non-theft, a continuous prayer, discipline, all became personified in this humble, vigorous, selfless, laughter-loving man of God. He never kept aloof or lost the common touch; never used long words or abstract nouns; never said a thing he didn't mean, nor propagated a theory that he didn't practice.[2]

He borrowed and quoted frequently the ideas contained in Mahabharta, Bhagavad Geeta, Vedas, Upanishads, etc. as well as the ideas of scholars like Plato, Ruskin, Tolstoy, etc. He has written widely. It is difficult to mention the names of books and Articles written by him.

ADMINISTRATIVE THOUGHTS

1. Responsive and Accountable Administration through Good Governance Based on Spirituality

Mahatma Gandhi underlined the importance of individuals in the Panchayati Raj Structure. To quote him: "In this structure composed of innumerable villages, there will be ever widening, never ascending, circles. Life will not be a pyramid with the apex sustained by the bottom, but will be an oceanic circle, whose centre will be the individual, always ready to perish for the village, the latter ready to perish for the circle of villages till at last the whole becomes one life composed of individuals, ever humble sharing the majesty of the oceanic circle of which they are integral units.

Gandhi outlined his concept of the 'ideal' society in an article in *Harijan* in 1946: Indian independence must begin at the bottom. Thus, every village will be a republic or Panchayat, having full powers. It follows, therefore, that every village has to be self-sustained and defending itself against the whole world. It will be trained and prepared to perish in the attempt to defend itself against any onslaught from without. Thus ultimately, it is the individual who is the unit. But this does not exclude dependence on willing help from neighbours or from the world. It will be free and voluntary play of mutual forces. Such a society is necessarily highly cultured in which every man and every woman knows what he or she wants and, what is more, knows that no one should want anything that the others cannot have with equal labour.

The Panchayat is the executive body of Gram Sabha to provide civic facilities to the people in its jurisdiction. Indian Independence must begin at the bottom. Thus, every village will be a republic or Panchayat, having full powers.

A very significant influence over the years on Government and public leaders in regard to development of rural local self-government has been of Mahatma Gandhi, the father of the Indian nation who advocated the revival of the traditional panchayats so that Gram Swaraj can become a reality. In his writings and statements he drew attention of the people and government to the urgent need for building panchayats as instrument for the government of the country and rebuilding the village panchayats playing the central role in encouraging and supporting productive and creative activities among the people. According to him, greater the power of the panchayat the better for the people as true democracy has to be worked from below by the people of every village. Panchayat approach thus became the objective for local rural government in India.

The Constitution of India, adopted on January 26, 1950, was meant to embody the ideals that had inspired the freedom struggle. Its Preamble promised "to secure to all its citizens: Justice, social, economic and political; Liberty;

Equality of status and of opportunity; and to promote among them all Fraternity assuring the dignity of the individual and the unity of the Nation." However, the Constitution itself created a hiatus by dividing the fulfilment of these promises through two different instruments, namely, Part III: Fundamental Rights (Articles 14 to 35), and Part IV: Directive Principles of State Policy (Articles 37 to 51). The Fundamental Rights, broadly speaking, cover political and civic rights but do not confer basic socio-economic rights, which are covered to a limited extent under Directive Principles. But this limited provision too has gone by default, because vide Art. 37, "The provisions contained in this Part IV shall not be enforceable by any court."

2. Role of the Executive

Role of the Executive in Combating Hunger and Violence: Y.P. Anand observes that: Gandhiji was wary of too much power being vested in the government structure: "The State represents violence in a concentrated and organized form . . .. it can never be weaned from violence to which it owes its very existence." Hence, there is the utmost need for transparency, integrity, and accountability in the State administration.

But the basic administrative structure and its overbearing attitude towards people has not changed after independence. That was the danger against which the Gandhiji had warned right from 1909 when he stated that change of political rule was no real Swaraj: "You want the tiger's nature, but not the tiger; that is to say, you would make India English. And when it becomes English, it will be called not Hindustan but Englishtan. This is not the Swaraj that I want." That there has been no basic change, is exemplified by the recent discovery of brutal killing of about 40 children in Nithari (Noida), practically an extended part of Delhi. For over two years the parents ran from pillar to post for their missing children but not even a police report was recorded, because they were children of poor people. In the same area, when a child of a rich family was kidnapped for ransom, the whole administration had stood up and recovered the child.

3. Economics of Non-Violence

Gandhiji had predicted in 1928 itself that Bolshevism could not last long: ". . . it aims at the abolition of the institution of private property. This is only an application of ethical principle of non-possession in the realm of economics - -. But from what I know of Bolshevism it does not preclude the use of force but freely sanctions it for expropriation of private property and maintaining the collective State ownership of the same. And if that is so. . . . the Bolshevik regime in its present form cannot last for long." But, if the rich do not "become guardians of the poor", non-violent non-cooperation is "the right and infalliable means", because the rich cannot amass wealth "without the co-operation of the poor." Gandhian concept of socialism is typically rooted in the Indian tradition: "Real socialism has been handed down to us by ancestors who taught: 'All land belongs to Gopal', where then is the boundary line? Man is the maker of the line and he can therefore unmake it." This is the tradition of fighting for social justice through satyagraha which Gandhiji had practiced all over the world as the only way through which a truly egalitarian social order can be established.

We have forgotten that Swaraj means the strengthening of the people, power going to the people, the awakening of the people to a sense of their individual worth and freedom and dignity. We have forgotten the definitions given by Gandhiji to Swaraj:

> 'Real Swaraj comes, not by the acquisition of authority by a few, but by the acquisition of the capacity by all to resist authority when it is abused'.

We are far away from this Swaraj based on the power of the people; our people are largely helpless and weighted down by the power of a callous and inefficient administration sitting on them; they are made to feel a glow of their power for a brief moment during the elections; and our democracy can be thankful that they have exercised that brief power wisely and boldly. It is imperative that all political and administrative steps are taken to make the people the source of power in our democracy, not just notionally, as we have done so far, but in the real sense, by making healthy and strong our local self-government institutions.

There must be an earnest and concerted effort by all the staff to put an end to all these serious evils in our administration; this can be achieved, and can be achieved only, by developing enlightened citizenship awareness, with its concomitant virtues of self-disciplines, punctuality, work-efficiency, talking less and working more, dedication to human services and welfare, imaginative sympathy, and impersonal loyalty to our democratic state and its noble constitution.

4. Democratic Decentralization

According to K.K. Panda, Gandhi had a humanist vision of India's future. A couple of years before he was assassinated he said, "Independence must begin at the bottom. Thus, every village will be a republic or panchayat having full powers. . . . In this structure composed of innumerable villages, there will be ever widening, never ascending circles. Life will not be a pyramid with the apex sustained from the bottom. But it will be an oceanic circle whose centre will be the individual always ready to perish for the village, the latter ready to perish for the circle of villages, till at last the whole becomes one life composed of individuals, never aggressive in their arrogance but ever humble, sharing the majesty of the oceanic circle of which they are integral units."

A political system like ours having perhaps world's lowest standard of living, widespread illiteracy, a living powerful tradition of feudalism, an acquiescing and unresponsive academic and bureaucratic structure, declining political credibility, weakening institutional systems, and above all, incidence of poverty that does not allow its dazed captive population to have an access to a meaningful life, people are slowly loosing their faith in the democratic political system. To avoid a violent systemic upheaval, the Gandhian methods of Swadeshi, Satyagraha, women empowerment, and village Swaraj programmes must be initiated. This is the only way to ensure both social democracy and political democracy. To conclude in the language of Dr. B.R. Ambedkar, "Political democracy cannot last unless there lies at the base of it social democracy. What does social democracy mean? It means a way of life which recognizes liberty, equality and fraternity as principles of life. These principles of liberty, equality and fraternity are not to be treated as separate items in a trinity. They form a union of trinity in the sense that to divorce one from the other is to defeat the very purpose of democracy." Perhaps Gandhi is the only answer today.

Based on Gandhi's well-known principle, "violence logically leads to centralization: the essence of non-violence is decentralization", he wanted that self-sufficient and self-governing villages should be the basic units of public administration in Free India. These primary political units should elect by adult suffrage, a *Panchayat,* ordinarily of five persons for a period of three years. The functions of the *Panchayats* should be very wide and comprehensive, covering almost all aspects of social, economic and political life of village community, so that villages can enjoy large measure of local autonomy. It should have administrative control over all its employees." It should also assess and collect land revenue, provide cheap and speedy justice, education, recreation and medical facilities and supervise co-operative farming irrigation and khadi and village industries.

To co-ordinate, guide, advise, supervise, the work of lower *Panchayats* and to perform functions of local nature, there should be Taluka (Tehsil), District, Provincial and All-India *Panchayats* connected with one another by the Presidents of the respective lower *Panchayats.* The President of All-India Panchayat would be the Head of the State and of government. He would have the power to appoint ministers from outside the memberships of Ail India Panchayat, who would be responsible for defence, currency, customs, running of key industries of national importance and co-ordination of provincial economic development plans. Thus, Gandhi envisaged complete political and administrative decentralization at the village level with an indirectly elected government at the top.[3]

5. Casteless and Classless Society Essential for Good Governance

The casteless and classless society he was striving to establish aims at the realization of both material and spiritual prosperities. He described the society that he was aiming as Ram Rajya. Non-Hindus and a section among his admirers failed to understand what he meant by Ram Rajya. Gandhi said, "By Ram Rajya, I do not mean Hindu Raj, I mean by Ram Rajya, a Divine Raj, the Kingdom of God." His faith in God was unshakeable. His god was not a personal god. He repeatedly chanted Ram nama but asserted that his Ram is not the Lord of Ayodhya. His Ram is the Almighty God which guides him to noble action and whose presence can be felt everywhere. The Ram Rajya he was advocating was an ideal social order where an ideal King Rules over his subjects without any distinction whatsoever. Truth, dharma and justice will be the dominant characteristics of such a society. Both the Pandit and the poorest of the poor will have equal say in the governance. Nobody will be discriminated against anybody.

Similarly, Gandhi believed, "There can be no Ram Raj in the present state of iniquitos inequalities in which only a few roll in riches, while the masses do not get even enough to eat", Does this Gandhian passion for social justice remain a far cry? No one knows. The ruler, in the modern context the state, like Lord Ram, Gandhi's ideal King—is Custodian of not only the physical domain of the people but also an inspirer of his people to higher realms of spiritual attainments.

Gandhi said in his advice: "I will give you a talisman, whenever you are in doubt or when the self becomes too much with you, apply the following test: Recall the face of the poorest and the weakest man whom you may have seen and ask yourself if the step you—contemplate is going to be of any use to him, Will he gain anything by it? Will it restore him to a control over his own life and destiny? In other words, will it lead to Swaraj for the hungry and spiritually starving millions?

In the schemes of thing Gandhi visualized, all are supposed to be partners and mutually supportive and 'dependent'. The trusteeship idea, an extension of Sarvodaya mooted by Gandhi has not been properly understood and implemented. It envisages the willingness on the part of those who have extra wealth to take care of the less privileged on the basis of the awareness that wealth like the other natural resources does not belong to any particular individual. All have equal right over all that nature possesses. Those, who have excess of what other don't have, should feel that they have to play the role of the custodians of society. The astute visionary that Gandhi was revealed in the manner in which Gandhiji reproduced in his journal the seven sins which a reader had sent him as a note. They are: Politics without Principles, Wealth without Work, Pleasure without Conscience, Knowledge without Character, Commerce without Morality, Science without Humanity and Worship without Sacrifice.[4]

6. Eradication of Poverty

It is noteworthy, within a short time after his return to India in 1915. Gandhi identified "poverty" as the main challenge for the India's independence and prosperity after freedom.

First, he realized that the secret of survival of India's people and polity is rural civilization and he believed western industrial civilization should be rejected. Second, Indian agricultural and village industries are at the heart of India's survival-oriented polity. Third, his approach led him to look for a symbol of people's knowledge and techniques for tackling poverty. He found Charkha as a perfect symbol as well as an idiom of action. Fourth, he realized that "outsiders".cannot deal with poverty. It is only the people in rural India who are qualified to deal with poverty and he identified the symbol as well as the tool for enabling the poor to respond to poverty.

Gandhi realized that these two sectors of Indian economy continue to be the repository of people's knowledge and skills with reference to poverty. The village industries are the concretized manifestation of the skills and knowledge and technique available in rural India. Second, the accumulated Lok Vidya relating agriculture is there among the rural population. He thought, both sectors have survival-oriented technique for a subsistence economy which enable the people to survive drought, famines and floods and exploitation.

This approach to the challenge of poverty is reflected in the concept and practice of Constructive Programme. Gandhi's Constructive Programme for the people in rural India during the period 1922-47 is another example. It is noteworthy that in the Constructive Programme, the role of outsiders and inputs from outsiders was minimal, and if any it was as one of catalysts. The Constructive Programme does not aim at a frontal attack on poverty as an economic phenomena, because Gandhi believed that poverty is not simply a result of economic under development.[5]

7. Co-operative System

The economy in the ideal society would function partly through cooperative societies. For Gandhi, "Ultimately, it is the individual who is the unit." However, "Inter-dependence is and ought to be as much the ideal of man as self-sufficiency. Man is social being. Without interrelation with society he cannot realize his oneness with the universe or suppress his egotism."

One of the basic principles of cooperation is non-violence. "Let it be remembered that co-operation should be base for non-violence. There is no such thing as success of violent cooperation. (Hitler) who also talked vainly of cooperation which was forced upon the people . . . . ." Voluntary cooperation will produce real freedom and a new order, vastly superior to the new order in Soviet Russia.

Another principle is honesty. Gandhi said, "Too often do we believe that material prosperity means moral growth. It is necessary that a movement which is fraught with so much good to India should not degenerate into one for merely advancing cheap loans. . . . We will not measure the success of the movement by the number of cooperative society formed, but by the moral condition of the cooperators . . . . . This will mean tracing the course of every pie lent to the members. Those responsible for the proper conduct of cooperative societies will see to it that the money advanced does not find its way into the today-seller's bill or into the pockets of the keepers of gambling dens."

Gandhi was strong advocate of cooperative farming. He said, "I firmly believe too that we shall not derive the full benefits of agriculture until we take to cooperative farming. Does it not stand to reason that it is better for a hundred families in a village to cultivate their lands collectively and divide the income therefrom than to divide the land anyhow into a hundred portions?"

Gandhi was deeply suspicious of the state. "The State represents violence in a concentrated and organized form. The individual has a soul but the state is a soulless machine, it can never be weaned away from violence to which it owes its very existence."

8. Essence of His Philosophy

Satyagraha to get justice—social, economic and political from Administrative system.

M.K. Gandhi, 'Satyagraha in South Africa': "None of us knew what name to give to our movement. I then used the term 'passive resistance' in describing it. I did not understand the implications of 'passive resistance' as I called it. I only knew that some new principle had come into being. As the struggle advanced, the phrase 'passive resistance' gave rise to confusion and it appeared shameful to permit this great struggle to be known only by an English name. Again that foreign phrase could hardly pass as current coin among the community. A small prize was therefore announced in India Opinion to be awarded to the reader who invented the best designation for our struggle. We thus received a number of suggestions. The meaning of the struggle had been then fully discussed in Indian Opinion and the competitors for the prize had fairly sufficient material to serve as a basis for their exploration. Truth (Satya) implies love, and firmness (agraha) engenders and therefore serves as a synonym for force. I thus began to call the Indian movement "Satyagraha", that is to say, the Force which is born of Truth and Love or non-violence, and gave up the use of the phrase 'passive resistance', in connection with it, so much so that even in English writing we often avoided it and used instead the word "Satyagraha" itself or some other equivalent English phrase. This then was the genesis of the movement which came to be known as Satyagraha, and of the word used as a designation for it."

Truth is the central concept of satyagraha. For Gandhi truth meant the manifestation of God in all reality. This reality has both a relative and an absolute connotation. While the relative truth is the reality perceived by an individual in a given circumstance; the ultimate truth is the sum total of all the relative truths. Thus the ultimate truth, manifests itself in many relative truths and this ultimate truth was equated with God by Gandhi. The adoption of Satyagrah was thus, for Gandhi, a means to progress towards God realization also.

Gandhi emphasized that when an individual adopts Satyagrah he should see to it that the demands he makes is consistent with truth. Thus a Satyagrahi's demand is at the same time the minimum and the maximum. There is no place for untruth in it; rather it strives to fight and remove untruth. For Gandhi, therefore, sincerity of the Satyagrahi is an indispensable part in the adoption and progress of Satyagraha. This sincerity was to be expressed by not merely holding an intense view on moral questions but more importantly by showing the willingness to accept the costs involved in realizing these principles.[6] To quote Gandhiji:

> "My mission is to teach by example and precept under severe restraint the use of the matchless weapon of Satyagraha which is a direct corollary of non-violence and truth. I am anxious, indeed I am impatient, to demonstrate that there is no remedy for many ills of life save that of non-violence. When I have become incapable of evil and when nothing harsh or naughty occupies, be it momentarily, my thought—world, then, and not till then, my non-violence will move all the nearest of the world. I have placed before me and the reader no impossible ideal or ordeal. It is man's prerogative and birthright." (*Young India*, 2-7-1925)

Among the many "experiments" Gandhi conducted in his life-time in his efforts to see 'God face to face', 'Satyagraha', is a distinct contribution he has bequeathed to humanity. Sarvodaya, Satyagraha, Ahimsa and Truth are the four pillars on which Gandhi built his edifice of global vision in which ethics, spirituality, morality, religion, equality, tolerance and compassion became the integrating and cementing foci to sustain this edifice which according to many critics of Gandhi is a Utopian and impracticable ideal

> "For the past thirty years I have been preaching and practicing Satyagraha. The principles of Satyagraha, as I know it today constitute a gradual evolution."

Satyagraha differs from Passive Resistance as the North Pole from the South. The latter has been conceived as a weapon of the weak and does not exclude the use of physical force or violence for the purpose of gaining one's end, whereas the former has been conceived as a weapon of the strongest and excludes the use of violence in any shape or form.

The term Satyagraha was coined by me in South Africa to express the force that the Indians there used for full eight years and it was coined in order to distinguish it from the movement then going on in the United Kingdom and South Africa under the name of Passive Resistance.

Its root meaning is holding on to truth, hence truth force, I have also called it love—force or soul—force. In the application of Satyagraha I discovered in the earliest stages that pursuit of truth did not admit of violence being inflicted on one's opponent but, that he must be weaned form error by patience and sympathy. For what appears to be truth to the one may appear to be error to the other. And patience means self-suffering. So the doctrine came to mean vindication of truth not by infliction of suffering on the opponent but on one's self. . . ."

"Thus Gandhi was emphasizing a new element in the moral fibre of humanity, which has much to learn from the Satyagraha movement. Those who believed that it has no relevance in the present day context has to acknowledge the truth of what Gandhi himself thought about it and how he developed it. To him Satyagraha is mainly educative to train the soul or develop character so as to reach near perfection. He prescribed hard training. He said, "In my opinion, the beauty and efficacy of Satyagraha are so great and the doctrine so simple that it can be preached even to children. It was preached by me to thousands of men, women and children commonly called indentured Indians with excellent results.[7]"

Gandhiji himself explained the term Satyagraha in these words:

> "Truth (Satya) implies love, and firmness (agraha) engenders and therefore serves as a synonym for force . . . the Force which is born of Truth and love or non-violence."

Satyagraha is often translated as "holding fast" in English. This raised the question: "To what values shall we hold fast?" Gandhi's two paramount values were truth and non-violence. To hold fast to non-violence, trained satyagrahis were trained to expect and to resist forces that would draw them into violence. Often we do not hear as much about holding fast to truth. But in the matter of truth, Gandhi taught that we should not assume that we own it. Instead, we should look for the truth in our opponent's perspective—something people find difficult to do, but can learn. Holding fast to truth does not mean being intransigent about our current beliefs, impressions, and positions. It means holding to the discipline of looking for the truth, even in arguments that are marshalled against us.[8]

In fact, Satyagraha is the most powerful and permanent weapon to solve political, social and economic as well as religious problems. It holds good even today in our democratic set-up against any perpetrated evil. Gandhi claimed that the Sarvodaya social order would be free from moral degradation, economic exploitation and political subjugation.

9. Satyagraha—A Science in the Making

1. "I am myself daily growing in the knowledge of satyagraha. . . . Satyagraha as conceived by me is a science in the making."
2. "In brief, the significance of Satyagraha consists in the quest for a principle of life."
3. "There are two ways of countering injustice. One way is to smash the head of the man who perpetrates injustice and to get your own head smashed in the process . . . . Everywhere wars are fought and millions of people are killed. The consequences is not the progress of a nation but its decline. . . . But through the other method of combating injustice, we alone suffer the consequences of our mistakes and the other side is wholly spared. This other method is Satyagraha."
4. "We can aim everything without hurting anybody and through soul—force or satyagraha alone."
5. "The course that a satyagrahi adopts in his fight is straight and he need look to one for help. He can, if necessary, fight by himself alone."
6. "For the battle of Satyagraha one only needs to prepare oneself. We have to have strict self-control.
7. "In brief, the aim of the satyagraha struggle was to infuse manliness in coward and to develop the really human virtues."[9]
8. True religion as the basis of Public Administration and Politics.

Gandhiji feels that let us have a great ideal, an ideal that will startle us with its greatness. That is only kind of an ideal to hold before our minds' eye and to work for. Little by little our imperfections and difficulties will vanish and instead of regarding life as a drudgery, instead of shrinking from it, we shall bless this life which offers so many opportunities. We shall find joy even in the little daily tasks and wherever we are placed we shall know happiness.[10]

Dharma, in the Indian tradition, commands morality in the sense of righteous conduct. As propagated by Emperor Ashok, it further implied inculcation and practice of virtue in the performance of assigned duties. To an extent, the normative morality would subjugate personal interests to community interests and particular aims to general aims of the society. Mahatma Gandhi has raised Dharma to a higher pedestal, signifying a quality through which we know "our duty in human life and our relation with other selves." Thus, ethics in public life is important to understand our place in society and the duties we owe to the society by virtue of what society gives us. The common people may not articulate it in as many words but this is built into their thinking process when they make an assessment of the conduct pattern of their representatives and leaders and the system over which the representatives have command.

He says, "I believe in absolute oneness of God and therefore also of Humanity . . . though we have many bodies, we have but one soul. The rays of the sun are many through refraction, but they have the same source. This unity is expressed both in the life of an individual and in social life. The spiritual law is constantly working behind all kinds of activities, individual, social, economic and political, and is, in fact, running through and unifying them all. He clearly says, "I believe in advaita. I believe in the essential unity of man, and for that matter of all that lives."[11]

10. Administration must Ensure Implementation of Policies-based on Ethics

Mahatma Gandhi is one of the beacon of modern humanity. He is a new star that rose on the horizon of the life of oppressed mankind, giving it a new hope. He is a religious, social and political leader, all in one, who does not distinguish between religious practice on the one hand and social and political ethics on the other, and who placed before India, and through India before the world, the idea that religious life is not merely a life of meditation but of active human service in social and political fields. He is a worshipper of Truth, and he has no definition of God but that of Truth. But this Truth is not to be found in any abstract realm but in the human situation itself. If it is to be realised at all, it has to be realised through activity amidst human affairs. There is thus a new emphasis on action; but all action in which spiritual Truth can be realised is ethical action, the fields of which are society and politics. Gandhi therefore is one of the greatest *karmayogins.* His teachings and life accord with the tradition that, during the *Kali* age, realisation is possible only through action, and not merely through gnosis or devotion. One's spirituality has to be embodied in ethical action; which means that it has to be confirmed by action. Otherwise, it may be imaginary or sentimental luxury. This is one feature of Gandhian thought that cannot be over-emphasized.[12]

11. His Ideal Constitution

In 1931, as the sole representative of Indian National Congress to the Second Round Table Conference he expressed his opinion on the type of constitutions he would like to have for a Free India.[13] I shall strive for a constitution which will release India from all thraldom and patronage. . . I shall work for an India . . . in which all communities shall live in perfect harmony. There can be no room in such an India for the curse of untouchability or the curse of intoxicating drinks and drugs. Women shall enjoy the same rights as men. . . . This is India of my dreams. . . . shall be satisfied with nothing else.

The objectives expressed in the Preamble are "perceptible vibration of Gandhian concept of independent India." His desire that the Constitution framed by the free-will of the Indians should provide social equality, economic and political justice and freedom of religion was—well reflected in the Resolution regarding Aims and Objects, moved by Pt. Nehru, Sir Alladi Krishnaswami Ayyar, during the debate on the Resolution said, "more than any argument, as the resolution before the House has received the blessings and support of Mahatma Gandhi, the architect of India's political destiny. . . . I trust that it will be carried with acclamation by the whole House without dissent. The Resolution, with some changes, was approved by the Assembly and took the form of Preamble. The aims and objects, laid in the Preamble and the ultimate source of the Constitution "We the people of India" are in no way different from Gandhian concept of Constitution.

CONCLUSION

Referring to Gandhi's seminal contribution to humanity Ram Manohar Lohia remarked: "In the context of this modern civilization to support you, even if you do not have arms to wield, you have got something inside you, which enables you to resist oppression and injustice and also to bear suffering manfully. It was this strange and powerful quality of Gandhi's actions in his last 30 years that fascinated the attention of modern man and made him believe that the future might still contain the ingredients of a new world."[14]

The greatest contribution of Gandhi in the context of the failure of modern civilization in eliminating violence and provide humanity the promised peace and plenty is his exposition of the vanity and hollowness of materialist world view of modern world and sought to restore the spiritualistic world view. Going by the spiritualistic view of life, Gandhi emphasized the organic view of life and pointed out that any action that is performed has its inevitable positive or negative consequence in all realms of human life and nature. Placing the spiritualistic worldview in the centre of human life, Gandhi explained the meaning of life, his inalienable nexus with nature and the values or norms that should be observed in all human activities.[15]

Gandhi's vision of a new society—sarvodaya—was based on the spiritual perception of the oneness of all life, sentient and non-sentient.[16] Gandhi envisaged the creation of a social order that promotes the accomplishment of the highest goal of human life. Such a new and transformed social order as would facilitate the greatest good of all Gandhi called Sarvodaya.[17] Highlighting the significance of Gandhian concept of Sarvodaya, especially in the light of recent research in environment science, R.R. Diwakar points out that, "Once we accept Sarvodaya as a concept for the evolutionary and all sided development, not only of man, but of all sentient beings (animal life and plant life) since man's own future depends on the health of the eco-system we will have to look upon the whole of the planet and everything on or in it, from that point of view. That is, the health and healthy growth of the sentient world had to be organized with a view to its being helpful for human evolution to higher moral and spiritual levels."[18]

In the beginning of the 21st Century no more analysis and debates are required to substantiate the relevance and importance of the evolution of a non-violent social order or the Gandhian legacy in its creation. The rosy picture of golden future promised by modern western civilization in its dual form of liberalism and socialism have turned out to be an illusion. The urgent need of the hour is whether we can rise above our verbal reiterations and symbolic acts in support of the creation of a just and non-violent social order and work collectively by transforming our life pattern and value preferences for the furtherance of the cause of a just social order. The world is ripe with positive climate. We cannot wait for the advent of another Mahatma. Thanks to revolutionary changes in means of communication the awareness of average man is higher than in the period of Gandhi.

For initiating such a collective and determined move for liberating the world from the clutches of violence in its manifold expressions, various movements that work in different parts of the world should form a consortium. The people in the developed as well as in the developing countries are directly and indirectly subjected to the violent onslaughts of globalization in the form of destruction of already shrunk production apparatus in poor countries - pushing thereby millions into poverty and dependence, depletion of water resources, forests, pollutions, monopoly on global media and intitutioalization and commercialization of knowledge.

"The generous and bountiful earth" as Mahatma Gandhi said, "will give enough for man's need but cannot cater fully to his greed." Man's greed has caused not only hunger and violence but also an alarming situation due to the collapse of human culture. I think that the cure for hunger and violence lies in building up the sinews of culture among our young people.[19]

The Samanyas, the generality of people, on the other hand, are those who engage themselves in the good of others so long as it does not involve the sacrifice of their own self-interest. There are those others, the manava-raksasas, devilish men, who sacrifice the good of others to gain their own selfish ends; but alas, what am I to say of those who sacrifice the good of others without gaining thereby any good even to themselves or to any one else!

Apart from those whom the world looks upon as divine incarnations, the satpurusa category includes men like Gandhiji. He might have remained a barrister and could have led a comfortable life. But he discovered himself in others and, dying to himself, lived for others. He dedicated himself to the work of rescuing from slavery and fear millions of his fellowmen, and making them realize the dignity and worth of their manhood and womanhood.

The Indian nation today, contrary to the expectation of the father of the Nation, Mahatma Gandhi, is not a peaceful country and despite the tremendous improvements it relegated in the various human development aspects, violence seems to be spreading like cancer. Violence of different sorts dominate the general scenario sending shock waves all around. Mass killings, rioting and destruction of others' property at the slightest provocation seems to have become the order of the day. No part of the India can claim to be free from this scourge.[20]

The odds before humanity appears to be imponderable. From religious violence, physical violence, economics of violence, etc. humanity has now moved over to a period of 'terrorist violence and counter-terrorist violence' which is more deadly. It is hoped that the power and glory of non-violence would continue to influence thinkers, social activists, policy-makers, administrators, writers as well as the common man, as is evident from the various campaigns and determined movements, led non-violently in different parts of the world now. The declaration of UNESCO of 2000 AD as the 'Year of Non-violence' is yet another milestone in humanity's striving towards building a non-violent world 'Vasudhaiva Kutumbakam' as espoused by Indian sages several centuries ago.[21]

On the one hand we have a resurgent India eagerly seeking its place in the world and on the other hand, we have a battered Bharat riddled with caste wars, political instability, social unrest and economic hardships. The bureaucracy is the new 'sahib' and the masses still don't realize their ownership to their resources. Thus, we are still far from the swaraj which our independence era leaders had envisioned. We have to move from gloating over the success of our parliamentary system and move towards strengthening grassroots political institutions.

Hence, Gandhi's definition stretched beyond mere political freedom and spread to encompass economic as well as moral freedom. By political freedom he meant the withdrawal of the British from India. But more important was economic and moral freedom. He felt that true independence can come only when people are economically secure and there is no exploitation of one class by the other. And by moral freedom he meant freedom from armed defense forces; where there was no need for armed forces to maintain law and order; where people had the sense to govern themselves. Such a broad conception of politics and freedom appears like a Utopia, which cannot be achieved. Such a deep understanding and self-restraint cannot develop overnight nor can it be successful if only a few understand its significance. The swaraj that Gandhi visualized would require lot of practice and discipline. It will be the natural and inevitable result of co-operative industry on the part of the whole nation. It will be the natural and inevitable result of an enlightened awakening amongst the masses of India. But half a dozen or 20 cities of India alone working together cannot bring swaraj. They did their best to formulate a constitution that would serve the country's best interests. After a lot of deliberation the multi-party democratic system was adopted, with a legislative assembly that would be elected by the people. The vision was to let the people elect their own government. However, the way democracy was run in the country, the parliamentary system developed but it also resulted in the centralization of power at the centre. For decade only a single party ruled the country. There was hardly a reasonable opposition to the Congress party and it was as if we had a single party rule in the country. Such a long stint in power further concentrated political power in the hands of a few; and the vision of political freedom for the common man remained just that—a vision. Gandhiji's dream of swaraj got lost in the glorified success of our parliamentary system. Even today we do not have successful local government which was what Gandhi has envisioned in his Hind Swaraj. The Panchayat Raj system has still not taken strong roots in the country and this has hampered the social and economic development of our village. Because we do not have strong political institution at the grassroot level, there is a dearth of leader who have risen from the lowest strata of our society. Strong political systems cannot be developed unless there are strong leaders who are capable of understanding the social and cultural dimensions of the society they are supposed to lead. The digital divide that we are so concerned about cannot be bridged unless there are sincere efforts to decentralize political power in a planned manner.

Relevance

Mahatma Gandhi's model of development would always remain relevant. The advanced countries engaged in multiplication of wealth through destroying human ecology would die their own death. Gandhiji wanted a full freedom to a village when the people work with their own hands.

In order to resolve conflicts, Gandhiji's philosophy is the answer. Gandhian philosophy says: create a situation where there would be less and less conflict. There are two theories propounded by Gandhi. He says the world has enough for everybody's need but not for anybody's greed. If you promote greed, some people would become richer and others would become poorer. This brings conflict. The first thing is don't create conflict. Gandhi's other theory is a model of development that says what should be made by hands should be made by hands and what should be made in village should be made in village. What cannot be made by hands, in village or in cottage industries, should be made in the big factories. This is the model of economy that makes villages powerful. Gandhi said India should be the nation of over 5 lakhs economically self-sufficient and self-managed villages. He never dreamt there would be Mumbai, Kolkata, Chennai, New Delhi and Prime Minister would dictate from centre to all villages. So, we did'nt follow the principle of Gandhi and through our current development model, we have created such an attitude that it brings conflict in our society. For instance, the Indian government is trying to conserve the jungle and asking the tribal groups to leave their places. This brings conflict. Why the government does not protect the forest and wildlife with the help of these tribal groups and Adhivasis?

Why the Dalits are fighting? Because the land they are tilling is owned by rich people. Basically, the land should be owned by the Dalits. The government has not been able to transfer the resources from the hands of rich people to the poor. Because of the wrong policies, the conflict has come now. So, the only way to address the conflict is to correct these policies. Military suppression is not the way a government should use. The leaders are elected to manage the governance, and the population and if they do not have that conscience then there is no reason for them to stay there any more. So, we need to address every problem through political dialogue.

Gandhiji is all in one. He was a great philosopher because he could see the present and future problems of the world clearly and he was able to give us directions on how to deal with these problems. He was a politician because he fought against the British regime, mobilized the people politically to free India and consequently liberated the country. He thinks, along with fighting for political freedom in India, he was fighting for freedom of humanity at large. He lived a very simple life. So he was a civilian as well. At times, you may even see him as a businessman because he was sensitive towards mobilizing financial resources, taking responsibility and accountability of this money and allocating it for movement appropriately. He was an expert in managing public money. Thus, he has played various roles in the society. That is the reason why Gandhi has been an inspiration for people of all walks of life.

Lots of people use Gandhi's name and many of them

have known him deeply. But there are also many people who take Gandhi as a theory. They say Gandhi is a past episode and Gandhi is a history. I say Gandhi is present and future. When he fought against British, he fought against injustice. Now there is a lot of injustice and exploitation and Gandhi is needed here. So, why don't you use Gandhian techniques now? They were relevant hundred years back and still relevant to fight against injustice. The best means to tackle injustice is peaceful uprising like his Satyagraha. In future society, these would become even more important. What I argue again and again is that don't use "Gandhi is the past." Many people are trying to present Gandhi as past and get rid of any responsibilities. What Gandhi did hundred years ago, we should do it now and our generation should be able to do that tomorrow. We should see radical Gandhi. Don't worship him; make him relevant to our age. That is not very new but people don't use that part of Gandhi.[22]

Since the nations in the world are engaged in destroying and exploitation of nature causing natural calamities and poverty in many parts of the world, therefore, Gandhiji does not seem relevant to them. However, in new millennium, Nations of the world would realize and follow his basic principle to ensure good existence on this planet—earth. His philosophy of Democratic decentralization that Swaraj to every village is ideal governance. Good Governance would not be possible as far as Union and State Governments do not transfer powers to villages and villagers so that they become their own masters.

It is high time that we stop glorifying Gandhi as a saint and put him on a pedestal to be revered but not followed. We should stop paying homage merely through words to Gandhi and his ideals on October 2 every year and instead focus on the building of political system that will provide political freedom to the grassroots. Instead of simply following him by being dressed in pure white khadi; let us come with innovative but truthful interpretations of Gandhi's political philosophy, so that our political systems can be managed more effectively and honestly.[23]

Notes and References

1. Verinder Grover, "Mohandas Karam Chand Gandhi: A Biography of his Vision and Ideas", New Delhi, Deep & Deep, 1998, Preface, XIV-XV.
2. R. De Loyoloo Fortucono, "End to a Life" in Varinder Grover (ed.) *op. cit.*, p. 294.
3. O.P. Minocha, "The Impact of the Gandhian Ideology on the Indian Constitution", in Verinder Grover (ed.) *op. cit.*, p. 55.
4. N. Radhakrishnan, Forward, Satyagraha, Centenary Reflections, N. Vasudawan (ed.) Indian Council of Gandhain Studies, Gandhian Media Centre, New Delhi, 2007, pp. 8-11.
5. Devdutt, An India without Hunger and Violence, on 27-28 January, 2007, at IGNOU.
6. Ronald Tercheck, Gandhian Politics in New Dimension and Perspectives in Gandhism, V.T. Patil (ed.) Inter-India Publications, New Delhi, 1989, p. 123.
7. Radhakrishnan, "Satyagraha, Century Reflections, *op. cit.*, pp. 1-5.
8. Charles Collyer, Satyagraha and Truth in Satyagraha, Centenary Reflected, *op. cit.*, p. 88.
9. Quoted from 1-7 are from Gandhi and South Africa, 1914-48, eds. Reddy and Gopal Krishna Gandhi.
10. Swami Parmananda, Secret of Right Activity, Madras, Ramakrishna Math, Year not mentioned.
11. *Young India*, 4-12-24.
12. P.T. Raju, The Four Basic Principles of Gandhi's Philosophy in Varinder Grover (ed.) *op. cit.*, p. 180.
13. Louis Fischer, Ed. The Essential Gandhi, An Anthology, George Allen and Unwin, London, 1968, pp. 196-97.
14. Rammanohar Lohia, Marx, Gandhi and Socialism, p. 156, Hyderabad, 1963.
15. K. Gopinatha Pillai, Non-Violent Global Orders, Searching a Step Further, in *Journal of Peace and Gandhian Studies*, January, 2004, p. 73.
16. M.P. Mathai, Mahatma Gandhi's World-View, p. 225, New Delhi, 2000.
17. *Ibid.*, p. 155.
18. R.R. Diwakar, Journey to Sarvodyaya, *Gandhi Marg*, Vol. 7, No. 4, 1985, p. 201.
19. Omchery, M.N Pillai, Role of Education in Combating Hunger and Violence in a Nation Dialogue", An India without Hunger and Violence, 27-28, January, 2007, IGNOU..
20. N. Radhakrishnan, Violent free society Campaign, in *Journal of Peace and Gandhian Studies*, *op. cit.*, p. 92.
21. *Ibid.*, p. 107.
22. Ahimsa Non Violence, Vol. II, No. 5, Sept-Oct. 2006, pp. 388-89.
23. Ipshita Bansal and Jaya Srivastava, The Four Pillars of Gandhian Political Edifice: Relevance For Contemporary Politics, in *IJPA*, January-March 2007, p. 66.

6

Jawaharlal Nehru (1889-1964)

Pt. Jawaharlal Nehru was born in Allahabad on 14th November, 1889 and this day is celebrated as Children's Day in India as he had great love for children and died on May 27, 1964.

India was indeed fortunate in having a political thinker and leader of the stature of Jawaharlal Nehru to shape her future and guide her destiny immediately after Independence. Independence was not a victory for him, it was relentless battle to fight poverty. The progress India has achieved since then, and the position that she now occupies in the international sphere, is largely due to his visionary approach and dynamic leadership during her infancy as an independent nation.[1]

IMPORTANT ACADEMIC WORKS

Soviet Russia (1919), The Discovery of India (1926), Glimpses of World History (1934), and Autobiography (1936). The letters which he wrote to Chief Ministers have also been published in three volumes under the title Letters to Chief Ministers (1947-64) and (1985-87). IIPA has brought out, Jawaharlal Nehru and Public Administration.

CHART 6.1

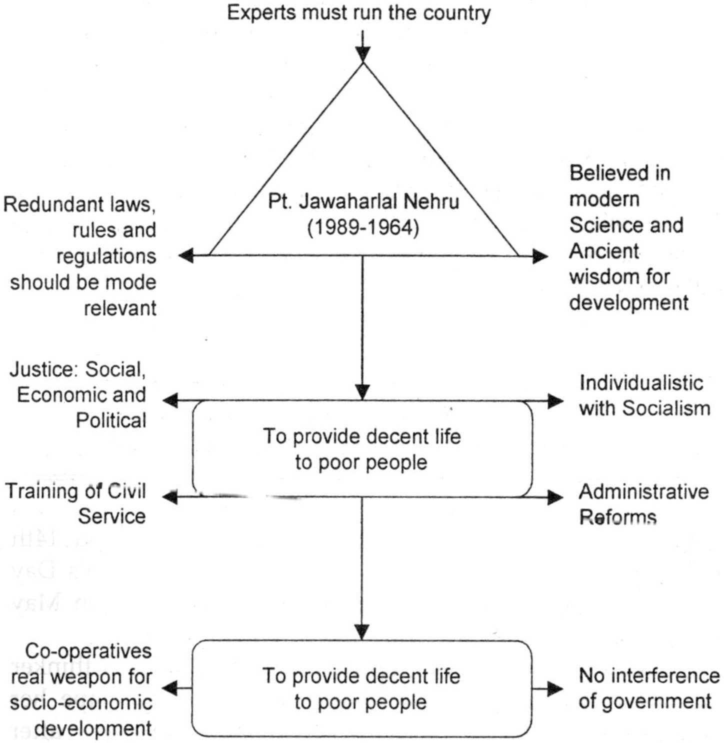

His view of public administration was dynamic and not static. Social change, according to Nehru, necessarily makes for administrative change also: "If all this is happening around us, obviously, the texture of human life is changing. If that changes obviously all this business of administration will necessarily be affected. Administration is not static; it is a changing, dynamic, revolutionary process to fit in with the changing times."

HIS IMPORTANT ADMINISTRATIVE THOUGHTS

1. Need of Experts in Administration based on Commitment

He wrote, "It seems to me quite essential that the ICS and similar services must disappear completely . . . The new

India must be served by earnest efficient workers" who did not attach much importance to the "money motive."

He was drawn into specialist-generalist controversy when a grievance was made that the engineers be given the status of secretaries. While not objecting to such a proposal he said: "I object to those who are specially qualified for a particular profession sitting quill driving . . . Our services are steeped in a system of gradation or caste system. . . . First Class engineers might be much more needed by us than any of our secretaries. . . . Secretaries are available in abundance, but engineers are few."[2]

Commenting on the civil servants craze for status-hunting he remarked, "In Delhi, you would have noticed there are no Directors—all are Directors-general." He looked upon the haphazard proliferation of bureaucracy as a sign of "maldevelopment." He said, "New Delhi is a jungle, a jungle of able men. Still a jungle you are lost in this jungle of administrative mazes and labyrinths . . . The way government organizations and departments multiply leads us nowhere but to waste."[3]

Pt. Nehru, the first Prime Minister of Independent India and many other important leaders like Pt. G.B. Pant, etc., did not like the idea that for building up a new India, the very machinery that was till now hampering and countering the freedom movement should be used. Pt. Nehru is on record to have said:

But of one thing I am quite sure that no new order can be built up in India, so long as the spirit of ICS pervades our Administrative Public Service. That spirit of authoritarianism is the ally of imperialism and it cannot co-exist with freedom. It will either succeed in crushing freedom or will be swept away by itself. Only with one type of State, it is likely to fit in and that is the Fascist type. Therefore, it seems quite essential that the ICS and similar services must disappear completely, much before we can start real work on a new order.[4]

Jahawarlal Nehru, while addressing the Fourth Annual General Body meeting of the Indian Institute of Public Administration, said:

In a period of dynamic growth, however, we want as civil servants persons who are not, if I may use the word without any disrespect, merely head clerks but people with minds, people with vision, people with desire to achieve, who have some initiative for doing a job and who can think how to do it. But the person who is to be completely neutral is a head clerk and no more. He would do his work efficiently as a head clerk, no doubt but nothing more. Can a person be neutral, I ask you, about basic things which we stand for, our state stands for, our plans stand for, e.g., a socialist pattern of society.[5]

A certain degree of informed zeal and identification with tasks entrusted to a functionary with a view to ensure higher levels of performance are the hallmark of excellence in public service. In the words of Jawaharlal Nehru:

No administrator, I suppose, or anyone else for the matter of that, can really do first class work without a sense of function, without some measures of a crusading spirit: I am doing this, I have to achieve this, as a part of a great movement in a big cause. That gives a sense of function, not the sense of the individual, narrow approach of doing a job in an office for a salary or wage, something connected with your life's outlook or anything, perhaps being interested, as people inevitably are, on one's personal preferment in that particular work.

"The methods of choosing people for services are still the old methods of choosing them for what may be called broadly the general administrative service and not for any specialized branch of service that we have today and that we are likely to have more and more in the future."[6]

Similarly, he was critical of the traditional emphasis on seniority since it interferes with efficiency: "we have also to do away with inefficiency. I agree that we should not be too hard but some way must be found to make it possible for the efficient and bright men to advance and the inefficient to be weeded out. Consideration of seniority is desirable to some extent but it is not wholly desirable because it pays regard only to the length of service or age to the detriment of efficiency. Things are different in science . . . it is commonly supposed that no big scientist does any creative work after reaching the age of 40. . . . Old minds maybe good but they are still old and they cannot bring a new outlook to these new tasks."

He observed: "The person who is becoming more and more important today is the engineer, the technical man, the scientist. In the old days, the person who was most important was the administrator. Now I do not mean to say that the administrator has become less important. . . . But the fact remains that the other types of specialized workers like engineers and the scientists are becoming more and more important. . . . There is a tendency, again derived from the British days, of treating the administrator at the top as far superior to a person engaged in any other occupation like engineering, science or education or anything. This is not a good tendency. Because, today our country is becoming more and more technical minded."[7]

2. Training of Civil Servants

Pt. Jawaharlal Nehru invited two experts Paul H. Applby and A.D. Gorwala to study administration and suggest methods of administrative improvements. Based upon their reports, Pt. Nehru set-up Indian Institute of Public Administration in 1954 at New Delhi. In his inaugural address he said, "Administration is meant to achieve something and not to exist in some kind of Ivory tower following certain rules of procedure and looking Narcissus like. The Test of administration is the welfare of the people." He wanted good training for civil services.

3. Faith in Administration that Promotes Socialism

Elaborating his concept of socialism in the Presidential Address at the Lucknow session of the Indian National Congress in 1936, he said:

I am convinced that the only key to the solution of . . India's problems lies in socialism. . . . I see no way of ending the poverty, the vast unemployment, the degradation and the subjection of the Indian people except through socialism. That involves vast and revolutionary changes in our political and social structure, ending vested interests in land and industry, as well as the feudal and autocratic Indian

States system. That means the ending of private property, except in a restricted sense, and the replacement of the present profit system by a higher ideal of co-operative service .. (and he thundered) . . . that the present order has reached the evening of its day, and it is upto us to try to mould the future as we would like it to be. . . .

In a significant passage he encapsulates the dilemmas of the modern statesman faced with the rival claims of democracy and socialism.

"We talk of a Welfare State and of democracy and socialism. These are good concepts but they hardly convey a clear and unambiguous meaning. Then the question arises as to what our ultimate objective should be? Democracy and socialism are means to an end, not the end itself. We talk of the good society. Is this something apart from the transcending the good of the individuals composing it? If the individual is ignored and sacrificed for what is considered the good of the society is that the right objective to have?

"It is agreed that the individual should not be so sacrificed and indeed the real social progress will come only when opportunity is given to the individual to develop, provided the individual is not a selected group but comprises the whole community. The touchstone, therefore, should be how far any political or social theory enables the individual to rise above his petty self and thus think in terms of the good of all."

Nehru wrote, while elaborating the objective of Congress Party in 1938: "The idea of the Congress is the establishment of a free and democratic society in India. Such a democracy involves an egalitarian society in which equal opportunities are provided for every member for self-expression and self-fulfilment and an adequate minimum civilized standard of life is shared by each member so as to make the attainment of this equal opportunity a reality. This should be the background or the foundation of our plan."[8]

"The moment we forget the human approach, somehow the foundation of thinking is removed."[9]

In his own words: "We talk of the good of society. In this something apart from and transcending the good of the individual composing it is not possible?" Nehru believed that "real social progress will come when opportunity is given to the individual to develop, provided the individual is not a selected group but combines the whole community."[10]

Ironically, Nehru had to resort to anti-civil liberty measures which consequently blurred the perceptions of common people in the Rule of Law in India. In the words of Nehru: "I have stood for the freedom of the individual and the group, and nothing pains me so much as that condition should arise in this country when civil liberties should be limited. . . . It pains me and hurts me that the very thing I condemned in the past should be indulged in by our governments."[11]

In a letter to Subhash Chandra Bose, he writes about himself in these words:

"I suppose I am temperamentally and by training an individualist and intellectually a socialist. . . . I hope that socialism does not kill or suppress individuality: indeed, I am attracted to it because it will release innumerable individuals from economic and cultural bondage."[12]

4. Laws Need Suit the Present Conditions to Provide Administration with Policies which Fulfil the Needs of Society

The existing laws in our country are too old to suit the existing conditions. These create problems in the way of progress. There is a need to change them to suit present requirements.

Writing in the *Glimpses World of History,* in 1934, Nehru wrote: "Laws are meant to fit existing conditions and they are meant to help us to better ourselves. If conditions change, how can the old laws fit in? They must change with changing conditions, or else they become iron chains keeping us back while the world marches on. No law can be an unchangeable law." In India, we are making use of law enacted 200 years back—a real tragedy.

5. Administrative Reforms

He is extremely critical of the formal organization laid down in rules made during British rule: "even in thinking purely of administration, here is something which is quite beyond my understanding it is so complicated—various departments traditions this and that. I confess I have not understood it at all; I feel lost in it. Once or twice, I had an occasion to look at the civil service rules and the like. I was astonished how the Government of India had continued to exist so long with these rules. It should collapse under them. In spite of the impediments that the rules put before it, it is a wonder how it has survived. There are three or four volumes with thousands of slips and the like. Only some selected high Pandits understand them. That is bad. In other words, the formal organization is highly complex, cumbersome and rigid, and so makes achievement difficult.

Nehru is highly critical of the existing procedures: "Take the Government of India, which has, I do not know how many, manuals of procedure, which some very highly talented people may understand, but most people do not. What are those manuals of procedure meant for? Apparently, I may use the word, perfection in administration. Ah! There must not be a mistake here, check, counter-check references and all that. This is all well-intentioned but if that results in the thing not being done or a great delay occurring in doing it, then the main thing is gone, in spite of the perfection aimed at."

"Wherever precedent, is the dominating factor, conditions are looked upon as static. Therefore, movement is slow and responsibility is spread out over anonymous individuals. That I think is a very important aspect for everyone of you, who is connected with administration, to consider, i.e. what your objective is. Is your objective the writing of a book or a fine manual of procedure. . . .? Or Whether your objective is to get the thing done . . .?"

In the face of social disorders he even found the legal system to be inadequate. On this behalf the following letter issued by Nehru to Chief Ministers is an illustration to the point:

"We have taken strong action frequently for the maintenance of public order. We have not hesitated to put people under detention or to proceed against them in law courts if they are offenders against public order. We have not shown the same earnestness in dealing with other anti-social activities, such as those indulged in by hoarders, black-marketers and those who indulge in corrupt practices . . . Perhaps our whole social structure and legal system have not been fashioned to meet such emergencies. If so, we shall have to think seriously of changing that structure or machinery . . ."[13]

He restated his position in *Whither India*:

India's immediate goal can, therefore, only be considered in terms of the ending of the exploitation of her people. Politically, it must mean independence and the severance of the British connection, which means imperialist domination; economically and socially it must mean the ending of special class privileges and vested interests. The whole world is struggling to this end: India can do no less, and in this way the Indian struggle for freedom lines up with the world struggle.

"Nehru's life work was to try to modernize this old land of ours to revive and free the latent energies of our people trapped in centuries of dead form, to change the ancient and sad face of the country into something that would once more vibrate with freshness, beauty and joy of life" said Asoka Mehta while discussing "Nehru on Social Justice and National Development."

He said: "It is perfectly clear that, under a democratic form of government different (political) parties come into power at different times, and I can understand that the civil servant should not be partial to any party. But he cannot be neutral about the basic issues. . . . In India, we are at present in a stage where all future developments depends upon the acceptance of certain basic assumptions and on intelligent and prompt and quick action."[14] He disliked expression like 'officials' and 'non-officials' which indicate a barrier between the administration and the people. While recognizing the importance of rules and regulations he felt that they tended to make the functioning of the government slow and complicated.

He observed: "If we have to deal with the rules framed not only in the pre-Independence days but long ago, in the remote antiquity, one might say, politically speaking, that we are bound hand and foot by something which has no place, no relevance today."[15] He recommended wider application of Work Study and O & M in administration.

In spite of the effort to make the decisions taken on administrative improvements as detailed and comprehensive as possible, the above still remains a 'statement of general principles. A great deal of work is required to be done to give them concrete shape. It is a continuing task and cannot evidently be detailed at a point of time in a statement of this nature. A Committee on Administration has been established at the Centre headed by the Cabinet Secretary. It will be its special function to progress the implementation of these decisions and to report periodically to the Cabinet.[16]

6. Industrial Development Based on Social Justice

Pt. Nehru spoke of this in Parliament in 1952 in the following terms: It is obvious that India be industrialized as rapidly as possible and industrialization includes, of course, all kinds of industry—major, middle, small, village and cottage. However rapid our industrialization may be, it cannot possibly absorb more than a small part of the population of this country in the next ten, twenty or even thirty years. Hundreds of millions will remain who have to be employed chiefly in agriculture. These people must, in addition, be given employment in small industries like cottage industries and so on. Hence, the importance of village and cottage industries, I think the argument one often hears about big industry *versus* cottage and village industry is misconceived. I have no doubt that we cannot raise the people's level of existence without the development of major industries in the country; in fact, I will go further and say that we cannot even remain a free country without them. Certain things, like adequate defence, are essential to freedom and these cannot be had unless we develop industry in a major way. But, we must always remember that the development of heavy industry does not by itself solve the problem of millions in this country.

He went on to say that "although the profit motive was at work very strongly and although there was probably greater suffering then, nevertheless, the approach was different. Perhaps the sense of social values was different. But, in the context of the world today, such a motive is becoming increasingly not only wrong from the economic point of view, but a vulgar thing from any sensitive point of view."

Now, the method of peaceful progress is a method ultimately of democratic progress. But keeping in mind the ultimate aim of democratic thought, it is not enough for us to say that we have given votes to all, and let the rest remain. The ultimate aim is economic democracy. The ultimate aim is putting an end to these great differences between the rich and the poor; the people who have opportunities and those who have none or very little. That must be kept in mind. In the ultimate analysis, everything that comes in the way of that aim must be removed—removed in a friendly way; removed in a cooperative way; removed by State pressure; removed by law—because nothing should be allowed ultimately to come in the way of your achieving that social objective.[17]

7. Socialistic Pattern of Society

He combined the socialist philosophy with the democratic values of capitalist society which is popularly described as the democratic socialism.

"In the society based on the principle of democratic socialism, socialism and democracy are the means for the creation of a society in which exploitation of one class by another is abolished so as to raise level of living of its people and in which the individual possesses an unfettered right to self-expression." The new pattern of society was described by the Congress at the Avadi Session in 1955 as the "Socialistic pattern of Society."

Nehru was firm believer in Socialism but he had his love for democracy also. Socialism demanded the centralization of all the means of production and distribution and vesting the ownership only in the hands of the State to wage the marathon war against poverty and the people have to sacrifice all non-economic values for waging the war successfully. Examples are Soviet Union and China. Nehru certainly did not want this type of war against poverty. He chose the socialistic pattern which will have the economic ideals of socialism and democratic values of capitalism. The combination of the ideals of socialistic and capitalistic economy resulted in the mixed economy. Nehru, the great visionary, gave this economic system to India which is being followed even today. Nehru was very much ahead of his time but, unfortunately, he did not live long to see the implementation of his ideas. The seeds of the economic fruits which India is reaping today were sown by none else than Jawaharlal Nehru.[18]

8. Foreign Policy

As far back as September 13, 1926, he had in a note defined the outlines of a foreign policy for India:

In developing our foreign policy we shall naturally first cultivate friendly relations with the countries of the East which have so much in common with us. With the European nations we are bound to develop further contacts. We have much to learn from them and closer intercourse will be to the advantage of both.

Looking far into the future of humanity Nehru envisioned a world federation almost on the eve of the devastating World War II—a dream still short of reality. On June 1, 1939 he wrote:

A faint glimpse of . . . word co-operation came to President Wilson of the USA twenty years ago and he sought to realize it. But the war treaties and the statesmen of that generation scotched the idea. . . . A world union is necessary today. Unhappily, it will not come because those in authority are children of the old world which has ceased to be and cannot think or act in terms of the new. Such a union . . . must be based on the fullest democracy and freedom, each nation having autonomy within its borders, and submitting in inter-national matters to the union legislature to which it sends its representatives.

Likewise, in 1940 he anticipated the emergence of a "real Commonwealth" and tracing its origin to the Indian ethos and history, on 18 December 1965 he declared:

Throughout her chequered history India has remembered the message of peace and tolerance. In our own time this message was proclaimed by our great leader and master, Mahatma Gandhi, who led us to freedom by peaceful and yet effective action on a mass scale. . . . The preservation of peace forms the central aim of India's policy. It is the pursuit of this policy that we have chosen the path of non-alignment. . . . We believe in non-aggression and non-interference by one country in the affairs of another and the growth of tolerance between them and the capacity for peaceful co-existence.

The imperatives for modernization, scientific and technological progress, tolerance and co-existence for world peace, and respect for human values are best summed up in Nehru's words excerpted from his speech on November 10, 1961 to the United Nations General Assembly at New York:

(The) truth is that violence and hatred are bad—bad for individuals and bad for everybody. The great men of the world have been those who have fought hatred and violence and not those who have encouraged it. . . . It really requires a new way of thinking, a new development of humanity . . . (The) world has made tremendous progress in many ways, progress which manifestly can cure the material ills of the world. But, what shall it profit the world if it conquers the material ills and then commits suicide because it has not controlled its own mind.

9. Planning

Even when confronted with these powerful challenges, Jahawarlal Nehru, the national freedom fighter now turned into nation-builder, did never lose sight of planning and economic developmental issues. In November 1947, he formed an economic programme committee of the Congress with himself as the Chairman which submitted a report in 1948, and on the basis of this report a Planning Commission was formed.[19]

Nehru himself told the Congress at Avadi (1955) towards the end of the First Plan that it had not been a plan "in the real sense of the term." The word socialism was not even mentioned during these years.

But the situation was not an irreversible one. It was at the Avadi session of the Congress that, uncle Nehru's inspiration, the well-known Avadi Resolution was adopted. The resolution announced that "planning should take place with a view to the establishment of a Socialistic Pattern of

Society, where the principal means of production are under social ownership or control, production is progressively speeded up and there is equitable distribution of national wealth." The resolution affirmed that the state would play a substantial part and stated that "the public sector must play a progressively greater part, more particularly in the establishment of basic industries."[20]

He pointed out in May, 1955, "It was therefore essential that the people should join them in their thinking about the plan. If the Government of the Planning Commission brought out the plan themselves and placed it before the public, the latter might not understand many things and might not accept some of them. On the other hand, when they are associated with the thinking of the plan they appreciate the difficulties and know that if they want something worthwhile they have to pay for it by hard work. In that way it became easier to tackle the question of resources." His belief in the democratic and peaceful method arose from his enormous faith in the Indian people. He felt that "if anything is put to them straight, honestly and in a way they are able to understand and if they are taken into confidence they can be made to do anything."[21]

The administrative structure is inadequate and inappropriate and also not responding and adapting itself to the needs of the developmental programmes. "We in the Planning Commission and others concerned have grown more experienced and more expert in planning. . . . I fear we are not quite so expert at implementation as at planning. . . . Now in this business of implementation, a very important factor is the administrative aspect.. the other aspect in implementation, in the vast plans that we have and which concern millions of people, is not a set of officials who implement them; you have to bring in a certain understanding of the public, a certain cooperation of the public.[22]

Speaking on the Draft outline of the Third Plan in the Rajya Sabha, Nehru reiterated the basic objectives of planning, in India and, in reply to those challenges the very idea of planning, stated: "A country situated as India is, as any more or less underdeveloped country is, cannot move ahead without hard planning and hard work. It cannot be left to the advocates of free enterprise." After achieving our Independence, we took to planning and drew up big project. In many cases implementation of these projects was delayed, giving rise to increase in cost. To some extent the fault lies with the administration because responsibilities were not properly allocated with the result that at every stage reference to a higher authority was required. We were repeatedly advised to delegate responsibility so that the man on the spot could take quick decisions. Something has been done in this direction but perhaps more is to be done. We have to consider how we can activise our administration so that decisions could be taken quickly at every level.[23]

With a dig at these advocates he said: "It is a matter of continual astonishment that we should have in this country relics and museum pieces of the past, mentally speaking."[24]

In 1937 he commented: "I believe that without . . . planning little that is worthwhile can be done."[25] Indeed, one of the ideas he brought from Soviet Union which he visited in November 1927 was of planning. Nehru's interest in and articulations on public administration were a by-product, so to say, of such broader concerns and orientations.

10. Public Enterprises

At the same time, he emphasized: "We have to avoid and prevent too much accumulation of wealth." With regard to the institutional perspective, he affirmed: "We want a socialist structure of society—socialist in the widest sense of the word—and that the principal means of production should be owned by the state or by the people. Where the principal means of production are in private hands, they may lead to private exploitation, to private monopoly and the like. That is why we are opposed to it."[26]

11. Co-operative Development

He considered co-operation as the best instrument for achieving these objectives and for the establishment of a democratic socialist order. He often repeated: "Co-operation to me is dearer than any other movement because it is something much more than merely an efficient and economic way of doing things, it equalizes and prevents disparities from growing. It is really a way of life and a way of life which is certainly not a capitalist way of life and which is not hundred per cent socialist though it is much nearer socialism than capitalism. Anyhow, it is a way of life and if we can extend that outside the economic field, shall I say, in regard to international intercourse, it is a way of mutuality. Cooperation is a kind of mutuality, a way of mutuality. It is a way of extension in the international field. Although perhaps the expression is not very apt, it is a way of peaceful co-existence. If people look at things in the co-operative way they are inevitably driven to ways of peace and not ways of conflict and war."

The world of co-operation will not again find a better champion that Pt. Nehru. Speaking at the Fourth Indian Co-operative Congress, he said, "Through co-operation alone can an individual, a small individual, keep his individuality intact, his freedom intact, and yet function in a big way and take advantage of science and technology."

He said, "Co-operation is not governmental control. Nothing can be more fatal than governmental control, which is the embrace of death—if it is governmental control, good or bad, it is not co-operation, whatever else it may be. If you examine the state of affairs in India today, you will find this demonstrated. Where people—non-governmental people—have taken the lead, have devoted themselves, the movement has flourished and grown. Where it requires nursing by the government all the time, it has not grown I will repeat—I will go on repeating—I dislike the association of government in co-operation except as an agency helping it by way of funds, etc.

12. Humanism

Thus, at that historic movement on the night of 14/15 August 1947, which marked a turning point in the long and tortuous history of mankind, Jawaharlal Nehru reiterated his conviction that political freedom is not an end in itself. To quote his historic words:

"A moment comes which comes but rarely in history when we step out from the old to the new, when an age ends and when the soul of a nation long suppressed finds utterances. It is fitting that at this solemn moment we take the pledge of dedication to the service of India and her people and to the still larger cause of humanity. . . . The service of India means the service of socialism, secularism and democracy, anti-colonialism and world peace, all flowed from his basic commitment to man and the spirit to man. For this he will be remembered in India and abroad as long as the history of the race survives."

13. Community Development and Democratic Decentralization

Community Development and Democratic Decentralization represented Panditji's main effort towards solving the dilemma of how to reconcile democracy with the needs of a technological age. Was everything to be dependent on a few planners and executives at the Centre? How were the people to be associated with the effort? Verdicts will vary on the way he set about this programme. May be he went too fast. May be no other halfway houses were practicable. May be the experiment has not been given sufficiently sustained trial. Are there any other lines open for achieving development without totalitarianism?[27]

Accordingly Nehru explained . . . 'the governance of a country does not merely consist in issuing orders from some high office, rather in reaching the minds and hearts of masses of people, of bringing about satisfactory human relations. Ultimately almost every problem can be resolved into one of human relations—the relationship of the individual with a group and of one group with another group'. In this approach, the key invariable was the human being behind the anonymous files in government. He emphasized, '. . .we have to deal with human aspect of every problem. We are apt to forget this, living in our ivory tower of government offices and dealing impersonally with files and papers, but behind these files and papers and the problems discussed in them lie human beings.[28]

14. Corruption

There is one matter I should like to speak to you about which I am very clear about that is that in India we have to be hundred per cent strict in regard to anything that savours of corruption. We should give no quarter to it. . . . I have often said in public and repeat it here that I am prepared to enquire into any allegation, any charge of corruption, for which there is some prima facie evidence. I cannot enquire into every charge that is hurled against one and all. If there is prima facie anything in it, I shall enquire, through whatever means I may possess. I shall enquire directly from New Delhi, and if after my initial enquiry anything substantial appears. We shall take action, and it just does not matter who the person concerned is, be he high or low.[29]

CONCLUSION

In the words of Dr. S. Radhakrishnan: "His life and work have had a profound influence on our mental make up, social structure and intellectual development."[30]

M.C. Chagla describes Nehru as a humanist and according to him: "A humanist is essentially a democrat not for any ideological reasons but because democracy essentially gives to the individual his self-respect and realization of his value as a separate personality and makes him feel that he is an equal with the highest in the land."[31]

To quote from the editorial of a reputed journal written after Nehru's death: "Nehru gave us the vision, it is for us, lesser men, to draw up the programmes and implement them."[32]

Nehru was a great visionary and he provided the fundamental ideas in the realm of economic policy for developing a strong and self-reliant India with a just social order. These ideas continue to be of great relevance and will remain so in future also. His contribution towards increasing economic capabilities of a country in various fields and laying strong foundations of a modern India has also undoubtedly been of great and far reaching significance. However, he did not follow-up his ideas vigorously and effectively enough for achieving social justice. This tendency is unfortunately still persisting. So, the most crucial need of the hour is to bridge the gap between professions and practice.[33]

Nehru was essentially a great visionary and he visualized a world which is happy and contented and is based on co-operation and equality. He was a prophet of lasting peace and universal fraternity. A man may die but not the ideas. Like Plato, Dante Kant, Rousseau and Gandhi, Nehru is immortal. While reflecting on his ideas and achievements, one is simply reminded of John Donne's immortal lines:

> "Death, be not proud . . .
> And Death shall be no more;
> Death, thou shall die."

Pt. Nehru is no more, but his ideas and thoughts shall be cherished for ever by the posterity as a part of the precious, heritage of humanity, and he will certainly be remembered as "the man who, with all his mind and heart, loved India and the Indian people, and they, in turn, were indulgent to him and gave him of their love most abundantly and extravagantly."[34]

Writing in his last Will and Testament he said:

> "I have received so much love and affection from the Indian people that nothing. I can repay even a small fraction of it, and indeed there can be no repayment of so precious a thing as affection. Many have been admired, some have been revered, but the affection of all classes of the Indian people, has come to me in such abundant measure that I have been overwhelmed by it."

K.R. Narayanan former President of India, observes: I then watched him go into the garden like a grand Mughal, meeting and talking to women and children, peasants and workers who had come from different parts of India to have the *darshan* of Jawaharlal Nehru. But his manner was not that of a Mughal descending from the throne to hear the complaints of the people, but of a great democrat and a wonderful human being wanting to meet and understand the people. It was for Nehru a dip into the ocean of India's humanity, a deep into the minds and hearts of the Indian people.

Memdouh Zike feels "I should like them to say, 'This was a man who, with all his mind and heart loved India and the Indian people, and they in turn were indulgent to him and gave him of their love most abundantly and extravagantly'."[35]

Relevance of Jawaharlal Nehru in 21st Century

Jawaharlal Nehru believed in that administration which is in tune with the present times. He wanted all the laws, rules and regulations must be changed and simplified to serve the common man. We, the students of Public Administration owe to him the following:

(a) Administration is a tool to serve the common man.

(b) His choice between Generalists and specialists was in favour of specialists, though he could not do anything practical about it. Even today, this controversy is going on. We must give proper respect and status to specialists who can be the architect of modern India.

(c) He believed in training of civil service to improve their efficiency and culture. For this he set-up Indian Institute of Public Administration in 1954.

(d) He believed in administrative reforms. He was fed up with the way Indian Administration functions. Even today, we are not in a position to give good governance to the people because of ineffective Government machinery. Inspite of plethora of Committees and Commissions set-up to improve administrative machinery, nothing happens in practice.

He was keen about unity of country which must be protected in future at all costs. However, in practice, he could not implement his ideas as an administrator.

Above all, finally, the Services—whether they are All India Services or State Services, they have to remember that the basic thing in India without which no great thing can be done at all, is the building up of the unity of India. That is quite essential and I want you to realise that. You all talk about it—of course, but I want you to realise it in all its importance and essential nature, whatever we have achieved in the past thirty to forty years in our struggle, in the last eight years of our Independence has been because in a large measure we have pulled together in India in spite of forces which disrupt and fissiparous tendencies. I think every member of the Services, whatever his Service may be, must understand and appreciate this; must understand that it is his duty to work for the unity of India, to break down barriers which come in the way of the unity of India and always to be a crusader in that behalf.[36]

In emphasizing continuity in planning, Nehru always recognized that new conditions would call for new forms of action. He saw change and continuity as two sides of the same coin. He would have been the first to see that the sequence of events which has led to the setbacks of the past two or three years in agriculture indicates also a new set of national priorities. It is clear that, in the next phase of development while exploiting the possibilities of industrial and technological growth to the maximum, the true core of national planning lies in agriculture, in human resources development, employment and education, and in the restructuring and deepening of the rural economy.[37]

Panditji, towards the end of his long political career, was criticized by many for being a weak Prime Minister, a naïve idealist and in the sphere of foreign relations as a leader who aspired to garner for India image and influence far beyond her innate strengths. This is a surfacial and short-sighted judgment of a person who more than anyone else laid the foundations of contemporary India. He was not infallible. Perhaps he was not successful in full measures in all that he dreamt and visualized for India but to paraphrase the Chinese poet Lao Tzu: "Often times he stripped himself of passion in order to see the secrets of life; and often times he regarded life was passion in order to see its manifold results."[38]

We shall always remember the ideas of Pt. Nehru to make India a great nation and a force to make human life on this earth peaceful and blissful.

Notes and References

1. Verinder Grover, Editor, 'Jawaharlal Nehru: A Biography of his Vision and Ideas', Preface, New Delhi, Deep & Deep, 1998.
2. C.D. Navaslmhaib (ed.), India is spokesman—From speeches and address by Pt. Jawaharlal Nehru, Macmillan, 1960. The speech was delivered as an inaugural address at the 24th Annual meeting of the Central Board of Irrigation and Power, on Oct. 26, 1953.
3. *Ibid.*
4. Jawaharlal Nehru, An Autobiography, London, The Bodley Head, 1953, p. 443.
5. V. Jagnadhan (ed.), Jawaharlal Nehru and Public Administration, IIPA, New Delhi, 1975.
6. *Ibid.*
7. Jawaharlal Nehru's Speech to Public services at Kurnool on 9th Dec., 1955.
8. Jawaharlal Nehru and Public Administration (Symposium Papers), IIPA, New Delhi, 1982, p. 36.
9. Jawaharlal Nehru Speech, Vol. III, Publication Division, Ministry of Information and Broadcasting, GOI, p. 86.
10. Jawaharlal Nehru Speeches, Vol. IV, p. 406.
11. Quoted in: Devas S., Nehru, Champion of Peace, Coimbtore Printing Works Ltd., Coimbtore, 1960, p. 164.
12. Jawaharlal Nehru, A Bunch of Old Letters, Asia Publishing House, Bombay, 1960, p. 363.
13. G. Parthasarthy, (ed.), Letters to Chief Ministers, Vol. 2, JLN Memorial Fund, New Delhi.
14. Jawaharlal Nehru Speeched at the Fourth AGM of IIPA, 5th April, 1948.
15. Jawaharlal Nehru speeches to Public Servants at Kurnool on 4th Dec., 1905.
16. Statement laid on the Tables of the Lok Sabha on 10th August, 1961 and Rajya Sabha on the 24th August, 1961 by the Prime Minister.
17. Text of the speech in moving the Resolution on the Report of the Planning Commission on containing the Five Year Plans in the House of People, Dec. 15,1952.
18. Sheik Ahmed Hussain and Om Parkash Kajipd, Nehru: A True Democrat, Socialist, in Varinder Grover (ed.), *Jawaharlal Nehru*, New Delhi, Deep & Deep., 1998, p. 410.
19. Ranjit Das Gupta, Nehru's and India's Struggle for Economic Independence in Varinder Grover (ed.), *op. cit.*, p. 516.

20. *Ibid.*
21. H.K. Paranjape, "Jawaharlal Nehru and the Planning Commission" on P.L. Sanjeev Reddy and R.K. Tiwari, (eds.) Jawaharlal Nehru and Public Administration, New Delhi, IIPA, 2004, pp. 230-33.
22. Indian Institute of Public Administration, Seventh Annual General Body Meeting, 27th August, 1961.
23. IIPA, Ninth Annual General Body Meeting, Aug. 13, 1963.
24. The Discovery of India, Signet Press, Calcutta, p. 878.
25. Jawaharlal Nehru, The Unity of India, London, Lindsay Drummal, Third Edition, 1948, p. 175.
26. Nehru, Problems of Third Plan, p. 45.
27. Vishnu Sahay, "Nehru as First Prime Minister and his impact on Public Administration" in P.L. Sanjeev Reddy and R.K. Tewari (Eds.), *op. cit.*, p. 161.
28. A.P. Saxena, Jawaharlal Nehru and his vision of Governance in P.L. Sanjeev Reddy and R.K. Tewari, *op. cit.*, p. 196.
29. Speech on the inauguration of the Bharat Sewak Samaj at Thiruvananthapuram, Dec. 28, 1952.
30. Quoted in Shashi Ahluwalia, Nehru, 100 Years, Man as Publications, New Delhi, p. 188.
31. *Ibid.*, pp. 203-04.
32. Nehru Era, The Economic Weekly, Special Number, July 1964.
33. M.L. Sudan, Nehru and Economic Policy, in Verinder Grover (ed.), *op. cit.*, p. 542.
34. R.N. Gupta, Jawaharlal Nehru and Co-operative Movement, in Verinder Grover, (ed.), *op. cit.*, p. 50.
35. *Statesman*, Calcutta, 21.1.1954.
36. Speech to an Audience of Public Servants, Kurnool, Dec. 15, 1955.
37. Tarlok Singh, Reassessing Nehru Perspective on Planning in P.L. Sanjeev Reddy and R.K. Tewari (eds.), *op. cit.*, p. 25.
38. J.N. Dixit, Panditji, As India's Foreign Minister: An Appraisal, quoted in Verender Grover (ed.), p. 673.

7

Sardar Vallabhbhai Patel (1875-1950)

Vallabhbhai Patel was born on 31 October 1875 at village Karamsad in Gujarat. In 1910, Vallabhbhai went to England to qualify for the Bar and joined the Middle Temple. In 1913, after passing the examination with distinction, he returned to India and started his practice at Ahmedabad. In 1917, Vallabhbhai gave up his lucrative practice and plunged into the National struggle as a comrade of Gandhiji.

Jawaharlal Nehru felt that "History will record it in many pages and call him the Builder and Consolidator of the new India and say many other things about him. By many of us he will perhaps be remembered as a great captain of Our Forces in the Struggle for Freedom and as one who gave us Sound Advice both in times of Trouble in Moments of Victory; a friend and colleague and comrade on whom one could invariably rely, as a tower of strength which revived wavering hearts when we were in trouble."

His death in Bombay on 15th December 1950, removed from the Indian scene one of the most outstanding figures of modern history.

CHART 7.1

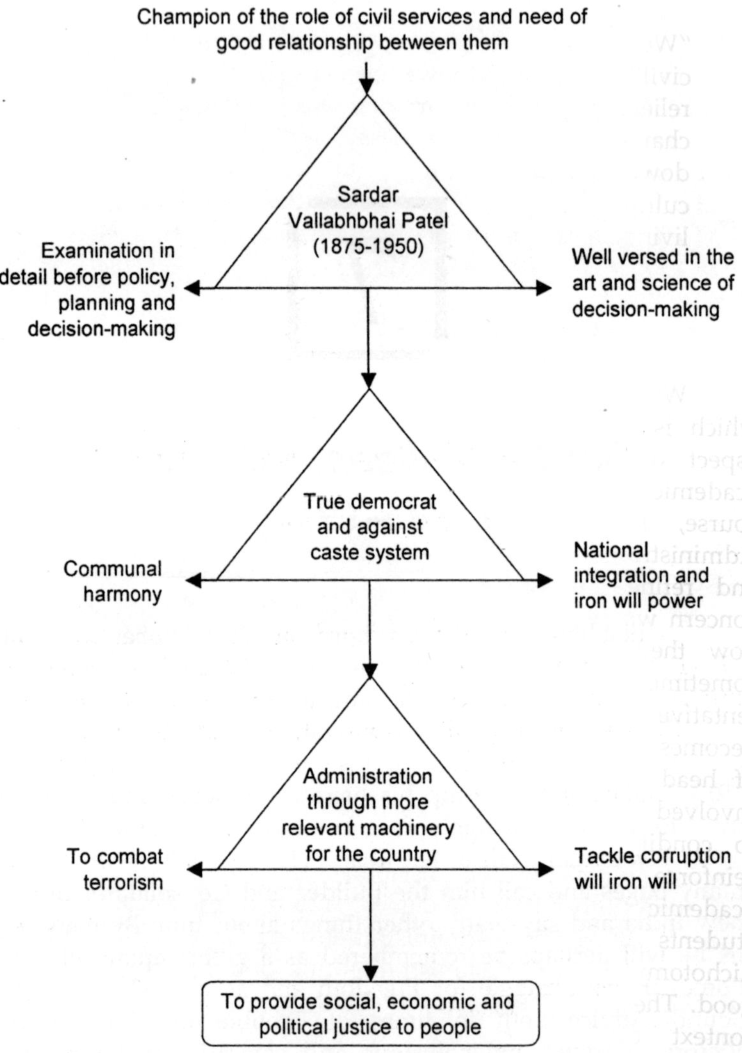

"What we have is not swaraj but only freedom from foreign rule. The still to win internal swaraj, abolish distinctions of caste and creed, banish untouchability, improve the lot of hungry masses, and live as one joint

> family—in short to create a new way of life and bring about a change of heart and a change of outlook."
>
> —*Sardar Patel*
>
> "We always speak of India's culture, of India's civilization, but do we ever pause to think that the relief of the poor, mutual aid amongst neighbours, charity to the helpless and kindness to the downtrodden have been the shining virtues of that culture and civilization? Let us ask ourselves if we are living in the spirit of those ancient virtues!"
>
> —*Sardar Patel*

MAIN ADMINISTRATIVE THOUGHTS

Without going into the semantics of it, administration—which is broadly the organization or management of any aspect of human affairs—can be viewed, firstly, as an academic study and, secondly, as the practice. The two, of course, have points of congruence and convergence. Administration as an academic discipline aims to improve and refine the administration in practice. Obviously, his concern was with the latter. But it is from the observation of how the mastermind works of a situation, that one is sometimes led to formulate some principals or at least tentative working rules of wider application. Besides, it also becomes interesting to judge the personal traits and qualities of head and heart which an administrator displays while involved in the actual administrative processes and which go to condition his success or otherwise. All this goes to reinforce ultimately the discipline of administration as an academic study. There is almost a broad consensus among students of public administration that the conventional dichotomy between administration and politics does not hold good. They constitute an interacting system and the politics context of administration is exceedingly relevant for administrative effectiveness. This becomes all the more pertinent when we aim to evaluate the contribution of one who was not merely an administrator, howsoever lofty or competent, not even simply a mighty politician but an outstanding statesman. The study of intellectual processes, as far as we can do so, of such a man adds to our understanding of the web of intricate relationships between politics and administration. Moreover, the tangible achievements of such a man may shape even the constitutional history and become an integral part of the administrative development of the country. From whatever angle of vision we look at, the many splendoured contribution of Sardar Patel to administration strikes the eye as lofty peaks.

In order to get a more balanced view of his contribution to administration, we have also to take into account his social ideas, his thoughts on socio-economic issues and the like since they directly impinge on the approach or the direction that has to be given to the policy as well as the programme by the apparatus of administration. Sardar Patel, as we have stated, was no administrator in the conventional sense. He was a statesman-administrator. In a way, he was the guardian not only of administrative requirements and proprieties but also of administrative effectiveness. As has been said, "It is in the effort at nation-building that his administrative finesse found expression as his capacity for organizational efficiency, enforcement of discipline and popular mobilization had flowered during the struggle for independence.[1]

1. Understanding and Perfect Implementation of Public Policies through the Application of Principles of Public Administration

As Dr. Rajendra Prasad observed: Like Mahatma Gandhi, he would look into the details of every problem that came up before him and he would not be satisfied unless he had probed the things to its depth. He was not the man who took what might be called a bird's eye view of a question, neglecting small details. He had also a fund of confidence in himself and in the people whom he led and he would not hesitate to take risks because he really felt that there was no risk involved. As things would, according to his collection, set themselves right. "Such an administrative perception is a unique contribution to the art and practice of administration."

2. Consolidation and Integration of Independent India

V.P. Menon, while referring to the Sardar's work in the Government, wrote: "When he took over the Home Minister in 1946 he had no experience even as a provincial minister, yet he showed at once a clear grasp of the essentials of administration. He knew how to exercise power and how to deal with men. He would have each problem fully discussed, hearing all sides, and would then take his decision, and once taken everybody knew it was final. He assigned a man his responsibility and then left the job to him, and everybody did his best because he could count on his being upheld."

"Handling of the rulers by the Sardar was the foremost factor in the success of the accession policy. The rulers soon came to recognize him as a stable force in Indian politics and as one who would give them a fair deal. Added to this, his unfailing politeness to the rulers, viewed against the reputation as the 'Iron Man of India'; endeared him to them and created such confidence that all accepted his advice without demur."

As Vaikunth L. Mehta said: "What made him great as a political administrator, while he remained a leader of men and a statesman, was his study of details, his knowledge of facts, combined with a deep insights, width of outlook and long-range vision. It is rarely that one comes across an individual of all these qualities that make for greatness-courage, knowledge of what is right, honour in action."

This is a perceptive appraisal of the Sardar as an administrator, but, as we have emphasized, it was the earlier phase of his political career which was, in a way, almost unconsciously, a preparation for his endeavour and success on his assumption of governmental responsibilities.

A greater testimony to this can be formed in the statement of our departed leader, Prime Minister Jawaharlal Nehru which runs as follows:

> "The greatest achievement of Sardar Patel is the metamorphosis he has wrought of the Indian States. These petty principalities disfigured the face of India and were the strongholds of British reaction. Within two years the Sardar has broken the century old barrier between Indian India and rest of the country."

As independent India's first Home Minister the Sardar had to deal with subversive and fissiparous activities of groups of people working secretly against country's integrity. Thanks to his able stewardship these elements were effectively kept in check. The Sardar could therefore say as he did.

"Countries adjoining India have an object lesson from us. Starting from small beginnings, the subversive agitations have burrowed big holes into social and administrative structures and have constituted themselves in some authorities and in others as a substantial threat to authority. In India fortunately we have, by our vigilance and the effective counter measures taken from time to time, succeeded in strictly localising these activities. . . . Success in this enterprise can obviously be secured only by rousing public consciousness to the dangers which threaten its existence by securing their co-operation and by maintaining the efficiency and intelligence of the police. . . . In order to hit back we have superiority in arms and equipment" (13.1.50).

N. Dhebar rightly observes that:[2]

The integration of the princely States was effected with singular tact and great magnanimity of heart. He saw to it that no one amongst the Princes felt let down. They were assured of a dignified place in the new social set-up with reasonable sources of income subject of course, to the concurrence of the Constituent Assembly and Parliament of India.

His firm decision-making capacity and bold and courageous policy made him 'Indian Bismarck'. His bold and courageous action in Hyderabad and Junagadh received applause from people. He wanted to amputate all infectious limbs before they poisoned the whole body. In a short span of four years he proved himself to be a great administrator. K.L. Punjab in 'The Indomitable Sardar' observed. "He had a quick eye for merit and could gauge the potentialities of each officer and know what use to make of him."[3]

3. Secular State[4]

Even with regard to the special safeguards provided for the Scheduled Castes and the Tribes, his objective was clear.

He told the Assembly that these classifications and the differences should be removed as rapidly as possible, and people should be brought to a level of equality. It was for the majority community to create by its generosity a sense of confidence in the minorities; and so also it was the duty of the minority communities to forget the past and to reflect on what the country had suffered because of the foreigner's measures to keep the balance between one community and another. He said:

> "If they really have come honestly to the conclusion that in the changed conditions of this country, it is in the interest of all to lay down real and genuine foundations of a secular State, then nothing is better for the minorities than to trust the good sense and fairness of the majority, and to place confidence in them. So also it is for us who happen to be in a majority to think about what the minorities feel and how we in their position would feel if we were treated in the manner they are treated. But in the long-run, it would be in the interest of all to forget that there is anything like majority or minority in this country, and feel that in India there is only one community."

I remember having read, a few years ago, an article by Edward Benes, former President of Czechoslovakia, in which he gave his conception of an ideal politician. "The ideal politician should have all the qualities of the real democratic leader combined with some of the qualities of the authoritarian leader", he said. Elucidating his point Dr. Benes added, "He must be something more than the man of analysis, of reason and of science, he must be not only an intellectual but also a man of decision and of courage."

The readers can see that in India Sardar Vallabhbhai is one of those leaders who satisfy all the above requirements.[5]

5. Sound Decision-making and Implementation

Girdhari Lal Verma observed that his firm decision-making capacity and bold implementation of policy made him "Indian Bismarck." His bold and courageous action in

Hyderabad and Junagadh received applause from people. He wanted to amputate all infectious limbs before they poisoned the whole body. In a short span of four years he proved himself to be a great administrator.[6]

6. A Perfect Democrat

Sardar Vallabhbhai Patel known as the Iron man of the Congress was essentially a man of democratic temperament. The Indian National Congress was a democratic organization of which the Sardar was one of the leading figures who guided the Congress in its fight for freedom and always insisted on the democratic ways of life. His idea of a welfare state in a democratic system was not what we find today in our country. The lot of the teeming millions has gone from bad to worse even after attainment of independence. The trend towards dictatorship which is clear from the ways the ruling party is following today, is the most unfortunate development which the great Sardar would have never tolerated.[7]

7. Role and Qualities of Civil Services

He realized the basic role of civil service and categorically stated: "An efficient, disciplined and contented services assured of its prospects as a result of diligent and honest work, is a *sine qua non* of sound administration under a democratic regime, even more than under an authoritarian rule. The services must be above party and we should ensure that political considerations either in its recruitment or in its discipline and control, are reduced to the minimum if not eliminated altogether.[8]

Girja Shankar Bajpai observed:

> "Time only strengthened these ties of trust between the Sardar and the service. This was due not only to this sense of the value to the administration of public servant of loyalty and integrity but to the keenness and warmth of his personal interest in their welfare A smaller man might have allowed old-time prejudices to raise a curtain of suspicion between him and those who had served an alien regime. It was another mark of the

Sardar's greatness that doubted the patriotism of no Indian unless the lack of it was proved. Trust, it has been said, begets trust, and distrust is its own cause. This is as true of Government as of human relations in other fields."

8. Civil Services in Independent India

In 1949, he stood up in the Constituent Assembly to defend it. "I wish to assure you that I have worked with them during this difficult period. I am speaking with a sense of heavy responsibility and I must confess that in point of patriotism, in point of loyalty, in point of sincerity and in point of ability, you cannot have a substitute. They are as good as ourselves. I wish to place it on record in this House that if, during the last two or three years, most of the members of the Services had not behaved particularly and with loyalty, the Union would have collapsed.[9]

Sardar Patel regarded the civil service as invaluable partner in the task of governance in Independent India. He openly exhorted the civil servants to function fearlessly and professionally in their relationship with the ministers. Equally, he warned the ministers not to choose time-seeking civil servants who anticipated the wishes of their ministers and tailored their advice merely to please them. Sardar Patel stood for the constitutional safeguards and guarantees for the civil service. This was to ensure the latter full protection necessary for its fearless functioning. Above all, Sardar Patel is the true architect of all-India service.

The All India Service is the name of the civil service which is recruited and initially trained by the Government of India but which is common to both the levels of government, and serve both of them. Its member is allocated to a provincial (or, state) government but rotates between the Government of India and the government of his allotted cadre. The nomenclature 'All India Service' was coined by the M.E. Gauntlet Committee on Division of Functions in 1918 when the Government of India Act, 1919 was on the anvil.[10]

The days when the service could be masters are over. . . Perhaps you are aware of saying regarding the Indian Civil

Service that it is neither Indian nor civil nor imbued with any sprit of service. . . . Your predecessors had to serve as agent of an alien rule; and even against their better judgement had some times to execute the biddings of their foreign employers. . . . A civil servant can not afford to, and must not, take part in politics. Nor must he involve himself in communal wrangles. To depart from the path of rectitude in either of these respects is to debase public service and to lower in dignity.[11]

He suggested the following to make civil services efficient:

Stability

"It would be a bad day if people did not look up to official holding high positions. Ministers come and Ministers go, but the permanent machinery (the Civil Service) must be good and firm, and have the respects of the people. The civil service is a source of stability."

Free and Frank Advice to Ministers "My Secretary can write a note opposed to my views. I have given that freedom to all my Secretaries. I have told them, "If you do not give your honest opinion for the fear that it will displease your Minster, then, please you had better to go. I will bring another secretary. I will never be displeased over a frank expression of opinion." These people are the instruments. Remove them, and I see nothing but a picture of chaos all over the country."[12]

Role of Prime Minister

Sardar Patel in a letter to Mahatma Gandhi said: "The Prime Minister's position is certainly pre-eminent; he is first among equals. But he has no over-riding powers over his colleagues; if he had, any Cabinet responsibility would be superfluous. In my view, the Prime Minister, as a leader of the party and the head of the whole administration, is inevitably concerned that cabinet decisions are effective and that there is no conflict between one Ministry and another, but the entire responsibility for implementing the policy of Government rests upon the ministers and Ministry under them which are concerned with the subject matter of the Cabinet decisions.

He continued that the Prime Minister had "the right to consult and advise on the lines of policy to be adopted and even the manner in which the policy is to be implemented . . . [but] the policy must be that of the ministry concerned and of the minister-in-charge, and the Prime Minister should influence action by way of consultation with the advice to the minister." Patel concluded: "I feel sure that this position of the Prime Minister not only fully safeguards his preeminence and makes him an effective head of the Administration, but is also fully in accord with democratic principles and rule of ministerial and Cabinet responsibility.[13]

He died on 15th December 1950 at Bombay following heart troubles.

CONCLUSION

John Gunther, the world renowned author, has paid a tribute to our great leader in the following words:

> "He is the party boss par excellence. Once Gandhi has determined the line to take, it is Patel who runs it through, as happened at Tripuri. Some one said about him once that his only 'culture' is agriculture. . . . He is a man of action, of practicality, the man who gets things done." (From "Inside Asia").

The best tribute that we can pay to this great son of India is to transform the administrative unity that he brought about into emotional integration and national solidarity. Even many years after his passing away, we are far from the goal he set before us.[14]

What greater and more glowing tribute can we pay to Sardar than what his own comrade Pt. Jawaharlal Nehru said of him in these moving words? "History will record it in many pages and call Sardar Patel the Builder and consolidator of the new India and say many other things about him. By many of us he will perhaps be remembered as a great captain of our forces in the struggle for freedom as one who gave us sound advice both in times of trouble and in moments of victory; a friend and colleague and comrade on whom one could invariably rely, as a tower of strength which revived wavering hearts when we were in trouble."

The Sardar's name will be inscribed in letters of gold in the history of independent India for the great role he played in achieving an integrated India. In a short span of three years the Sardar managed to bring more unity and consolidation to this country than it had for centuries. But to him unity and integration were not ends in themselves. They were the means to create a society which is free from exploitation, free from caste and class conflict and to realise a social and economic order based upon truth and non-violence and one which guaranteed equal opportunities to everyone to realize his potential to the full.[15]

He was a man of action. "His teachers were the facts of life; not books or doctrines." According to circumstances, his approach to administration could be manipulative, preventive, anticipatory or creative. He not only saved India from "the danger of fragmentation" but "gave her a united entity and a homogenous administration."

First, it is the clarity of objectives and understanding of the instrumentalities and the strategy to achieve the objectives set. Second, it is the power of rapid analysis, capacity to grasp all the facts and essentials of a situation and their mutual relationship. Third, it is the sense of timing, i.e., when the crucial step or decision is to be taken. Fourth, it is the capacity to think ahead and anticipate moves or problems. Again, it might involve a fine sense of discrimination as to when and how far to give a point away without compromising a principle. Fifth, it is the capacity to judge people, willingness to take responsibility, desire to delegate responsibility to inspire confidence, to impart watchful guidance, to give credit or recognition and protection or support as needed. Sixth, "it is the capacity not only to understand people but to lead them—to be the conductor of the orchestra." The leader is not only the follower. He multiplies his capacity through team-work and sets trends and even gives judgement against fleeting passions or opinions—a fairly exacting and at times a thankless task. Last, there are personal qualities of imagination, perseverance, equanimity of temperament, sense of dedication to causes higher than self, etc. We really find all of them in varying measures reflected in Sardar Patel.[16]

Vallabhbhai Patel's was a many sided genius. He was a mass leader, statesman, administrator, and an astute diplomat. Above all he was an ardent nationalist and patriot who devoted his whole life to the service of India. He was not a saint like his Master Mahatma Gandhi, nor an idealist like his colleague Pandit Jawahar Lal Nehru. But he had the knack of setting forth Gandhiji's ideas and ideals, in a language that went straight to the heart.

Another quality of Patel was his balanced judgement and sound common sense. He was free from wishful thinking and never went in for cheap popularity. He did not say sweet words just to please people but believed in plain speaking. His popularity rested on his integrity, truthfulness, self-denial and self-effacement. He was a down to earth peasant and had completely identified himself with the masses. The masses, too, had immense faith in him and knew that he said only what he meant. He believed in action and not in tall talks. It will take centuries for India, may the world, to produce another such statesman.

Soon after Patel's death the *Manchester Guardian* wrote, "Without Patel Gandhi's idea would have had less practical influence and Nehru's idealism less scope. Patel was not only the organizer of the fight for freedom but also the architect of the new state when the fight was over. The same man is seldom successful as rebel and statesman. Sardar Patel was the exception."[17]

Relevance

As Prime Minister Jawaharlal Nehru, with his deep insight into history, said in the Indian Parliament when this Titan breathed his last: "History will record his (Sardar Patel's) achievements in many pages and call him the builder and consolidator of the new India and say many other things about him. By many of us, he will perhaps be remembered as a great captain of forces in the struggle for freedom and as one who gave us sound advice both in times of trouble and in moments of victory, a friend and a colleague and comrade, on whom one could inevitably rely, as a tower of strength which revived wavering hearts when we were in trouble." A Shining symbol of nishkama karma (selfless service), Vallabhabhai Jhaverbhai Patel's name will ever remain inscribed on the roll call of honour of history as one of the greatest nation-builder and statesmen of India through the ages.

India is faced with a number of problems? How to come out of them to make India a developed nation? What is needed is to follow the principles, practices and philosophy of Sardar Patel. His philosophy helped the nation to come out of chaos in difficult periods. What we need is that the politicians and Civil Service must follow the administrative thought of Sardar Patel to take the country to new heights.

Terrorism is raising its head in various parts of the country. Only administrative leadership of the stature of Sardar Patel can eliminate it. The leadership to day has made the bureaucracy also defunct and the result is lawlessness. There is a need to revive the ideals and qualities of Sardar Patel to keep the country united. National integration and development is the top priority which was practically achieved by the strenuous and sincere efforts of Sardar Patel

Prime Minister Jawaharlal Nehru congratulated Sardar Patel as an "Architest of Indian Unity" and paid him a glorious tribute in these words: 'Sardar occupied a unique position in the party and the Government. He had attained that height not by a single, surprising miracle, but by ceaseless endeavour and unflinching loyalty to the goal of national independence."

The Sardar stood by the bureaucrat, saying: "The very instrument from whom we have to take work, we have been continuously quarrelling with. If that is so, we are not doing a service to the country. We are doing disservice." Dorothy Norman wrote: "The moment one spoke with him one knew that one was dealing with an honest man, that whether or not one agreed with him, one knew he would say only precisely what he believed."

We must follow Patel's idea to make bureaucracy functional and not as dead woods. Until and unless, there would be good relationships between political masters and the bureaucrats nothing can be achieved.

Pt. Nehru, the first Prime Minister of Independent India and many other important leaders like Pt. G.B. Pant, etc., did not like the idea that for building up a new India, the very machinery that was till now hampering and countering the freedom movement should be used. Pt. Nehru is on record to have said:

But of one thing I am quite sure that no new order can be built up in India, so long as the spirit of ICS pervades our Administrative Public Service. That spirit of authoritarianism is the ally of imperialism and it cannot co-exist with freedom. It will either succeed in crushing freedom or will be swept away by itself. Only with one type of State, it is likely to fit in and that is the Fascist type. Therefore, it seems quite essential that the ICS and similar services must disappear completely, much before we can start real work on a new order.[18]

Sardar Patel, the then Home Minister, however, held an opposite view. He foresaw the dire necessity of "All India Services" in independent India. Therefore, he convened a "Provincial Premiers Conference" in October, 1946 to take a decision on All India Services. While presiding over the conference, he said:

My own view as I have told you, is that it is not only advisable, but essential, if you want to have an efficient service, to have a Central Administrative Service, in which, we fix the strength as the Provinces would require them and we draw a certain number of officers at the Centre, as we are doing at present. This will give experience to the personnel at the Centre leading to efficiency and administrative experience of the district, which will give them an opportunity to contact with the people. They will thus keep themselves in touch with the situation in the country and their practical experience will be most useful to them. Besides their coming to the Centre will give them a different experience and wider outlook in a larger sphere. A combination of these two experiences will make the service more efficient. They will also serve as liaison between the Provinces and the Government and introduce certain amount of freshness and vigour in the administration, both at the Centre and in the Provinces. Therefore, my advice is that we should have an All India Service.[19]

Again speaking in the Constituent Assembly, he warned:

There is no alternative to this administrative system. . . The Union will go, you will not have a united India, if you have not a good All India Service, which has the independence to speak out its mind, which has a sense of security that you will stand by your work. . . . If you do not adopt this course, then do not follow the present Constitution. Substitute something else . . . this Constitution is meant to be worked by a ring of service, which will keep the country intact. There are many impediments in this constitution, which will hamper us. But in spite of that, we have in our collective wisdom come to a decision that we shall have this model, where the ring of a service will be such that will keep the country intact. . . . These people are the instrument. Remove them and I see nothing, but a picture of chaos all round the country.[20]

Sardar's tenure as Home Minister and Deputy Prime Minister proved to be very short. But in that short time he laid the foundation of united India and left an indelible imprint on the evolution of independent India. The nation will be ever grateful to him for his singular contribution. The example that he left behind as a political administrator should be a perennial source of inspiration and guidance to India's political administrators for all times to come.

Sardar Vallabhbhai Patel was a multi-splendoured personality, who left an indelible mark of his ingenuity in every walk of Indian public life. History may or may not do justice to his contribution, but he stands head and shoulders above several of his contemporaries who had more opportunities, but accomplished much less in their endeavours. As the first Deputy Prime Minister of free India he set high standards of probity and norms of integrity for his government. Events tested his mettle quite rigorously and every time he came out with flying colours. The nation owes a deep debt to this statesmanship. Today when the follies of history are taking their terrorist revenge, the nation should rediscover the rich heritage of an indomitable Sardar and learn to nip all criminality in the bud.[21]

Sardar Patel could not find time to pen down his

administrative thoughts, but his attitude to solve administrative problem clearly depict that he could not do that without sound administrative thoughts in his mind. I rate him as a first rate administrative thinker who did not believe in futile ideas but practical ideas based on facts which proved fruitful. He is a source of inspiration and guidance to India's political administrators for all times to come.

Notes and References

1. T.N. Chaturvedi, Sardar Patel's Contribution to Public Adminstration in Verinder Grover (ed.) in *Verender Patel, A Biography of His Vision and Ideas,* New Delhi, Deep & Deep, 1998, pp. 191-93.
2. U.N. Dhebar, Sardar Vallabhbhai Patel, The Architect of India's Unity in Verinder Goel, (ed), *op. cit.,* p. 238.
3. Girdhari Lal Verma, Sardar Patel, Iron Man of India in Verinder Grover, ed. *op. cit.,* 251.
4. B. Shiva Rao, "Sardar Patel and the Constitution" in Verinder Grover, ed., p. 401.
5. Mubarak Singh, Sardar Vallabhbhai Patel: The Man of Few Words and Many Triumphs, in Verinder Grover (ed.), p. 215.
6. Girdhari Lal Verma, Sardar Patel, Iron Man of India, in Verinder Grover (ed.), p. 25.
7. J.B. Kriplani, Sardar Patel, The Great Democrat, in Verinder Grover (ed.) p. 32.
8. Patel's letter dated 27th April, 1948 to Pt. Jawaharlal Nehru.
9. The Constituent Assembly Debates, Vol. X, No. 1, 10 Oct., 1949, p. 50.
10. S.R. Maheswari, Sardar Vallabhbhai Patel: The Author of All India Service in P.L. Sanjeev Reddy and S.N. Mishra (ed.), *Sardar Vallabhbhai Patel: The Nation Builder,* IIPA, New Delhi, 2004, p. 252.
11. The Bombay Chronicle, 21 April, 1947, Quoted in Krishna, S., Sardar Vallabhbhai Patel: India's Iron Man, Harper Collins, New Delhi, 1995, p. 476.
12. *Ibid.,* p. 481.
13. Das, Durga (ed.), Sardar Patel's Correspondence, Vol. VI, Navjivan Publishing House, Ahmedabad, 1973, pp. 9, 13, 22.
14. Mubarak Singh, *op. cit.,* p. 220.
15. Jagjivan Ram, Sardar as I knew Him, in Verinder Grover (ed.), p. 552.
16. T.N. Chaturvedi, Sardar Patel, S., Contribution to Public Administration, in *IJPA,* Oct.-Dec., 1977, pp. 872-73.
17. P.L. Sanjeev Reddy and S.N. Mishra, Sardar Vallabhbhai Patel, The Nation Builder, New Delhi, *IIPA,* Preface, p. 18, (eds.)

18. Jawaharlal Nehru: An Autobiography, London, The Bodily Head, 1953, p. 443.
19. Sardar Patel, Proceedings of the Premier's Conference, October, 1946.
20. Constituent Assembly, Vol. X, No. 3, Oct. 10, 1996, quoted in Lata Sinha, Role and Rationale of All India Services in *IJPA*, Oct.-Dec., 1990, pp. 822-24.
21. P.D. Sharma, Sardar Patel, A Gandhian Bismarck and His Policy of Bloodless Iron, in P.L. Sanjeev Reddy and S.N. Mishra (eds.), p. 172.

8

Max Weber (1864-1920)

Max Weber (1864-1920) was born in a well-to-do family at Erfurt in East Germany in 1864. His father being interested in politics, economics and law had great impact on his thinking. His father was a leader of the National Liberal party in Germany, and a member of the erstwhile 'parliament' of his country. Many visitors—intellectuals and political leaders—used to come to their house.

He was appointed a professor of economics in a German University in 1900. Weber fell ill and was forced to give up his post. But he continued writing and doing research even when he was not working. He visited U.S. in 1904 on his own expenses. He returned to teaching in 1918 but he died two years later in 1920.

Max Weber was a contemporary of Taylor, Fayol, and the Gilberths. His work, first published in Germany in 1921, provides further insight into the ideals of the classical management writers. But unlike most of these writers, Weber was not a practicing manager, but an intellectual.

CHART 8.1

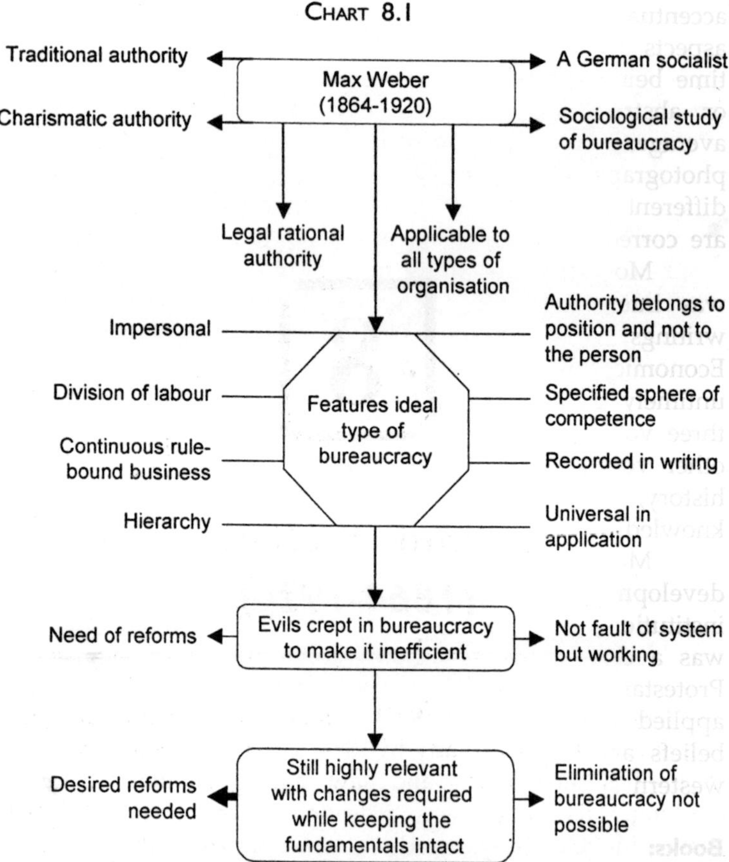

WEBER'S CONTRIBUTIONS TO RESEARCH METHODOLOGY

Let us begin by understanding the meaning of Verstehen.

He has combined the methods of the natural and the cultural sciences. Natural sciences explain facts by finding out their causes. Cultural sciences understand the meanings of facts. Weber's method of research involves grasping the facts from outside and interpretatively understanding the inside story.

For constructing ideal types, one has to define certain salient features of the situation. These are brought out, accentuated, exaggerated and maximised. The remaining aspects are understated, minimised, left out of view for the time being. These ideas are used to construct word pictures or abstract models. These models are based neither on averages nor on proportions. These are not exact replicas or photographs of the reality. We can construct a number of different ideal types of the same phenomenon. All of them are correct.

Most of his writings are not all sociological themes. He was interdisciplinary in approach. Among his sociological writings we can mention a monumental volume on Economics and Society which he could not finish due to his untimely death. Collections of his papers were published in three volumes one of these deals with sociology of religion, other volumes include his writings on social and economic history, sociology and social policy, and sociology of knowledge.

Max Weber was deeply interested in the origin and development of political, economic, legal and religious institutions of the Western societies. He suggested that there was a close connection between the rise of capitalism and Protestantism—an off-shoot of Christianity. And then he applied this idea to study the relationship between religious beliefs and values, and economic development in the non-western societies of China, India and West Asia.

Books:

1930 The Protestant Ethics and the spirit of Capitalism.
1947 The Theory of Social and Economic Organization.
1948 From Max Weber: Essays in Sociology, (ed. By H.H. Herth and C.W. Mills).

ADMINISTRATIVE THOUGHTS

Weber classifies authority in three ways, e.g. Traditional, Chrismatic and Legal rational. Let us explain them. If obedience is based on tradition we have traditional authority. Thus if subjects obey a tribal authority, the latter is being legitimated by tradition.

I. Traditional Authority

Such authority is based on the traditional privileges and prerogatives being sacrosanct, and the orders of those exercising such authority being perfect in a moral sense. What has always been there since times immemorial is respected, because it has been like that. Old conventions and precedents are followed. Orders of persons in authority are obeyed. Traditions permit a master a lot of leeway for wilful acts. The master is merciful to some persons. He cold-shoulders others without provoking them to offer resistance. But by over-stepping the limits laid down by traditions, the master can jeopardize his own authority. Eventual resistance is not directed against the system. It is directed against the person of those who deviate from the traditions.

Chrismatic Authority

Charisma is a Greek word. It means gift of grace, or inspiration. It rests on the sacred or heroic or exemplary character of somebody bestowed with supernatural powers.

The charismatic leader's followers belonging to his inner circles spread myths about his miraculous powers. He then exercises his leadership with their active support.

Although the transformational leadership concept dates back at least to Max Weber's discussion of charismatic leaders in the first decades of the century, The concept received relatively little research attention until recently. One of the notable early contributions to systematic analysis of the subject is Robert J. House's theory of charismatic leadership.

House's theory suggests that charismatic leaders have very high levels of referent power and that some of that power comes from their need to influence others. The charismatic leader has "extremely high levels of self-confidence, dominance, and a strong conviction in the moral righteousness of his/her beliefs"—or at least the ability to convince followers that he or she possesses such confidence and conviction. House suggests that charismatic leaders communicate a vision or higher-level ("transcendent") goal that captures the commitment and energy of followers. They are careful to create an image of success and competence and to exemplify in their own behaviour the values they espouse.

They also communicate high expectations for followers and confidence that followers will perform up to those expectations.[1]

When a charismatic leader remains unsuccessful over a period of time, and his lead does not help his followers, it is believed, that the supernatural power behind him has withdrawn its support. This deprives him of his charisma. His followers desert him.

Rational—Legal Authority

Under system of legal authority obedience, "is owed to the legally established impersonal orders. It extends to the persons exercising authority of office only by virtue of the formal legality of their commands, and only within the scope of the authority of the office."

Weber often uses the term rational legal authority. In his view the tradition and charismatic system place major obstacles in the way of rational, suitable and calculable action. The term rational means endowed with reason. In a system of legal authority actions have to be based on laws and rules and reasons have to cited. Hence Weber often uses the term legal and rational together.

The orders of those possessing such authority, like a manager, are obeyed according to rules. Laws may be enforced through the willing cooperation of those in authority, in expectation of certain rewards, or under fear of punishment. Rules and regulations do not contradict each other. They are uniformly applicable to everybody under the same circumstances. Those in authority are office-holders. Nobody is above law. Bureaucracy is an example of rational-legal authority. All three types of authority discussed above are ideal types.

During the 1920s Weber correctly predicted that the growth of the large-scale organization would require a more formal set of procedures for how to administer them. At the time, managers had few principles they could apply in managing organizations. He therefore creates the idea of an ideal or "pure form" of organization, which he called bureaucracy. This term did not refer to red tape and inefficiency-bureaucracy, for Weber, was in favour of the most efficient form of organization.

Bureaucracy is the purest form of rational-legal authority. It runs routine business with technical means and professional skills, with its stability, discipline, precision and reliability, it increases calculability and rationality. It hinders irrational decisions. It is mechanism for achieving the goals laid down by those who control it. Its parts are interchangeable. It can be easily re-organised to attain the same or different goals.

FEATURES OF LEGAL-RATIONAL AUTHORITY-BUREAUCRACY

1. Continuous Organisation

Individual employees come and go, but the organisation continues as usual. Nobody is inevitable. The organisation is based on division of labour which lead to specialization of functions, and allocation of responsibilities. A bureaucrat is a full-time employee even though his office-timings are fixed but can be called at any time. His appointment is not honorary. Normally he is entitled to leave and holidays. But these can be denied to him in case of exigency, i.e. pressing official necessity. Bureaucracy is a career based on upward movement based on merit.

2. Division of Labour (Specific Spheres of Competence)

An enterprise or a department is a unit. Officers, clerks and workers in it are assigned definite spheres of competence, according to their professional qualifications. An officer's orders are valid only within his limited sphere of competence. He is not allowed to arrogate to himself somebody else's authority. Only the chief can make public statements. He is responsible for what his bureau does or fails to do.

Adam Smith[2] and Max Weber[3] recognized that the division of labour is essential to maximizing the output of workers and machines. Division of labour means dividing large tasks into smaller packages of work to be distributed among several people. This work specialization allows an employee to master a task in the shortest time with a minimum of skill. It also allows human labour to become inter-changeable, which contributes greatly to organizational efficiency.

Division of labour creates many different and often narrow jobs, which intensifies the need for effective managerial coordination. William Whyte studied the interrelationships of specialized jobs in the restaurant industry (cooks, waitresses, counterworkers, and runners) and observed significant stresses among these positions and the need for careful coordination.[4]

Scott and Mitchell observed that job specialization at executive levels often creates problems of segmenting the organization into "enclaves of authority and influence.[5]

Efforts to weld areas of executive specialization into a consistent, synchronized part of an overall organization are frequently resisted by managers as an undue infringement on their jurisdictions. Thus specialization brings about jealously guarded functional segments in the organization.[6]

However, the advantages of a division of labour have outweighed its disadvantages over the years by improving efficiency, contributing to mass production techniques and bringing about a high level of industrial and service output.

3. Hierarchy

The employees are placed in a hierarchy. The subordinates are subject to disciplinary control by their superordinates, the higher officers. The lower officers have to obtain orders from their superiors in a disciplined manner. Insubordination is punishable. They have to proceed through proper channel even when they want to appeal to their higher officers against wrong orders from their officer incharge.

According to Weber, "the organization of offices follows the principle of hierarchy that is, each lower office is under the control and supervision of a higher one." He also mentions that "the whole administrative staff under the supreme authority are organized in a clearly defined hierarchy of offices." The literal meaning of hierarchy is the rule or control of the higher over the lower. A hierarchy means a graded organization of several successive steps or levels, in which each one of the lower levels is immediately subordinate to the next higher one and, through it, to the other higher steps right up to the top.

4. Rules

Operations are governed "by a consistent system of abstract rules . . . (and) consist of the applications of these rules to particular case." According to Weber, these rules are more or less suitable, exhaustive and can be learnt. Weber says, "The reduction of modern office management to rules is deeply embedded in its very nature. The theory of modern public administration, for instance, assumes that the authority to order certain matters by decree which has to be legally granted to public authorities does not entitle the bureau to regulate the matters by decree which has been legally granted to public authorities does not entitle the bureau to regulate the matters by commands given for each case but only to regulate the matter abstractly. This stands in extreme contrast to the regulation of relationship through individual privileges and bestowals of favour which is absolutely dominant in patrimonialism at least in so far as these relationship are not fixed by sacred tradition. Thus system of rules is designed to assure uniformity in the performance of every task." Explicit rules and regulations define the authority of each member of organization.

5. Impersonality

The ideal official conducts his office (in) "a spirit of formalistic without hatred or passion and hence without affection or enthusiasm." An official is expected to have a detached approach free from personal considerations. If he develops strong feelings, about some subordinates or clients these are likely to influence his official decisions. The detachment is fostered by the fact that the administrative staff is completely separated from ownership of the means of production or administration. Thus, there is clear distinction between the personal property and residence of an official from the property and place of the office.

6. Career System

Employment in the bureaucratic organization

constitutes career. There is a system of promotions according to seniority or achievement, or both. Employment in bureaucratic organizations is based on technical qualifications and protected against arbitrary dismissal. Promotion according to seniority encourages the development of loyalty to the organization. Employees come to identify with the organization and exert greater efforts in advancing its interests.

7. Rights belong to the Office and not to the Official (Impersonal)

All the rights belong to the position and not its incumbent. He had to discharge according to the rules of the position.

8. System of Procedure for Dealing with the Work

"According to Weber a Bureaucracy is more efficient than organizations having traditional or charismatic system of authority. Weber compares the bureaucracy with a machine. "The fully developed bureaucratic mechanism compares with other organizations exactly as does machine with non-mechanical modes of production."

9. Capitalism

Weber emphasizes relationship between capitalism and bureaucratization as follows: "Today, it is primarily the capitalist market economy which demands that the official business of the administration be discharged precisely, unambiguously, continuously and with as much speed as possible. Normally, the very large, modern capitalist enterprises are themselves unequaled models of strict bureaucratic organization. Business Management throughout rests on increasing precision, steadiness, and above all, the speed of operations. This, in turn, is determined by peculiar nature of the modern means of communication, including among other things, the news service of the press. The extraordinary increase in the speed by which public announcement as well as economic and political facts are transmitted exerts a steady and sharp pressure in the direction of speeding up the temper of administrative reaction transmitted exerts a steady and sharp pressure in the direction of speeding up the temper of administrative reaction towards various situations. The optimum of such reaction time is normally attained only by a strictly bureaucratic organization."

According to Max Weber . . . . Technical superiority over any other form of organization. Precision, speed, unambiguity, knowledge of the files, continuity, discretion, unity, strict subordination, reduction of friction and of material and personal costs—these are raised to the optimum point in the strictly bureaucratic administration, and especially in its monocratic form.[7]

This consists on the one hand of technical knowledge, which by itself is sufficient to ensure it a position of extraordinary power. But in addition, to this bureaucratic organisations . . . . have the tendency to increase their power still further by the knowledge growing out of experience in the service.[8]

However, the pure power interests of bureaucracy exert their efforts far beyond these areas of functionally motivated secrecy. The concept of the 'office secret' is the specific invention of bureaucracy, and few things it defend so fanatically as this attitude which, outside of the specific areas mentioned, cannot be justified with purely functional arguments. In facing a parliament, the bureaucracy fights, out of a sure power instinct, every one of that institution's attempts to gain through its own means (as for example) through the so-called 'right of parliamentary investigation' expert knowledge from the interested parties. Bureaucracy naturally prefers a poorly informed, and hence powerless, parliament—at least insofar as this ignorance is compatible with the bureaucracy's own interests.[9]

CONCLUSION

Bureaucracy is the purest form of rational-legal authority. It runs routine business with technical means and professional skills, with its stability, discipline, precision and reliability, it increases calculability and rationality. It hinder irrational decisions. It is mechanism for achieving the goals laid down by those who control it. Its parts are interchangeable. It can be easily re-organised to attain the same or different goals.

Today we often think of bureaucracies as vast, impersonal organizations that put impersonal efficiency ahead of human needs. We should be careful, though, not to apply our negative connotations of the word bureaucracy to the term as Weber used it. Like the scientific management theorists, Weber sought to improve the performance of socially important organizations by making their operations predictable and productive. Although we now value innovation and flexibility as much as efficiency and predictability, Weber's model of bureaucratic management clearly advanced the formation of huge corporations such as ford. Bureaucracy was a particular pattern of relationships for which Weber saw great promise.

Early managers and management writers sought the "one best way" a set of principles for creating an organizational structure that would work well in all situations. Max Weber, Frederick Taylor, and Henri Fayol were major contributors to the so-called classical approach to organizational design. They believed that the most efficient and effective. organizations had a hierarchical structure in which members of the organization were guided in their actions by a sense of duty to the organization and by a set of rational rules and regulations. When fully developed, according to Weber, such organizations were characterized by specialization of tasks, appointment by merit, provision of career opportunities. for members, routinization of activities, and a rational, impersonal organizational climate. Weber called this a bureaucracy.

Weber praised bureaucracy for its establishment of rules for decision-making, its clear chain of command, and its promotion of people on the basis of ability and experience rather than favoritism or whim. He also admired the bureaucracy's clear specification of authority and responsibility, which he believed made it easier to evaluate and reward performance. He and other classical writers, alongwith their contemporaries in management, lived in a time when this approach to organizational design had precedent in government civil services. The term bureaucracy has not always carried the modern negative connotation—a framework for slow, inefficient, unimaginative organizational activity.

Need of Bureaucratic Reforms

Development of public administration in that manner should be accompanied by initiating administrative reforms on a large scale in a "case-by-case" approach, applying the following administrative principles:[10]

- Administrative action should be user-oriented,
- Expertise and authority should rest with those who are closer to the customers or users,
- Competition between services should be allowed and institutionalized, and
- Internal organizational readaptation measures should be followed by a managerial approach through efficient use of financial and personnel resources.

To realize these principles in everyday life of public administration, management analysis of the government organization and that of public enterprises becomes necessary. As a part of serious efforts to upgrade governance and to reform bureaucratic authorities, the modern state has to simplify the organizational structures and administrative procedures, and prepare job profiles of the personnel.

Vincent Ostrom observes, "When the central problem in Public Administration is viewed as the provision of public goods and services, alternative forms may be available for the performance of those functions apart from an extension and perfection of bureaucratic structures. Bureaucratic structures are necessary but not sufficient structures for a productive and responsive public service economy. He thus opts for the public choice theory in which the individual is the unit of analysis and methods which are effective in economics are adopted.

Relevance

Though many evils have crept in Max Weber's model of bureaucracy but still it is most relevant, rational, practical and efficient.

Max Weber, pointed out in the early 21st Century that the then emerging legal-rational bureaucratic form of authority was more technically efficient than other forms of authority, such as charismatic or traditional leadership, and was, therefore, an 'ideal' type of authority. The basis of this authority rested on "a belief in the legality of patterns of normative rules, and the right of those elevated to authority under such rules to issue commands."[1] Since this authority was derived from Law, there was no arbitrariness in its functioning. It was totally impartial and just. The bureaucracy depended on institutional memory (carefully preserved written record) of work regardless of who was performing it.

In short, "the decisive reason for the advance of bureaucratic organization has always been its purely technical superiority over any other form of organization, precision, speed, unambiguity, knowledge of files, continuity, discretion, unity, strict subordination, reduction of friction and personal costs . . . these are raised to an optimum point in the strictly bureaucratic organisation."[11]

However, many issues have crept in as this model was followed religiously and not in its true spirit. The need was felt for lubricating the model through administrative reforms.

The World Bank has tried to introduce rationalist reforms in bureaucracies in the Third World. which comprises the following:

- Installing in civil services personnel information and management systems which are more tightly lined to payrolls, and including clear and appropriate career development schemes;
- Staff audits to determine what personnel is on hand;
- Improved training systems;
- Revision, usually meaning simplification, of legal framework governing the civil service; and

> Getting the right people into administration, partly by stronger incentives to attract and retain them, partly by changing objectives and procedures in an effort to make the work situation more challenging and rewarding.

Unless there are simultaneous and corresponding changes in social, political and economic spheres, Third World bureaucracies will resists any move to change the *status quo*. In fact, several countries have attempted to reform the system through a series of Administrative Reform Commissions but since they were mainly composed of senior bureaucrats, and 'political will' for such a reform has been markedly lacking, there has been little success in inducing rationality into system.[12]

In developed countries, there has been a lot of experimental movement away from the Weberian ideal to post-bureaucratic organisations. These organisations expose and manage their information and knowledge sources, have an empowered and participative workforce, aim at maximizing efficiency and effectiveness, and are responsive to the people. Dynamism, flexibility and innovativeness are the hallmarks of these organisations, which have to compete successfully with the private sector for survival. Traditionally valued concepts liked bureaucratic routines, public service ethics, and professional codes of conduct are assessed as costs rather than benefits. However, it must be pointed out that though there is a growing anti-bureaucratic stance among politicians, academicians, private entrepreneurs and taxpayers in rich countries, the Weberian model cannot be completely written off. It is still the most dominant model and it will be a long time before it can be completely replaced by the post-bureaucratic organisation.

Max Weber would remain relevant for all times to come, as no organization whether in government, religious, private sector can function without following the rational bureaucratic model. However, we may keep in mind that impurities and problems emerge as the time and circumstances change. We can modify the model but still it must be rational. The theoretical perspective of Max Weber

Bureaucratic model is really ideal. However, practice needs to change with the change in times and circumstances. As Government of India enacted Right to Information Act, 2005 to make bureaucracy transparent. In this way, we can bring in desired changes while keeping the model intact.

Notes and References

1. James A.T. Stoner *et. al., op. cit.,* p. 489.
2. Adam Smith, The Wealth of Nations, New York, Modern Library, 1917.
3. Max Weber, The Essentials of Bureaucratic Organization: An Ideal Type Construction", In *A Reader in Bureaucracy* ed. Robert, Merton *et. al.,* Free Press, 1952, pp. 18-27.
4. William F. Whyte, Human Relations in the Restaurant Business (New York: McGraw Hill, 1948).
5. William G. Scott and Terrence Mitchell, Organization Theory (Homewood, III, Richard D. Irwin, 1976), p. 39.
6. *Ibid.,* p. 39.
7. Weber, Max, Economy and Society, Vol. 2, Bedminister Press, New Jersey, 1968, p. 713.
8. Weber, Max, Economy and Society, Vol. 1, Bedminster Press, New Jersey, 1968, p. 225.
9. *Ibid.,* pp. 990-93.
10. OECD, Public Management Development: Update, 1992, Paris, OECD, 1992; and A. Peter Aucoin, "Administrative Reform in Public Management: Paradigms, Principles, Paradoxes and Pendulums", *Governance,* Vol. 3, 1990, pp. 115-37.
11. O.E. Hughes, Public Management and Administration: An Introduction, New York, St. Martin's Press, 1994.
12. Anuradha Balram, Examining Substitution of the Weberian Model, in *IJPA,* April-June, 2000, p. 156.

PART B

9

Theories of Organisation

Fred N. Kerlinger defines theory as "a set of interrelated constructs (concepts), definitions and propositions that presents a systematic view of phenomena by specifying relations among variables, with the purpose of explaining and predicting the phenomena."[1]

As Easton puts it: "The accumulation of data through acceptable techniques does not alone give us adequate knowledge. Knowledge becomes critical and reliable as it increases in generality and internally consistent organisation, when, in short, it is cast in the form of systematic generalised statements applicable to large number of particular cases."[2]

There are many systems of organisations. It is difficult to discuss everyone of them and in detail. We are discussing here six important theories briefly:

1. Traditional—Ever Relevant Theories
2. Scientific Management
3. Classical Theory
4. Human Relations Theory
5. Bureaucratic Theory
6. Systems Theory
7. Contingency Theory

CHART 9.1

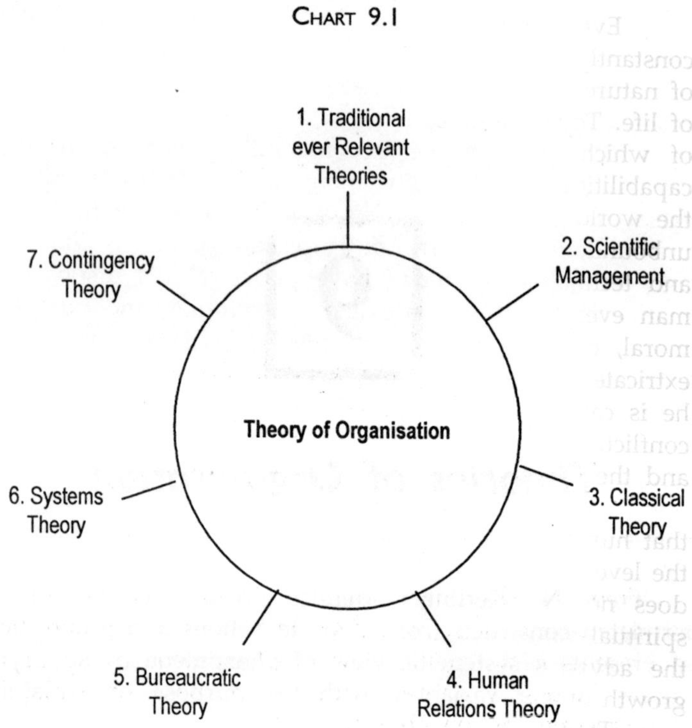

1. TRADITIONAL—EVER RELEVANT THEORIES

Indian thinkers like Lord Krishna, Lord Rama, Swami Vivekananda have propounded theories, concepts and philosophy which are relevant for all time, i.e. eternal. Traditional theories lay emphasis on perfection and the aim is not merely material advancement but adhering to values. Materialism is wonderful, no doubt, but it burdens man with endless anxiety and craving to possess more, to acquire and aggrandize and to indulge with slavish attachment. Work in life becomes worship if it is in the service of the nation, poor, hungry and the helpless and not for self.

Ever since the dawn of civilization, man has been constantly engaged in the pursuit of unraveling the mystery of nature with a view to arriving at the fundamental values of life. Today, the world is in a state of turmoil, the causes of which seem to be beyond man's comprehension and capabilities. Paradoxically enough, man seems to be lost in the world of plentitude. His soul is starved in the midst of unbounded materialistic pleasures and comforts that science and technology of today have placed at his disposal. Now man everywhere is bedeviled by complex and complicated moral, cultural and social issues. The harder he strives to extricate himself out of the web of these problems, the more he is caught and involved in it. Underneath the morass of conflicting values lies man's quest for the real meaning of life and the destiny to which it leads.

With all the scientific and technological revolutions that humanity has achieved so far, we have not risen above the level of satisfying the bare physical needs of man. Science does not help us to discuss the fundamental moral and spiritual values of life or 'how to live' and here we see that the advancement of science has led to mankind lopsided growth and development.

Traditional literature is full of material required for management and administration. Their focus has always been on truth, beauty and goodness.

The mechanical steps which are incorporated in a sporadic manner to improve our system would lead us to more problems and decay. The need is to follow the eternal principles of Human Excellence as contained in Bhagavad Gita, Vedas, Upanisads and other literature aiming at building character and spirituality, which would impel individuals to lead a detached, moral, contended life and service to people and animals, non-possessive, simple life. There is no magic or formula which can transform our present governments into Ethical Governments until and unless all those who are in Government as well as the people outside the Government follow ethical, moral and spiritual values and service to humanity as the cardinal principles of life. The present day reforms are an eyewash to quiten the people temporarily and are superficial in nature. The permanent solutions are possible if we take the help of the basic principles enshrined in ancient Sanskrit literature (Ram Rajya in Ramayana).

Common people imitate the standards set by the elect. Democracy has become confused with disbelief in great men. The Gita points out that the great men are the path-makers who blaze the trail that other men follow. The light generally comes through individuals who are in advance of society. They see the light shining on the mountain heights while their fellow sleep in the valley below. They are, in the words of Jesus, the "Salt", the "Leven", the "Light" of human communities. When they proclaim the splendor of that light, a few recognize it and slowly many are persuaded to follow them.

We shall study some thoughts of great men like Lord Krishna, Lord Rama, Swami Vivekananda who fall in the category of Ever-relevant.

2. SCIENTIFIC MANAGEMENT

With the advent of Industrial Revolution, sometimes in the middle of the eighteenth century, there was an attempt to develop management to reap the benefits of industrialization. The new scientific management emphasized rational decisions and discarded the decisions based on tradition or intuition. Many eminent persons, mostly with engineering background like, Frederick Taylor (1856-1915), Henry Lawrence Gantt (1861-1919), Harrington Emerson (1853-1931), France Bunker Gilbreth (1868-1924), Lillian Moller Gilbreth (1878-1972), and others have laid the foundation of the scientific management.

The scientific management stressed rationality, predictability, specialisation and technical competence. Its focus was on the design and operation of production processes at the "shop" level of the organisation. There are three assumptions of scientific management:

(1) That improved practice will come from the application of the scientific method of analysis to organisational problems;

(2) The second assumption pertains to the relation of worker to his work. There is a primary focus on work itself and not on the particular person doing the work. The good worker is viewed as one who 'accepts' orders, but does not 'initiate' actions. The worker is told how to do his job based upon scientific analysis of the job.

(3) Each worker is assumed to be "economic man." He is interested in maximising his monetary income.

Scientific management does not emphasize integration and coordination of higher levels of organisation.

Taylor's Philosophy of the Scientific Management

Taylor is generally acknowledged as the 'Father of Scientific Management'. Scientific Management is also known as Taylorism because Taylor was the first to introduce scientific method at the workshop level. Taylor's ideas, based on experiences and experiments, are contained in his two important books: Shop Management and Principles of Management. He advocated the application of scientific methods to take care of the problems of management. In his paper, 'Principles of Scientific Management', Taylor mentions the indispensability of scientific method in management.

(i) Firstly, to point out through a series of simple illustrations, the great loss which the whole country is suffering through inefficiency in almost all of our daily acts.

(ii) Secondly, to try to convince the reader that the remedy for this inefficiency lies in systematic management, rather than in searching for some unusual or extraordinary man.

(iii) Thirdly, to prove that the best management is a true science, resting upon clearly defined laws, rules, and principles, as a foundation. And further to show that the fundamental principles of scientific management are applicable to all kinds of human activities, from our simplest individual

> acts to the work of our great corporations, which call for the most elaborate cooperation. And, briefly, through a series of illustrations, to convince the reader that whenever these principles are correctly applied, results must follow, which are truly astounding.

The most important thing in Taylor's scientific attitude is his stress on the change of attitudes through 'mental revolution'. It would be most appropriate to reproduce the meaning and need of mental revolution in his own words in his testimony before the House Committee in 1912, "Scientific management is not any efficiency device, nor is it any bunch or group of efficiency devices. It is not a new system of figuring costs; it is not a new scheme of paying men; it is not a piecework system; it is not a bonus system; it is not a premium system; it is not holding a stop-watch on a man and writing things down about him; it is not time study; it is not motion study nor an analysis of the movements of men; it is not the printing and ruling and unloading of one or two of blanks on a set of men and saying 'Here's your system; go use it!' It is not divided foremanship or functional foremanship; it is not any of the devices, which the average man calls to mind when scientific management is spoken of. Now, in its essence, scientific management involves a complete mental revolution on the part of the workingman engaged in any particular establishment or industry—a complete mental revolution on the part of these men as to their duties toward their work, toward their fellowmen, and toward their employers. And it involves the equally complete mental revolution on the part of those on the *management's* side—the foreman, the superintendent, the owner of the business, the board of directors—a complete mental revolution on their part as to their duties toward their fellow workers in the management, toward their workmen and toward all of their daily problems."[3]

Taylor's approach to scientific management may be summarised as follows:

(a) The development of a true science of management (organised knowledge) needs to replace the rules of thumb based on tradition and intuition. This would produce 'standardisation' of work methods for each task, which would avoid *ad hocism.*

(b) Securing group harmony and not discord through allocation of definite work to workers to suit their mental calibre. He never overlooked the fact that "The relations between employers and men form without question, the most important part of this art."[4]

(c) Achieving human 'cooperation' rather than chaotic individualism.

(d) Working for maximum 'output' rather than restricted output.

(e) Provision of scientific education and development of the workers. It is the duty of management to make training arrangement for workers for their development.

(f) Equitable division of work and responsibility between management and workers. Management should concentrate on its functions—planning, organising, controlling and determining the methods of work.

Henry Gantt and Others

Henry Lawrence Gantt gave his major attention to man as an important element of productivity and developed the concept of motivation in his famous books, *Industrial Leadership* (1916) and *Organising for Work* (1919). He is best known for development of graphic methods of depicting plans and was the forerunner of modern management techniques like PERT. Gantt developed time and motion study and ergonomics. He believed that inefficiency and low productivity arise from "ill-directed and ineffective motions."

Mrs. Lillian Moller Gilbreth, acclaimed as 'first lady of management' in her famous books, Primer of Scientific Management (1912), and Motion Study (1911) emphasised the human factor in administration. Her renowned work, *The Psychology of Management* stressed the importance of human element in productivity.

Harrington Emerson in his books, *Efficiency as a Basis for Operation and Wages* (1911) and *The Twelve Principles of Efficiency* (1913), advocated twelve principles—first five relating to 'interpersonal relations' and the other seven relating to 'system' of management, to eliminate wanton and wicked waste from government and industries. There are also many others who developed upon the ideas of Taylor.

Scientific management, thus, was the outcome of 'quantification' of work based on work norms, derived out of rigorous time and motion studies and the payment of wages to workers in proportion to their output. Scientific management contributed to the theory of the organisation in a big way. Though many scholars are critical of this approach, still scientific management is of great relevance in improving productivity. Developing countries, like India, where industrial activities are on a take-off stage, need to adopt scientific management to achieve optimisation. The modern management techniques like work study, method study, work measurement, programme evaluation and review techniques have been derived from scientific management. The organisation can be designed well with the knowledge of scientific management. Scientific management keeps the organisations in order and helps in planning, decision-making, coordination and control effectively.

Nigro and Nigro are of the view that "one of the scientific management's enduring contributions to modern managerial thought and practice is the idea that efficiency and goal accomplishment are the products of systematic research and evaluation."[5] Empirical research and controlled experimentation with alternative methods were central elements in scientific management. These experiments intended to discover the "best way" to carry out specific tasks. "This approach carried beyond the design of technical systems to selection and training of employees. Once efficient procedures were devised, it was the management's responsibility to implement appropriate selection and training systems and to see to it that the psychological and physical traits of workers matched the requirements of their jobs."[6]

CLASSICAL THEORY

The classical theory, also known as structural theory, engages its attention on the development of universal principles of formal organisation. The chief proponent of this theory is Henri Fayol, who is known as father of 'modern operational-management theory'. Besides, Luther Gulick, L.F. Urwick, J.O. Mooney, A.C. Reiley, M.P. Follett and Oliver Sheldon also advocated this theory. Let us discuss about them.

Henri Fayol, a French industrialist born in 1841, wrote three books and a number of research papers on management. His acute observation on management appeared under the title *Administration Industrial et Gene 'rale'* in 1916 in French. Its English translation was made available in restricted form in 1929. In the USA, its English translation was made available only in 1949.

Fayol stressed that management, one of the six activities of an enterprise: (i) technical, (ii) commercial, (iii) financial, (iv) security, (v) accounting, and (vi) managerial-involving five functions: (a) planning, (b) organisation, (c) command, (d) coordination, and (e) control—with sixteen managerial duties and fourteen principles, constitutes a complete theory of management. Let us mention his main ideas.

Mental Qualities and the Need for Training

Fayol mentions the following six qualities, which are essential for managers and advocates the need for training:

1. Physical health, vigour and appearance.
2. Mental ability to understand and learn, judgement, mental vigour and adaptability.
3. Moral firmness and willingness to accept responsibility.
4. General acquaintance with matters not belonging exclusively to the function performed.
5. Special knowledge of the function being handled, be it technical, commercial, financial or managerial.

6. Experience knowledge arising from the work proper?

To quote his views on training, "Everyone needs some concept of administration; in the home, or in affairs of the State, the need for administrative ability is in proportion to the importance of the undertaking and, for individual people, the need is everywhere greater in accordance with the position occupied. Hence, there should be some generalised teaching of administration: elementary in the primary schools, somewhat wider in the post-primary schools, and quite advanced in higher social educational establishments."

Principles of Management

Let us mention briefly the Fourteen Principles advocated by him:

(i) *Division of work:* It leads to specialisation and better work performance.
(ii) *Authority and Responsibility:* He favoured the parity of authority and responsibility.
(iii) *Discipline:* Discipline among employees is essential for productivity.
(iv) *Unity of Command:* An employee should receive orders from his superior only.
(v) *Unity of Direction:* There should be one head and one plan for each activity.
(vi) *Subordination of Individual Interest to General Interest:* The interest of the group needs to prevail over the individual interest.
(vii) *Remuneration of Personnel:* It should be fair and should afford maximum satisfaction both to the employees and the organisation.
(viii) *Centralisation:* The extent of concentration or dispersal of authority will depend on individual circumstances enabling to give the best overall yield.
(ix) *Scalar Chain:* It denotes the line of authority from top to lower level for the purpose of communication. It can be short-circuited to meet the needs.

(x) *Order (Placement):* Each employee occupies a job wherein he can render the best service.
(xi) *Equity:* It is the combination of kindliness and justice in a manager, which he should apply while dealing with the subordinates.
(xii) *Stability of Tenure of Personnel:* High turnover is detrimental to organisational development.
(xiii) *Initiative:* It is the ability to think afresh. Fayol wants managers to sacrifice 'personal vanity' to increase zeal and energy among the employees.
(xiv) *Esprit de corps:* It is the need for team work, "In union there is strength."

It may be added that Fayol never mentioned that this was a complete list. Principles can be added or subtracted according to need, but codification of principles is indispensable.[8]

Fayol made a distinction between 'General Principles of Management' and 'Elements of Management' numbering five. The work of J.D. Mooney and A.C. Reley, *Onward Industry* (1931); The *Principles of Organisation* (1939), formulated elements of organisation into a logical pattern of principle, process and effect numbering nine, drawn mostly from Church and military organisations.

Oliver Sheldon, in his work *Philosophy of Management* (1923), mentions that management is a matter of principles, primarily both scientific and ethical. To quote him, "It is important, therefore, that we should devise a philosophy of management, a code of principles, scientifically determined and generally accepted, to act as a guide, by reason of its foundation on ultimate things for the daily practice of the profession. Management must link up all its practitioners into one body, pursuing a common end, conscious of a common purpose, actuated by a common motive, adhering to a corporate creed, governed by common laws of practice, sharing a common fund of knowledge."[11]

Mary Parker Follett's views on management thought are like a bridge connecting the classical movement and social systems movement. Follett blended the theory, fact and ideal, beautifully.

Luther Gullick enumerates ten principles of organisation, while Lyndall Urwick in his book, *The Elements of Public Administration* (1943) listed 29 principles of management and a list of sub-principles, based on the fourteen principles of Fayol, Mooney and Reley's principle of process and effect, Taylors' principle of management, ideas of Follett and Graicunas: (1) investigation, (2) forecasting, (3) planning, (4) appropriateness, (5) organisation, (6) coordination, (7) order, (8) command, (9) control, (10) coordination, (11) authority, (12) scalar process, (13) assignment of functions, (14) leadership, (15) delegation, (16) functional definition, (17) determinative, (18) applicative, (19) interpretative, (20) the general interest, (21) centralisation, (22) staffing, (23) spirit, (24) selection and placement, (25) rewards and sanctions, (26) initiative, (27) equity, (28) discipline, and (29) stability.[9]

He mentioned that the main point is that it focuses on a logical scheme of various 'principles of administration' formulated by different authorities. The fact that such 'principles'—worked out by persons of different nationalities, widely varying experience and, in the majority of cases, no knowledge of each other's work—were susceptible to such logical arrangement, is in itself highly significant.[10] These principles are an extension of Urwick's co-author Luther Gulick's seven functions, coined under the word (POSDCORB).

The classical theory has been dubbed as 'mechanical' theory and has been accused of ignoring the social and psychological motives of the people within it. There is not much truth in it. Classical thinkers never regarded human beings as an inert instrument or management a closed system. The theory has advocated concrete principles, which are being applied both in developed and developing countries with modifications to suit ecological conditions. As has been seen from the summaries of various management pioneers, certainly from the time of Taylor, none overlooked the human factor or treated it in a mechanical way.

HUMAN RELATIONS THEORY

This theory is a reaction to formalism and focuses on basing organisation on human values, which are of cardinal importance. It takes into account the social, psychological and informal needs of the people. The theory is based on Hawthorne experiments, which were conducted in the USA in the late 1920s and early 1930s, at the Western Electric Company at Hawthrone (near Chicago), under the guidance of Elton Mayo and his colleagues of the Harvard Business School. The study found that 'human behaviour' must be recognised as a key factor in raising production. Elton Mayo has been rightly titled as the father of human relations movement. Roethlisberger, while mentioning the contribution of Elton Mayo, has said: "The manager is neither managing men nor managing work, he is administering a social system." Many other eminent thinkers, like McGregor, Argyris have also favoured human relations theory. We mention here the following essentials of human relations theory:

(i) The need for recognition of 'human' element and the well-being and motivation of the working teams.

(ii) Good supervision is exercised with proper understanding *of the subordinates.*

(iii) It is important to have proper communication and consultation between the managers and the workers. This creates a sense of participation and involvement among the employees. There should be a means of keeping the management informed of what the employees are thinking, fearing, hoping, and equally of keeping the employees informed of what the management is thinking or proposing to do.

(iv) The Hawthorne experiments showed that economic incentive is far less powerful than the personal or social incentives.

(v) The flow of work and arrangements of operations should give full play to the informal organisation of the workers.

In Argyris's view, an organisation following these principles would be able to achieve efficiency as well as keep their employees satisfied. He says: "Every individual has 'psychological energy' to expend. Exerting that energy in a way that helps him fulfil his own social and egoistic needs is what motivates an individual. Therefore, provided a company is structured in such a way that an individual is able to meet these self-fulfilment needs, the psychological energy will be used in the company's interests. If the reverse is the case, the psychological energy can easily be used to thwart the company's aims."

McGregor, however, points out that man's motivation is far too complex and varied to be explained away wholly by the aforementioned assumptions. In line with other thinkers of social psychology school, McGregor describes his alternative model of motivation as theory. The assumptions of theory Y may be stated as:

1. The average man is not really against doing work.
2. The ordinary man can show self-control and self-direction depending upon the involvement in the work he is doing.
3. The average man craves for self-actualisation, and it is the responsibility of the management to provide genuine conditions for satisfying his creative abilities and yearnings.
4. The ordinary man under suitable conditions would willingly shoulder responsibility.
5. The average man is capable of making significant contributions to the solution of many administrative problems but his potentialities are not fully utilised.

McGregor's assumptions in theory Y roughly correspond to what Maslow and Argyris have stated about human motivation. The running theme of all these thinkers has been to show that adequate attention has not been paid, so far, to the actual potentialities, creativity and responsible behaviour with which the ordinary man is endowed. That way, McGregor has successfully discarded the assumption of classical schools of thought. Human relations can be improved through:

(i) Participation
(ii) Job enlargement and enrichment
(iii) Positive reinforcement
(iv) Effective organisational climate
(v) Building morale
(vi) Decentralisation and delegation

The human relations theory, though covered an important ground to improve organisational effectiveness, still cannot be used independently to design an organisation. This theory can supplement classical or bureaucratic theory and help to remove the irritants from them. The extent of the use of this theory would depend upon the social and psychological needs of the people working within it. This theory was designed in the context of experiments conducted in an environment of advanced country. It may not be out of place to mention that in developing countries like India, monetary incentive may still be more productive than social and psychological incentives. What is needed is the conduct of Hawthorne-like experiments in different regions of the country to locate the role of social and psychological motives. Upon the output of such research, the value of the theory can be judged.

BUREAUCRATIC THEORY

The subject of bureaucracy occupies a key position in the study of public administration to explain authority-control relationship in formal organisations. M. de Gournay, an economist of France, first coined the word Bureaucracy in the eighteenth century to refer to "a fourth or fifth form of government" in which "officers, clerks, secretaries, inspectors and attendants are not appointed to benefit the public interest.[12] Indeed the public interest appears to have been established such that offices might exist."[13] Harolds J. Laski,[14] defines the term bureaucracy as, a system of government, the control of which is so completely in the hands of officials that their power jeopardises the liberties of ordinary citizens. The characteristics of such a regime are a passion for routine in administration, the sacrifice of flexibility to rule, delay in the making of decisions and a refusal to embark upon experiment. In extreme cases the members of a bureaucracy may become a hereditary caste manipulating government to their own advantage.

Max Weber, the German social scientist, made sociological study of bureaucracy. His two important works in English are: *The 'Theory of Social and Economic Organization* translated and edited by M. Henderson and Talcot Parsons and *From Max Weber: Essays Sociology* translated and edited by R.H. Gerth and C. Wright Mills. He thinks that once it is fully established, bureaucracy is among those social structures, which are the most difficult to eliminate. Bureaucracy is an ideal type as it is based on impersonal and rational basis.

He classifies the authority as Traditional, i.e., resting on an established belief in the sanctity of immemorial traditions and the legitimacy of the status of those exercising authority under them, Charismatic, i.e. "resting-on the devotion to the specific and exceptional sanctity, heroism or exemplary character of an individual person, and of the normative patterns or order revealed or ordained by him" I and Legal, i.e., "resting on the premises of legality of patterns of normative rules and the right of those elevated to authority under such rules to issue commands." Legal authority is superior and more logical than charismatic. To quote Max Weber, "In contrast to any kind of bureaucratic organisation of offices, the charismatic structure knows nothing of a form or of an ordered procedure of appointment or dismissal. It knows no regulated 'career', 'advancement', 'salary', or regulated and expert training of the holder of charisma or of his aids. It knows no agency of control or appeal, nor does it embrace permanent institutions like our bureaucratic 'departments' which are independent of persons and of purely personal charisma."[15]

Let us examine the features of bureaucracy enumerated by Max Weber. To quote Max Weber, "The ruled, for their part, cannot dispense with or replace the bureaucratic apparatus of authority once it exists. For this bureaucracy rests upon expert training, a functional specialisation of work, and an attitude set for habitual and virtuoso-like mastery of single yet methodically integrated functions." If the official stops working, or if, his work is forcefully interrupted, chaos results, and it is difficult to improvise replacements from among the governed who are not fit to master such chaos. This holds for public administration as well as for private economic management. More and more the material fate of the masses depends upon the steady and correct functioning of the increasingly bureaucratic organisations of private capitalism. Everywhere the modern state is undergoing bureaucratisation.

According to Weber, bureaucracy has certain characteristics, such as adherence to rules, hierarchy, separation of office and incumbent and selection by merit. He stressed that bureaucracy is capable of attaining the higher degree of efficiency and is, in this sense formally, the most rational means of carrying out imperative control over human beings. It is superior to any other form in precision, in stability, in the stringency of discipline, and in its stability.[16] The salient features of a bureaucracy are:

Impersonal Order

The authority is inherent in the post and not the individual who performs the official role. An official is supposed to have a detached approach, free from personal considerations.

Rules and Regulations

Organisations are to function within the framework of rules and regulations. Rules must be followed meticulously. Functions are clearly spelled out in rules. *The* 'objective' discharge of business primarily means a discharge of business according to calculable rules and without regard for *persons*."[17]

Hierarchy

The organisation of offices follows hierarchy that is the lower offices are under the control of the higher ones.

Contract

Officials are appointed through contract on the basis of professional qualifications. They are entitled to salary and pension rights. There is a career structure.

Control

There are necessary disciplinary system, checks, unified control.

Division of Work Leading to Specialisation

The activities of the organisation are distributed as fixed official duties. This leads to specialisation.

Efficiency

Weber's ideas on efficiency and rationality are closely related to his ideal type of bureaucracy. "The decisive reason for the advance of bureaucratic organisation has always been its purely technical superiority over any other form of organisation. The developed bureaucratic mechanism compares with other organisations exactly as does the machine with the non-mechanical modes of production."[18]

Neutrality

Bureaucracy is apolitical and neutral. Prof. Frederich mentions the following features of bureaucracy; (i) differentiation of functions, (ii) qualifications for office, (iii) hierarchial organisation and discipline, (iv) objectivity of method, (v) precision and consistency involving adherence to rules, and (vi) exercise of discretion involving secrecy.

We can conclude, in the words of Weber: "Experience tends universally to show that the purely bureaucratic type of administrative organization—that is, the monocratic variety of bureaucracy—is, from a purely technical point of view, capable of attaining the highest degree of efficiency and is in this sense formally the most rational known means of carrying out imperative control over human beings. It is superior to any other form in precision, in stability, in the stringency of its discipline, and in its reliability. It thus makes possible a particularly high degree of calculability of result for the heads of the organisation and for those acting in relation to it. It is finally superior both in intensive efficiency and in the scope of its operations, and is formally capable of application to all kinds of administrative tasks."[19]

The excellence of a bureaucratic organisation lies in its Technical superiority over any other form of organisation. Precision, speed, unambiguity, knowledge of the files, continuity, discretion, unity, strict subordination, reduction of friction and of material and personal costs—these are raised to the optimum point in the strictly bureaucratic administration and especially in its monocratic form.[20]

Criticism

The Max Weber theory has been criticised by most of the administrative thinkers. Mention may be made of Robert Merton, Talcot Parsons, Peter Blau, Robert Presthus, H.C. Creel and A.B. Spitzer, Simon, Barnard, La Palombaro, etc.

Carl Friedrich has observed, "Weber sets forth his ideal type as mental constructs which are neither derived by a process of deductive rationalisation from higher concepts, nor built up from empirical data by relevant inference, nor demonstrably developed as working hypotheses from such data."[21] The main criticisms levelled against bureaucracy are:

(a) Red tape leading to delays, postponement of decisions, circuitous course of reference and delay,
(b) Abuse of power,
(c) Class consciousness,
(d) Inefficiency,
(e) complexity, and
(f) Insensitivity.

Most of the ills of bureaucracy can be cured through administrative improvement and reforms. Bureaucracy is a necessary evil. We should try to remove the irritants. Bureaucracy can be improved through executive development programmes. How is it that bureaucracy in Private Sector is more efficient than in Government Sector? How is it that bureaucracy in advanced countries is more responsive than in developing countries? The answers to these would provide the necessary material for reform in state bureaucracy.

R.N. Haldipur has rightly said: "Bureaucracy, while it has faced many a challenge in the past, will have to be forward looking, human in content and flexible enough to lend stability while moving forward to keep the momentum of change, going fast enough to see that every tear from the faces of the millions is wiped out and the hungry man gets at least one square meal per day. Here Gandhi's advice could serve as a guiding light to the bureaucrat in his day-to-day and moment to moment functioning."[22]

M.P. Barber observes: "Weber's pioneering analysis of bureaucracy has stimulated much further analysis and research, and these studies make it possible critically to review and bring about some modifications which will give bureaucracy a dynamic aspect and enable an organisation to serve the needs it was created to serve."[23]

Fred W. Riggs observes that Weber's ideal type construct of bureaucracy assumes a relatively autonomous administrative system and thus is not particularly relevant to the study of developing societies. In developing countries, the administrative structures do not enjoy sufficient autonomy from other social structures whereas in developed societies they are comparatively more autonomous. Thus in developing countries the administrative structures become multifunctional and are likely to perform a variety of "extra administrative functions" and less strictly "administrative" ones. In such a situation it is difficult to study the administrative sub-systems on the basis of ideal type constructs of Weber. Riggs thus argues that new conceptual constructs are to be developed to study such societies which have a mixture of primitive and modern structural characteristics.[24]

SYSTEMS THEORY

We have discussed theories of management, which are based on isolated and disjointed attempts, concentrating on few variables. A need was felt to formulate a system's theory of organisation, which can take care of all the variables. The system approach was first used by scientists in the study and explanation of the scientific phenomenon.

The term 'system theory' owes its origin to the eminent biologist, Ludwig Yon Bertalanft'y (1901-72), who defined system as "a set of element standing in interaction." Colin Cheray defines it as "a whole which is compounded of many parts, an ensemble of attributes."

Webster defines a system as "A set or arrangement of things so related or connected as to form a unity or organic whole."

As Robert Chin observes, "Psychologists, sociologists, anthropologists, economists, and political scientists have been 'discovering' and using the system model. In so doing, they find intimations of an exhilarating 'unity' of science, because the system models used by biological and physical scientists seem to be exactly similar. Thus, the system model is regarded by some system theorists as universally applicable to physical and social events, and to human relationships in small or large units."[25]

A system is (a) a group of entities, (b) these entities are functionally interdependent, (c) the system does not exist and function in a vacuum, it is surrounded by a variety of other objects and systems which constitute its environment; (d) the functioning of the system affects, and is vitally affected by the environment. Systems theory aims at integration of sub-systems. The theory, in its application, is holistic, congruous, and inclusive. It views phenomena in the physical, biological, and social world in terms of hierarchies of systems, sub-systems, and supra-systems in ceaseless interaction with one another. With its emphasis on synthesis, convergence, and integration of knowledge, process, and represents a thinking.[26]

Nigro and Nigro say that systems framework starts with the proposition that all social organisations share certain characteristics, the most important ones are mentioned below:[27]

1. Organisation as open systems, constantly seek and import resources (input) in both human and

material form, and transform these inputs into products and services, using internal social and technological process (throughputs).

2. Organisations, as open system, export products to the external environment and outputs usually become the inputs of organisations.
3. Organisation structure develop around patterned activities that form stable and predictable input, throughout and output cycles.
4. Over time, structural differentiation and task specialisation are common system responses to "the search for resources and adaptiveness, and as the organisations become more complex, managerial structures for coordination and control became more elaborate.
5. Feedback in the form of information about environmental responses to organisational activities (outputs) is used to keep the system on course with regard to its goals and to evaluate the performance of the organisation and its sub-units.

The system approach can be used profitably by all the disciplines to study phenomenon in their own area. Robert Chin mention "Psychologists, sociologists, anthropologists, economists, and political scientists have been 'discovering' and using the system model. In doing so, they find intimations of an exhilarating 'unity' of sciences, because the system models used by biological and physical scientists seem to be exactly similar. Thus, the system model is regarded by some system theorists as universally applicable to physical and social events, and to human relationships in small or large units."

The systems can be open and closed. Biological and social systems are open systems, i.e., they are in continued interaction with the environment and are moving to complexity through differentiation and specialisation, and are dynamic. Physical systems are closed systems, i.e., they are non-responsive to their environment and are static. The closed systems interact with tangible objects while open systems interact with intangible phenomenon. We may keep in mind that the system theory is concerned with only such roles that interact with one another and not those that are performed in isolation. The writings of Mary Parker Follett, Chester Barnard, Herbert Simon, and Karl Marx indicate in a rudimentary form their interests in the system theory of management.

Systems Theory and Management

The system approach looks at the organisation as a total system, comprising a number of interacting variables. Under this approach, organisation is viewed not merely as a formal arrangement of superiors and subordinates, or a social system comprising informal organisation and people's influence on each other, but as a total system of formal organisation, individuals, social system, the physical setting (man-machine systems) and the environment, all constantly interacting with each other. The systems approach studies the organisation as an integrated whole encompassing many sub-systems, and considers each system as a part of a still larger system.

Management seeks utilisation of resources, economically and efficiently, through the organisation. An organisation comes into existence to meet the objectives in an environmental context. An organisation has many sub-systems, of which management is one. The organisation has its input system and environmental linkages, here classified into four functional linkages, which link it with the task-environment, enabling linkages which link it to the source of power, diffused linkages link it with clients, and normative linkages link it with the philosophy. The sub-system of the organization relates it to laying down immediate and long-term objectives, setting performance standards and determining output. Management has its own sub-systems like planning, organising, staffing, coordinating, budgeting, decision-making, communication, etc. The management sub-system is deeply intertwined with the organisational sub-system. System theory in management implies application of the system approach to management of organisations in its totality. It includes all the internal and external sub-systems. It deals with input and output of resources in all its manifestations—technical, organisational and institutional.

System theory in management has many limitations, as it deals with complex and ever-changing phenomena. The selection of variables and their inter-connections are not subject to control. It does not offer a unified philosophy. Models based on the system theory of management cannot comprehend social phenomenon. However, with the help of new electronic gadgets, it is possible, to some extent, to develop the system theory of management. It is hoped that the system theory of management may be perfected over a period of time. We may conclude, in the words of C.L. Sharma, "Management of organisations would remain an exasperating, frustrating, and challenging task and experience, intuition, and judgement would continue to play an important role. Because of the interplay of human element, the discipline of management, unlike natural sciences, is not likely to develop predictive laws. Nonetheless with the introduction of the computer, the increased application of quantitative methods, and the proliferation of the findings of behavioural sciences, there is a movement towards making management—the decision-making, component of an organization—an identifiable, observable, measurable and verifiable process. Systems Theory is a strand of this movement that seeks to develop the science of management."

CONTINGENCY THEORY

It has been seen that no predetermined theory of organisation can serve its purpose for all times, as situations and times are changing fast. Organisation theory today suggests that organisations may be designed according to technology and environment. Technology has produced a great change in many sub-systems. The same is true about the environment. Contingency theory of management follows contingency theory of leadership.

Despite the advance made in the general systems development and the trend for both the quantitative and behavioural approaches to move towards a system base. Contingency Management Theory seems better suited to lead management out of the present theory jungle. Contingency management approaches fall somewhere between 'simplistic, specific principles' and 'complex vague notion'. The contingency approach to organisation design is based on the premise that there is no single design that is the best for all situations. The contingency designs are conditional in nature. Technology, economic, and social conditions, and human resources are some of the variables that must be considered in a contingent organisation design. The overall goal of a contingency theory of management would go to match quantitative and behavioural systems approaches with appropriate situational factors.[28]

CONCLUSION

We have discussed some of the important theories of organisation with their main themes. The question as to which theory is more important is a difficult issue. The relevance of the theory would depend upon the prevailing atmosphere, objectives of the organisation and the quality of people. For a developing country like India, scientific management theory appears to be better, since it needs clarity and specificity, and these can be provided by scientific management. In Union and State Governments, we find that, at many places, the staff is surplus while at other places, the work is suffering because of the shortage of staff. How can we improve it—only through scientific management. Another serious issue is the harassment of the masses by the people in administration, as the work has not been defined carefully and disposal cannot be checked. Through scientific management, we can achieve this objective, through its tools like planning, coordination, control, etc. Besides, the bureaucracy and classical theories are also good in so far as they provide us the framework and principles of administration. We can modify the bureaucratic principles to suit our needs. Behavioural approach can supplement these theories and help in enhancing their efficiency. Systems theory of management, though in its elementary stage, can be useful with the help of electronic gadgets. Contingency theory can help in constantly changing environment and technology. We may conclude by saying that all the theories are important. The relative use of these theories would depend upon a number of variables which need to be taken into account in making a decision.

Social scientists in India are mostly using Western models. Yogendra Singh rightly mentions, "One might think that the Western 'reference model' continues to flourish in the Indian social science today as much as under the colonial regime. Indian social scientists did enter into periodical sessions of self-appraisal of their role and some thoughtful discussions have followed, but with very few exceptions most social scientists remain prisoners of the academic habits formed by their Western orientation in matters of conceptualisation, selection of problems and selling the products of their research."[29]

However, while applying these theories, we must keep in mind the ecology prevailing in India. J.P. Subramanian, in his Article, 'Management: Theories and their Limitations' in *Business India*, November 3-16, 1986, has rightly said that:

"While the pattern of industrialisation and modernisation adopted in India makes western management theories and techniques seem relevant, the environmental factors—social, cultural, economic and political—operating on organizational behaviour in India are so different that there are *bound to* be significant limitations to their applicability. The values and attitudes germane to one *culture* often become incongruous with another culture." The studies by Burns and Stalker and Lawrence and Lorsch[30] are important contributions to environment-related theories of organisation.

Thus, there is a need to adopt a theory of management which is congenial to our current socio-economic and politico-administrative situations.

Notes and References

1. Quoted in Felix A. Nigro and Lloyd G. Nigro, *Modern Public Administration;* Harper and Row Publishers, New York, 6th edition, 1984; p. 141)
2. David Easton, *The Political System,* Scientific Book Agency, Calcutta, 1971, p. 55. .
3. Taylor, Frederick, *Testimony,* pp. 26-27, 29-30.

4. Taylor, Frederick, *Shop Management*, p. 25.
5. Felix A. Nigro and Lloyd G. Nigro, Modern Public Administration; *op. cit.*, p. 146.
6. *Ibid.*
7. Fayol, Henri, *Administration Industrielle et Gene 'rale'*, p. 7.
8. Fayol, *op. cit.*, p. 19.
9. See, I. Urwick, *The Elements of Administration*, pp. 118-23.
10. Urwick, *op. cit.*, p. 7.
11. Oliver Sheldon, *The Philosophy of Management*, p. 280.
12. Max Weber, "The Essentials of Bureaucratic Organisation: An Ideal Type Construction" in RK. Merton, *et. al.*, (ed.), *Reader in Bureaucracy* (New York, The Free Press, 1952), p. 24.
13. Albrow, Martin, *Bureaucracy*, London, Macmillan, 1970, p. 16.
14. Harold J. Laski, 'Bureaucracy', *Encyclopaedia of the Social Sciences*, 1937 edition, Vol. 2, selected from pp. 70-72, quoted in Lepawsky, Copyright 1930, The Macmillan Company, *op. cit.*, p. 189.
15. R.H. Gerth & C. Wright Mills (trans. and ed.), from *Max Weber's Essays in Sociology*, Oxford University Press, 1940, p. 246.
16. Webermax, "The Essentials of Bureaucratic Organisation. An Ideal Type Construction" in R.K. Merton, *et. al.* (ed.) Reader in Bureaucracy, New York, The Free Press, 1952, p. 24..
17. Gerth and Mills, *op. cit.*, p. 215.
18. *Ibid.*, p. 214.
19. Weber, *Essays in Sociology*, p. 337.
20. Boston: Houghton Miffin Co., 1964, p. 73.
21. Carl Friedrich, 'Some Observations on Weber's *Analysis of Bureaucracy*' in Robert K. Merton (ed.), *Reader in Bureaucracy*, New York Press, 1952,
22. R.N. Haldipur; 'Bureaucracy's Response to New Challenges', *IJPA*, Vol. XXII, No.1, p. 13.
23. M.P. Barber, *Public Administration*, London, McDonald, 1979, p. 96. Fred, W. Riggs, Administration in Developing Countries: The Theory of Prismatic Society.
24. *Ibid.*
25. Robert Chin, "The University of System Models and Developments Models for Practioners", in Warren G. Bennis, *et al.* (eds.), *The Planning of Change*, Holt, Rinehart, and Winston, New York, 1976.
26. *Ibid.*
27. Felix A. Nigro and Lloyd G. Nigro, *Modern Public Administration, op. cit.*, p. 163.
28. Fred Huthars, "The Contingency Theory of Management" in *Business Horizons*, June, 1973, pp. 66-67.

29. Yogendra Singh, "The Role of Social Science in India: A Sociology of Knowledge", *Sociological Bulletin*, No. 22, (March 1973), p. 256.

30. T. Burns and G.M. Stalker, *The Management of Innovation*, London: Tavistock, 1961.

10

Woodrow Wilson (1856-1924)

INTRODUCTION

Woodrow Wilson is considered to be the father of the discipline of Public Administration. He was a political scientist at Bryan Mawar College. Leonard D. White says, "Wilson introduced the idea of administration." Allen Schick says, "Wilson launched Public Administration as a generic course." Dwight Waldo comments: "The publication of Woodrow Wilson's famous essay marks the birth of public administration as a self-conscious inquiry." Thus, Wilson was a pioneer and the founder of the study of the science of administration.

Public administration has been in existence since the birth of civilized society. However, public administration as an academic discipline took its birth in the USA in 1887, when Woodrow Wilson published his article, 'The Study of Public Administration' in *Political Science Quarterly*, June 1877, Vol. 2, (pp. 197-222), which made a distinction between politics and administration. This article is considered a significant trail-blazing effort. The paper became a bacon light for the specialization of Public Administration. Through

CHART 10.1

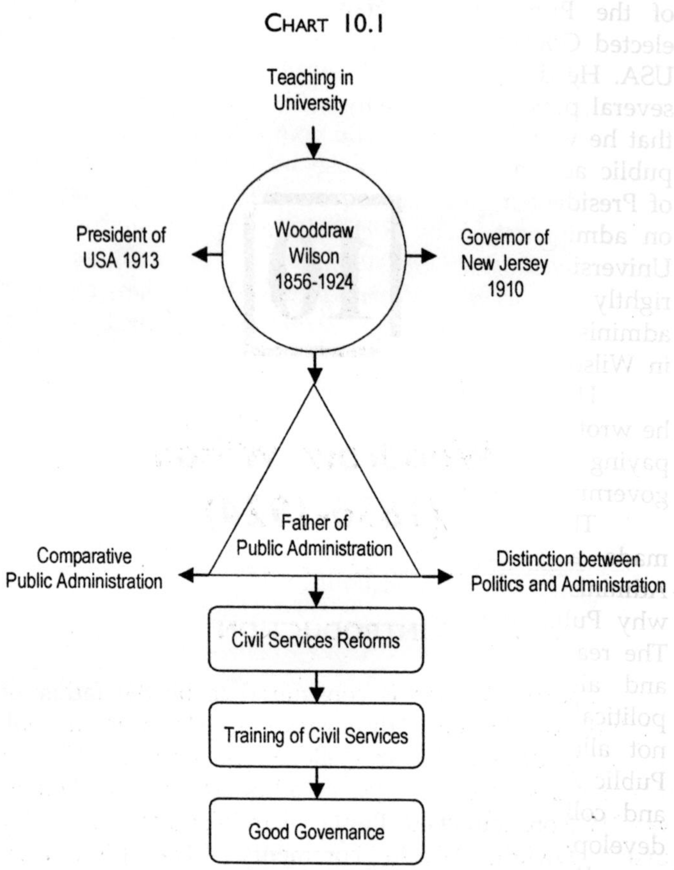

this article, Wilson helped in the establishment of public administration as a recognized field of study. That is why Wilson is known as the father of public administration. The paper before its publication was presented before the historical and Political Science Association in Ithaca, New York at the invitation of its President, Charles K. Adams of Cornell University and also a former teacher of Woodrow Wilson.

Woodrow Wilson was born on Dec. 28, 1856 in Virginia, USA. He studied Politics, Government and Law. He graduated from Princeton in 1879 and got Ph.D. in 1886. He was a Professor of Political Science (1886-1902), and President of the Princeton University (1902-1910). In 1910 he was elected Governor of New Jersey and in 1913 as President of USA. He died in 1924. He wrote eight books and published several papers. If we analyse his life, it is quite crystal clear that he was the person who combined theory and practice of public administration because he assumed the highest office of President in USA. Woodrow Wilson had attended lectures on administration by Richard T. Ely at the Johns Hopkins University during 1982-1983. In his autobiography Ely has rightly remarked: "When I talked of the importance of administration, I felt that I struck a spark and kindled a fire in Wilson."

His famous essay, "The Study of Administration" that he wrote more than a century ago in 1887 was a landmark in paying special attention to increased efficiency in government.

The distinguished administrator and scholar indeed made a pioneering contribution to the study of Public Administration as a scientific subject. He wondered as to why Public Administration as a discipline emerged so late. The reason he thought was limited functions of Government and also public administration is considered a part of political science: Even today in India, Political Science does not allow public administration to come of age. Though, Public Administration in India is taught in many universities and colleges but still political scientists do not allow it to develop.

Wilson viewed administration from Legal angle. To quote him, "Public Administration is the detailed and systematic application of law. Every particular application of law is an act of administration." In his word in The State (1899), Wilson reiterates that administration executes the laws, and the legislature makes them. Without legislation administration must limp and with administration legislation must tail of effect.[1]

THE BEGINNING PERIOD

In the development of modern administrative thought, thinkers from varied fields have made their contribution, such as behaviouralists, systems scientists, business managers and Public Administrators. In the early nineteenth century the development of management theory was a new phenomenon. In 1886, Henry R. Towne felt that administration was of equal importance as engineering, established discipline, came about as a radical new approach.

THE STUDY OF ADMINISTRATION

According to Koontz and others, a number of scholars attempted to bring about increased efficiency in government by means of improved personnel practices and better management. A leading light of this new movement was Woodrow Wilson who in 1885 and later, propagated the idea of efficient government. His works titled "Congressional Government" (1885) and "The Study of Administration" (June 1887) attracted particular attention to bring more and more economy and efficiency in government and laid emphasis on organization, personnel practices, budgetary controls, planning, etc. Other Public Administrators and Political Scientists had also joined in.

Wilson Writes, "Administration is the most obvious part of government: it is government in action, it is executive, the operative and the most visible side of the government." He said that "the science of administration is the latest fruit of that study of the science of politics. He further says that we are having now what we never had before, a science of administration." According to Wilson, "We must Americanise it and that not formally, in language merely, but radically, in thought, principle and aim as well. It must learn our constitution by heart; must get the bureaucratic fever out of its veins; must inhale much free American air."

DISTINCTION BETWEEN POLITICS AND ADMINISTRATION

Wilson firmly believed that the focus of Public Administration was different than that of those who were concerned with how Constitution should be framed. He differentiated between the two and stated that it was getting harder to administer a Constitution than to frame one. Wilson proclaims, "The field of administration is a field of business. It is removed from the hurry and strife of politics. Administrative questions are not political questions." Wilson himself observes, "It is the object of administrative study to discover, first, what government can properly and successfully do, and secondly, how it can do these proper things with the utmost possible efficiency and at the least possible cost either of money or of energy." Right in the beginning of his famous essay he brought out the distinction between politics and administration and that the two were separate from each other. And it goes to his credit that he propagated Public administration as an independent and separate discipline of study. He wanted more attention be paid to it to further refine it and enrich it as a distinct subject. One of the most significant developments in the theory and practice of public administration since the post-war period is the increasing role that the administrative arm of government plays in public policy-making. There are two schools of thoughts with regard to the role of administration in policy formulation. The first is of the view that policy-making is exclusively a political function, while administration is concerned only with the implementation of the policy. According to the second school of thought, politics-administration dichotomy is not possible and administration cannot be completely separated from policy formulation. Luther Gullick was one of the first exponent of this view.

Wilson says that "Most important to be observed is the truth already so much and so fortunately insisted upon by our civil service reformers; namely that administration lies outside the proper sphere of politics. Administrative questions are not political questions. Although politics sets the tasks for administration, it should not be suffered to manipulate its offices. The field of administration is a field of business. It is removed from the hurry and strife of politics; it at most points stands apart even from the debatable ground of constitutional study. It is a part of political life only as the methods of the counting-house are a part of the life of society; only as machinery is part of the manufactured product. But it is, at the same time, raised very far above the dull level of mere technical detail by the fact that through its greater principles it is directly connected with the lasting maxims of political wisdom, the permanent truths of political progress.[2]

In his study of the relationship between administration and politics, his views vary as at some places he appears to say that the two are separate and at others that these are not. For example, he stresses at one place that "no lines of demarcation, setting apart administrative from non-administrative functions can be run between this and that department of government without being run uphill and down, daze over dizzy heights of distinction and through dense jungles of statutory enactment, hither and thither around 'ifs' and 'buts', 'whens' and 'howevers' until they become altogether lost to the common eyes, then in 1891 he expressed the view that no topic in the study of government can stand by itself—least of all perhaps administration whose part it is to mirror the principles of government in operation. . . . Administration cannot be divorced from its connections with the other branches of Public Law without being distorted and robbed of its true significance. Woodrow Wilson only reasserted that public administration cannot be purely independent; it affects and is affected by other subjects like political science, law, sociology, psychology, etc. However, his ultimate aim was to promote administrative science which was essential to run the government efficiently. Its foundations are those deep and permanent principles of politics." These views of Wilson make it clear that on one side he appreciated the deep connections, inseparability and interdependence between administration and politics, but at the same time he was attempting to carve out a separate discipline of public administration. He also pointed out that newer and newer functions were being undertaken by administration, so it must be studied more deeply so that those were better performed. Wilson firmly believed that administration is a science. He said that "the science of administration is the latest fruit of that study of the science of politics. He further says that we are having now what we never had before, a science of administration."

CIVIL SERVICE REFORMS

When Wilson wrote his essay in 1887, the USA had already passed The Pendleton Act of 1883 which had brought about greater attention towards the merit system of recruitment in the federal civil service. Wilson too was a strong proponent of civil service reform and said that civil service ought to be "cultured and self-sufficient enough to act with sense and vigour and yet . . . to find arbitrariness or class spirit out of the question" is an apt description in democracy. He was among the fore-runners of civil service reforms in the USA and was the first to propound the concept of a politically neutral civil service. So he could also be credited with laying an intellectual foundation of the modern personnel administration.[3]

Wilson very wisely delineated the correct direction for the development of civil service in a democracy. He observed: "Bureaucracy can exist only where the whole service of the state is removed from the common political life of the people, its chiefs as well as its rank and file. . . . The ideal for us is a civil service cultured and self-sufficient enough to act with sense and vigour, and yet so intimately connected with the popular thought, by means of elections and constant public counsel, as to find arbitrariness or class spirit quite out of the question.[4]

Comparative Public Administration

He was also founder of Comparative Public Administration. He wanted that Americans should study public administration of other countries and take good principles from them which can make administration of USA better.

Wilson asserted that transplanting of foreign systems into the American polity would not work. "But why should we not use such parts of foreign experience as we want, if they be in any way serviceable? We are in no danger of using them in a foreign way. We borrowed rice but we do not eat it with chopsticks. We borrowed our whole political language from England, but we leave the word "kings" and "lords" out of it. We can borrow the science of administration with safety and profit if only we read all fundamental differences of condition into its essential tenets. We have only to filter it through our constitution, only to put it over a slow fire of criticism and distil away its foreign gases."

"It is best on the whole to get entirely away from our own atmosphere and to be most careful in examining such systems as those of France and Germany. Seeing our own institutions through such media, we see ourselves as foreigners might see us were they to look at us without preconceptions. Of course, so long as we know only ourselves, we know nothing."

Woodrow Wilson opined that "the way of sharpening a knife should be learned even from a murderer." He warned, "Our own politics must be the touchstone of all theories . . . arrangements not only sanctioned by conclusive experience elsewhere but also congenial to American habit must be preferred without hesitation to theoretical perfection."

The major thoughts of Woodrow Wilson may be summarized as follows:

1. Administration is becoming increasingly important for the well-being of society.
2. Administration can be described as 'science'.
3. Man can learn and be imparted training in principles and techniques of administration.
4. The tasks of administration are non-partisan, detailed and managerial.
5. There are administrative processes and techniques which are universally applicable and are thus common to all modern governments.
6. Administration is a field of knowledge which can be acquired in colleges and universities.
7. Administration is separate from politics.
8. Administrative study should include the experiences of other governments.

CONCLUSION

According to Dwight Waldo, Wilson's essay which he

modestly called "semi-popular introduction to administrative studies" is the most significant work in the history of Public Administration, a source of seemingly endless stimulation and controversy. Others rightly said that he "was a pioneer and a real founder of the study of the science and the art of public administration in this country", i.e. USA.

In the words of Darnel W. Martin, "No one including White, Dimock—identified Wilson as the founder of the study of Public Administration."[5] Paul Van Riper further says, "The 1887 work had no influence whatever on the evolution of either, the theory or practice of public administration in the United States until well after the 1950's." Riper concludes, "In reality, any connection between the essay and the later development of the discipline is pure fantasy."[6]

Louis Brownlow, himself a distinguished consultant, thus praised Wilson's famous essay: ". . . . In that one essay he laid down as a programme of study which . . . Every one . . . . Who is interested in either the art or science of public administration, would do well to read again and to heed."[7] Wilson "was a pioneer and a very founder of the study of the science and the art of public administration in this country." (USA)

Woodrow Wilson essay paves the way for further study and development of Public Administration. We see today the study of Public Administration has become of cardinal importance not only in USA but throughout the world. Since Woodrow Wilson, Public Administration has expanded both in magnitude and diversity. The stability of the universe depends upon a good administrative system.

Relevance

Woodrow Wilson realized as early as 1887 that administration is of basic significance for the development of the country. He attributed the status of science to Public Administration. His influence on the study and practice of public administration multiplied.

The publication of Frank J. Goodnow's book, Politics and Administration, in 1900 supported the ideas of Wilson. The book mentioned that politics concentrates on policies or expressions of the State's will, whereas administration has to deal with the execution of these policies. As a result of these developments, public administration was made a part of the study of political science as a separate field of study. This momentum grew with the publications of books like Introduction to the Study of Public Administration in 1926 by L.D. White, Principles of Public Administration in 1927 by W.F. Willoughby, The Frontiers of Public Administration in 1936 by M.E. Dimock, Constitutional Government and Politics in 1937 by C.J. Fredrick, etc.

Simultaneously, there appeared many publications based on empirical studies in the context of industry. These publications contributed substantially to administrative theory. Some of these are—The Philosophy of Management by Oliver Sheldon (1923), Papers on the Science of Administration by L. Gulick and L. Urwick (1937), Onward Industry by J.D. Mooney and A.C. Reiley (1931), The Elements of Administration by L. Urwick (1943), General and Industrial Administration by Henry Fayol (1949), The Theory of Social and Economic Organisation by Max Weber (1947), Administrative State by Dwight Waldo (1948), etc.

Fayol observes: "The meaning which I have given to the word 'administration', and which has been generally adopted, broadens considerably the field of administrative science. It embraces not only the public service but also enterprises of every size and description, of every form and every purpose. All undertakings require planning, organisation, command, coordination and control, and in order to function properly, all must observe the same general principles. We are no longer confronted with several administrative sciences, but with one which can be applied equally well to public and to private affairs."[8]

In spite of all these developments, public administration as a discipline is still in a growing stage in both developed and developing countries. The need of the discipline has been supported by the increasing functions of the Government. Let us mention briefly the developments of governmental activities at the union level in India. The growth of public administration has been on the increase beyond expectation, especially in the developing countries like India wherein we adopted the definition of public administration as the instrument to provide services from the cradle to the grave. As a result of this approach, the Government machinery in terms of infrastructure, departments, institutions, personnel, finances, etc. increased beyond proportion.

Let us now discuss the growth and developments in the discipline of public administration:

(a) Public Administration as an independent discipline has been started by more than 30 universities at the under-graduate, post-graduate, M.Phil. and Doctoral levels. The enrolment of students is increasing at a very fast rate. Many educational institutes, including the Indira Gandhi National Open University, are imparting full-fledged M.A. courses and other degree level courses through distance education.

(b) A large number of doctoral research works have been carried out, covering vast spectrum. Under the guidance of the author alone, 25 doctoral theses have been completed in the areas of Railways, Cooperatives, Public Health, Power-Supply and Agricultural Administration. Out of these, a large number have been published. Thus, the scientific inquiry into various areas of public administration is being done on a big scale.

(c) Public administration is being studied as a part of different subjects also, like Political Science, History, Sociology, etc. at the post-graduate level.

(d) Many senior civil servants and defence personnel are pursuing M.A., M.Phil. and doctoral courses in Public Administration. This has helped the discipline to get into practical aspects of administration. The Indian Institute of Public Administration has started an M.Phil. in Social Sciences—a residential course of 9 months for senior civil servants. Such courses have tried to forge intellectual unity between theory and practice of public administration.

(e) A large number of training institutes at the Union and State levels have been set-up to impart knowledge of theory and practice of public administration to civil servants both technical and non-technical. All these institutes have been designated as 'Institutes of Public Administration'. These institutes have provided the opportunity to the faculty in public administration to lecture at these institutes and, in the process, get the opportunity to understand the practice of administration. The author was the first Professor of Haryana Institute of Public Administration, Gurgaon.

(f) Many reports of committees and commissions are available, which touch on various aspects of public administration scholarly. First and Second Administrative Reforms Commissions (ARC) reports covering the entire administration from the Union to the field levels, and major activities of the Government can well be said to be a "Treatise on Indian Public Administration."

(g) Faculty members are publishing their research works in the forms of books and articles in journals, which are adding to the theory and practice of public administration. The author has published about fifty books given in the beginning.

(h) The UN is bringing out literature on different aspects of public administration, in the context of developed and developing countries, which serves as source for training and guidance. For example, the publications of World Health Organisation on different aspects of administration of health services arc superb. The United Nations section on public administration has published a large number of reports, which are very useful documents for study, practice and research in public administration.

In view of the observations made above, we can definitely say that public administration is an established academic discipline. However, there are certain weaknesses (as are bound to be in a budding discipline), which can be taken care of by the faculty of this discipline. We present here some issues and suggest remedial actions, which can help in optimising the potentialities of this budding discipline.

Dimock says: "It does not take much thought to realize that popular government can only be made competent enough through proper administration to survive the complexities and confusion of a technological civilization."

Paul Pegeon observes: "Public administration ensures the continuance of the existing order with a minimum of effort and risk. Its fundamental aim is to carry on rather than to venture along new and untried paths. Administrators are, therefore, the stabilizers of society and guardians of tradition."

A.D. Gorewala remarks: "In a democracy there can be no successful planning without a clear, efficient and impartial administration."

Fred Riggs highlighted the importance of comparative public administration by asserting that American Public Administration must get viewed as a sub-field because public administration is global in scope. Riggs says: "The new paradigm for 'public administration' must be 'comparative', i.e. global, since the solution of the problem to which it addresses itself will require increasing communication between scholars and practitioners in all countries. The American dimension (will be viewed as) a 'sub-field' or a practical aspect of the broader subject . . ."[9]

In short, public administration is no longer treated as being exclusively concerned with the system of public administration in a single country. An understanding of Indian Public administration or any other country's system of administration is possible only when the study finds itself placed in a cross-cultural setting.

Woodrow Wilson would remain fore-runner for the development of Administration science which is the heart of development. He will always guide the posterity in understanding and implementing the science of administration. We shall always remain indebted to Woodrow Wilson in promoting an independent science of administration.

Relevance

Woodrow Wilson would always remain relevant as he is the person who first recognized the importance of Public Administration in USA and wanted experts in the Public Administration to implement the policies laid down by Government. Woodrow Wilson is rare who got the opportunity to study, and teach public administration in a university as well as practice Public Administration as Governor and President of USA, highest office in the world. His views ignited the fire among various thinkers and today the discipline of public administrations has become important both in the Universities and Government. He is known as the father of the discipline of Public Administration.

Notes and References

1. Woodrow Wilson: The State, London, D.C. Health and Company, 1899, p. 569.
2. Express Wilson's views about the science of public administration and dichotomy of politics and administration.
3. Maheshwari, S.R., Administrative Thinkers, *op. cit.*, pp. 72-74.
4. Wilson, Woodrow, "The Study of Public Administration", Annals of American Government, 1955, Washington, D.C. p. 19, (reproduced).
5. Martin, Daniel, W., 'The Fading Legacy of Woodrow Wilson', in *Public Administration Review*, Vol. 48, No. 2, March-April, 1988, pp. 632-33.
6. Van, Ruper, Paul, P., 'The American Administrative State', in *Public Administration Review*, Nov.-Dec., 1983, pp. 477-90.
7. Brownlow, Louis, "Woodrow Wilson and Public Administration", in *Public Administration Review*, Vol. XVI, No. 2, 1956, p. 81.
8. Fayol, Henri, The Administrative Theory in the State', in *Papers in the Science of Administration*, eds. L. Gullick and L. Urwick, New York, Columbia University Press, 1937.
9. Quoted in Tummala, Krishna K. (ed.), Administrative Systems Abroad, Univeristy Press of America, Washington, D.C., 1982.

11

Henry Fayol (1841-1925)

F.W. Taylor, the father of scientific management focused his attention on the problem of the shop floor, while Henry Fayol concentrated on the problems of top management. He was first to formulate and develop the universal principles of administration applicable to both government and private administration. He is the original exponent of the functional principles of organisation. That is why he has been called Fayol, the Universalist.

He is generally hailed as the founder of the classical management school—not because he was the first to investigate managerial behaviour, but because he was the first to systematize it. Fayol believed that sound management practice falls into certain patterns that can be identified and analyzed. From this basic insight, he drew up a blueprint for a cohesive doctrine of management, one that retains much of its force to this day. (see Chart 11.1)

With his faith in scientific methods, Fayol was like Taylor, his contemporary. While Taylor was basically concerned with organizational functions, however, Fayol was interested in the total organization and focused on management, which he felt had been the most neglected of business operations.[1]

CHART 11.1

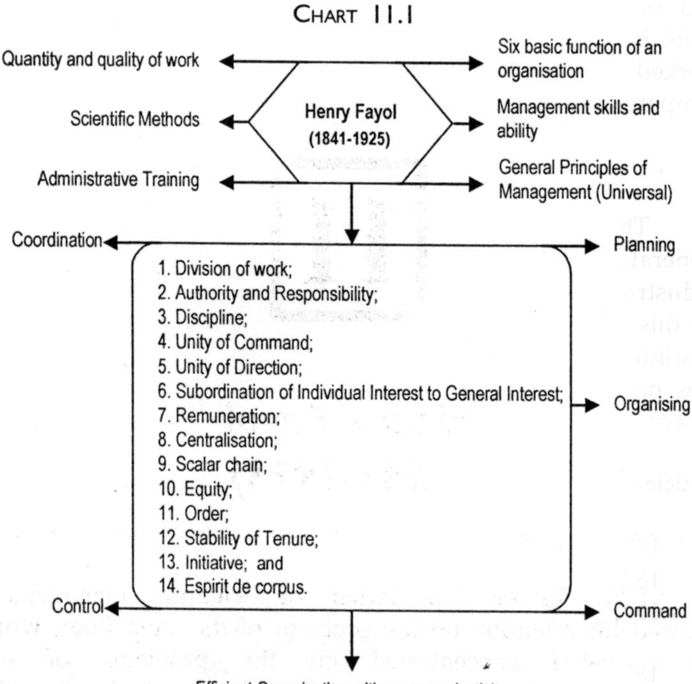

Talyor has also pointed out that managers and non-managers must have complete understanding about the quantity and quality of work to be accomplished within a given period. He indicated that the answer to this question was needed: What constitutes an honest day's work? From this answer, a basis for mutual understanding would be provided and a focal point around which to build better management and labour relations would be available. Many believe this question is as valid today as it was when Taylor suggested.[2]

FAYOL'S LIFE AND CAREER

Henri Fayol was born in 1841 in a French middle class family. After his graduation in 1860 in mining engineering, Fayol was appointed as an engineer in a mining company. (S.A. commentary-Fourchambault) in 1860. From 1860 to 1872 he worked as Junior Executive. Thereafter, he was promoted as Manager and in 1888 he was appointed Chief Executive, i.e. Managing Director, in which capacity he worked from 1888 to 1918. He remained director of the company until his death in December 1925.

MAIN WORKS

The most outstanding of his writings is his book General and Industrial Management (1916). "Administration Industrielle et General." His reputation to a large extent rests on this single short publication which is still being frequently reprinted. This book was translated in English in 1929 and was not available in the USA until 1949. In 1921, Fayol was awarded a Noble Prize for his research in Metallurgy.

Articles in the Bulletin of the Societe de l'Industrie Minerale

1874 Note on the Timbering of the Commentary pits.
1877 Planning mine galleries
1878 Note on the erection, removal and replacement of timbering.
1879 Structural changes and spontaneous combustion in coal exposed to air.
1882 Note on the elimination of night shifts in the working of large seams.
1885 Note on subsidence due to mining.

Scientific Publications on the Geology of Coal Measures

Proceedings of the Academie des Sciences:

1881 Four geological studies of the Commentary coal measure. Bulletin of the Societe de I'Industrie Minerale.
1885 Five Issues containing the full text of a geological study of the Commentary coalfield, subsequently published as a book in three volumes.
1893 Bulletin of the Societe Geologique de France
1888 Summary of the theory of deltas and history of the formation of the Commentary basin.

Publications on Administration:

1900 Paper on administration to the Congress des Mines et de la Metallurgie.

1908 "Discourse on the General Principles of Administration", Jubillee Congress of the Societe de I'Industrei Minerale'.

1916 "Administration industreille et generale'. Bulletin of the Societe del I'Industrie Minerale.

1917 "Improtance of the administrative function in the conduct of business." Paper to the Societe d'Encouragement pour I'Industrie Nationale. "A discourse on Higher Education." Paper to the Soceite des Ingeniers Civils de France.

1918 "The Reform of the Public Services." Paper to the Cercle du Commerce et de l'Industrie. "Positive administration in Industry." Article in La Technique moderne.

1919 "The Industrialization of the State." Bulletin of the Societe de I'Industrie Minerale.

1920 Lectrues on Administration at the Ecole superviure de guerre and at the Centre des hautes e tudes militarie. Published privately.

1921 Administrative Reform of the Posts and Telegraphs. Pamphlet. "The State cannot administer the Posts and Telegraphs."

1922 "The Theory of Administration in the State." Paper to the Second International Congress of Administrative Science.

1925 Administration, industrielle et generale. Republished in book form by Donod Freres. Publication of Un grand ingenieur—Henri Fayol by Henri Verney, a study celebrating the sixty-fifth anniversary of his graduation.

1929 First English translation of Administration, industrielle et generale by the International Management Institute, Geneva.

1937 English translation of "The Theory of Administration in the State", published in USA. Papers in the Science of Administration.

ADMINISTRATIVE THOUGHTS OF FAYOL

Administrative Theory: Universal

A distinction was made between administration and management in English speaking countries as the former was aimed at Government activities while management was for private business. However, Fayol draws no distinction.

To quote him[3]: "The meaning which I have given to the word administration and which has been generally adopted, broadens considerably the field of administrative Science. It embraces not only the public service but enterprises of every size and description, of every form and every purpose. All undertakings require planning, organisation, command, co-ordination and control, and in order to function properly, all must observe the same general principles. We are no longer confronted with several administrative sciences, but with one which can be applied equally well to public and to private affairs."

Let us now discuss the main features of his administrative philosophy.

Six Basic Functions of a Business Organization

Fayol found that activities of an industrial enterprises could be divided into six groups: (1) technical (production); (2) commercial (buying, selling and exchange); (3) financial (search for an optimum use of capital); (4) security (protection of property and persons); 5. Accounting; (6) managerial (planning, organization, command, co-ordination and control). Fayol observed that last of these—the managerial activity was the most important and deserved the most analysis.[4] He rightly stressed that the first five functions are to be guided and controlled by the management activity. He laid great stress on managerial action which can optimize the other five.

Management Skills and Ability

Fayol was very much conscious of the human factor in Management. He has mentioned six types of abilities which the executives must possess. In his view each managerial function must be backed by a corresponding special ability. In his own words, "To every group of activities or essential functions there exists a corresponding special ability. These could be identified: technical ability, commercial ability, financial ability, managerial ability, etc. each of these is based on a combination of qualities and of knowledge which may thus be summarized:

1. Physical qualities: health, vigour and dress.
2. Mental qualities: ability to understand and learn, judgement, mental vigour and adaptability.
3. Moral qualities: energy, firmness, willingness to accept responsibility, initiative, loyalty, tact, dignity.
4. General education: general acquaintance with matters not belonging exclusively to the function performed.
5. Special knowledge: that peculiar to the function, be it technical, commercial, financial, managerial, etc.
6. Experience: knowledge arising from the work proper. It is the recollection of lessons which one has oneself derived from things."

GENERAL PRINCIPLES OF MANAGEMENT

Fayol observed, "The real reason for the absence of management teaching is absence of theory, without theory no teaching is possible. Everyone needs some concepts of management in the home and in the affairs of state."

Fayol formulated detailed 'Principles of Management'. On the basis of his experience, he has laid down fourteen important principles for an administrator. Though he identified fourteen principles, he was quite flexible in his views: "There is nothing rigid or absolute in management affairs, it is all a question of proportion . . . therefore, principles are flexible and capable of adaptation to every need, it is a matter of knowing how to make use of them, which is a difficult art requiring intelligence, experience, decision, and proportion." The fourteen principles enunciated by Fayol are as follows:

1. Division of Work

This is well known principle of specialization. Divisions of work promotes efficiency. Fayol advocated for division of work. According to him, "Specialisation belongs to the natural order . . . The worker always on the same part, the manager concerned always with the same matters, acquire an ability, sureness, and accuracy which increase their output. Each change of work brings in its train an adaptation which reduces output . . . yet division of work has its limits which experience and a sense of proportion teach us may not be exceeded.[5] The more people specialize, the more efficiently they can perform their work."

2. Authority and Responsibility

Authority is the right to give order and the power to get obedience. Fayol wrote: "Responsibility is a corollary of authority, it is its natural consequence and essential counterpart, and wherever authority is exercised responsibility arises." Authority should be commensurate with responsibility.

3. Discipline

Foyal considered discipline, as "respect for agreements which are directed at achieving obedience, application, energy and the outward marks of respect." Authority is of two types: one that stems from the official position and the other that results from personal knowledge, character and competence. Again Fayol has given us a scintillating expression: He says: 'Discipline is what managers make it.' If managers are disciplined in their own work, the entire organisation becomes disciplined. If the manager is slack and slovenly in his work, people also become indifferent towards their work.[6] Fayol thought essential to have supervisors who are competent, impartial and social.

4. Unity of Command

The workers should receive orders only from one source. Emphasizing on the importance of unity of command, Fayol wrote, "should it (unity of command) be violated, authority is undermined. Discipline is in jeopardy, order disturbed and stability threatened. This rule seems fundamental to me and so I have given it the rank of a principle." According to him, "A body with two heads is in the social as in the animal sphere as monster and has difficulty in surviving."

5. Unity of Direction

By Unity of direction Fayol meant "one unit and one plan" for group of activities having the same objective. Fayol wrote, "unity of direction (one unit, one plan) must not be confused with the unity of command (one employee should have orders from one superior only). Unity of direction is provided for by sound organization of the body corporate, unity of command turns on the functioning of the personnel. Unity of command cannot exist without unity of direction, but does not flow from it."[7]

6. Subordination of Individual Interest to General Interest

Subordination of Individual Interest to General Interest: According to Fayol, "the interest of one employee or group of employees should not prevail over that of the concern. The superiors should set an example in firmness and goodness. The agreements between the employers and employees should be fair, and there should be constant vigilance and supervision."

7. Remuneration

This principle of Fayol states that the remuneration and methods of payment should be fair to both employees and employers, time, job piece rates, bonuses, profit sharing and other methods should be used to afford the maximum possible satisfaction to employees.

8. Centralisation

He believes in combining centralization and decentralization as per the need of the organisation. According to him, "Everything that goes to increase the importance of subordinate's role is decentralization. Everything which goes to reduce it is centralization." He wrote, "What appropriate share of initiative may be left to intermediaries depends on the personal character of the manager, on his moral worth, on the reliability of his subordinates, and also on the condition of the business . . . Seeing that both absolute and relative values of manager and employees are constantly changing, it is understandable that the degree of centralization or decentralization may itself vary constantly.[8]

9. Scaler Chain

Fayol thinks of this as a "chain of superiors" ranging from the ultimate authority to the lowest ranks. This chain describes the flow of authority. It should not be departed from needlessly. The line of authority is the route followed—via every link in the chain—by all communications which start from or go to the ultimate authority. However, in large organizations following this path often is too lengthy. An alternative "gang plank" is suggested by Fayol.

Fayol, however, made one exception. With the prior consent of their respective bosses, two employees on different chains can enter into direct contact across 'the gang plank', reach a decision and inform their bosses of the decision. "The use of the gang plank is simple, swift, sure." Henri Fayol however, expresses, his fear about the limited usefulness of gang plank in public administration than in private administration. This is because the aim of an organization is vague and unclear in government. Thus, "each section tends to regard itself as its own end, neglects its relationship with other sections, and becomes isolated, cloistered, aware only of the line of authority. This is another reason that the top level authority does not encourage its own direct subordinates to invoke the 'gangplank' themselves.[9]

10. Order

Fayol said that there should be a place for everything and everyone. At the same time everything and everyone should be in their place. This boils down to: "Right man in the right place." He believed that this kind of order "demands precise knowledge of the human requirements and resources of the concern and a constant balance between these requirements and resources. This balance becomes more difficult, the bigger the business.

11. Equity

According to Foyal, equity results from the combination of kindliness and justice. He felt that managers should strive to instill a sense of equity throughout at all levels of organization to evoke loyalty and devotion from employees. He said: 'Desire for equity and equality of treatment are aspirations to be taken into account in dealing with employees'.

12. Stability of Tenure of Personnel

Fayol points out that instability of tenure constitutes the cause and effect of bad management. Efficiency can be promoted by a stable workforce. He opines that often "a mediocre manager who stays infinitely is preferable to outstanding managers who merely come and go." Government of India is considering the stability of Tenure of All India Services to promote efficiency.

13. Initiative

This principle is conceived of as the thinking out and execution of a plan. Fayol said that "it is one of the keenest satisfactions for an intelligent man to experience and one of the most powerful stimulants of human endeavour." He exhorts managers to "sacrifice personal vanity" in order to permit subordinates to exercise it. In this way, they will feel satisfied and develop a feeling of belongingness.

14. Espirits de Corps

Fayol decried the abuses of written communication and "divide and rule" policy. The communication as far as possible should be direct and oral. The manager should encourage espirit de corps and cohesiveness among his subordinates. The erring employees should be set right by oral directions and not by demanding written explanations. Written explanations complicate the matters.

ELEMENTS OF MANAGEMENT

Fayol indicated that all management activity is made up of five elements: planning, organizing, commanding, coordinating and controlling. He regarded these elements of management as its functions. They are applicable not only to business but also to political, religious, military, philanthropic and other undertakings. They are briefly discussed as under:

(a) Planning

It is to forecast the future. He says that plan of action is "the result envisaged, the line of action to be followed, the stages to go through and methods to use. It is a kind of future picture wherein proximate events are outlined. He summed up "the plan of action facilitates the utilization of the firm's resources and the choice of best methods to use for attaining the objective. It suppresses or reduces hesitancy, false steps, unwarranted changes of course and helps to improve personnel. It is a precious managerial instrument."[10]

(b) Organising

Fayol was also the originator of the organizations chart. He stressed the need for a clear definition of roles, duties and responsibilities should be precisely defined.

Fayol classifies these activities into two categories: (1) the material organisation, and (2) the human organisation. The latter includes both personnel leadership and organisation structure.

Fayol pointed out that the organizer (manager) had sixteen managerial duties to perform:

1. Ensure that the plan is judiciously prepared and strictly carried out.
2. See that the human and material organization is consistent with the objective, resources and requirements of the concern.
3. Set-up a single, competent and energetic guiding authority.
4. Harmonize activities and co-ordinate efforts.
5. Formulate clear, distinct, precise decisions.
6. Arrange for efficient selection.
7. Define duties clearly.
8. Encourage a liking for initiative and responsibility.

9. Have a fair and suitable compensation for services rendered.
10. Make use of sanctions against faults and errors.
11. See to the maintenance of discipline.
12. Ensure that individual interests are subordinated to the general interest.
13. Pay special attention to unity of command.
14. Supervise both material and human order.
15. Have everything under control.
16. Fight against excess of regulations, red tape and paper control.

(c) Command

Fayol says that for every manager, the object of command is to get the optimum return from all employees of his unit in the interest of the whole concern. He adds that the manager who has to command should:

1. Have a thorough knowledge of his personnel.
2. Eliminate the incompetent.
3. Be well-versed in the agreements binding the business and its employees.
4. Set a good example.
5. Conduct periodic audits of the organization and use summarized charts to further this.
6. Bring together his chief assistants by means of conferences at which unity of direction and focusing of effort are provided for.
7. Not get engrossed in details.
8. Aim at making unity, energy, initiative and loyalty prevail among personnel.

(d) Co-ordination

Fayol had stressed the need for unity of command and control in organizations. Co-ordination is of cardinal importance in the running of organization. Co-ordination across the organisation should be affected by periodic meetings of departmental heads. All discussions in these conferences should be focused on specific problems such as the attainment of plan targets.

Mooney observed, "The supreme coordinating authority must rest somewhere and in some form in every organization. . . . It is equally essential to the very idea and concept of organization that there must be a process, formal in character, through which this coordinating authority operates from the top throughout the entire structure of the organized body.

It consists of working together and 'harmonizing' all activity and efforts so as to facilitate the working of the organisation. Essentially, the objective of coordination is to ensure that one department's efforts are coincident with the efforts of other departments, and keeping all activities in perspective with regard to the overall aims of the organisation.[11]

(e) Control

Its objective is to obtain conformity with the plan adopted, the instructions issued and principles established. In the process, weaknesses and errors have to be rectified and their recurrence prevented. For control to be effective it must be done within a reasonable time and be followed up by sanctions. He uses the term control in the wider French sense of watch, monitor, check, audit and obtain feedback.

Henry Fayol says that "control consists in verifying whether everything occurs in conformity with the plans adopted, the instructions issued and principles established. It has for its object to point out weaknesses and errors in order to rectify them and prevent recurrence."

NEED OF ADMINISTRATIVE TRAINING

Fayol wanted the Compulsory teaching administrators including technical people

To quote Fayol: Everyone needs some concepts of administration; in the home, in affairs of the State, the need for administrative ability is in proportion to the importance of the undertaking and for individual people the need is everywhere greater in accordance with the position occupied. Hence, there should be some generalized teaching of administration: elementary in the primary schools, somewhat wider in the post-primary schools, and quite advanced in higher educational establishments.

Administration has universal application as it applies to all forms of group activity.

He wrote: 'There is no one doctrine of management for business and another for affairs of State; management is universal. Principles and general rules which hold good for business hold good for the State too, and the reverse applies.'

Emphasis on Human Side

Fayol also stressed human side and said that there is no limit to the number of principles of administration. Every administrative rule or device which strengthens the human part of an organisation or facilitates its working takes its place among the principles for so long as experience proves it to be worthy of this important position.

Claude S. George says: "He opened the door to the development of the functional school of thought and brought clarity into the muddled thinking on the nature of top management."

In the words of Peterson, they are 'modes of action'. These principles have been developed in several areas of management. Advocates of classical theory of management relied heavily on these principles, treating them as prescriptive fundamental truths with universal validity and applicability for different situations. These principles are applicable to all types of organizations such as economic, non-economic, social, religious and political and provide guidance to managers working at different levels.

Harwood F. Merril, who edited an excellent reader on the subject entitled Classics in Management (1960) called Fayol "the Francis Bacon of management literature."

Professor Megginson states that there exists a systematic body of knowledge that constitutes the core principles of management that are true in all managerial situations; these principles are universally applicable in business, government, religious, social or any other type of organization. They are relevant at all levels of management, from foreman to executives.

D.S. Pugh mentioning the contributions of Fayol, thus,

sums up: "Fayol's pride of place in this field is due not so much to his principles of how to manage, enduring though these are, as to his definition of what management is. He is the earliest known proponent of a theoretical analysis of managerial activities—an analysis which has withstood almost a half century of critical discussion. There can have been few writers since who have not been influenced by it, and his five elements have provided a system of concepts with which managers may clarify their thinking about what it is they have to do."

Daniel Wren Writes: "His notion of an administrative theory applicable to all types of organized undertaking was an important milestone in the history of management." According to Alber Lepawsky, "The twentieth century has yet to produce as balanced a combination of able practitioners and keen student of administration as Henry Fayol."

Fayol was also careful to state that his principles should not be considered as rigid rules. He observes:

There is nothing . . . absolute in management affairs. Seldom do we have to apply the same principles twice as in identical conditions; allowance must be made for different changing circumstances.[12]

E.F.L. Brech makes the following significant observations on Henri Fayol: The importance of Fayol's contribution lay in two features. The first was his systematic analysis of the process of management; the second, his firm advocacy of the principle that management can, and should be taught. Both were revolutionary lines of thought in 1908, and still little accepted even in 1925.

It may be noted that these principles of management are not absolute, due to the nature of discipline to which they belong, they form a theoretical body of management knowledge which call upon the managers to gather the required know-how and skills for their efficient application. These principles are of crucial importance for managers in understanding problems and conditioning their styles and approaches in decision-making and problem-solving. In the words of Terry: "They are capsules of selected management wisdom to be used carefully and discretely."

The scientific management school has contributed tremendous management knowledge to us. Its essence is the development of an inquiring mind with the resultant intelligent searching for more knowledge, more facts, more relationships. Historically, it is associated with economic considerations such as cost, time use, and efficiency, but the method it uses is basic in the research of other disciplines such as chemistry, physics, psychology, and sociology. Hence, the scientific method is found in more than the scientific management school. Advocates of scientific management firmly believe better management is possible, and they seek to find it by using the scientific method. Yet they realize the best management is never permanently attained because continuous new knowledge paves the way for constant improvement. Scientific management enjoys wide use but is by no means universal.

Relevance

Henry Fayol will remain relevant for all times to come. The principles and elements listed by Fayol based on wide research are applicable to all areas whether health, education, industry, business, etc. Henry Fayol cautioned that these principles and elements can be adjusted to suit the given situation. Administration is of great significance to promote efficiency and effectiveness. Let me illustrate with disaster management. If there is an earthquake of the same magnitude in USA, Japan and India, the losses would be negligible in USA and Japan while India would suffer huge losses. Why? The answer is simple that is poor administration in India.

Recently the Government of India has taken a decision to suitably adapt Incident Command System[13] (ICS) as per requirements of India to handle disaster management efficiently in collaboration with USAID in a project "Disaster Management Support Programme."

In India, most of our health institutions, educational institutions, social welfare, etc. are not performing well because the persons who are heading these organizations lack understanding of elements and principles of public administration. Effort has been made by Union and State

Government to provide training to them to make them excellent technical administrators but due to lack of seriousness on the part of trainees and trainers, the condition is not improving. The only answer to come out of the chaos in technical areas for non delivery of services is to give emphasis on serious training and successor planning. For example, if a Vice-Chancellor is appointed, he is appointed a week earlier leading to chaos as he is asked to perform the duties with which he has no acquaintance. What is the result? Failure of Higher Education.[14]

Relevance of Henry Fayol would increase in 21st century as the administration is going to be most important to handle affairs in the context of globalization, liberalization and privatization. China has made a great progress and is in the process of becoming a super-power. The credit for it goes to their central, provincial, city and village party schools where training in elements and principles of administration are imparted.

Management science has made the decision-making process explicit. It provides the factual data relating to the past, on the basis of which events to take place in the future are predicted and the policies formulated accordingly. Occasions arise when an executive finds that his decisions need modifications and correction. Management science helps the executives to make the changes speedily and economically.

Scientific management has effected a whole range of improvements in output and introduced new ways and means of minimizing wastes, thus contributing directly to the well-being and prosperity of an organization. In the areas of coordination, and control too, management science has led a great impact. The rationalized systems for data collection, flow of information, decision-making and implementation are proving of great help in the managerial function of control. Standardized procedures, budgets, performance norms and instant reporting systems—all these ensure more effective co-ordination.

The new trends in management have brought about rapid and dynamic changes in the level of economic activity—changes in personnel and work situations, changes in production and distribution. These changes are indeed a challenge to the managers who have to take stock of the relevant economic situations, business ethics and morals, public relations and devise new ways of functioning to meet the new requirements.

Henry Fayol's principles of management are basic in MBA teaching, M.A. Public Administration. Without these, the courses would lack luster. Administrators and Managers are always busy in dealing with these principles as only through these principles, administration and management can achieve results.

Thus, Fayol would always remain alive through his Administrative and Management thoughts and his influence would increase as the time passes.

Co-ordination: Within and among various agencies/ departments of the state/central governments is, of course, paramount. No doubt, this is being done. But let us remember that in the confusion and chaos which follows such devastation, it is not unknown for such coordination to collapse, particularly at the district level. This sometimes can even lead to an erosion of the hierarchal structure which is most effective for decision-making under such disaster conditions.

Based upon past experiences in dealing with disasters, we mention a number of problems and weaknesses that are visible.

(a) Professional teams with training are not provided to authorities at all levels.
(b) Specific teams with specialized tasks are not ready, rather teams carry out all types of activities causing confusion.
(c) Inadequate Resource Inventory.
(d) Action takes place only after the disaster as no exercise of professional teams is done like military operations.
(e) Lack of effective communication in Net-work.
(f) Absence of unity of command and wide span of control.
(g) Lack of designated facilities.
(h) No financial discipline

INCIDENT COMMAND SYSTEM (ICS) (SEE CHART 11.2)

Evolution

Incident Command System (ICS) was developed in early 1970s in the United States in response to a series of major wild land fires in southern California. As a response, several agencies collaborated to form the (FIRESCOPE) Firefighting Resources of California Organized for Potential Emergencies to address these difficulties and this interagency effort resulted in the development of ICS model of management.

CHART 11.2

Incident Command System (Major Organization Functions)

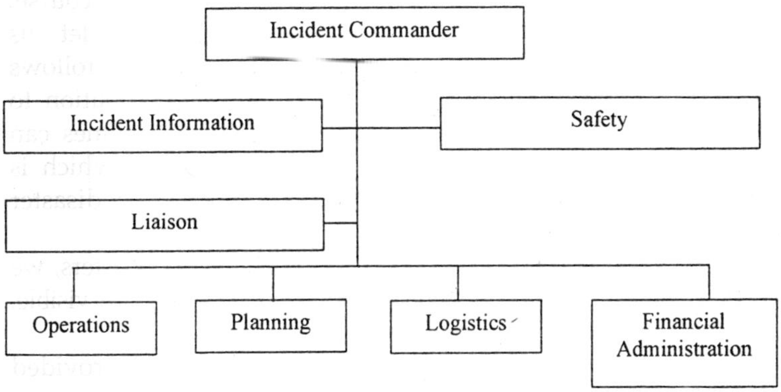

Source: Centre for Disaster Management, LBSNAA, Mussoire, Introductory Workshop and brain Storming at Colombo, Sri Lanka, 11-12 January, 2006, p. 20.

The Incident Command System (ICS) is an on-scene, all-risk, flexible modular system adaptable to any scale of natural as well as man-made emergency/incidents. The ICS seeks to strengthen the existing disaster response management system by ensuring that the designated controlling/responsible authorities at different levels are backed by trained Incident Command Teams (ICTs), whose members have been trained in the different facets of emergency/disaster response management. The ICS will not put in place any new hierarchy or supplant the existing system, but will only reinforce it. The Members of the ICT will be jointly trained for development as a team. When an ICT is deployed for an incident, all concerned agencies of the Government will respond as per the assessment of the Team. This system therefore enables proper co-ordination amongst the different agencies of the Government. The five Command functions in the Incident Command System are as follows[15]: (See Chart 11.3)

CHART 11.3

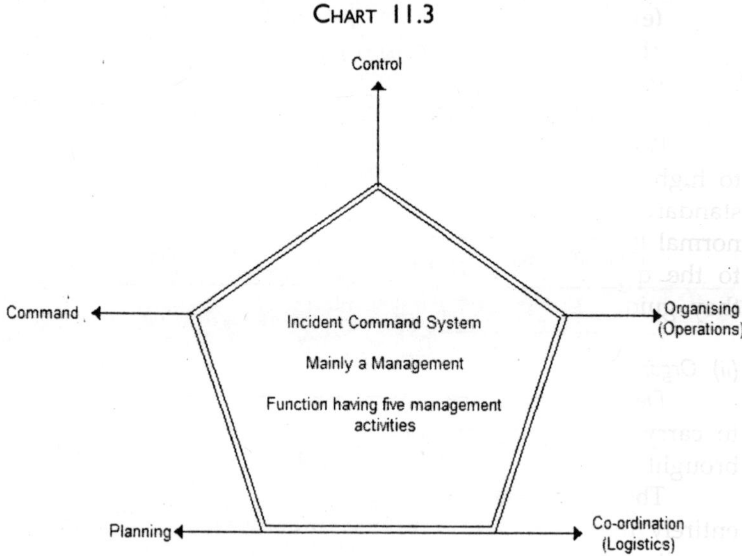

(i) Incident Command

Has overall responsibility of the incident. Determines objectives and established priorities based on the nature of the incident, available resources and agency policy. Under this, the commander has the main responsibility to define objectives, prioritise them and take overall responsibility. The Incident commander must posses emotional intelligence. Emotional intelligence is concerned with achieving one's goals through the ability to manage one's own feelings and emotions, to be sensitive to, and influence other key people, and to balance one's motives and drives with conscientious and ethical behaviours. The following are the characteristics of EI:

(a) Inter-personal sensitivity covering competencies like listening and sensitivity.
(b) Motivating, including impact and energy.
(c) Emotional Resilence.
(d) Influence and Adaptability covering both influencing and negotiating ability and being adaptable in various types of situations and cultures.
(e) Decisiveness and assertiveness.
(f) Integrity.
(g) Leadership including motivating other people.

Peter Drucker defined it as the lifting of man's visions to higher sights, the raising of man's performance to higher standard, the building of man's personality beyond its normal limitations. According to Chester I. Bernard, "It refers to the quality of the behaviour of the individuals whereby they guide people on their activities in organized efforts."

(ii) Organising

Develops tactical organization and directs all resources to carry out the Incident Action Plan. Likert has beautifully brought forth this point. To quote him:

The performance and output of any enterprise depend entirely upon the quality of the human organization and its capacity to function as a tightly knot, highly motivated, technically competent entity, i.e. as a highly effective interaction-influence system. High productivity, high quality products, high earnings, and successful use of research and development are not accomplished by impersonal equipment or computers. These goals are achieved by human beings. Successful organizations are those making the best use of competent personnel to perform efficiently all the tasks required by the enterprises.

(iii) Planning

Develops the Incident Action Plan to accomplish the

objectives. Collects and evaluates information, and maintain status of assigned resources. Cyril, L. Hudson has given a comprehensive definition of planning in the following terms:

"To plan is to produce a scheme for future action, to bring about specified results, at specified cost, in a specified period of time. It is a deliberate attempt to influences, exploit, bring about, and control the nature, direction, extent, speed and effects of change. It may even attempt deliberately to create change. It is a carefully controlled and co-ordinated activity. Plan implementation is an integral part of planning process. It requires responsibility for translating the objectives of plan into action. However, looking from the broader point of view, the plan implementation requires cooperation, coordination and commitment at all levels of the implementing machinery, starting with the ministries at the union and State levels, through to various non-secretariat organizations in the field at district, block or village level. It is at the implementation level that the difficulties creep in, resulting into the lower output. Implementation must be watched properly and timely action should be taken to improve administrative, technical, financial or personnel inadequacies. Planning and implementation are intimately connected. To quote Mr. Goetz: "Plans alone cannot make an enterprise successful. Action is required; the enterprise must operate. Plans can, however, focus action on purposes. They can forecast which actions will tend towards the ultimate objective . . . which tend away, which will likely offset one another, and which are merely irrelevant. Managerial Planning seeks to achieve a consistent and coordinated structure of operations focussed on desired ends. Without plans, action must become merely random activity, producing nothing but chaos."

A common tautology that permeates the field of Planning is that implementation is one of the most crucial aspects of any planning exercise. Within the development context, where resources of all types are generally scarce successful implementation can represent the most critical of all issues in the process of planning, growth and development.

Experience with the Five Year Plans has demonstrated

that from the very start of the planning process, implementation is generally slow, even half-hearted, and there is a wide gap between the results achieved and the planned targets. Many of the schemes have consequently to be carried over to the next plan. It is a happy sign that the Government of India is keen to lay greater stress on implementation and that the highest priority is being given in the Plans to "operationalize the Plan."

(iv) Logistics and Co-ordination

Provides resources and all other services needed to support the organization. Resources are an essential requirement to take immediate action for disaster management. Without Logistics, commander and his staff cannot function. The exercise of the availability and need of resources is an essential exercise. In emergency situation, we must know before hand where the resources are stored or from where these can be purchased.

We must ensure that all the logistics are available and are in functionsal form. We have failed in logistics in previous disasters causing great loss to people and property.

(v) Finance/Administration and Control

Monitors costs related to the incident, provides accounting, procurement, time recording, cost analysis and overall fiscal guidance. Administration is at the core of all human affairs. Its principal aspects are the formulation of policy and then its implementation for the attainment of the stated objectives in an optimum manner. It is the systematic ordering of affairs and the calculated use of resources aimed at making the desired things happen and forestalling everything to the contrary. According to Robert McNamara, former President of the World Bank, "Management is in the end, the most creative of all the arts—for its medium is human talent itself."[16]

Financial Administration is a branch of Public Administration, which can help an organization in the 'management' of financial resources, through the application of well thought out principles, practices and rationalized techniques of raising, allocating and utilizing financial resources for the fulfilment of organizational objectives, systematically and scientifically. It may be defined as the art and science of policy-making, planning, decision-making, coordination, control of the processes of securing adequate resources, ensuring their safe custody, genuine allocations among different areas of socio-economic development, effective utilization and avoiding the pilferage of resources and duplication of efforts to attain the objectives of the disaster management in Government. In short, we may define financial administration as the technique of maximizing financial output and the optimization of financial resources.

According to Prof. M.J.K. Thavraj: "Finance is the lifeblood of all magnetized socio-economic formations ranging from nuclear families to complex, national and international organizations. Financial administration relates to the system, which generates, regulates and distributes the monetary resources needed for the sustenance and growth of an organization. In this respect, financial administration is similar to the circulatory system in complex living organisms."[17]

Financial administration is a systematized and specialized branch of knowledge of the techniques, which can help in administering financial resources for optimum performance. It is becoming more and more complex day-by-day. Until and unless we understand all the implications of such an administrations, we may not be able to reap the potential benefits of the financial resources employed in an organization like ICS. A large number of training institutes have sprung up in all the countries at all levels to impart training in financial administration. Thus, financial administration is a definite art, which can be learnt and practiced to produce pre-designed output. It is an art as it can help to direct and guide the administrators in the formulation and implementation of financial policies of an organization efficiently and systematically.

In his preface, Shri Rajiv Raj and Mishra, IAS to Introductory Workshop and Brainstorming Consultation at Colombo, Sri Lanka, observed that Incident Command System is essentially a management system that seeks to organize various emergency functions in a single framework. The significance of this framework lies in its provision for smooth coordination between different management components. The approach in ICS is to appreciate that emergency functions such as rescue, relief, logistics, information and communication, etc. are specialized task which differ substantially in content from routine administrative jobs and therefore require adequate training beforehead. Further all such functions need to be integrated in a management framework so that such response does not suffer from disjointed efforts and affect overall performance.[18]

Sh. S.S.L. Hettiarachchi in an Introductory Workshop and Brainstorming consultation at Colombo, observes that the Incident Command System (ICS) by definition as a Standardized Emergency Management System designed to allow users to adopt an integrated organizational structure equal to the complexity and demands of any emergency, irrespective of its type and magnitude. We recognize the fact that all emergencies are highly chaotic, very dynamic in character and on many occasions associated with an unparalleled degree of surprise. The ICS by its very functional mechanism provides accurate information, high degree of accountability, and a platform for planning, cost effective operations and logistical support for any emergency.[19]

David Summer from US Department of Agricultural, Forest Service underlines the important features of ICS in the above mentioned workshop.

- Clear objectives and priorities
- Defined operational objectives and organization
- Incident Action Plan
- Common Terminology
- Common communications
- Uniform Position Descriptions
  - o Roles and responsibilities defined
  - o Clear lines of authority, chain of command and reporting requirements
- Standardized personnel qualifications and training—national coordinating group.[20]

Henry Fayol is one of the very few thinkers who based upon his research developed the principles of management and elements of administration which have influenced all individuals and organizations. These are taught in all the universities, colleges, training institutions. He showed that following these principles we can increase our productivity. We shall always remain indebted to him.

"Management principles are flexible and capable of adaptation of every need: it is a matter of knowing how to make use of them, which is a difficult art requiring intelligence, experience, decision and proportion. Compounded to tact and experience, proportion is one of the foremost attributes of the manager." Elsewhere he wrote: "There is nothing rigid or absolute in managerial matters; everything is a question of degree."[21]

Daniel Wren writes: "His notion of an administrative theory applicable to all types of organized undertaking was an important milestone in the history of management." According to Alber Lepawsky, "The twentieth century has yet to produce as balanced a combination of able practitioners and keen student of administration as Henry Fayol."

Notes and References

1. James, A.F., Stoner *et al.* Management, (Sixth Edition), 1998, New Delhi, Prentice Hall of India, pp. 35-37.
2. Terry and Franklin, Principles of Management, Delhi, A.I.T.B.S., 2003, p. 23.
3. Henry Fayol, The Administrative theory in the State, in papers in the Science of Administration eds. L. Gulick and L. Urwick, New York, Columbia University Press, 1937.
4. Henry Fayol, General and Industrial Management, (London: Sir Issac Pittman's and Sons, 1949, Trans. by Stores) p. 3.
5. *Ibid., op. cit.,* 22.
6. C. North Cote Parkinson, *et. al.,* Great Ideas in Management, p. 50.
7. General and Industrial Management, *op. cit.,* p. 69.
8. *Ibid.,* p. 33.
9. Shriram Maheshwari, "Administrative Thinkers, Macmillan, Delhi, 2003, pp. 140-41.
10. *Ibid.,* p. 50.
11. Fayol, *Ibid.,* pp. 97-98.
12. Fayol, *op. cit.,* 19.

13. Based on the Elements of Administration propounded by Henry Fayol.
14. Prof. Nirmal Singh, "Principles of Management", Deep & Deep Publishers, 2002, pp. 41-42.
15. GOI, Ministry of Home Affairs, LBSNAA, Source Book on "District Disaster Management", p. 85.
16. Speech of Millsap's College, Jackson, Mississippi, February 24, 1960.
17. MJK Thavraj, Financial Management of Government, New Delhi, Sultan Chand, 1978, p. 1.
18. Centre for Disaster Management, LBSNAA, Mussoire, Introductory Workshop and Brainstorming at Colombo, Sri Lanka, 11-12 January, 2006, Preface.
19. Introductory Workshop and Brainstorming Consultation at Colombo, Sri Lanka, 11-12 Jan. 2006.
20. David Sumer, *Ibid.*, p. 19.
21. Henry Fayol, *op. cit.*, p. 19.

12

Federick Winslow Taylor (1856-1915)

The work of Taylor (scientific management) is in terms of techniques and takes the point of view of the Engineer and prescribes procedures for the efficient organization and conduct of routine work. Taylor has indicated mainly three things: (1) Time and methods study should be used to find one best way of performing a job, (2) That workers should be enabled to perform the job in the best way and at a good place by providing him an incentive, and (3) Specialized experts (Financial foreman) should be used to establish the various conditions surrounding the workers' task, methods, machine, speed, task priorities, etc. Since this kind of work encompasses primarily physical variables this theory has been referred by some as physiological organization theory.

By the end of the nineteenth century the industrial revolution was almost more than a century old. The scientific and technological advancement had brought about revolutionary changes not only in the field of industry but also in the field of transportation and commerce. It changed the lives of people. However, there was no parallel revolution in management and administration to take advantage of industrial revolution.

CHART 12.1

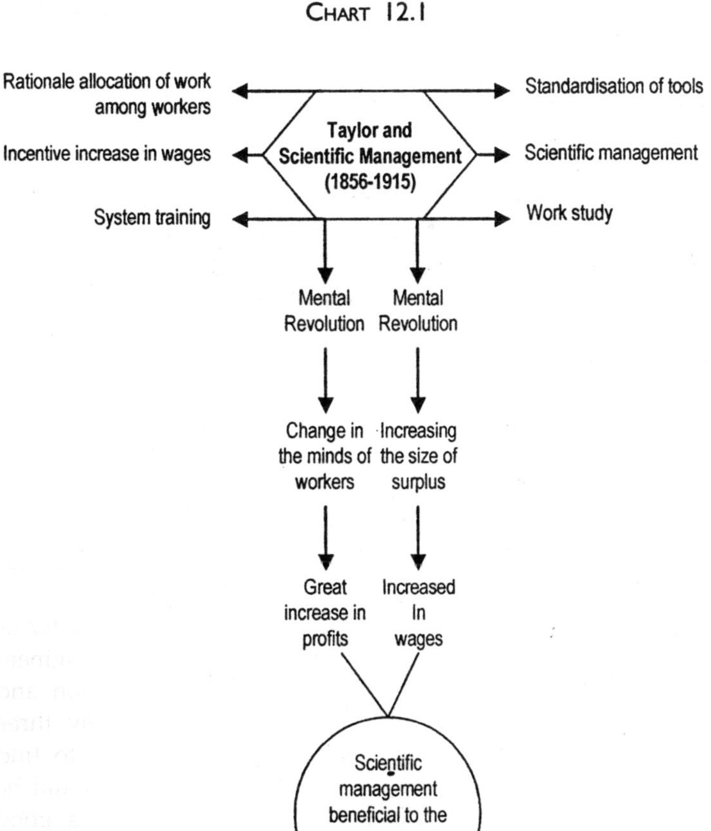

Managerial inefficiency was rampant in these organizations, which threatened the existence of big organizations. The industrialists took hold of the scientific knowledge for increasing efficiency. The need was to find ways and means to get work out of workers and tools used for production and raise productivity.

In the words of Anthony Tillete: During that period, labour was the main source of efficiency, the workshop was the main unit, work measurement was the major tool for improvement."

During his career spanning a period of 26 years Taylor conducted a series of experiments in three companies: (i) Midvale Steel, (ii) Simonds Rolling Machine, and (iii) Bethlehem Steel

Taylor began his career in the 1870s as an apprentice in a small machinery-making shop in Philadelphia where he was employed by the Midvale Steel Company from 1878 to 1889 beginning as a labourer and then progressing to clerk, machinist, gang boss, foreman, chief draftsman and finally chief engineer. Taylor's God was efficiency and highest possible productivity. He worked as consulting engineer after 1889. His one of the best assignments was with the Bethlehem Steel Company between 1889 and 1901. Taylor had developed various new processes of manufacturing, getting about a hundred patents. He left the practice in 1901 and until his death in 1915, he devoted all of his time to the cause of "scientific management." Taylor is called the Father of Scientific Management Approach.

Frederick Winslow Taylor was born in a German town, Pennsylavania on March 20, 1856 in a cultured and well to do family. He received his education in France and Germany and attended Philips Exeter Academy. Although he passed the Harvard entrance examinations with 'honours', he could not continue his academic pursuits because of impaired eyesight owing to too much study by kerosene light.

Books

- 1903 Shop Management.
- 1905 Concrete: Plain and Reinforced (with S.F. Thompson).
- 1911 Principles and Methods of Scientific Management.
- 1912 Concrete Costs (with S.F. Thompson).
- 1913 Scientific Management.

Papers

- 1895 "A Piece Rate System." Trans. ASME, Vol. 16, pp. 56-903.

1903 "Shop Management", Trans. ASME, Vol. 24, pp. 1337-1480.

1905 "On the Art of Cutting Metals", Trans. ASME, Vol. 28, pp. 31-35.

1911 "The Gospel of Efficiency", Article in the American Magazine, Vols. 71 & 72.

TAYLOR'S MANAGEMENT THOUGHT

Philosophy of Scientific Management

Taylor defined Management as knowing exactly what you want men to do and then seeing that they do it in the best and cheapest way. The relations between employers and men form without question the most important part of this art.[1]

In the words of Taylor, "The changes from the rule of thumb management to scientific management involves, however not only a study of what is the proper speed for doing the work and a remodeling of the tools and the implements in the shop, but also a complete change in the mental attitude of all men in the shop towards their work and towards their employers."[2]

Taylor further pointed out that "It is only through enforced standardization of methods, enforced adoption of the best implements and working conditions and reinforced co-operation—that this faster work can be assumed. And the duty of enforcing the adoption of standards and of enforcing this co-operation rests with the management alone. The management must also recognize the broad fact that the workmen will not submit to this more rigid, standardization and will not work extra hard, unless they receive extra pay for doing it."[3]

He viewed no conflict between workers and management. High payment to workers was in the interest of employers as they were compensated by high productivity.

Taylor stated: Scientific management has for its very foundation the firm conviction that the true interests of the two are one and the same; that prosperity for the employer cannot exist through a long-term of years unless it is accompanied by prosperity for the employee, and *vice versa;*

and that it is impossible to give the worker what he most wants—high wages—and the employer what he wants—a low labour cost—for his manufacturers.[4]

Talyor's First paper on "A Piece Rate System" was considered as the outstanding contribution to the principles of wage payment. He proposed a new system consisting of three parts: (a) observation and analysis of work through time study to set the 'rate' or standard, (b) a differential 'rate' system of piece work, and (c) paying men and not 'positions'. In his second paper on "Shop Management" he discussed at length workshop organization and management.

He focused attention in this paper in "Shop Management" to his philosophy of management. Frederick Taylor and the scientific management school studied the problem of inefficient production by designing reward systems to encourage high performance by managers and workers. Taylor and his followers believed that workers, in general, were lazy, aimless, and mercenary. The challenge was to get them to the factory by paying decent wages and simplifying tasks. Taylor constructed output controls and designed an incentive system of bonuses to be paid to workers who beat their quotas. Management's major task was to closely supervise workers and to ensure that they met production quotas and adhered to company policies and rules. "In short, the underlying motivational assumption of the traditional model was that, for a price, workers would tolerate the routinized, highly fractionated jobs of the factory.[5]

Frederick Winslow Taylor was among the first of what historians today call the classical management writers; he developed a set of principles that became known as scientific management. Taylor's basic theme was that managers should study work scientifically to identify the "one best way" to get the job done. His framework for scientific management was based on four principles:

1. *The "one best way"*: Management, through observation and "the deliberate gathering . . . of all the great mass of traditional knowledge, which in the past has been in the heads of the

workmen," finds the "one best way" for performing each job.

2. *Scientific selection of personnel*: This principle requires "the scientific selection and then the progressive development of the workmen." Management must uncover each worker's limitation, find his or her "possibility for development," and give each worker the required training.
3. *Financial incentives*: Taylor knew that putting the right worker on the right job would not by itself ensure high productivity. Some plan for motivating workers to do their best and to comply with their supervisors' instructions was also required. Taylor proposed a system of financial incentives, in which each worker was paid in direct proportion to how much he or she produced, instead of according to a basic hourly wage.
4. *Functional foremanship*: Taylor called for a division of work between manager and worker such that managers did all planning, preparing, and inspecting, and the workers did the actual work. Specialized experts, or functional foremen, would be responsible for specific aspects of a task, such as choosing the best machine speed, determining job priorities, and inspecting the work. The worker was to take orders from each of these foremen, depending on what part of the task was concerned.

Taylor further says that "Scientific management fundamentally consists of certain broad general principles, a certain philosophy, which can be applied in many ways, and a description what any one man or men may believe to be the best mechanism for applying. These general principles should, in no way, be confused with the principle themselves."[6]

Taylor applied work study and standardization of tools as well as training to achieve efficiency.

Work Study

Work Study aims at the elimination of inefficiency in the functioning of management and administration through ensuring optimum utilization of resources—men, money and material. It is probably the most well known and widely published analytical technique used in works management. Lord Mountbatten, in a message to the Defence Institute of Work Study, said, "Work Study is a really effective service in management. It will pay dividends which are handsome, speedy and beyond expectations. But, it must have, for its success, the unstinted support of management." Work study is a generic term for those techniques, particularly method study and work measurement, which are used in the examination of human work in all its contexts, and which leads systematically to the investigation of all the factors which affect the efficiency and economy of the situation being reviewed in order to effect improvement."[7]

Taylor based his management system on production line time studies. Instead of relying on traditional work methods, he analysed and timed steel worker's movements on a series of jobs. Using times study as his base, he broke each job down into its components and designed the quickest and best methods of performing each component. In this way he established how much workers should be able to do with the equipment and materials at hand. He also encouraged employers to pay more productive workers at a higher rate than others, using a "scientifically correct" rate that would benefit both company and worker. Thus, workers were urged to surpass their previous performance standards to get more pay. Taylor called his plan the differential rate system.

Standardisation of tools—Standardisation of tools for the jobs to be done was done by Taylor which improved efficiency.

SELECTION AND TRAINING OF WORKERS

Mental Revolution

In order to make the principles of scientific management successful, it is the first and foremost important task to bring about change in minds of workers and management to which Taylor called "Mental Revolution"

To quote in Taylor's own words:

"Scientific management is not any efficiency device, not a device of any kind for securing, efficiency; nor is it any bunch or group of efficiency devices. It is not new system of figuring costs; it is not a new scheme of paying men; it is not a piecework system; it is not a bonus system; it is not premium system; it is not scheme for paying men; it is not holding a stop watch on a man and writing things down about him; it is not time study; it is not motion study nor an analysis of the movements of men; it is not the printing and ruling and unloading of a ton or two of blanks on a set of men and saying, "Here's your system; go use it."

The great mental revolution that takes place in the mental attitude of the two parties under scientific management is that both sides take their eyes off the division of the surplus as the all-important matter and together turn their attention towards increasing the size of the surplus until this surplus becomes so large that it is unnecessary to quarrel over how it should be divided. They come to see that when they stop pulling against one another, and instead, both turn and push shoulder to shoulder in the same direction, the size of the surplus created by their joint efforts is truly astounding. They both realize that whey they substitute friendly cooperation, mutual helpfulness for antagonism and strife, they are together able to make this surplus to enormously greater than it was in past and that there is ample room for a large increase in wages for the workmen and an equally great increase in profits for the manufacturer.[8] Both had a common interest in increasing productability.

To achieve these planning ends and to exercise strict control over the workers, Taylor introduced the concept of functional specialists. Taylor suggested that each workman should receive his daily orders and assistance directly from eight different bosses. Four of these bosses in the planning office were the time and cost clerk, the instruction card clerk, the order of work and route clerk, and the shop disciplinarian. They were held responsible to send their orders and receive their returns usually in writing. Four others in the workshop were the gang boss, the speed boss, the repair boss and the inspector. They were responsible to help the men personally in their work, each specialist helping in his own particular line or function.

"Now, in its essence, scientific management involves complete mental revolution on the part of working men connected in any particular establishment or industry . . . and it involves equally complete mental revolution on the part of those on the management's side—the foreman, the superintendent, the owner of business, the board of directors . . . and without his complete mental revolution on both sides scientific management does not exist. The great revolution that takes place in the mental attitude of the two parties under scientific management is that both sides take their eyes off the division of the surplus as the all-important matter, and together turn their attention towards increasing the size of the surplus."

Functional Foremanship

Taylor separated manual workers from Supervisors as different qualities are required for each job. He attached more importance on the mental aspect of planning.

Incentive Wage Payment

Taylor provided for a system of reward and punishment. He felt that payment to workers should be paid according to the output which he called piece meal rate or differential piece work. Under this system one piece rate if he produced the already determined pieces but another rate if he produced more pieces.

No Emphasis on Human Factor

Taylor was more concerned with productivity than thinking about human beings. He was impersonal in formulating his scientific management. Taylor accepted human relations approach but could not put in practice due to more emphasis on productivity.

To quote him, "No system can do away with the need of real men. No system of management, however good, should be applied in a wooden way. The proper personal relations should always be maintained between the employers and men; and even the prejudices of the workmen be considered in dealing with them."

The opportunity which each man should have of airing his mind freely and having it out with his employers, is a safety-valve; and if the superintendents are reasonable men, and listen to and treat with respect what their men, have to say, there is absolutely no reason for labour unions and strikes.

It is not the large charities (however generous they may be) that are needed or appreciated by workmen so much as small acts of personal kindness and sympathy, which establish a bond of friendly feeling between them and their employers."[9]

Management by Exception

He wanted that the manager should not supervise those activities which have become routine or standards performance. He should rather concentrate on items which show varied standards and performance.

Taylor's Scientific Management

The following four principles are the basics of his philosophy of scientific management:

1. The development of a true science of management, so that, for example, the best method for performing each task could be determined.
2. The scientific selection of the workers, so that each worker would be given responsibility for the task for which he or she was best suited.
3. The scientific education and development of the workers.
4. Intimate friendly co-operation between management and labour.

It is modesty of Taylor that he said that he is not the only person who pioneered scientific management. There are many others as well. To quote him:

During the course of an enquiry of a Congressional Committee in 1912, Taylor categorically stated that he did not lay any claim to a monopoly on scientific management. He replied, "I should not say . . . . My gracious, I do not believe there is any man connected with scientific management who has the slightest pride of authorship in connection with it. Everyone of us realizes that this has been the work of 100 men or more, and that the work which any one of us may have done is but a small fraction of the whole. . . . It is a matter of evolution of many men, each doing his proper share in the development, and I think any man would be disgusted to have it said that he had invented scientific management, or that he was even very much of a factor in scientific management.[10]

Inspite of all this, he is considered the father of scientific management.

CRITICISM

1. Against Trade Unionism—He is supposed to have worked against trade unionism and collective bargaining.

2. Managers were not given promotion with adequate training, etc. To quote Bertram M. Gross, "The Managers did not appreciate his scornful comments on rule-of-thumb method. Those who had fought their way to high managerial positions without the benefit of higher education were sensitive to Taylor's stand that unless assisted by highly trained experts they were unqualified to manage."[11]

The critics have pointed out the following main weaknesses in Taylor's philosophy:

(a) Taylor's approach was directed towards the lowest operating level of the organization. He placed the emphasis on small work groups at lower levels. It did not emphasise to the relationship between managerial organization and the performance of managerial functions.

(b) Taylor's approach is purely physiological and mechanical one. It did not emphasize the human aspects of the problem.

(c) Taylor assumed the worker as "economic man" and he failed to understand and to try harness the worker's greater psychological needs. He omitted the concept of "whole man."

(d) Taylor tried to individualize the worker. He assumed that group behaviour was undesirable. He did not realize that social satisfaction may also play an important role in organization.

(e) Taylor's piece-rate wage plans aroused fears of speed up and unhealthy pressure upon workers. They often created inequitable situations.

(f) He largely ignored the group processes and informal organization that were found by human relationists to be important.

(g) Taylor was regarded as anti-union, although he did say that his principle were widely applied, there would be no need of unions.

(h) Some critics said that Taylor equated men with machines. His concept of man was defective. He lost sight of man's feelings and emotions. He generated workers' hostility.

(i) Taylor did not dwell on organizational integration at the worker-management, and higher levels to the extent that Fayol, Urwick, Follett and other administrative theorists did.[12]

Speaking on "Scientific Management and the dictatorship of the Proletariat" in June 1919, Lenin said:

The possibility of socialism will be determined by our success in combining soviet rule and Soviet organization and management with the latest progressive measures of capitalism. We must introduce in Russia the study and teaching of the Taylor school and its systematic trial and adoption.

We may conclude with the words that Taylor was the founder and exponent of scientific management and that is why he is called the father of scientific management.

Relevance

Federick W. Taylor, probably the greatest contributor to

scientific management joined the society of mechanical engineers in 1886 and used this organization to develop and test the ideas he formulated while working in various steel firms. It was in one of these firms, Midvale Steel Company that he observed men producing far less than their capacities. Taylor believed this waste was due to ignorance of what constituted a fair days work. At that time there were no studies to determine expected results per worker (work standards) and the relationship between work standards and the wage system. Taylors Personal dislike for waste caused him to rebel at what he interpreted as inefficient labour and management practices based solely on hunch commonsense and ignorance. Many techniques and principles of scientific management have become integral part of quantitative approach such as time study, motion study, work study, specialization and standardization.

He believed that the key to harmony was seeking to discover the one best way to do a job, determine the optimum work pace, train people to do the job properly and reward successful performance by using an incentive pay system. Taylor believed that co-operation would replace conflict of workers and managers know what was expected and the positive benefits of achieving mutual expectations.[13]

His ideas for solving problems and making decisions, through science and not through rule of thumb which are of great significance for all times. He further believed that harmony in functioning and any kind of disagreement should be reduced to minimum.

A recent visit of the author as a part of high delegation of Indian Institute of Public Administration to China from 24th April to 2nd May 2007 revealed that China is progressing very fast. How? Politicians and civil servants are given intensive training in central, provincial city and village party schools. They are engaged meticulously following Taylor's principles of scientific management to accelerate development. Government Machinery is not wasting any time in unnecessary activities. That is why, Chinese people are getting the benefits of development. For developing countries, scientific management is essential.

To the modern student of management, Taylor's ideas

may not appear to be pioneering given the times in which he developed them, however, his ideas were and continue to be, lasting contributions to the way work is done at the shop floor level. He urged managers to take a systematic approach in performing their job of co-ordination. His experiments with stop watch studies and work methods stimulated many others at that time to take similar types of studies.[14]

Scientific Management is of great significance for developing countries: Employees in government, business, industry, health and educational institutions are a great liability on state exchequer. They get their salary and other fringe benefits whether they do any work or not. Even employees remain absent without leave, etc. causing low productivity. Such a situation in developing countries like India poses a matter of concern. What can we do? The only answer is Taylor and his philosophy of scientific management. India must pay its employees only if they perform, if they work and discharge their duties. If India wants development and not populist approach the Indian Government has to be strict.

Words written or spoken are of no use unless put to action. Robert Chambers has rightly observed, "It is action that matters . . . but knowing does not guarantee a change of feeling; and a change of feeling does not guarantee a change of behaviour. So we come to the final, paradoxical, reversal; to start by acting. . . . Not everything can or should be foreseen. It is often best to start, to do something, and to learn from doing."

We have defined clearly the thrust of the public policy in India in the Preamble to the Constitution of India which reads as:

"WE THE PEOPLE OF INDIA, having solemnly resolved to constitute India into a SOVEREIGN, SOCIALIST, SECULAR, DEMOCRATIC REPUBLIC and to secure to all its citizens JUSTICE—social, economic and political;

LIBERTY of thought, expression, belief, faith and worship;

EQUALITY of status and of opportunity;

And to promote among them all

FRATERNITY assuring the dignity of the individual

and the unity and integrity of the nation, do hereby enact and give ourselves the following constitution."

India must make its people work to become an advanced country. Taylor's call for 'Mental Revolution' on the part of workers and managers is a constructive message for the good of both the parties and in turn to the society at large. The workers and managers, like partners of the industrial venture, should abandon their squabbles over the distribution of the fruits of their labour (product) and should collaborate on maximizing the quantum of production in true co-operative spirit. The moment this shift in the consciousness of both occurs, the dream of mental revolution would be realized. Thus, scientific manager would transform the society. In such a society where mutual mistrusts and squabbles will disappear and both workers and capitalists will live happily. In actual practice things did not go the way Taylor wanted. However, Taylorism brought orderliness to a great extent in the chaotic conditions prevailing in the industrial world. His gospel of scientific rationality could not appeal to capitalists. Labour also remained hostile to his doctrine.

The modern assembly line pours out finished products faster than Taylor could ever have imagined. This production "miracle" is just one legacy of scientific management. In addition, its efficiency techniques have been applied to many tasks in non-industrial organizations, ranging from fast-food service to the training of surgeons.[15]

Taylor also pointed out that managers and non-managers must have complete understanding about the quantity and quality of work to be accomplished within a given period. He indicated that the answer to this question was needed: what constitutes an honest day's work? From this answer, a basis for mutual understanding would be provided and a focal point around which to build better management and labor relations would be available. Many believe this question is as valid today as it was when Taylor suggested it.

With the advent of Frederick W. Taylor and the scientific management school of thought began the formal, broader study of management as a discipline akin to physics, history, mathematics, and other fields of study. From this and earlier developments, numerous schools of management thought have evolved and still exist today.

Taylor's management philosophy can inject efficiency in the management of delivery of services in developing countries especially India, e.g. Doctors, teachers and other workers in villages are getting salary without proper work. Thus Taylor would always remain relevant where inefficiency is to be curbed.

Notes and References

1. F.W. Taylor, Shop Management, p. 21.
2. F.W. Taylor, The Principles of Scientific Management, p. 103.
3. *Ibid.*, p. 83.
4. F.W. Taylor, "The Principles of Scientific Management", p. 13.
5. Richard M. Steers and Lyman Porter, Motivation and Work Behaviour, (New York, McGraw Hill), 1975, p. 16
6. Taylor, *op. cit.*, pp. 28-29.
7. The definition given here is that adopted in the British Standard Glossary of Terms in Work Study, ILO: Introduction to Work Study, Revised Edition, Geneva, 1974, p. 35.
8. Taylor Testimony, pp. 26-27, 29-30, vide Harward F. Merill, Classic in Management (Bombay, Taraporwala Publishing Ltd., 1980), p. 6.
9. Taylor, "Shop Management", pp. 28-29.
10. F.W. Taylor, "Testimony Before the Special House Committee", Scientific Management, p. 282.
11. Bentram M. Gross, "The Managing of Organization: The Administrative Struggle, Vol. I, New York, The Free Press, 1964, p. 125.
12. Hicks and Gullett, "Organisation: Theory and Behaviour", 1975, 180.
13. Lyndall Urwick, The Golden Book of Management, (London, Newman, Neame Ltd., 1956, pp. 72-79).
14. Edivin A. Loke, "The Ideas of Federick W. Taylor: An Evaluation", *Academy of Management Review*, January 1982, pp. 14-24.
15. Initiative, Subordinates should be given the freedom to conceive and carry out their plans, even though some mistakes may result.

13

Luther Gullick and Lyndall Urwick

INTRODUCTION

Gullick and Urwick made a substantial contribution to administrative thought through their formulation of Administrative Principles.

Luther Gullick was born in Oska Japan in the year 1882 and obtained his Ph.D. in 1920 from Columbia University. D.Litt. in 1939 and LL.D. in 1954. He was a member of President's Committee on Administrative Management. He served in Defence Council in the First World War. His main association was city research institute at New York for forty years. He served as the Administrator for New York City during 1954-56 and President of Institution of Public Administration, New York during 1960-62 and its Chairman from 1960-82. He also served as Professor in many universities.

He authored a number of books, some of them are:

1. Administrative Reflections from World War II.
2. Metropolitan Problems and American Ideas.
3. Modern Management for the city of New York and papers on the Science of Administration.

CHART 13.1

Principles of Management Universally Applicable to all Organisation

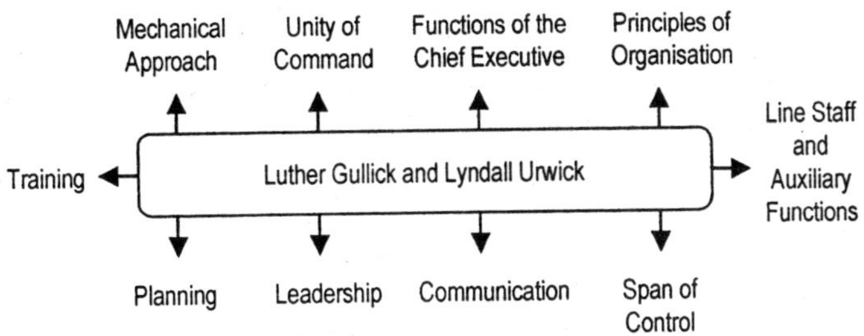

With the advent of industrial revolution, in 19th Century, there was a need of the principles of Administration to manage the emerging industrial and business enterprises. Attempts were made by F.W. Taylor, Max Weber and Henry Fayol. Gullick and Urwick consolidated the works of earlier thinkers and brought out "Papers on the Science of Administration" in 1937, which is considered as a landmark in the development of the science of administration.

Urwick is an internationally known management thinker and consultant, whose contributions to management thought are overwhelming. He was born in Britain in 1891 and served as a Lt. Col. during the First World War in British Army. He is a man of varied and rich experiences. He was educated at Oxford. He served as Professor in the University of New South Wales, General Secretary, International Committee of Scientific Management; Chairman, Committee on Education for Management and Director of the American Management Association.

He had bright careers as a British military officer, as a civil servant, and as a management consultant. He has been leading exponent of classical theory of organization.

He is greatly influenced by the ideas of earlier writers like Taylor and Fayol. He tried to integrate the theories propounded by earlier writers on management. He has not made original contributions to management. His work is the synthesis of so many thinkers of management.

His books include the following:

1924 Dynamic Administration: The Collected Papers of Mary Parker Follett (Co-ed.)
1929 The Meaning of Rationalisation
1933 Management of Tomorrow
1937 Papers on the Science of Administration (Co-ed.)
1944 The Elements of Administration (Co-ed).
1945 The Making of Scientific Management (Vols. I, II and III, Co-auth.)
1952 The Theory of Organisation
1956 The Golden Book of Management (ed.)
1956 The Pattern of Management

CONTRIBUTION TO MANAGEMENT THOUGHT

Urwick concentrated more to the discovery of the principles for designing the organization.

1. Principles of Organisation

Urwick identified eight principles of orgnisation, viz. (1) the 'principle of objectives—orgnaisation should be an expression of a purpose; (2) the 'principle of correspondence', authority and responsibility must be co-equal; (3) the 'principle of responsibility'—responsibility of superiors for work of subordinates is absolute; (4) the scalar principle; (5) the 'principle of the span of control'—a superior cannot superwise directly the work of more than five or six subordinates whose works interlock; (6) the 'principle of specialization'—limiting one's work to a single function; (7) 'principle of coordination', and; (8) the 'principle of definition'—a clear prescription of every duty.

In U.K., Lyndall Urwick, a distinguished Executive and Management Consultant wrote a book, "The Elements of Administrative in which he tried to integrate the concept and Principles of Taylor, Fayol, Mooney, A.C. Reily and other early management thinkers. Luther Gullick and Lyndall Urwick edited a volume called Papers on the Science of Administration (1937), which is a monument piece of work. They are rightly called the architects of organizations, for they were first to formulate the basic principles for designing organizations. To start with, Gullick discusses the questions, "what is the work of the executive?" His answer was POSDCORB a verbal artifact made up of the initial letters of seven fundamental administrative activities:

Planning is working out in broad outline the things that need to be done and the methods for doing them to accomplish the purposes set for the enterprise.

Organising	Selecting the formal structure of authority through which work subdivisions are arranged, defined and coordinated.
Staffing	Selecting and training staff and providing proper working conditions.
Directing	Making decisions and issuing specific orders and instructions.
Coordinating	Interrelating various parts of work.
Reporting	Preparing reports on the progress of various activities.
Budgeting	Fiscal planning, accounting and control over expenditure.

The task of the executive can be described in various ways. But this is a very simple and useful way of understanding the different tasks of the executive.

He is credited in integrating the views on administrative system propounded by different scholars in different countries which in itself is unique. To quote him:

"The main point is that it focuses on a logical scheme of various 'Principles of Administration' formulated by different authorities. The fact that such 'Principles'—worked out by persons of different nationalities, widely varying experience and, in the majority of cases, no knowledge of each other's—work were susceptible to such logical arrangement, is in itself highly significant.[1]

He further added that these principles can be applied to any organisation of any type. To quote him:

"There are principles . . . which should govern arrangements for human associations of any kind. These principles can be studied as a technical question irrespective of the purpose of the enterprise, the personnel composing it, or in constitutional, political or social theory underlying its creation."

Let us discuss other important aspects:

Fitting People to Structure—Machine Model of Man

Urwick opined that an organisation should be like a machine which should be well designed. He ignored the importance of human beings in comparison to administrative structure.

Urwick attached much importance to the structure and design of administration while ignoring the role of human beings in it. He remarks that "it is impossible for humanity to advance its knowledge of organization unless the factor on structure is isolated from other considerations, however artificial such an isolation may appear."

Urwick observed, "It may be objected that . . . the organizer . . . can't sit down in a cold-blooded spirit and draw an ideal structure, an optimum distribution of duties and responsibilities, and relationships, and then expect the infinite variety of human nature to feed into it." I am convinced that a logical scheme of organisation, a structure based on principles which take priority over personalities, is in the long-run far better both for the morale of an undertaking as a whole and for the happiness of individuals, than the attempt to build one's organisation around personality."

Delegation

Executives must learn to delegate. This is essential in order to ensure that they have enough time and energy to concentrate on the most important task in hand. The other advantage is this that their subordinates can use and develop their knowledge and skills by shouldering responsibility. Delegation therefore can lead to a more efficient and speedy execution of work.

He emphasized delegation principles. In his opinion authority and responsibility must be co-terminus, co-equal and well defined. He states, lack of the courage to delegate properly and of knowledge how to do it, is one of the most general causes of failure in organisation.

Chief Executive

At the top of every organisation there must be one person, a supreme commander, who will make final decisions and resolve all conflicts. This alone will ensure that there is proper direction, control and consistency in the conduct of a business. This work cannot be entrusted to a committee.

Leadership

Urwick's views on leadership are well known. According to him, a leader should have four functions to his role:

(i) he embodies and represents the organisation he serves;
(ii) he initiates thought and action;
(iii) he administers routine; and
(iv) he interprets to others the purpose and meaning of what is to be done.

Span of Control

According to Urwick, no one can supervise the work of more than five or six persons if their work is interlocked. As several variables are involved, this figures is liable to change but the fact remains that this limitation needs to be kept in view while designing organizations.

To quote him: "No superior can supervise directly the work of more than five or, at the most, six subordinates whose "work interlocks." Urwick encouraged Graicunas in developing his mathematical analysis of relationships.

Communication

Urwick emphasizes clear-cut communication in simple language. In his view, everyday experiences should not be written in technological style. He decries the tendency to complicate the language. His views on this score are worth recording:

"One of the more unfortunate consequences of this tendency to complicate language is that it is apt to undermine the style of academic writers even when they are not writing technically'.

Line and Staff Functions

Gulick and Urwick feel that the special staff units do not exercise any direct authority and that their job is to render technical advice and provide timely and adequate information. The objective of these staff agencies is to discharge knowing, thinking and planning functions and they must get the things done by 'authority of ideas'. The general staff is also necessary to assist the executive in the tasks of command, control and coordination. They must draw up and transmit orders, follow up operations and help coordinate the work of staff specialists without themselves taking on any specialized functions.[2]

Training

He felt the importance of training requirements at the different levels of management in industry. He writes: "Nothing in managing touches more closely on the prospects of industrial society than the problem of the training and the selection of those who will administer business. Upon its solution depends not only co-operation in the present, but the ultimate acceptance by mankind of the machine technology as a way of life."

Urwick strongly stressed that nothing in managing touches more closely on the prospects of industrial society than the problem of the training and the selection of those who will administer business. Upon its solution depends not only cooperation in the present, but the ultimate acceptance by mankind of the machine technology as a way of life.

Urwick said that unless it is prepared to place good management within the machinery of government in the forefront of the agenda and to stimulate its servants to place greater emphasis on the executive as opposed to the political virtues, the best intentions are negatived by its inability to drive faster a machine designed for a far more leisurely age.

Unity of Command

This principle simply states that no one should have more than one boss. If one has to work under different bosses, it is bound to lead to confusion, because the various bosses may give contradictory orders and the subordinate will find it impossible to comply with them.

Urwick's contribution is in the field of organisation also. In his book "The elements of Administration" (1943), he listed 29 principles of management. These are also known as classical principles of organisation. He used the terms "management" and "organisation" interchangeably. Urwick's 29 classical principles of organisation are as follows:

1. Investigation,
2. Forecasting,
3. Planning,
4. Appropriateness,
5. Organisation,
6. Coordinative,
7. Order,
8. Command,
9. Control,
10. The Coordinative Principle,
11. Authority
12. Scalar Process,
13. Assignment of functions,
14. Leadership,
15. Delegation,
16. Functional definition,
17. Determinative,
18. Application,
19. Interpretative,
20. The General Interest,
21. Centralization,
22. Staffing,
23. Esprit,
24. Selection and placement,
25. Rewards and sanctions,
26. Initiative,
27. Equity,
28. Discipline, and
29. Stability.

CONCLUSION

Analyzing Urwick's work, Philip Sadler writes: "The

principles which Urwick gathered together have come to be known as the "classical" principles of management. They are based on a combination of experience and philosophy rather than rigorous research and have been widely criticized for this. They have attracted criticism on other grounds also. First, the underlying assumption of their work—that there exists a common set of principles applicable to management in all types of situation—has been frequently challenged. Second, their work is criticized (perhaps unfairly) on the grounds that the world in which they had their experience no longer exists and that the principles they derived from that experience have little or no validity for the contemporary organization operating in the modern business environment."

C.S. George evaluates Urwick in his book in these words: "It sometimes happens that men who express the right theory at the right time make a greater contribution than the pioneer whose ideas were disregarded because they were decades ahead of their time. This is how Urwick has served the management continuum."

The principles postulated by Urwick are not scientific L.D. White says that the terms line, staff, and auxiliary agencies, hierarchy, authority, centralization, etc., are useful terms for describing or classifying administrative situations, they are no more. They provide no guidance as to whether a given system more or less should be highly centralized, nor as to whether auxiliary agencies should be given more or fewer duties or authority. They are not rules. They suggest only working rules of conduct with wide experience seems to have validated.[3]

According to Gulick, some of the difficulties arise from (a) the uncertainty of the future—as to the behaviour of individuals and of people; (b) the lack of knowledge, experience, wisdom and character among leaders and their confused and conflicting ideas and objectives; (c) the lack of administrative skill and technique; (d) the vast number of variables involved and the incompleteness of human knowledge, particularly with regard to man and life; and (e) the lack of orderly methods of developing, considering, perfecting and adopting new ideas and programmes.

Relevance

Luther Gullick and Lyndall Urwick have come out with the science of administration or the principles of administration. The world "POSDCORB" has been coined by them. It is being taught to all students of business management and public administration. They were pioneers in consolidating thoughts of earlier thinkers like Taylor, Fayol and Max Webber. They discussed the functions of Chief Executive, Line, Staff and Auxiliary agencies.

They are with us and are being widely used both in theory and practice. However, these principles are being modified to suit the present conditions and in tune with development of science and technology.

Notes and References

1. Urwick, The Elements of Administration, 1943, p. 7.
2. D. Gvishian, "Organization and Management, Moscow, Progress Publishers, 1972, p. 198.
3. L.D. White, An Introduction to the Study of Administration", New York, Macmillian Company, (III Ed.) *op. cit.*, 1948, p. 37.

14

Chester I. Barnard
(1886-1961)

Chester I. Barnard belongs to the Human Relations School of Administrative Thought. He was pioneer in developing the philosophical groundwork of management by using the interdisciplinary approach, i.e. ideas of sociology, psychology, abstract reasoning and physical sciences. His ideas centre around as to what is an organization both as a formal as well as an informal entity. He emphasized more on the informal aspects of an organization. Individuals essentially come together due to a common purpose and organizations are mainly cooperative systems. Barnard also elaborated the theory and structure of formal organization. He focused on behavioural view of organizations. Chester Irving Barnard is prominent among the organizational theorists. He is one of the very few administrative thinkers who propounded organizational principles and theories based on personal experience. He is considered the spiritual father of the social system school, which has influenced many organizational thinkers of 20th century.

In 1927, he was appointed the first chairman of the New Jersey Telephone Company. During 1931-33 and in 1935 he worked as director of State Rehabilitation Organisation,

CHART 14.1

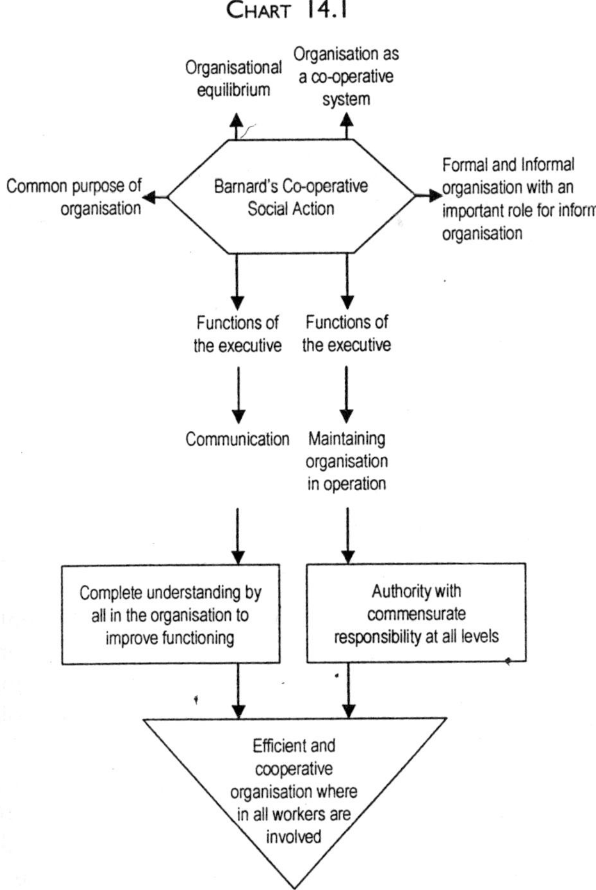

New Jersey and in 1946 as a member of the Atomic Energy Commission of the State Department. Between 1948 and 1952, after retirement from the Bell Company, he worked as President of the Rockefeller Foundation. Thus, he occupied many positions both in government and private administration and earned seven honorary 'doctorates' even without a bachelor's degree. He occupies a distinctive place in the history of administrative thought. His experiences in various capacities in different organizations afforded him an opportunity to understand administrative processes in the government.

Barnard's formal educational career was not very inspiring as he was impatient about implementing his own ideology. Although he attended Mount Hermon Academy and entered Harvard University in 1906 yet he left it three years later without obtaining degree. He had no patience with college rules which required him to take a pre-requisite to a course he had already passed with honours. Later in June 1909, Barnard entered the employment of American Telephone and Telegraph as translator and engineer. Then he joined Pennsylvania Bell Telephone Company, where he got initiated in the field of general management.

Publications

His famous writings are as follows:

1938 The Functions of the Executive
1940 The Nature of Leadership
1948 Organization and Management

CONTRIBUTION TO MANAGEMENT THOUGHT

Organization as a Co-operative System

The individual human being is limited by his biological factors, as well as physical and social. Barnard defined organisation as a system of consciously coordinated activities of two or more persons. As a system, it is held together by some common purpose by the willingness of certain people to contribute to the operation of the organisation, and by the ability of such people to communicate with each other.[1]

Barnard had viewed it as the means by which people can be linked together in an organization to achieve the objectives of the programme.

Barnard, while rejecting the viewpoint that man is mainly motivated by economic incentives, analyses the multiplicity of satisfactions and identifies four specific inducements viz., (1) material inducements such as money, things or physical conditions; (2) personal non-material opportunities for distinction, prestige and personal power, (3) desirable physical conditions of work; and (4) ideal benefactions, such as the pride of workmanship, sense of adequacy, altruistic service for family or others, loyalty to organisation and patriotism and aesthetic or religious feelings and the satisfaction of the motives of faith or revenge.[2]

He further stated, "The same principles that govern simple organization may be conceived as governing the structure of complex organizations which are composite systems. He treated organization as a 'living body' and his interest was in the functioning of an organization. He was not concerned with finding out the best way to administer an organization."

In his own words, "The efficiency of the co-operative system is the capacity to maintain itself by the individual satisfaction that it affords. This may be called its capacity of equilibrium, the balancing of burdens by satisfaction that results from its continuum."

The most effective method of overcoming these limitations, in the view of Barnard is cooperative social action. This requires that he may adopt a group for non personal purpose and take into consideration the process of interaction. With this basic premise those individuals must cooperate, Barnard builds up his theory of organisation.

Barnard stated that by examining the formal organization, it was possible to provide for cooperation and accomplish basically three goals:

(a) to insure the survival of an organization by the "maintenance of an equilibrium of complex character in a continuously fluctuating, environment of physical, biological and social materials, elements and forces" within an organizaton;
(b) to examine the external forces to which such adjustments must be made; and
(c) to analyse the functions of executives at all levels in managing and controlling formal organizations.

FORMAL AND INFORMAL ORGANISATION

Barnard defined an organization as "a system of consciously coordinated activities of forces of two or more persons. He was highly critical of the classical organisation theory which according to him was too descriptive, superficial and artificial. This definition is applicable to all types of organizations.

He further stated, "the same principles that govern simple organisation may be conceived as governing the structure of complex organizations which are composite systems. He treated organisation as a 'living body' and his interest was in the functioning of an organisation. He was not concerned with finding out the best way to administer an organisation."

Formal Organisation

Members in a formal organisation are assigned authority through a formal system of rules and regulations. The distribution of authority can easily be depicted through organisational charts, and rules as laid down in the organisational manual. For example, a university is a formal organisation governed by the university calendar, 'approved by a competent authority. In a formal organisation, structure, procedure, status, communication channels and superior subordinate relationships are defined minutely to avoid confusion. These formal organisations are, however, becoming complex, i.e., over-organised.' Their management is becoming problematic. Many new techniques like management by objectives (MBO), organisational development (OD), interpersonal communication through Transactional Analysis (TA), organisational change management, etc. are being suggested to make the formal organisation function efficiently. The purpose of all these new techniques is to remove excess of formalism from the formal organisation, so that these may function as per the needs of the personnel.

Informal Organisation

One of the first scholars to recognize the importance of informal structures was Chester Barnard. He noted that informal relationships help organization members satisfy their social needs and get things done.

Formal organisation is a tip of the iceberg in the totality of organisations. It is very difficult to understand the functioning of an organisation until and unless we examine the role of informal organisation. To quote Dubin, "The formal organisation is but the skeleton of the total organisation. We must also see the subordinate groups of people within it." He summarised these four functions of informal groups for their members; viz.

1. They are the natural units where the actual operations for getting things done are determined.
2. They provide simultaneously the climate for supporting experiments with new methods of work.
3. They establish and maintain norms of behaviour for members.
4. They provide each member with sympathetic human consideration, which supports his self image, personality and integrity.[3]

Informal organisations are the product of group behaviour and a system of activity of human beings. It is impossible to understand organisational behaviour without taking into account human and social features of an organisation. Informal organisation arises from the social interaction among the members of an organisation and, as such, it is indefinite and beyond the scope of exact measurement. We can understand the functioning of informal organisations with the help of behavioural science, which includes knowledge in the fields of psychology, sociology and anthropology, with links to some part of political science and economics. There are various techniques, which can help us in understanding the subtle working of an informal organisation.

Human interactions develop in many directions. This results in the development of different informal organisations within a formal organisation. These cannot be depicted through formal charts. However, these have more hold on the personnel in the informal organisation rather than the formal one.

Informal organisations are the product of the complexity of the formal organisations wherein employees find it difficult to satisfy their varied needs. They want to come out of the drudgery of mechanical life. They also want to protect themselves collectively against the attitudes and wrong actions of officers above them.

The actual working of any organisation is not according to the formal plan. The informal relationship of the persons working in the organisation may be different from the formal expected relationship. It is better to encourage healthy informal relationships among personnel in an organisation.

According to Chester I. Barnard, the initial existence of an organizations depends upon three elements.

(a) Willingness to Co-operate

He believed that willingness to co-operate is always fluctuating, willingness to cooperate, positive or negative, is the expression of the net satisfactions or dissatisfactions experiences or anticipated by such individuals in comparison with those experienced through alternative opportunities.[4]

(b) Common Purpose

Chester Barnards feels that willingness to co-operate is not possible without some common purpose.

Unless there is such an objective it cannot be known or anticipated what specific efforts will be required of individuals, nor in many cases what satisfactions to them can be in prospect . . . . The necessity of having a purpose is axiomatic, implicit in the words "system", "coordination", "cooperation." He further says that a purpose does not incite cooperative activity unless it is accepted by those whose efforts will constitute the organization.

According to Barnard, "an objective purpose that can serve as the basis for a cooperative system is the one that is believed by the contributors to be the determined purpose of the organization."

(c) Communication

Communication promotes the achievement of purpose and makes it dynamic. Communication determines scope of organisation.

Chester I. Barnard, a strong proponent of the acceptance view, has defined the conditions under which a person will comply with higher authority: A person can and will accept a communication as authoritative only when four conditions simultaneously occur: (a) he can and does understand the communication; (b) at the time of his decisions he believes that it is not inconsistent with the purpose of the organization; (c) at the time of his decision he believes it to be compatible with his personal interest as a whole; and (d) he is able mentally and physically to comply with it.[5]

In the context of administration and management, William Scott defined communication as a process which involves the transmission and accurate replication of ideas ensured by feedback for the purpose of eliciting actions which will accomplish organisational goals.[6] To quote Goddard:

"Efficient communication is essential to all aspects of effective administration. Staff must be adequately and correctly informed about plans, methods, schedules, problems, events and progress. It is necessary that instructions, knowledge, and information be passed on for practical application to all concerned, and that they are so clearly presented as to make misinterpretation or misunderstanding impossible. Proper and adequate communication is not just in one direction. It requires two-way passage. Administrators must be certain that they know and understand the problems of workers for whom they are responsible. Communications must flow from the bottom upwards, as well as from the top down."[7]

Broadly speaking, communication is the means through which intentions of the programmes are translated to ensure fruitful results. It may even be looked upon as the means by which special information inputs are fed into social systems. It is the means by which behaviour of the personnel engaged in the programme is modified; change is effected, information is made productive and goals are achieved. Barnard has viewed it as the means by which people can be linked together in an organisation to achieve the objectives of the programme.[8] Newman and Summer have viewed communication as an exchange of facts, ideas, opinion, or emotions by two or more persons.

COMMUNICATION MANAGEMENT

Communication management means the designing of communication strategy, procedures and contents in advance, according to the nature and objectives of the organisation, to smoothen its operations and avoid misunderstanding and other complicated problems, which could be generated out of the communication gap.

Types of Communication Network

Communication network is of two types—formal and informal. Formal communication is authoritative and well defined as to who will communicate with whom, when and how. All the procedures are well laid out. Formal communication is effective in normal and routine situations. However, organisations cannot cope with rigid and inflexible communications to meet urgent and spontaneous needs. Informal channels develop network where formal channels are not well designed. Informal communication develops strong bonds. It may supplement, at times, formal channels of communication. Informal communication, however, sometimes carries rumour and distorted information, which may damage the goodwill and prestige of the organisation. Thus, there is a need to make use of both the channels of communication as per the needs of the organisation."

In Barnard's words, "they are inter-dependent aspects of the same phenomenon—a society is structured by formal organization, formal orgnaisation are vitalized and conditioned by informal organizations." What is asserted is that there cannot be one without the other. If one organization fails, the other will necessarily disintegrate. Barnard considers the following as the functions of informal organization, viz., communication; maintenance of cohesiveness through regulating the willingness to learn and the ability of the objective authority; and maintenance of the feeling of personal integrity, self-respect and independent choice.[9]

The task facing managements at present is skillfully to blend together the formal organization with the informal in order to minimize conflict and to encourage healthy adjustment and co-ordination. This can be achieved by managerial recognition of the importance that informal groups have upon individual attitudes and morale. The supervisor should encourage the formation and growth of informal groups; he should see that they are properly informed about policies and procedures. If proper encouragement is given to informal groups they will respond in positive rather than negative ways .

We can thus conclude by saying that we must synthesize the merits of both formal and informal groups to get proper understanding of the nature of an organization. Keith Davis has rightly said, "the informal organization needs to be strong enough to be supportive, but not strong enough to dominate." In short, we can say that we must try to synchronise formal and informal goals

Organizational Equilibrium

It means that the persons who work for the organisation must get the benefits out of it. In his own words: "The efficiency of the co-operative system is the capacity to maintain itself by the individual satisfaction that it affords. This may be called its capacity of equilibrium, the balancing of burdens by satisfaction that results from its continuum."

Barnard believed that individual and organizational purposes could be kept in balance if managers understood an employee's zone of indifference—that is, what the employee would do without questioning the manager's authority. Obviously, the more activities that fell within an employee's zone of indifference (what the employee would accept), the smoother and more cooperative an organization would be. Barnard also believed that executives had a duty to instill a sense of moral purpose in their employees. To do this, they would have to learn to think beyond their narrow self-interest and make an ethical commitment to society. Although Barnard stressed the work of executive managers, he also focused considerable attention on the role of the individual worker as the basic strategic factor in organization. When he went further to emphasize the organization as the cooperative enterprise of individuals working together as groups, he set the stage for the development of a great deal of current management thinking.[10]

It may also be added that the equilibrium is not static. Changes in environment can disturb the equilibrium. As he points out: "This external equilibrium has two terms: first, the effectiveness of the organisation which compromises the interchange between the organisation and individuals. Thus, the elements stated will vary with external factors, and they are at the same time interdependent; when one is varied, compensating factors must occur in the other if the system of which they are components is to remain in equilibrium, that is, to persist and survive."

It may of great interest that Barnard feels that the persons in an organisation do not merely work for material rewards. Barnard feels, "It seems to me to be a matter of common experience that material rewards are ineffective beyond the subsistence level excepting a separate limited proportion of men; most men neither work harder for more material things, nor can be induced thereby to devote more than a fraction of their possible contribution to organisation efforts."

Barnard lays great emphasis on pride of workmanship, opportunity of distinction and prestige, feeling of belongingness, etc. Organisation must motivate the persons to achieve these excellent qualities.

4. Functions of the Executive

To Barnard, Executive work "is not of the organization, but the specialized work of maintaining the organization in operation. The executive functions serve to maintain a system of cooperative effort. They are impersonal. The functions are not, as so frequently stated, to manage a group of persons.[11]

Barnard feels that the executive plays the role of nervous system to keep the organisation functional. He says: It exists to maintain the bodily system by directing those actions which are necessary more effectively to adjust to the environment, but it can hardly be said to manage the body, a large part of whose functions are independent of it and upon which it in turn depends."[12]

Executive responsibility then is that capacity and ability of leaders by which reflective ideas, hopes desire largely emerge from themselves. They are compelled to bind the wills of men to the accomplishment of purposes beyond their immediate end and beyond their times. Barnard repeatedly emphasized how important it was that individual be induced to co-operate. This inducement can take the forms of an order, but if so it would be accepted as authoritative only. This may not be successful. We must ensure his cooperation which can be forth coming if he: (i) understood it, (ii) believed it to be consistent with the purpose of the organization, (iii) believed it to be compatible with his own present interest, and (iv) was able to comply with it.

Barnard set about developing a theory of how to get workers to cooperate. How do you get the individuals to surrender their personal preferences and to go along with the authority exercised by supervisors?[13] He believed the answer could be found in what he called the person's zone of indifference, a range within each individual in which he or she would willingly accept orders without consciously questioning their legitimacy.[14] Barnard saw willingness to cooperate as an expression of the net satisfactions or dissatisfactions experienced or anticipated by each person. In other words, organizations had to provide sufficient inducements to broaden each employee's zone of indifference and thus increase the likelihood that orders would be obeyed.

But Barnard, in a clear break with the classicists, said that material incentives by themselves were not enough: "The unaided power of material incentives, when the minimum necessities are satisfied, in my opinion, is exceedingly limited as to most men."[15] Several other classes of incentives, including "the opportunities for distinction, prestige, [and] personal power" are also required.

Barnard classified the functions of the executive under three heads, viz., (1) maintenance of organization communication, (2) securing essential services from the individuals, and (3) the formulation of purpose and objectives.[16]

Maintenance of Communication

This involves the following steps:

I. Defining the Organizational Position

It entails designing of organizational charts, specification of duties, division of labour, specializations, co-ordination and securing the kind and quality of service which can be brought under a co-operative system. This is accomplished through careful employee selection, the use of positive and negative sanctions and securing the co-operation of the informal organisation. The informal organisation reduces formal decisions and minimizes 'undesirable influences.'

These communication factors are as follows:

1. The channels of communication should be definitely known.
2. There should be a definite formal channel of communication to every member of an organization.
3. The line of communication should be as direct and short as possible.
4. The complete formal line of communication should be competent.
5. The persons serving as communication centres should be competent.
6. The line of communication should not be interrupted while the organisation is functioning.
7. Every communication should be authenticated.

Formulation of purpose and objectives is quite important. This includes policy formulation, laying down of objectives and assignment of responsibility, and so on. The persons serving at the lower level should be indoctrinated, so that they are quite conversant and alive to the objectives of the organisation

Securing Essential Services from Individuals

It involves firstly recruiting of persons into co-operative relationships with the organisation and getting services from them for which they were brought. For this many techniques as desired are used like incentives, disincentives, morale, motivation supervision, control, educational training.

To him Executive work "Is not of the organization, but the specialized work of maintaining the organization in operation. . . . The executive functions serve to maintain a system of cooperative effort. They are impersonal. The functions are not, as so frequently stated, to manage a group of persons."

THE THEORY OF AUTHORITY

Authority in the organisation is essential to achieve co-ordination, effectiveness and efficiency. A Shrewd Executive named Chester Barnard wrote in his classic work, "Functions of the Executive" that managers are essentially powerless unless their followers grant them the authority to lead.

According to Barnard "Authority is the character of communication (order) in a formal organization by virtue of which it is accepted by a contributor or member of the organization as generating the action he contributes, that is as governing and determining what he does or is not to do, so far as the organization is concerned."

Authority is the right or power of a person to command other people to do things and to get work done from them. 'Responsibility' means a job for which one is responsible or accountable. Since it would not be just to hold a person responsible for performing a task without first giving him/her the authority necessary to get the job done, responsibility should always be commensurate with authority. This parity is not mathematical but rather co-extensive, because both relate to the same assignments. According to Earnest Dale, "Authority should be equal to responsibility. That is, if man is responsible for the results of a given operation, he should be given enough authority to take the action necessary to ensure success."[17]

In 1938, Chester Barnard began writing about organizations being "cooperative systems" and proposed the "acceptance theory or bottom-up theory of authority." He argued that management has only as much authority or power as subordinates are willing to accept and to the extent they consent to comply with directives. Barnard suggested that at least four conditions must be met for subordinates to comply with authoritative communication:

1. The communication is fully understood.
2. At the time of decision, the employee believes the directive is consistent with the objectives of the organization.
3. At the time of decision, the employee believes the command is compatible with personal interests and objectives.
4. The employee believes he or she is physically and mentally capable of complying with the communication.[18]

According to Henri Fayol, authority is the right to give orders and the power to get obedience, Mooney calls it "The Supreme Co-coordinating Power." Herbert Simon speaks of authority as the power to make decisions to guide the action of others. Koontz and O'Donnel state, "Authority is the key to the management job. Since managers must work through people to get things done, management theory is necessarily concerned with a complex of superior-subordinate relationship and is, therefore, founded on the concept of authority."

Absolute authority, though having the legal right to command, fails to create interest among employees. The trend today is to make use of authority in collaboration with colleagues or developing teamwork. Teamwork would encourage participation, leading to following benefits:

(a) Participation encourages involvement goals;
(b) Participation produces the free flow of communications for an informal workforce and atmosphere;
(c) Control systems are primarily for self-monitoring and guidance and not needed for external control;
(d) It produces high degree of mutual respect and trust among organisational members;
(e) Through participation, employees are likely to obtain stronger motivation towards an objective. Even those who disagree will feel compelled to

observe loyalty by the sheer weight of the group opinion; and

(f) A high degree of subordinates, which process yields personal commitment and confidence is shown in subordinates which facilitates interpersonal process.

An employee's participation would build his morale and ultimately his efficiency. An ILO document mentions that the "individual worker is not just a cog in the very big wheel, but that his personal effort is essential for the achievement of the overall production plan."[19]

Authority in an organisation means the power to take decisions, communicating them for implementation and thus influencing their behavioural pattern. How far authority is accepted and obeyed depends on the capacity and judgment of the superior and subordinates? He has to take his subordinates with him. He has to create his own image in the minds of the subordinates, so that there exists identification of purpose in the members of the organisation. Authority is exercised to achieve the purposes of the organisation. This is not possible unless the person accepting authority is able to understand as to what is expected of him. The exercise of authority will be smooth if the person exercising it is able to inspire confidence among other members of the organisation. Subordinates should dream as the superiors do.

Barnard does not agree with the traditional concept of authority; and introduces 'acceptance' as the basis of his theory of authority. He defines authority as "the character of a communication (order) in a formal organization by virtue of which it is accepted by contributor or 'member' of the organizations as governing or determining what he does or is not to do so, as far as the organization is concerned."

EFFECTIVENESS AND EFFICIENCY

A major contribution made by Chester Barnard lay in the difference that he made between effectiveness and efficiency.

Effectiveness depends on the alignment of the effort

and goals of an individual department or employee with those of the organisation as a whole. Effectiveness relates to the accomplishment of the cooperative purpose, which is social and non-personal in character. Efficiency relates to the satisfaction of individual motives and is personal in character. The test of effectiveness is the accomplishment of a common purpose or purposes; effectiveness can be measured. The test of efficiency is the eliciting of sufficient individual wills to cooperate.[20]

Barnard views authority as a character of communication and defines it as follows: "Authority is the character of a communication (order) in a formal organization by virtue of which it is accepted by a contributor to or 'member' of the organization as governing the action he contributes; that is, as governing or determining what he does or is not to do so far as the organization is concerned . . ."

If a directive communication is accepted by one to whom it is addressed, its authority for him is confirmed or established. It is admitted as the basis of action. Disobedience of such a communication is a denial of its authority for him. Therefore, under this definition the decision as to whether an order has authority or not lies with the persons to whom it is addressed, and does not reside in "persons of authority" or "those who issue the orders . . ." The concept of formal authority developed by Henri Fayol and his associates was not fully endorsed by behaviourual scientists. They argued that formal authority vested in the position of the manager, is just as nominal authority. It becomes real authority only when it is accepted by subordinates, whose activities are commanded by exercising authority. According to the advocates of acceptance theory, an authority seems to be meaningful and real only when it is used effectively. For example, if the manager having formal authority gives orders and instructions to his subordinates and the subordinates do not comply with them, it renders whole exercise ineffective.

All this suggests that there are definite limits of authority in an organization. No one, not even a manager, can decide and enforce an activity which is beyond the capacity, either mentally or physically, of the subordinate to perform. A manager who orders a shop employee to manually lift an object weighing 1,800 pounds cannot enforce compliance. Nor will the object be lifted even though the subordinate agrees with the request. Likewise, a manager cannot expect compliance with a request for a stockroom helper to operate a gear-cutting machine.[21]

CONCLUSION

William Wolf has commended this work in the following words:

Chester I. Barnard's book itself is a sociology of management. Its style of writing was purposely pitched at a 'high level of discourse'. Barnard was writing for social scientists, not for practitioners. He believed that the field of management was lacking in concepts and was clouded by ambiguous and even erroneous thinking. In a sense, he hoped that the functions would set things right and guide the social scientists to more realistic studies of organisation and management."[22]

The functions of the Executive is a highly significant work, a classic in the field written in a period following Mayo and his associates. Barnard introduced social concepts into the analysis of managerial functions and processes. By painstaking scientific exploration he formulated a logical network of definitions and concepts, with heavy applications of sociology to the management of organizations. He combined theoretical studies with active administrative work. His remarks, conclusions and evaluations demonstrate unusually profound understanding of the complexity of administrative processes.

In the words of Mooney and Reiley, ". . . the real leader finds it easy to delegate authority, and is quick to do so whenever he perceives its necessity, but he remains very conscious of the fact that three is one thing he cannot delegates, namely, his own authority and the responsibility which it includes. It is in the fact this very sense of responsibility, which makes him so ready to delegates any task as soon as the total task begins to exceed his own unaided powers. Such men are the true organizers; we might call them the born organizers. Organising genius seems to know instinctively that it must operate through the principle of delegation in order to achieve a real collective efficiency in the pursuit of the common objects.

Barnard was an acute thinker who could explain the subtleties and complexities of the working of organizations. He is seen at his best in his analysis of the decision-making process. He argues that the decision-making process has two aspects—logical aspects and non-logical aspects—which are inextricably interwoven.

Relevance

The philosophy of Chester I. Barnard is quite relevant today and there is a need to introduce co-operative system in organizations.

Cooperation implies that a well differentiated and specialized society with diversified human needs and activities may be so organized that 'each may work for all and all for each'. The present world is a scene of exploitation of the poor by the rich.

The word 'cooperation' has been derived from the Latin word Cooperate which means to work together to labour together, to endeavour for some common purpose. The Webster Universal Dictionary defines Cooperation as an association of a number of persons for a common benefit, especially in carrying on some branch of trade or industry, etc. the profit being shared, as dividend among the members.[23] In the Encycolopaedia of Social Work in India, Cooperation has been regarded as one of the most important agencies for promoting economic and social welfare. It helps to transform the social order voluntarily and, in the process, builds up the moral and material strength of the people.[24]

Co-operatives envisage participation of all employees with complete understanding and considering themselves as an important part of the organization.

What are we seeing today that there are large number of problems in making the organization run efficiently especially in developing countries. Chester I. Barnard has rightly given us a model of cooperative management which can serve as a tool of organization development.

The objectives of a typical organization development

programme are:

(i) to increase the level of the trust and support among individuals and groups throughout the organization;

(ii) to create an open, problem-solving climate throughout the organization—where problems are confronted and differences are clarified, both within group and between groups in contrast to "sweeping problems under the rug."

(iii) to increase the level of personal enthusiasm and satisfaction in the organization;

(iv) to attain better collaboration and cooperation between inter-department persons and/or groups;

(v) to increase the openness of communication laterally, vertically and diagonally;

(vi) to increase the level of self and group responsibility in planning and achievement of goals through optimum resource utilization; and

(vii) a shift in values so that human factors and feelings come to be considered as legitimate.[25]

The new millennium needs Chief Executive/Leaders as suggested by Chester I. Barnard who can keep the organizations in equilibrium. For Barnard Chief Executive is most important to provide leadership, motivation and partnership of all engaged in an organization.

Leaders are responsible for the organisation's moral climate, which in effect, reflects the moral development of the leader as well as the followers. The leader's moral development is a result of character formation through the practice of virtue in public as well as private life. The moral development of followers can be facilitated by the leader through the use of morally appropriate influence strategies and tactics which are motivated and guided by moral intent. Ethical leadership therefore, manifests itself in three dimensions: The leader's motives, the leader's influence strategies and the leader's character formation . . . The endeavour to cultivate virtues and abstain from vices in order to build up their own inner strength.[26]

China is adopting co-operative system in its development programmes in rural and urban development. The author was highly impressed by personality visiting and seeing co-operative system at work. There is no conflict between the manager and the workers.

Notes and References

1. Functions of the Executive, *op. cit.*, p. 6.
2. *Ibid.*, pp. 142-46.
3. Dulen, R. (Ed.), Human Relations in Administration, New Delhi, Prentice Hall of India Pvt. Ltd., 1970, p. 107.
4. Chester I. Barnard, The Functions of the Executive (Cambridge, Mass: Harvard University Press, 1976), p. 6.
5. Chester I. Barnard, The Functions of the Executive, 30th Anniversary ed. (Cambridge, Mass: Harvard University Press, 1968, p. 165.
6. Scott, William, G., Organisation Theory, Richard D. Irwin, Homewood, III, 1967, p. 153.
7. Goddard, H.A., Principles of Administrative Applied to Nursing Service, World Health Organisation, Geneva, 1958, p. 85.
8. Barnard, Chester I., The Functions of the Executive, Cambridge Harward University Press, 1968, pp. 226-27.
9. Herbert A Simon, Administrative Behaviour, *op. cit.*, p. 81.
10. See Chester I. Barnard, The Functions of the Executive (Cambridge, Massachussets: Harvard University Press, 1938).
11. Chester I. Barnard, Functions of Executive, *op. cit.*, pp. 215-16.
12. Chester I. Barnard, Functions of the Executive, *op. cit.*, p. 217.
13. Sumatra Ghoshal and Christopher Barlett, "Changing the Role of Top Management: Beyond Structure to Processes", *Harvard Business Review*, Jan.-Feb. 1995, p. 96.
14. John Holland, Making Vocational Choices: A Theory of Careers (Upper Saddle River, N, Prentice Hall, 1973); see also Johan Holland, Assessment Booklet: A Guide to Educational and Career Planning, 1990.
15. Edgar Schein, Career Dynamics: Matching Individual and Organisational Needs (Reading, MA: Addison-Westley, 1978, pp. 128-29.
16. Chester I. Barnard, Functions of the Chief Executive, pp. 175-81.
17. Dale Ernest, Management—Theory and Practice, 1973, Tokyo, McGraw Hill, p. 149.
18. Terry and Franklin, *op. cit.*, p. 220.
19. ILO, International Labour Conference, 33rd Session, Provisional Records, p. 34.
20. Barnard, Chester, "The Functions of the Executive, Harvard University Press, Cambridge, 1938, p. 60.

21. Terry and Franklin, *op. cit.*, p. 220.
22. W.B. Wolf, How to Understand Management, An Introduction to Chester I. Barnard, Lucas Publishers, Los Angles, 1968, p. 4.
23. Webester Universal Dictionary, p. 308.
24. Encyclopaedia of Social Work in India, Vol. I, the Planning Commission, GOI, New Delhi, 1968, p. 164.
25. S.K. Bhatia and Nirmal Singh, Principles and Techniques of Personnel Management/Human Resource Management, Deep & Deep, New Delhi, p. 106.
26. R.N. Kaungo and M. Mendonce, Ethical Leadership in Three Dimensions, in *Journal of Human Values,* IIM, Calcutta, Vol 4, No. 2, July-Dec. 1998, pp. 136-37.

15

Herbert A. Simon
(1916-2001)

Simon a distinguished American Political and Social scientist is a well-known authority in the field of Administrative Behaviour and Public Administration. He has made notable contributions to the science of administration by writing a number of papers and some thought-provoking books. He passed away in February 2001. At the time of his death, he was the Richard King Mellon University Professor at Carniqie Mellon University Pitsburg of Computer Science and Psychology. He was awarded Nobel Prize for Economics in 1978.

Herbert Simon then proceeds to make a frontal attack of administrative principles. He observes:

Administratie description suffers currently from superficiality, oversimplification, lack of realism. It has confined itself too closely to mechanism of authority and has failed to bring within its orbit the other equally important modes of influence of organizational behaviour. It has refused to undertake the tiresome task of studying the actual allocation of decision-making functions. It has been satisfied to speak of 'authority' , 'centralization', 'span of control', 'function', without seeking operational definitions of these terms.

CHART 15.1

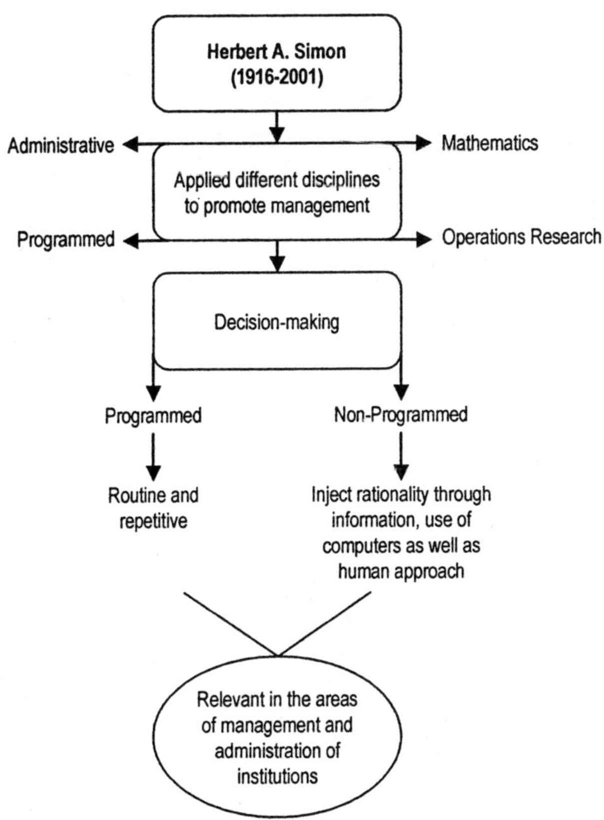

In 'Foreword' written by C.I. Barnard to Simon's book Administrative Behaviour, Barnard wrote: "In this book Professor Simon gives us an important contribution to the social science of formal organization and administration. His objective, as he says in the Preface, is to construct a set of tools—a set of concepts and a vocabulary—suitable for describing an organization and the way an administrative organization works. His interest has been primarily in the field of public administration; but to achieve his purpose adequately he has taken into account experience in other kinds of formal organizations such as military, commercial and industrial and private non-profit organizations. This makes his conclusions generally applicable and his work useful for describing administrative behaviour in all types of organization . . . the chief value of Professor Simon's exposition for the general reader and for men of affairs lies in the clarity, comprehensiveness, and generality of his description of organization, of the administrative process, of the nature of decisions, and of the elements of value and fact entering into decisions."

Simon is one of the those political and social scientists whose contribution are most important in the field of Public Administration and Decision-making. Until administrative description reaches a higher level of sophistication, there is little reason to hope that rapid progress will be made towards the identification and verification of valid administrative principles. His following books are most important.

Simon's Books

1. Measuring Municipal Activities in Co-authorship with Clarence Ridley.
2. Administrative Behaviour, 1945.
3. Public Administration, 1950 in Co-authorship with D. Smithburg and V. Thompson.
4. Organization, 1958 in co-authorship with James. G. March.
5. The New Science of Management Decision, 1960.
6. The Sciences of the Artificial (1969).
7. Human Problem Solving (1972).
8. Representation and Meaning (1972).
9. Models of Thought (1979).
10. Models of Bounded Rationality (1982).
11. Reasons in Human Affairs (1983).

He has contributed in diverse fields such as science theory, applied mathematics, operations research, economics, administration, decision-making, etc. his perceptive thinking in management has been unique. In fact his contributions encompassed all aspects of administration.

HIS MAIN CONTRIBUTIONS TO ADMINISTRATIVE THOUGHT

1. Decision-making

Simon equates organisation with decision making and considers it as the heart of administration. He asserts that The task of 'deciding' pervades the entire administrative organisation, quite as much as does the task of 'doing'—indeed, it is integrally tied up with the latter.

In a complex organization, there must be genuine goodwill between the superiors and the subordinates. This requires leadership equipped with technical knowledge. Leadership must be innovative. We can sum up in the words of Simon, who suggests that the process of decision-making includes three identifiable and essential phases. "The first phase of decision-making process-I shall call intelligence activity (borrowing the military meaning of intelligence). The second phase—inventing, developing and analysing possible course of action—I shall call design activity. The third phase —selection of a particular course of action from those available—I shall call, choice activity.[1]

Programmed and Non-Programmed Decision

Decisions have been classified differently by different writers Simon has classified decisions into programmed and non-programmed decisions. According to Simon, "decisions are programmed to the extent that they are repetitive and routine and a definite procedure has been worked out for handling them. . . If a particular problem recurs often enough, a routine procedure will usually be worked out for solving it . . . Decisions are non-programmed to the extent that they are novel, unstructured, and consequential. There is no cut and dried method for handling the problem because it has not arisen before or because its precise nature and structure are elusive or complex, or because it is so important that it deserves a custom-tailored treatment." The process of decision-making in respect of programmed decisions is simplified by decision rules as no judgement or discretion is needed to find out solution of such problems. It simply becomes a matter of identifying the problem and applying decision rules for getting it solved. Programmed decisions remain consistent for a relatively longer period of time and over many situations.

Non-programmed decisions are made with respect to problems which are unique, non-repetitive and about which required knowledge and information are not available. Such decisions are made under new and unfamiliar circumstances, less frequently compared to programmed decisions. Since non-programmed decisions are made with regard to new situations, it renders standard and pre-determined procedure and rules ineffective and irrelevant. And it calls for a lot of experience, creativity, innovativeness, farsightedness and judement.

Drucker classified them into generic and unique decisions, Generic and unique resemble programmed and non-programmed decisions respectively. Delbecq classified decisions into routine decisions, creative decisions and negotiated decisions.

Programmed decisions may also not be so mechanical. We need to have some discretion, however small these may be.

Rationality in Decision-making

Rationalist Approach

This classical approach presupposes that a number *of* alternatives are available, based on mathematical analysis and logic. This approach considers reason as a superior source *of* knowledge and expands the ability *of* the manager to avoid unsought and undesired consequences.

A variant of this theory is the approach *of* March and Simon in viewing the organization seeking a satisfying solution rather than an optimum one. According to this view, "The central concern *of* Administrative theory is with the boundary between the rational and the non-rational aspect of human social behaviour. Administrative theory is peculiarly the theory of intended and bounded rationality of the behaviour of human beings who satisfy because they have not the wits to maximise."

In trying to describe the factors that affect decision making, Herbert Simon, among others, has proposed a theory of bounded rationality. This theory points out that decision makers must cope with inadequate information about the nature of the problem and its possible solutions, a lack of time or money to compile more complete information, an inability to remember large amounts of information. and the limits of their own intelligence.

Instead of searching for the perfect or ideal decision, managers frequently settle for one that will adequately serve their purposes. In Simon's terms, they satisfy, or accept the first satisfactory decision they uncover, rather than maximize, or search until they find the best possible decision. What the effective decision-maker learns to do is to satisfy with a clear sense of goals for the organization in mind.[2]

The rationalist approach is recommended by Dror also. He mentions its five limitations as:

1. Too strong dependence on quantifications.
2. Impossible to deal with conflicting values.
3. Precise criteria indispensable.
4. Special characteristics of the political resources.
5. Inability to deal with large and complex system.

Herbet A. Simon is of the view that the computer can help us in making programmed decisions. It is very difficult for the top executives of complex organizations to take rational decisions as the variables are numerous. Simon lists the following developments in the adoption of electronic computer in programmed decision-making:

(a) The electronic computer is bringing about, with unexpected speed, high level of automation in the routine, programmed decision-making and data processing that was formerly the province of clerks.
(b) The area of programmed decision-making is rapidly extended as we find ways to apply the tools of operations research to types of decisions that have upto now been regarded as judgemental particularly, but not exclusively, middle management decisions in the area of manufacturing and warehousing.

(c) The computer has extended the capability of the mathematical techniques to problems far too large to be handled by less automatic computing devices, and has further extended the range of programmable decisions by contributing the new technique of simulation.

(d) Companies are just beginning to discover way of bringing together the first two of these developments—of combining the mathematical techniques for making decisions about aggregative middle management variables with the data processing techniques for implementing these decisions in detail at Clerical levels.

The combination of the above mentioned four developments, is resulting in data processing factories for producing in a highly mechanized way, the programmed decisions.

2. Humanistic Approach

The humanistic process is discussed by Chester Bernard in his book, "Functions of the Executives." He states that the ultimate decision may not be the result of logical processes, but may be determined by an approach developed within a framework of social and environmental conditions, past and present. Perceptions and past experience, highly influence the decision-making in this approach. The basic elements of the humanistic solution to a problem are:

(i) The Social setting or environment of the decision-making.
(ii) The nature of the decision-making.
(iii) The goals of the decision.
(iv) The social impact of the decision.

3. The Integrative Approach

An integrative decision process combines both the rational and humanistic, the economic and social, authoritarian and the autonomous in such a way that all members of the work group feel better. This approach is most successful when decisions are made by those who do the work at the scene of the action rather than by those occupying executive offices, a long way from the firing line. Rational, ethical, economic and social considerations must be considered concurrently during the decision-making.[3]

All decisions must be rational in general parlance and for this to achieve, there is need of appropriate means. To him it requires a total knowledge and anticipation of the consequences that will follow on each choice. It also requires a choice from among all possible alternative behaviours. If appropriate means are chosen to reach desired ends, the decision is rational. However, there are many complications to this simple test of rationality. For it is difficult to separate means from ends because an apparent end may only be a means for some future end. This is commonly referred to as the means end chain or hierarchy."[4]

Simon feels that it is difficult to take decisions rationally.

He mentioned three reasons for it.

First, the end to be attained by the choice of particular behaviour alternatives are often incompletely or incorrectly stated through failure to consider the alternate ends that could be reached by selection of another behaviour. . . . Second, in actual situations a complete separation of means from ends is usually impossible. . . . Third, the means-end terminology tends to obscure the role of the time element in decision making.[5]

Simon differentiates between different types of rationality. A decision is:

(1) objectively rational where it is correct behaviour for maximizing given values in a given situation;
(2) subjectively rational if the decision maximizes attainment relative to knowledge of the subject;
(3) consciously rational where adjustment of means to ends is a conscious process;
(4) deliberately rational to the degree that the adjustment of means to ends has been deliberately sought;

(5) organizationally rational to the extent that it is aimed at the organisation's goals; and

(6) personally rational if the decision is directed to the individual's goals.[6]

In Simon's view, "behaviour is determined by the irrational and non-rational elements that bound the area of rationality. The area of rationality is the area of adaptability to these non-rational elements."

Simon, however feels "Ideally this involves upward, downward and sideways channels. For decision-making to function adequately, communication in all three channels must be a two way process. Simon favours the channel of informal communication. These informal channels are based on the social as distinct from the formal pattern of relationships and carry advice, information, 'unofficial orders', and the norms and values of the informal organization." We have to be careful from various problems faced in the process of communication However, there are problems of communications in formal organization, Simon observes.

"From warning, difference in the frame of reference of the persons receiving a communication, difference in status which cause a filtering and distorting influence upto difficulties linked with geographic distance and biased processing of the information both by the senders and receivers. Moreover, as Simon further notes, the constant pressure of work makes it impossible to pay due attention to all communications", "including channels for oral and written communications, paper flow, records and reports and manuals. Adequate channel of communication is necessary for decision-making functions. The organization structure includes the specification of a formal system of communications."

The Formal and Informal Organizational Structure

Organization charts are useful for showing the formal organizational structure and who is responsible for certain tasks. In reality, though, the organization chart cannot begin to capture the interpersonal relationships that make up the informal organizational structure. Herbert A. Simon has described this as "the interpersonal relationships in the organization that affect decisions within it but either are omitted .from the formal scheme or are not consistent with it. For example, during a busy period, one employee may turn to another for help rather than going through a manger. Or an employee in sales may establish a working relationship with an employee in production, who can provide information about product availability faster than the formal reporting system. And anyone who has worked in an organization knows the importance of secretaries and executive assistants, which are never shown on an organization chart.[7]

Role of Information Technology

Simon also advocated the role of information Technology in decision-making

In these high tech times, marked by a revolution in informatics and electronics, an effective administrator has to be a 'knowledge worker' in the service sector, which is 'knowledge' or 'information industry'. In such an industry, we receive information, process information and produce information as an output of decision-making. The time has come when there is hardly any 'scope' of 'arbitary' and 'ego-based' decision-making. The behaviour of subordinates will be controlled not perhaps through the code of conduct rules but through better knowledge and information on the part of the boss. Hence, the information skill of the decision-maker in getting information, in storing information and using information is going to be the crux and future decision making scenario.[8]

T.K. Rama Chandran in his Article, "Information and Systems Management in Government" in the Administrator, Oct.-Dec. 1997 rightly suggests the role of information system in decision-making. He says that millions of man hours and rupees are lost because the right information is not available to the right person at the right time. Decisions are therefore, based on half-baked information and is perhaps out of date; inaccurate or misleading. . . During a drought a few hundred bore wells were to be dug and a proposal to purchase some drilling rigs was put up for urgent clearance. When he asked as to how many bore wells were in existence, nobody seemed to know. Then he wanted to know how many rigs were already available and their locations. Again nobody knew. However, the purchase had to be made and there was no alternative but to go ahead with the order. Here was a case of decisions having to be taken without necessary and sufficient information being available with all the concomitant implications in terms of higher cost and inefficiency of resources use that the nation can ill-afford.

Herbert A. Simon says : "Information should be gathered upto the point where the incremental cost of additional information is equal to the incremental profit that be earned having it."

The new decision-making techniques will alter the manager's job. Decision-making will be rationalized. it will become an impersonal process. Routine business activities will be directed in the manner traffic is controlled by automatic signals today. The personal element in giving orders will gradually disappear. Moreover, people prefer to work in an atmosphere which is free from personal domination. The new organization may then be a more congenial place to work.

Simon says, "With advances in computer technology, more and more complex decision will become programmed. Even a completely unprogrammed decision, made once and for all, can be reached via computer techniques by building a model of the decision situation. Various courses of action can then by simulated and their effects assessed. 'The automated factory of the future'. Simon maintains, 'will operate on the basis of programmed decisions produced in the automated office beside it.' However, Computers cannot take rational decisions.

Simon says:

"Real understanding is obtained by analyzing the managerial process in terms of decisions. If complete rationality were impossible then the whole theory of decision-making and management would be 'Always select that alternative, among those available, which will lead to the most complete aehievement of goals."[9]

"Decision are something more than factual propositions. To be sure, they are descriptive of a future state of affairs, and this description can be true or false in a strictly empirical sense; but they possess in addition an imperative quality—they select one future state of affairs in preference to another and direct behaviour towards chosen alternative. In short, they have ethical as well as "factual content."

Science of Administration—Simon's main focus was to develop science of administration which can be value free and based on facts rather than hunches.

In his "A Comment on the Science of Public administration Review" (1947), Simon proposed:

A pure science of administration would attempt to answer such questions as: "What factors determine the degree of efficiency achieved by an organization?" "Under what circumstances is public responsibility secured in a government agency?" The answers to these questions do not depend upon the value system of the inquirer.

However, the pure science of administration may divorce from social reality and relevance.

Simon was the first to argue that: "most of the propositions that make up the body of administrative theory today share . . . this defect of proverbs. For almost every principle one can find an equally plausible and acceptable contradictory principle. Although the two principles of the pair will lead to exactly opposite organisational recommendations, there is nothing in the theory to indicate which is the proper one to apply.

He further observes:

"Administrative description suffers currently from superficiality, oversimplification, lack of realism. It has confined itself too closely to mechanism of authority and has failed to bring within its orbit the other equally important modes of influence of organisational behaviour. It has refused to undertake the tiresome task of studying the actual allocation of decision-making functions. It has been satisfied to speak of 'authority', 'centralisation', 'span of control', 'function', without seeking operational definitions of these terms'.

Until administrative description reaches a higher level of sophistication, there is little reason to hope that rapid progress will be made towards the identification and verification of valid administrative principles."

The ultimate purpose of decision-making is to ensure rational, feasible, acceptable and practical decisions. According to Mr. L. Mehl there are three zones of decisions.[10]

(a) Calculable Zone

In this zone, the processing of elements is done in a reasonable and precise manner, i.e., in the logic deductive sense. In this zone, large number of technocrats work and their results are often reliable and somewhat quick.

(b) Uncertain Zone

It suggests a state where the information available is always in an incomplete from mostly dominated by the generalist administrators.

(c) Axiologic Zones

It is the area of ultimate reality where the decision is taken and made public.

Most of the decisions involve risk, adventure and uncertainties. Therefore, to improve decision-making we must reduce the uncertain zone as far as possible. It is not possible to eliminate the uncertain zone altogether in a democratic form of government. Therefore, the only possibility is that the calculable zone could be extended to reduce the uncertain zone. In social sciences value hazards are inherent and no decision-maker can be completely free from the elements of risks and uncertainties but we should see that the rationality component of the decision should be maximized and all efforts should be directed to eliminate value judgements which may enter due to incomplete knowledge and information.

Speedy and realistic decision-making is one of the essentials of efficient administration. In a big and complex organization, the number of decisions to be taken from time to time is so large and the points at which the decisions are to be implemented are so many that it becomes necessary to distribute decision-making powers among a number of organs, rather than concentrate these in one organ. This is expected to prevent the emergence of bottlenecks which bedevil highly centralized power structures.

In simple words, an organizations is said to be centralized, if most of the powers of decision are vested in the top level, so that the lower ones have to refer most problems to the head of the organizations, for his immediate decisions. A decentralized organization, on the other hand, is one in which the lower hands are allowed to decide most of the matters which come up, reserving comparatively a few bigger and more important problems only for those higher up. The essence of centralization or decentralization, therefore, lies in the distribution of the power of decision-making. It should be noted that no organization can be completely centralized or decentralized.[11]

Fesler states that greater the degree of decentralization:

1. Greater the number of decisions made lower down the management hierarchy;
2. More important the decisions made lower down the management hierarchy, for example, greater the sum of capital expenditure that can be approved by the plant manager without consulting any one else, greater the degree of decentralization in the field;
3. More functions affected by decisions at lower levels. Thus, companies which permit only operational decisions to be made at separate branch plants are less decentralized than those which also permit financial and personnel decisions at branch plants; and
4. Less checking required on the decision-centralizations is greater when no check at all must be made, less when superiors have to be informed of the decision after it has been made; still less if superiors have to be consulted before the decision is made. The fewer people to be consulted and the lower they are on the management hierarchy, the greater the degree of decentralization.[12]

Prof. Herbert A. Simon was also interested in Operations Research as it can help in making rational decision.

Operational Research is the methods of science to complex problems arising in the direction and management of large systems of men, machines, materials and money in industry, business, government and defence. The distinctive approach is to develop a scientific model of the system incorporating measurements of factors such as chance and risk, with which to predict and compare the customers of alternative decisions, strategies or controls. The purpose is to help management determine its policy and actions scientifically."

The success of whole management depends upon decision-making. Herbert A Simon would be providing help if managers understand his writing and put it into practice.

Effective Organizational Climate

Simon feels that organization affects the people who work for it in the five different ways:

(i) The organization divides work among its members; giving each employees particular task, it limits and concentrates his attention on that task.

(ii) The organization establishes standard practice; by working out detailed procedures it relieves employees of the need to determine such procedure, each time they are crossways;

(iii) The organization transmits authoritative decisions by dispatching such decisions downward, upward and crossways;

(iv) The organization provides a communication system; and

(v) The organization trains and indoctrinates its members by providing for the internalization of influence relating to knowledge, skills and loyalty; training enables employees to make decisions as the organization would like them to be made.

Relevance

Herbert A Simon, a distinguished Political and social scientists is a well-known authority in the field of administrative behaviour and Public Administration and most valued contributor to administrative thought lies in the enunciation of his views on decision-making. Simon treats decision-making as synonymous with managing. He holds that decision-making is the heart of administration and "the vocabulary of administrative theory must be derived from the logic and psychology of human choice." His book Administrative Behavour has gained worldwide recognition. It has been translated into 12 languages: German, Italian, Spanish, Portuguese, Japanese, Dutch, Korean, Swedish, Polish, Finnish, French and Chinese. The earliest translation was in German in 1955. Its translation into Chinese has been the most recent, only in 1988. Published first in 1945, the book has been in print ever-since.

In 'Foreward' written by C.I. Barnard to Simon's book Administrative Behaviour, Barnard wrote: "In this book Professor Simon gives us an important contribution to the social science of formal organization and administration. His objective, as he says in the Preface, is to construct a set of tools—a set of concepts and a vocabulary—suitable for describing an organization and the way an administrative organization works. His interest has been primarily in the field of public administration; but to achieve his purpose adequately he has taken into account experience in other kinds of formal organizations such as military, commercial, and industrial and private non-profit organizations. This makes his conclusions generally applicable and his work useful for describing administrative behaviour in all types of organization. . . . the chief value of Professor Simon's exposition for the general reader and for men of affairs lies in the clarity, comprehensiveness, and generality of his description of organization, of the administrative process, of the nature of decisions, and of the elements of value and fact entering into decisions."[13]

Simon would always remain relevant in future times to come which is evident from translations of his book. His view of Administrative behaviours is excellent. Rational decision-making is the heart of management which was emphasized by Simon.

CONCLUSION

Simon observes: "It is fatal defect of the current principles of administration that, like proverbs, they occur in pairs (e.g. specialization by place and specialization by function). For almost every principle one can find an equally plausible and acceptable contradictory principle." It needs to be emphasized that Administrative Behaviour makes a watershed in the history of administrative thought. Simon has laid the foundation of a really scientific science of administration which requires for its steady development concepts and tools and rigorous methods of organizational analysis.

Simon recognizes the "importance of centralized decision-making as a means of coordination of professional competence and responsibility. In his view, centralization delays decision-making, obstructs communication channels and diverts the attention of management from significant to insignificant problems. Such dysfunctional influence on motivations is one of the important weaknesses of centralization.

Prof. Herbert A. Simon would remain relevant in future as he emphasizes on rational decision-making. He classified decision as Programmed and unprogrammed but his effort has been to make unprogrammed decision as rational as possible.

Decision-Makers in the new millennium should not merely be satisfied with the efficient and effective decisions, but their decisions should act as initiators of changes in polity to ensure a satisfaction of the people. An effective decision-making/implementation produces satisfaction. Otherwise there is dissatisfaction, reflected in stress, hypertension, germinating avoidance/escapist style, percolating ultimately into the life style of a decision-maker, producing general discontentment, frustration and perhaps, a life without any rudder to attain undecided mission.[14]

The decision-makers have to go beyond traditional administration. T.N. Rastogi in his Article, "Changing Scenario of Management Discipline" rightly mentions the need of new ideology for Decision-makers. To quote:

"Management, which I call knowledge industry, is what management does through POSDCORB in its seven-fold functional mechanism. This may also be filled into my favourite VIBGYOR model hinging on the matrix of humanization with the rainbow colours in all their splendor when professional managers as change agents in their respective colour will ensure their professional wisdom to bring about a complete transformation of Indian economy in its globalized structural shape in the overall scheme of globalization. I conclude with the dictum of the good old pagan, Plato, May my store of gold be such as none but the best can bear."[15]

In the new Millennium, administrators can take the help of the following to take decisions in tune with the changed times.

(a) Exploding material on management.
(b) Expanding modern technology to process variables to arrive at decisions.
(c) Understanding the changing needs of the society.
(d) Pressure of globalization and privatization.

Notes and References

1. Herbert A. Simon, The New Science of Management Decisions, Harpee and Row, New York, 1960, p. 2
2. James, A.F. Stoner, *et. al.*, *op. cit.*, p. 253.
3. Herbert Simon, Administrative Behaviour, *op. cit.*, p. 81.
4. Fred Luhans, Organisational Behvaiour: A Modern Behavioural Approach to Management, Tokyo, Mc.Grow Hill, Kogak Usha Ltd., 1973, p. 191.
5. Herbert A Simon, "Administrative Behaviour", *op. cit.*, p. 63.
6. *Ibid.*, pp. 76-77.
7. James A.F. Stoner, *et al.*, *op. cit.*, p. 334.
8. N.K. Kulshreshtha, Management in Public Administration, The Decision Anatomy, X-rayed, in IJPA, January-March, 1994, p. 45.
9. H.A. Simon, Administration Behaviour, *op. cit.*, p. 240.
10. L. Mehl, Article in Institute International Administration Publique, October-December 1968.
11. F.M. Marx, *op. cit.*, p. 252.
12. Earnest Koontz and Cyril O'Dannell: Management: A System and Contingency Analysis of Managerial Functions, McGraw Hill, London, 1976, pp. 204-06.
13. G.S. Sudha, Management and Administrative Thinkers"—Doctrines and Philosophies, Indus Valleys Publications, p. 169.
14. N.K. Kulshrestha, "Management in Public Administration: The Decision Anatomy X-Rayed", in *IJPA*, January-March, 1994, p. 34.
15. T.N. Rastogi, *IJPA*, January-March, 2000, p. 19

16

Mary Parker Follett (1868-1933)

Mary Parker Follett, a versatile genius having keen and deep insights into the issues of management and industry was born in 1868, in Boston, USA. She got education in Political economy, Political Science, Philosophy and Law from Cambridge College. Her approach to management was psychological and social. It is surprising that she had no contact with those who were concerned with the Hawthorne Experiments. "But the findings of those investigations, when they appeared in their full form in 1930s the conclusions drawn from the Hawthrone Studies can be recognized as reflecting principles of a fundamental tenet that Follett had advanced from her own observations of the industrial situation."

She was a great writer. She took care to present her original ideas in simple and lucid style. Her main concern was human philosophy and character. She believed in togetherness and group thinking in management. She felt the need of harmony between owners and labourers which she thought is possible through integration.

Follet was convinced that no one could become a whole person except as a member of a group; human beings

Versatile Genius

Mary Parker Follett (1968-1933)

Simple and Lucid Style

First Lady Administrative Thinker

Resolution of Conflict

Compromise

Domination

Real Method is Integration

Leadership (To draw from each fuller potentialities)

Law of the situation depersonalising order

Other Administrative Thoughts

Authority (consent of Subordinates vital sense of belongingness)

Co-ordination (Synchronised Efforts)

Control effective unity

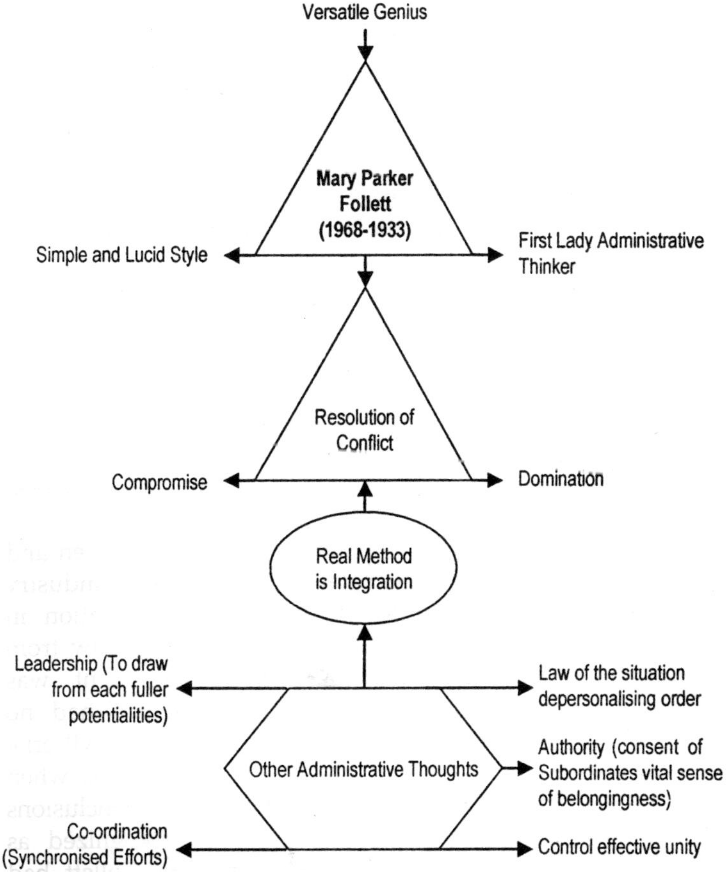

grew through their relationships with others in organizations. In fact, she called management "the art of getting things done through people."[1] She took for granted Taylor's assertion that labour and management shared a common purpose as members of the same organization, but she believed that the artificial distinction between managers (order givers) and subordinates (order takers) obscured this natural partnership. She was a great believer in the power of the group, where individuals could combine their diverse talents into something bigger. Moreover, Follett's "holistic" model of control took into account not just individuals and groups, but the effects of such environmental factors as politics, economics, and biology.

Follett's model was an important forerunner of the idea that management meant more than just what was happening inside a particular organization. By explicitly adding the organizational environment to the theory, Follett paved the way for management theory to include a broader set of relationships, some insider the organization and some across the organization's borders. A diverse set of modern management theories pays homage to Follett on this point.[2]

Her writings include the following:

1909 The Speaker of the House of Representatives, New York.
1920 The New State, N.Y. and London, Longman.
1924 Creative Experience, N.Y. and London, Longman.
1927 Business Management as Profession (Edited by Henry C. Metcalf), Chicago A.W. Shah & Co.
1941 Dynamic Administration: The collected Papers of Mary Parker Follet. (Edited by M. Metcalf and L. Urwick) London, Pitman, N.Y., Harper & Sons.
1949 Freedom and Coordination: Lectures in Business Organization by Mary Parker Follet (Edited by L. Urwick), London Pitman.

Follett is regarded as 'prophet' in management philosophy. Harold Pollard wrote: "In the field of management thought there can be no one more deserving of this title than Follett. Almost everything she said and wrote in the 1920s has been 'rediscovered' and amplified by the psycho-sociologists of the 1950s and 1960s. But in her day and age, she was almost a lone voice crying in the wilderness.[3]

MAIN CONTRIBUTION TO ADMINISTRATIVE THOUGHT

Constructive Conflict

Conflict is inevitable in life and at work.

Mary Parker Follett advances the idea of "constructive conflict recognizing thereby that conflicts should be regarded as a normal process in any activity of an organization by which socially valuable differences register themselves for the enrichment of all concerned." It can be used constructively or destructively

To Follett, conflict is neither good nor bad and has to be considered without passion or ethical prejudgments. Conflict is not warfare, but is only an appearance of difference—difference of opinions, of interests not only between employer and employee but also between managers, between directors or wherever differences appear.[4]

Interactionists not only accept conflict, but also encourage it in a regulated way. This approach that a minimum level of conflict needs to be maintained to shake the group out of its complacency and to make them innovative and creative. A large number of social scientists like Robins (1973, 1978), Boulding (1971), Dalton (1950), Katz (1974), McGregor (1967), Schimidt (1974), Pareek (1982), and other opine that 'conflict generates a climate, wherein stagnant organizations are rejuvenated.'

While the behavioural approach accepted conflict, the interactionist view encourages conflict on the ground that a harmonious, peaceful, tranquil and cooperative group is prone to becoming static, apathetic and non responsive to need for change and innovation."[5] Thus, groups require disharmony as well as harmony, dissociation as well as association and conflicts within them are by no means altogether disruptive factors."[6]

Resolution of Conflict

Follett feels that conflicts can be solved by the following three methods, i.e. Domination, Compromise and integration.

(a) Domination

Dominance is identical with "power over" that is "the power of some person or groups over some other person or group."[7] Dominance leaves habits and beliefs unchanged.

Domination is based on the huge power available with one party as compared to the other. It makes use of this power to manipulate and exploit individuals. In this way, the less powerful party cannot dictate and hence accept domination even without liking it.

(b) Compromise

In this method both parties part with something and compromise is reached at some point which they are supposed to agree. This is traditional method of resolving conflicts. There is no distinct winner or loser or because each party is expected to give up something of value for a concession. It is based on a simple give and take process and typically involves negotiation and a series of sacrifices. The amount given up by each party in conflict, however, will be in direct relation to its strength.

Bargaining can lead to the resolution of a conflict, but usually without much openness on the part of the groups involved and without much real problem-solving. Typically, in bargaining each side begins by demanding more than it really expects to get.

For bargaining to be practical at all as a conflict resolution strategy, both parties must be of relatively equal power. Otherwise, one group simply will force its will on the other, and the weaker group will have no means of obtaining concessions from the stronger one. Bargaining also is more likely to work if there are several acceptable alternatives that both groups are willing to consider. Otherwise, bargaining is likely to end in a deadlock.[8]

(c) Integration

According to Follett compromise does not create but only deals with the existing, whereas integration creates something new, leads to invention, and to the emergence of the new value.

In Follett's words, "the first rule for obtaining integration is to put your cards on the table, face the real issue, uncover the conflict, bring the whole thing into the open.

BASES OF INTEGRATION

Follett describes three steps for integration.

1st Step

In the first step, there is a need to bring the differences in the open rather than suffering with them.

We cannot hope to integrate, she asserts, "sour differences unless we know what they are."[9]

Care must be taken to bring the vital points in the open rather than unimportant points. It means to analyse real issues affecting conflict.

2nd Step

The second step is the breaking up the whole into their constituent parts. It means analyzing the concrete issues in question.

To Follett, all language used is symbolic, and therefore, one should be on one's guard to know as to what is being symbolized. Integration not only involves breaking up of the whole but sometimes one has to do the opposite. It is important to articulate the whole demand, the real demand which is being obscured by miscellaneous minor claims or by ineffective presentation.

3rd Step

Anticipation of conflict is the third step. Anticipation of conflict does not mean the avoidance of conflict but responding to it differently. The responses and reactions of the two parties to each other and the way that those responses and reactions affect the evolving situation must be fully realized. According to Follett, the major objective of management should be the attainment of integrative unity. A business should function smoothly and noiselessly like a well-designed, well-constructed, well-lubricated machine. There should be perfect coordination between its various parts. There will be some amount of friction, for no movement is possible without friction. There are conflicting interests in every business but these should be so reconciled as to achieve maximum efficiency.[10]

By dominance only one side gets what it wants by compromise neither side gets what it wants;[11] by integration we find a way in which both side may get what they wish. In this way one is domination, which means a victory for one side or the other. The second is compromise which means each side gives up something in order to have peace. The third is integration which means neither side sacrifices any thing and both sides gain. Integration occurs when difference are brought into the open when facts are presented. The first rule then for obtaining integration, is to put your cards on the table, face the real issue, uncover the conflict and bring the whole thing into the open. In this way this involves breaking the demands and interests of the both sides and finding the whole demand, which is being[12] obscured by miscellaneous minor claims or by ineffective presentation. Thus integration means the creation of a novel solution that penalizes no one and that becomes the only sure base for progress.

Mary Parker Follet says It is realized that greater participation in the affairs of the organizations is not a simple matter and for it to be effective, not only will it be necessary to create appropriate machinery and procedures but changes will also have to be brought about in the management attitudes and skills of staff in upper echelons of administration. The polarization of differences of views of the management and the employees can only be avoided by using the medium of staff organizations for the better ventilation of their grievances and the expression of their needs and problems. We must encourage the process of integration of management as it would lay the solid foundations for harmounious relationships and lesser staff problems.

Obstacles to Integration

Integration is difficult to achieve as it requires, intelligence, and an art and science to solve the obstacles in the way of integration. Only deep insight and mature judgment can help to reach integration. The difficulty to integration arises from the fact that people enjoy and like domination rather than integration. Another difficulty in achieving integration is the emphasis laid on theory rather than practical solution.

Fourth problem is the use of language. Language used, Follett says, must be suitable to reconciliation and should not arouse antagonism and perpetuate the conflict. Sometimes language used even results in new disputes which were not there earlier and making situation more complicated.

Other obstacles are the undue influence exerted by leaders and lack of training to those who are engaged in the process of integration. Training is needed in the art and science of co-operative thinking, to understand the technique of integration.

Follett says that there are four important steps in giving orders: (1) a conscious attitude—realize the principles through which it is possible to act on in any matter; (2) a responsible attitude to decide which of the principles we should act on; (3) an experimental attitude—try experiments and watch results; (4) pooling the results. In order that the orders are accepted.[13]

Follett suggests three things viz., (1) building up of certain attitudes; (2) providing for their release; and (3) augmenting the released response as it is being carried out.[14]

To Follett, both giving and receiving orders is a matter of integration through circular behaviour. There are two dissociated paths in the individual. Therefore, before integration can be made between order giver and order receiver, there is need for integration to be made within the individual. An order should seek to unite, to integrate the dissociated paths.[15]

Follett creative experience discusses about circular response. She says:

"The concept of circular response developed in creative experience in later essays and lecturers, is her principal contribution to the analysis of failures of integration. Circular response rests upon the theory that the unit of social analysis is the pattern of relations between actor conceived as a single situation produced by a union of their interests. No response by an actor is wholly predictable for he must continually modify his behaviour to adjust to expect responses of others, who constitute his environment. This modulation to both the activity and the sentiments of the actors in an environment, constitutes circular response. As Follett puts it . . . "The most fundamental thought about all this is that reaction is always reaction to relating. I never react to you but you plus me; or to be more accurate, it is plus—you reaction to a you—plus —me." Yet the actual response is still more circular. I can never fight you. I am always fighting you plus me. Employees do not respond only to their employers, but to the relation between themselves and their employer circular behaviour on the basis of integration gives us the key to constructive conflict."

LAW OF THE SITUATION: (DEERSONALISING ORDER)

Mary Parker Follett, an early contributor of theories of administration, first developed the concept of "law of situation." In this, she referred to the fact that real authority stems from the situation itself and not from any inherent authority vested in the administrator who view the scene.[16] At one place Mary P. Follett said that, "One person should not give order to another person but both should agree to take their orders from the situation. How can we avoid two extremes; to great bossism in giving orders, and practically no orders given?. . . . My solution is to depersonalize the giving of orders to unite all concerned in a study or situation, to discover the law of the situation obey that . . . One person should not give orders to another person, but both should agree to take their orders from the situation. If orders are simply part of the situation, the question of some one giving and some one receiving does not come up. Both accept the orders given by the situation."[17]

In a paper published in 1919, Mary Parker Follett used the phrase "law of the situation" to express the same general idea. Actually, most practicing managers consider the individual situation in carrying out their managerial duties, but they perhaps neglect some situational factors. As more knowledge is gained about which factors should be taken into account in what situations, the caliber of management will improve and the manager will be able to manage with more certainty than at present. With increasing knowledge about the various psychological, sociological, and technical circumstances of various situations, the contingency school will offer much to our theory and practice of management.

Power

She defines power as "the ability to make things happen, to be a causal agent, to initiate change. Power is the capacity to produce intended effects. It is an instinctive urge inherent in all human beings. She makes a distinction between power over and power with.[18] The former may tend to be 'coercive-power' while the latter is a jointly developed coactive power'.[19]

Management: Writers and political scientists talk about "the delegation of power" or the separation, transfer, or conferring power. Follett maintains and they are wrong and they fail to distinguish between power and authority. Power is defined by Follet, "simply the ability to make things happen, to be a casual agent, to initiate change." Its sources and uses should be carefully studied. In any case, whether it is good or bad depends on the purposes for which it is used.

Power with is superior to power-over as it is a self-developing entity which promotes better understanding, reduces friction and conflict and encourages cooperative endeavour. However, Follett does not think it possible to get rid of power over, but thinks that one should try to reduce it. This can be accomplished, according to Follett, by integrating the desires, obeying the law of situations and through functional unity. In a functional unity, each has his functions and he should have the authority and responsibility which go with that function. Follett also believes that power can never be delegated or handled out or wrenched from someone as it is the result of knowledge and ability. But, she feels, we can create conditions for the development of power.[20]

Authority

Mary Parker Follett analyses the underlying forces which find their expression in what is popularly referred to as authority. It is her conclusion that the influence exerted by an individual is derived ultimately from the nature of the task itself and from the situation in which the task is to be performed. Furthermore what appears as authority and is displaced in a specific decision is in reality but the final outward expression of an entire series of tasks, action, and decision which have preceded this is so called decision or act of authority. Although she discusses delegation and acknowledge expertise as a base for authority. Miss Follett makes the point that authority is a far more complex concept than had previously been believed and its roots lie deep in the task and the situation in which it occurs. This belief in function as source of authority and responsibility, and the conclusion that final authority as evidenced by the decision itself is but one step in an entire process of particular importance to anyone studying organization behaviour and structure.[21]

According to her authority stems from the task being performed and from the situation, and suggests that function is the true basis from which authority is derived. Therefore, she says that central authority i.e., derivation of authority from the Chief Executive should be replaced by authority of function in which each individual has final authority within the allotted functions. She feels that the authority can be conferred on others and such conferment is not delegation. She expresses in clear terms that 'delegation of authority' should be an 'obsolete expression'.[22]

Control

Control is an important method to achieve organizational goals. Unlike classical thinkers, Follett believes in fact-control rather than man-control and in correlated-control than super-imposed control.[23]

Her concept of control was based on unity and cooperation among all elements, material and people, in a given situation. She said that 'the aim of organization engineering is control though effective unity.' She argued that control cannot be established without bringing the integrative unities, which are self-regulating, self-directing organism. The managers must not pay attention to single elements, but complex interrelationships; not persons, but situation. In business, social control must develop from the process of integration.[24]

Co-ordination

Perhaps the most original and constructive thought on the concept of coordination has been that of Mary Parker Follett, who has shifted principles from techniques and clarified the conditions for creating synchronized effort. [25]

Follett favours "collective planning on a national or even international level," but at the same time she feels that central government planning imposed the top down is doomed to failure. She said, "The opposition of *laissez faire* is not coercion but coordination," and "coordination is by its very nature a process of auto governed activity the reciprocal relating of all the factors in situation." She pointed out three principles for achieving coordination as follows.[26]

1. Direct Contact

The principle of direct contact states that coordination must be achieved through interpersonal vertical, and horizontal relationships of the people in an enterprise: "Cross relations between heads of departments instead of up and down the line through the chief executive." People exchange ideas, ideals; prejudices, and purposes, through direct personal communication much more efficiently than by any other method, and with the understanding gained in this way, they find means to achieve both common and personal goals.

2. Co-ordination in the Early Stages

The second principle stresses the importance of achieving coordination in the early stages of planning and policy-making, so that policy may be created by responsible people, rather than later meetings and then can only try to resolve differences between policies already evolved by isolated groups. Follett said that, "The process of the interpretation of policies must begin before they are completed, while they are still in the formative stage."

3. Reciprocal Relationship

The third principle states that all factors in the situation are reciprocally related. This means equal attention to all variables in the social system.

"Coordination in these various forms is a continuing process, since in any complex social environment there exists many points of creativity and established policies can never be executed as designed but must constantly be reformed in consonance with basic goals." Finally, all those principles must be underpinned by information based on continuous research. Follett said that "the information itself would not be a form of control, for there would be a tendency to act in accordance with information given if it were accepted as accurate."

Planning

According to Follett, national planning need not be in opposition to individual. If national planning is based on the principle of "the interpenetration of authority instead of super-authority it could give scope to individual initiative by showing in the way to combine effectively with other individual initiative by a process not of compromises but integration."[27]

Leadership

The leaders' main function is to evoke, that is to draw out from each of his people, their fullest potentialities. Everybody has some capacity, some ability and some potential for development. The leader sees to it that he develops it and uses it for organizational work. The leader is like a good teacher. He guides and inspires his subordinates. His men therefore work with him enthusiastically. The Annual Report of Larsen and Tubro Ltd., 2006-07 follows the ideas of Follett. To quote the report: The quality of leadership more than any other single factor determines the success or failure of an organization. . . . People whose talent are not exploited become disenchanted and disruptive. The important thing is that managers must involve employees; employees' lead employees.

Follett has very perceptively observed that the skills of

the executive are not painted on the outside. A good executive is like an iceberg. His skills and abilities are not immediately visible. He needs to possess many intangible qualities, such as good judgement, foresight, understanding of men, courage and coolness. Theses qualities are not immediately evident.

She believes that the old ideas of leadership are changing because of the changes in the concept of human relations, and developments in management.[28] To Follett, a leader is not the president of the organisation or head of the department, but one "who can see all around a situation, who sees it as related to certain purposes and policies, who sees it evolving into the next situation, who understands how to pass from one situation to another.[29] Leadership is the activity of influencing people to strive willingly for group objectives. According to her, a leader is "the man who can energize his group, who knows how to encourage initiative, how to draw from all what each has to give."[30] He is "the man who can show that the order is integral to the situation.[31] Leadership goes to the man who can grasp the essentials of an experience and, as we say, "can see it as a whole" and "to whom the total inter-relatedness is most clear.[32] He is the expression of a harmonious and effective unity which he has helped to form and which he is able to make a going concern.[33] Such people, Follett feels, are found not just at the apex but throughout the organisation. According to Follett, coordination, definition of purpose and anticipation are the three functions of the leader.[34] A leader has also to organize experience of the group and transform it into power.[35] Follett stresses that leaders are not only born but can be made through education and training in organisation and management.

Follett goes on to state: "the real function of the leader is to heighten individuality, to draw out others' capacities, to increase their freedom, and to give them driving force and to crate group power rather than to exercise personal power. She was in favour of multiple leadership based on integrative thinking, adapting to the evolving situation.

Follet' s contribution is thus described by Pauline Graham, her biographer. Her achievement was that she created a philosophy of management embedded in the full complexity of human nature . . . her purpose . . . was to understand all of them (the elements of management) in their intricate dynamic interactions, the better to integrate and unify them into the more effective working whole.

Profession in the Making

Follett sees certain tendencies in the direction of the professionalization of business management. Among these are "the developments of Scientific Management," the growth of Specialization. The decline of arbitrary trend toward conscious business cycles, and the recognition that management is more fundamental element in industry than either stockholders or bankers. But a true profession is based on the motive of service and foundation of science. Here much more should be done. The Annual Report of Larsen and Torbro 2006-07 based upon the ideas of Follett feels that corporate social responsibility is of great interest. . . . Another happy smile, another twinkle in the eye, another vibrant life another soaring spirit—that is the vision for tomorrow.

B. THE SCIENTIFIC FOUNDATION

With respect to Science, two major steps are needed. First of all, the Scientific standard must be applied to business and management. It must include not only operations but also management itself. It must deal not only with the technical side, but also with the personnel and human relations side. In fact the technical side itself cannot be properly understood if not discovered from human side.

In different pioneering work of developing standards of service and building a body of organized knowledge, managers themselves must play the major role. "All professions have been developed by the work of their own members." The managers must contribute to the development of their profession not merely by activity in a management association. "The way in which you give every order, the way in which you make every decision, the way in which you meet every committee in almost every act you perform during the day you may be contributing to the science of management.[36]

Sense of Belonging

In case a worker is not accepted as a member by his group and is treated as an outcast, he cannot be happy and may not be able to work. The strongest human urge is to have friends and colleagues. The quest for fellowship is eternal. Without friends, the worker becomes solitary and utterly helpless. Even after retirement, people call at their offices and factories to meet their former colleagues and friends whom they miss greatly. The sense of belonging to a group gives one a feeling of security. It is the basis of all team work in factories.

Critical Appraisal

Mary Parker Follett provided a psychological approach to management rather than trying to resolve conflict through the usual easier methods of domination or compromise she suggested the new method of integration to deal with conflict. In her views conflict was not something negative, to be avoided or abhorred. But it should be viewed in a constructive manner to arrive at solutions acceptable to all, if possible. She also gave her law of situation and explained why order giving in traditional sense was resented by every body in general and by those working in organizations particularly. In her view order giving should be de-personalized. She also distinguished between power and authority. Follett made a significant contribution towards establishing business as a career and profession.

A few writers on organization classed Follett as a 'classical' thinker. But Follett herself criticized the classical theory of management for its one-sidedness, mechanism, and for ignoring psychological aspects.[37] She threw all real social, class conflicts off the scale and considered only psychological conflicts rising mainly from lack of understanding, misapprehensions and differences in the personnel qualities. Her ideas on integration were criticized as being illusory.[38] She was also criticized for not interpreting social content of organisation scientifically. Baker observed that Follett was never a systematic writer, she threw out interesting ideas more or less randomly and, therefore, the thread of consistency was hard to find and harder to follow.[39] Not all her readers would see where her thoughts would lead them.

D. Gvishiani, who states in his *Organisation and Management* that Follett, 'made a positive contribution to the theory of management' but 'her approach was purely empirical and did not interpret the social content of organization scientifically.[40]

What happened was that the level of production of each worker was informally determined by the group, which the research showed was armed with its own customs, norms and social control. This was informal organisation.

Follett's contribution to administrative theory is "seminal and indeed prophetic."[41] As Metcalf and Urwick have observed, 'her conceptions were in advance of her time'. They are still in advance of current thinking. But they are a gold-mine of suggestions for anyone who is interested in the problems of establishing and maintaining human cooperation in the conduct of an enterprise.[42]

Follett drew many of her illustrations from the actual problems and experiences of business management. Though originally a student of political science, she deserted this field and its terminology altogether. For the rest of her life, she was lecturing on business administration and related subjects. Follett was convinced of three things, as pointed out by Lyndall Urwick. First, all such problems, whether they occur in the home or the Home Office are fundamentally problems in human relations. Secondly, while every human being is different, there is a sufficiently large common factor in human reactions to similar situations to permit the development of principles of administration. Thirdly, and in consequence, those principles must be sought wherever human endeavours to pursue a common objective give rise to the necessity for organisation.[43]

CONCLUSION

Urwick comments on her work in the following words, "It was her special merit to turn from the traditional subject of study—the state or the community as a whole—progressively to concentrate on the study of industry. In this context she not only evolved principles of human association and organisation especially in terms of industry, but also convinced large numbers of businessmen of the practicality of these principles in dealing with their current problems. Her approach was to analyse the nature of the consent on which any democratic groups is based by examining the psychological factors underlying it. This consent, she suggested, is not static but a continuous process generating new and living group ideas through the interpenetration of individual ideas.[44]

Professor Wills comments, "Much of what Follett said in her writings has become accepted and may now seem commonplace. But the interested managers in problems which writers such as Taylor were not dealing with, and indeed, considered unimportant. She took large questions and tried through examples and suggestions to make the problems susceptible to science. Her writings are a rich reward for anyone who takes them up. The simplicity of the anaysis must not be allowed to conceal their true value and relevance.[45]

The ideas of Mary Parker, Follett Were accepted by eminent thinkers later on as highly relevant. Mary Parker Follett, in Creative Experience and Dynamic Administration, writes that it is possible to conceive conflict as not necessarily as wasteful outbreak of incompatibilities, but a normal process by which socially valuable differences register themselves for the enrichment of all concerned.

Rensis Likert in his book, "New Patterns of Management", has rightly said that conflict and differences of opinion always exist in a Healthy, virile organization, for it is usually from such differences that new and better objectives and methods emerge. Differences are essential for progress, but better, unresolved differences can immobilize an organization. The central problem, consequently, becomes, not how to reduce or eliminate conflict, but how to deal constructively with it. Effective Organizations have extra-ordinary capacity to handle more conflict.

Mary Parkert Follett ideas are relevant in 21st Century. She advocated ideas far ahead of her times. The dynamics of the conflict plays a vital role in the modern analysis of organizational behaviour. Conflict can lead to innovation and change; it can energize people to activity, develop protection for something else in the organization (in the divide and conquer sense), and be an important element in systems analysis of the organization.[46] Traditionally the Management of Organisational conflict was based on simplistic assumptions. Formal authority and classical restricting were used in an attempt to eliminate it. The more modern approach is to assume the inevitability of conflict, recognize that it is not always bad for the organization, and try to manage it effectively rather than merely try to eliminate it. Even we may promote conflict for temporary purpose to ensure organizational efficiency. Care must be taken so that conflict may not become suicidal to existence of the organization. In brief, we can say that absence of conflict leads to stagnation, but unending conflict is responsible for chaos. Therefore, the conflict must be managed as it is not conflict itself that is problematic but its mismanagement which is detrimental to the effectiveness of an organization. To conclude in the words of Aparna Chattopadhyay,[47] with the dawn of the twenty-first century, we are witnessing enormous global changes at the average workplace which is becoming more challenging than ever before. Understanding human behaviour in its diversity has become imperative for human resource development and organizations. Today, the knowledge of the work styles is essential for effective leadership. Without this knowledge, a leader or manager may not understand his or her followers; as a result he or he may send those followers information in a way that does not make them feel understood, appreciated, respected, acknowledged or validated. On the other hand, with the knowledge of his or her followers, a leader can adapt his or her response, create rapport, and lead the followers to develop their own talents and abilities. The leader must never follow a blanket strategy for dealing with different workers having different work styles. His approaches must cater to the different needs of different kinds of his workers.

In India, large business Organizations are adopting integration approach to solve conflicts.

Relevance

Mary Parker Follett, First lady administrative thinker

has enriched the literature of public administration and business management which would meet the present and emerging needs of new millennium. Her innovative idea of conflict resolution through integration is real and practical provided it is taken in the right spirit. Most of conflicts become suicidal for organization causing great upheavals and losses. Mahatma Gandhi also believed in such type of integration where both sides agree peacefully, voluntarily and without any condition. Integration promotes cohesion, love, affection and harmonious relationship within an organization.

In addition her new approach to leadership, co-ordination, control would bring new diversification to the discipline of Public Administration. Authority arises from the law of the situation and not the person is correct both in theory and practice. Order is depersonal as it comes from the situation. Thus she propounded practical implications of these concepts.

Mary Parker Follett feels that Public Administration and business management can be a good profession provided we make our principles based on scientific foundation and feel belongingness.

Mary Parker's Follett, an eminent, illustrious thinker who came out with innovative theory and made us understand its practical applications, is sure to guide the academia and practitioners in 21st Century to promote excellence, creativity and innovation.

Glenn L. Starks in his article, "Managing Conflict in Public Organizations" in The Public Manager, Winter 2006-207 clearly defines that Managers in every type of organization have to deal with conflict, but those in public organizations are subject to more of it than their counterparts in private and non-profit organizations. In extremely bureaucratic environments, with ever-increasing pressures to do more with less, subject to layers of laws and regulations, and under constant public scrutiny, public agencies face a barrage of factors that catalyze internal and external conflicts. Being able to recognize, tackle, and resolve conflicts in thus a critical skill for public administrators.

Dealing with conflict, of course, is seldom an easy task. In fact, it requires skills that not many public managers

Conflict Resolution Techniques

Definition	*Pros*	*Cons*	*Use*
	Confronting (or collaborating)		
Everyone's interests are met	Builds, commitment, satisfies all parties, and ensures common goals	Takes time, energy, and focus	When all interests are too important to be compromised, it is possible to satisfy all parties without sacrificing anything of value to the organization, constituents, or customers; and each party can be trusted to be considerable of the needs of the other.
	Compromising (for synergizing)		
Each party agrees on some issues at the expense of others.	Can improve trust and team building, each party achieves, some degree of satisfaction, and work can continue	Important issues can be ignored, long-term focus lost, and those with unreasonable interests rewarded and those with reasonable interests punished; if constantly used, parties may begin with unreasonable offers knowing the compromise will result in what they really want, and one party may be obliged to another for a future favour	When there is not time to conduct extensive negotiations, a temporary solution is needed, and it is important to reach a consensus on priority issues.

	Smoothing (or accommodating)		
One party sets their interests aside to satisfy the other	Enables quick agreement and ends the conflicts	The interests of one party are neglected, causing it to feel resentment and that the other owes a favour	When it's obvious one party's interests are more important
	Forcing (or competing)		
One party wins through power or coercion and the other loses	Quickly ends the conflicts	Short-term solution, the conflict can resurface later, and loser feels resentment and may seek retribution	Quick resolution is a must; the future relationship of the parties will not be compromised or is not important; healthy, safety, or issues vital to the organization's welfare are at stake; and laws, regulations, or organizational policies dictate the solution
	Avoiding (or withdrawing)		
Conflict is set aside or ignored	Quickly, simply, and easily deals with the problems	Short-term solution and the conflict remains and can grow worse over time	The cost to resolve the conflict outweights the benefit, the conflict can't be resolved now, dealing with the issue will cause more harm than good, more is accomplished by delaying the issue; and the problem will go away if ignored.

Source: Glenn L. Starks, Managing Conflicts in Public Organization, in the Public Manager, Winter 2006-07, p. 59.

possess. Some don't recognize its existence, and others choose to ignore complex issues, avoid confrontations, or feel powerless to make change. Sadly, ignoring conflicts, won't resolve them even if the conflict itself goes away, side effects can linger, such as a manager's reputation for infectivity or a negative impact on teaming. This article offers public administrators a structured process for managing organizational conflict.

Mary Parker Follett method of resolving conflict has been modified by Glown L. Starks. Collaboration is equal to integration. She is even relevant as modern thinkers who follow her methods:

Notes and References

1. See Mary P. Follett, "The New State (Gloucester, Massachustts, Peter Smith, 1918); Henry C. Metcalf and Lyndall Urwick, eds. Dynamic Administration (New York) Harper & Brothers, (1941); and L.D. Parker, "Control in Organizational Life. The Contribution of Mary Parker Follett", Academy of Management Review, pp. 736-45.
2. James A.F. Stoner *et. al.*, Management, Sixth Edition, New Delhi, Prentice Hall, 1998, p. 38.
3. Harold R. Pottard, Development in Management Thought, London, Heineman, 1982, p. 161.
4. Henry C. Metcalf and Lyndall Urwick, Dynamic Administration: The Collected Papers of Mary Parker Follett, New York, Harper and Row, 1940, p. 30.
5. S.P. Robbins, Organizational Behaviour, Englewood Cliffs, N.Y. Prentice Hall, 1983, p. 38.
6. Lewis Coser, The Functions of Social Conflict, The Free Press, Glencose, III, 1956, p. 31.
7. Mary Parker Follett, The New State, N.Y., Longman, p. 30
8. P. Lawrence and J. Lorsch, Organization and Environment, Boston, Harward Business School, Divisions of Research, 1967.
9. Henry C. Metcalf and Lyndall Urwick, Dynamic Administration, The Collected Papers of Mary Parker Follett, New York, Harper and Row, 1940, p. 42.
10. C. North Cote Parkinson, *et al.*, Great Ideas in Management, Vision Books, New Delhi, 1999, p. 37.
11. H.B. Mavnard (ed.), Top Management Handbook.
12. Sheeman Kreep, Pattern in Organisation Analysis.
13. Henry C. Metcalf and Lyndall, Urwick, *op. cit.*, p. 51.

14. *Ibid.*, pp. 51-52.
15. *Ibid.*, p. 56.
16. H.B. Mainard (ed.), TOP Management Handbook (USA, McGraw Hill), p. 714.
17. Mary Parkert Follett, Dynamic Administration, pp. 58-59.
18. Dynamic Administration, *op. cit.*, p. 99.
19. *Ibid.*, p. 101.
20. Henry C. Metcalf and Lyndell Urwick, pp. 112-13.
21. Albert K. Wickorbery, Management Organization, Bombay, The Times of India Press, 1970, pp. 127-28.
22. M.P. Follett, Freedom and Co-ordination—Lectures in Business Organization, London, Management Publication Trust Ltd., 1949, p. 9.
23. May Parker Follett, The Process of Control, in Gullick and Urwick (eds.) Papers on the Science of Administration, New York, Institute of Public Administration, Columbia University, 1937, p. 161.
24. G.S. Sudha, Management and Administrative Thinkers, Jaipur, Indus Valley Publications, 2004, p. 101.
25. Koontz O, Donnell, Principles of Management, McGraw Hill, 1972, p. 50.
26. International Encyclopaedia of Social Sciences, p. 501.
27. Follett, Dynamic Administration, p. 60.
28. Henry C. Metcalf and Lyndell Urwick, *op. cit.*, p. 247.
29. *Ibid.*, p. 266.
30. *Ibid.*, p. 247.
31. *Ibid.*, p. 275.
32. *Ibid.*, p. 279.
33. S.A. Sapre, Mary Parker, Follett, Her Dynamic Philosophy of Management, Bombay, Govt. Central Press, 1975, p. 38.
34. Henry C. Metcalf and Lyndal Urwick, *op. cit.*, pp. 260-66.
35. *Ibid.*, p. 258.
36. Great Ideas in Management, *op. cit.*, pp. 43-46.
37. D.Grishiani, Organization and Management, A Sociology Analysis of Western Theories, Moscow, Progress Publishers, 1972, p. 28.
38. *Ibid.*, p. 25.
39. R.J.S. Baker, Administrative Theory and Public Administration, London, Hindustan University Liberty, 1972, p. 44.
40. Gvishiani D, Organization and Management, Progress Publishers, Mascow, 1972, p. 24.
41. R.S.S. Baker, Administrative Theory and Public Administration, *op. cit.*, p. 44.
42. Hesrye Metcalf and Lyndol Urwick, *op. cit.*, p. 1

43. Urwick, A Republic of Administration in Public Administration, Vol. XIII, No. 3, July 1935, p. 267.

44. The Golden Book on Management, pp. 132-133.

45. Gordon Wills, *op. cit.*, p. 252.

46. Joseph A. Hilterer, Managing Conflict in an Organisation, Proceedings of the 8th Annual Midwest Management Conference, South Illions University, Business Research Bureau, 1965, in Max S. Watman and Freed Huthans, Emerging Concepts in Management, The McMillian 1969, p. 192.

47. Arpana Choudhry, *Hindustan Times*, July 6, 2000.

17

George Elton Mayo (1880-1949)

INTRODUCTION

Elton Mayo studied the effects of non-material incentives on productivity. He pioneered the human relations school. He believed that "effective management involved leading men, and not manipulation robusts." His main thrust was on interpersonal relations. Elton Mayo was born in 1880 in Adelaide in Australia. He had obtained his M.A. degree in logic and philosophy from the University of Adelaide in 1899 and became teacher at Queensland University. Later on, he studied medicine in Edinburgh, Scotland and became a research associate in psychopathology.

After visiting a few countries in West Africa, Mayo returned to his native land. He made a beginning with the printing business but gave it up immediately to study Psychology at Adelaide University. Mayo successfully organized psychiatric treatment to the soldiers who suffered from shell shock during the First World War. He was appointed Chairman of Philosophy Department at the University of Queensland in 1919 based upon his work on soldiers. While working in the University he taught, in

CHART 17.1

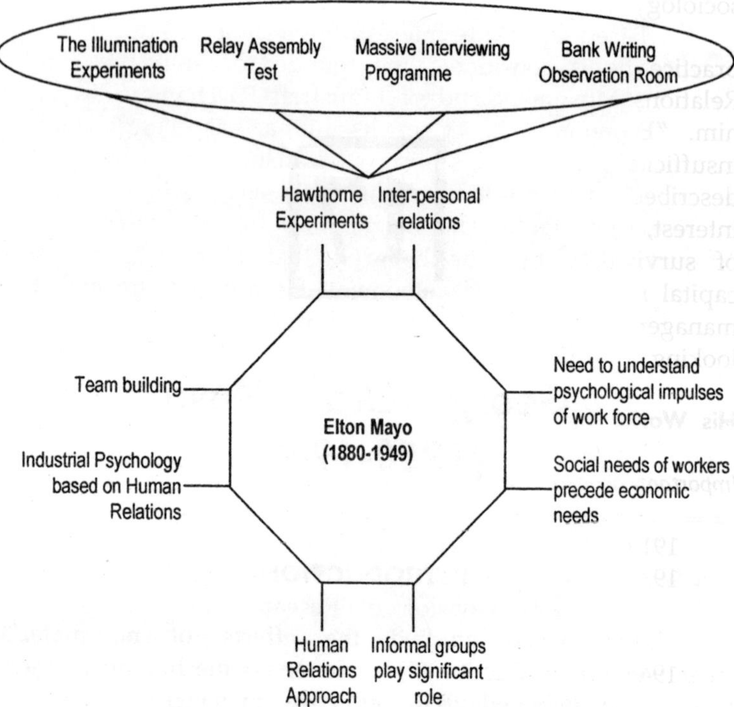

addition to Philosophy, other subjects like Logic and Ethics. He wanted the managers to pay attention to human problems at work place. Shortly afterwards Mayo emigrated to America and joined the faculty of the Wharton School of Finance and Commerce of the University of Pennsylvania. Later, in 1926, Mayo became Professor of Industrial Research at Graduate School of Business Administration, Harvard University. He concentrated all his attention on private industrial establishment and was supported by Rockefeller and Carnegie Foundation Grants throughout his career. He applied psychological approach to industrial problems.

Under the influence of eminent psychologists Pierre Janet and Sigmund Freud, Elton Mayo viewed organisation as a social system and not merely a production unit and worker as the most important functionary in it as the success of the organisation depends mainly on him. He developed the discipline of Industrial psychology and industrial sociology.

Based upon his interest, environment, education and practice he is considered the founder of both the Human Relations Movement and of Industrial Psychology. To quote him. "Economic Theory in its human aspect is woefully insufficient, indeed it is absurd. Humanity is not adequately described as a horde of individuals each actuated by self interest, each fighting his neighbourer for the scarce material of survival." Thus, he believed that Human rather than capital is the key to development. He advised the industrial managers to be humanistic in approach rather than merely looking after physical infrastructure.

His Works

Important academic works

1919 Democracy and Freedom.
1933 The Human Problems of an Industrial Civilization, Boston: Division of Research, Harvard Business School.
1945 the Social problems of an Industrial Civilization, Boston: Division of Research, Harvard Business School.
1947 The Political Problems of an Industrial Civilization.
1948 Some Notes on the Psychology of Pierre Janet.

Important Papers

1929 "What is Monotony?" the Human Factory, Boston: Massachusetts Society for Mental Hygiene.
1930 "Changing Methods in Industry" the *Personnel Journal*, Vol. XX, No. 1.
1939 "Frightened People", *Harvard Medical Alumni Bulletin*, Vol. XIII, No. 2.
"Routine Interaction and the Problem of Collaboration", *American Sociological Review*,

Vol. IV.

1941 "The Descent into Chaos," Boston, Harvard Business School.

1945 "Supervision and What it Means." Lecture given at McGill University, January 30, Studies in Supervision, Montreal McGill University.

Experiments/Studies Undertaken

Hawthorne studies in the Western Electric Company in Chicago—The study (1927-32) is considered to be a classic in the history of Industrial Management theory and practice. This was conducted by Elton Mayo in active collaboration with the management consultants and a group of clinicians.

In the Western Electric company, in USA (Chicago) engaging large number of labourers, productivity was low, labour unrest and other connected problems were on the increase. Management was perplexed and in view of the above mentioned problems; management, therefore thought to invite industrial consultants.

HAWTHORNE INVESTIGATION

The management decided to consult eminent professors of sociology from Harvard University under the leadership of professor Elton Mayo. The investigations carried out by these experts are called Hawthorne Experiments which were carried out for five years from 1927-32. Elton Mayo and his co-researchers endeavoured research when neither the designers nor the execution of such studies had developed much. Professor Elton Mayo, first of all, took executives of the company to an out of the place restaurant where good quality onion soup was served instead of the usual restaurant. This helped professor Elton Mayo to build excellent rapport with the management—the first essential feature of investigation—developed faith in him and his team. This is the cardinal principle of research. Professor B. Wallance Donham said that the Mayo's research has been carried out in an effort to get a better and more basic knowledge of human relations and how to improve them.

There were four major phases of this study.

1. The Illumination Experiments,
2. Relay Assembly Test Room,
3. Massive Interviewing Programme, and
4. Bank Wiring Observation Room.

(1) Illumination Experiments—This experiment continued for 2½ years

The consultants attributed the low productivity to defective, unsatisfactory physical conditions of work such as poor ventilation and inadequate illumination . To start with they decided to investigate whether productivity was affected by illumination. They made a number of experiments. In one case they deliberately reduced the intensity of illumination to that of ordinary moonlight. But surprisingly enough, there was no change in productivity. They could not explain the strange phenomenon.

(2) *(i) The First Relay Assembly Test Room Experiment*

Of the various investigations carried out at Hawthorne, this was the most important one. In this investigation, variations in the output of the work of five girls assembling a small telephone part were minutely studied. Their working conditions were changed from time to time. The weekly working hours were reduced from 48 hours to 40 hours and 40 minutes. Rest pauses were introduced and varied from time to time. They were given free lunches. Even a five day week was introduced. At the end of the experiment all concessions were withdrawn and the girls reverted to the original conditions.

The most surprising part of the story is that contrary to expectations the girls did not raise a hue and cry because the concessions were withdrawn. On the contrary, they set a new record in production. Originally the average output per girl per week was 2,400 pieces. Now the figure jumped up to 3,000. This was something undreamt of. It just showed what people can do more when they are given recognition and appreciation.

(2) *(ii) The Second Relay Assembly Group*

The experiments conducted in the first assembly test room experiment were conducted on other groups to retest the above factors. During the nine weeks, 13 per cent increase in output took place on an average.

(2) *(iii) The Mica Spitting Group*

This experiment was started three months earlier than the second relay assembly test. Here five girls were placed in other test room over a period of 2 years, changes were introduced to physical environment 5 times. The output increased to 15 percent.

The experiments brought forth the ideas that there had been change in social interaction and development of informal relationships which helped in increase of productivity. In the words of Mayo, ". . . .the itemized changes experimentally imposed . . . . could not be used to explain the major changes. . . . The continually increased production." Mayo, therefore, concluded that "the work satisfaction depends to a large extent on the informal social pattern of the work group. Where norms of co-operativeness and high output are established because of a feeling of importance, physical conditions have little impact."

The relay assembly test studies led the researchers to conclude that the social situations of the workers, not just the working conditions, influenced behviour and performance at work. The researchers discovered, for instance, that in countless ways, their observations had inadvertently made the workers feel they were special. The observer had changed the worker's situation by "his personal interest in the girls and their problems. He had always been sympathetically aware of their hopes and fears. He had granted them more and more privileges.[1]

3. Massive Interviewing Programme

The clinical phase—The interview schedule of 80 topics was structured. After some time, respondents were asked to discuss freely those issues with which they were pre-occupied. Some interviews were conducted amongst supervisors also.

The broad conclusions of this study which was extensive, intensive and well groomed are given below:

(i) The early discovery that the interview aids the individual to get rid of useless emotional complication, i.e. stresses and strains and help to state problem clearly and precisely.

(ii) The interview has demonstrated its capacity to aid the individual to associate more easily in informal groups. In addition individuals can be free with fellow workers or supervisors with whom they are in daily contact.

(iii) The interview not only helped the individual to collaborate better with his own group, it also developed his desire and capacity to work better with the management. This double loyalty to group and management can be used if the management is wise enough and take necessary steps.

(iv) Interview doesn't take action but contributes in facilitation of communication both up and down the line. It clears emotional distortion and exaggeration and his work manifestly aids locate objective statement and grievances that lies beyond the various complaints.

(v) Finally interview proves to be a source of information which can be of great objective value to management.

Elton Mayo clearly demonstrated that the interviewing techniques is the key to understand the dynamic of human behaviour at work. Based upon this management can take rational decisions in the interest of workers and company. The impact would be higher productivity and satisfaction to workers.

4. The Bank Writing Observation Group

These were carried out between Nov. 1931 and July 1932.

The bank wiring observation room was another very

significant study in the Hawthorne Investigations. It was concerned with the working of a group of 12 workers, 2 inspectors and 1 supervisor. The study brought out certain revealing features of the organisation. The official production records did not reflect the correct state of affairs. Side by side with the official organisation, there existed an informal organisation. Workers had evolved their own norms of production and ignored the official norms in various ways. Work would be slowed down for one reason or another, real or imaginary. They had their own leader in preference to the official foreman. The foreman was therefore placed in a quandary. The management insisted on higher production while the informal organisation resisted any such move. The foreman had to bear the brunt of the attack from both directions.

"The industrial worker, whether capable of it or not, does not want to develop a blackboard logic which shall guide his method of life and work. What he wants is more nearly described as, first, a method of living in social relationship with other people and second, as part of this an economic function for and of value to the group. . . . Socialism, Communism, Marxism would seem to be irrelevant to industrial events of the twentieth century. These doctrines probably express the workers, desire to recapture something of the lost human solidarity. . . . As we lose the non-logic of a social code, we must substitute a logic of understanding. In all critical posts in communal activity, we had intelligent persons capable of analysing an individual or a group attitude in terms of, first, the degree of logical understanding manifest; second, the non-logic of social codes in action; and third, the irrational exasperation symptomatic of conflict and baffled effort. If we had an elite capable of such analaysis, very many of our difficulties would dwindle to vanishing. . . . Our leaders tend to state these problems in terms of systematic economics, and since the gravity of the issue is human and social and not primarily economic, their statements are not relevant."[2]

From 1933 to 1943 many research inquiries were conducted by the Harvard Research Group. Out of which Mayo chooses to refer to three—a study of a large department store, a study of unemployment in Western Pennyslvania and a study of a small rapidly expanding manufacturing concern. The first and the second may be said to have given strong support to the belief that the study of working groups is vital to the understanding of any management worker relationship. The third possesses a particular interest, in that it is served to demonstrate the urgent need of a systematic ordering of operations as business grows in size.

Profs. Miller and Form have summarized other conclusions from Mayo's researches as sunder:

(a) Work is a group activity.
(b) The social world of the adult is primarily patterned about work activity.
(c) The worker's attitudes and effectiveness are conditioned by social demands from inside and outside the work plant.
(d) Change from an established to an adaptive society tends continually to disrupt the social organization of work plan and industry generally.
(e) Group collaboration does not occur by accident; it must be planned for and developed. If group collaboration is achieved, the work relations within a work plant may reach a cohesion which resists the disrupting effects of adaptive society.[3]

The studies, as Drucker has put it, are still the best, the most advanced and the most complete works in the field of human relations. Indeed, it is debatable, whether the many refinements added since by the labour of countless people in industry, labour unions and academic life have clarified or observed the original insight.[4]

The total contribution of Mayo is such a phenomenon that he is regarded as one of the founding fathers of human relations concept in the administrative thought. He was a behavioural scientist long before the term became popular.[5]

Mayo observed, "If our technical skills are to make sudden and radical changes in our methods of working we must develop social skills that can balance these moves by effecting social changes in our methods of working. We cannot live and prosper with one foot in the twentieth century and the other in the eighteenth."[6] He asserted, "if our social skills (that is, our ability to secure cooperation between people) had advanced step by step with our technical skills, there would not have been another European War."[7]

MAYO'S CONTRIBUTION TO MANAGEMENT THOUGHT

(1) Human Relations Approach

Elton Mayo helped in understanding the importance of human factor in administration. In addition man is not a machine, a statistics or a mere abstraction but a living being with emotions. The researchers concluded that informal work group—the social environment of employees—have a positive influence on productivity. Many of Western Electric's employees found their work dull and meaningless, but their associations and friendships with co-workers, sometimes influenced by a shared antagonism toward the "bosses," imparted some meaning to their working lives and provided some protection from management. For these reasons, group pressure was frequently a stronger influence on worker productivity than management demands.[8]

(2) Informal Groups Play an Important Role in the Organizations

Elton Mayo appreciated that an individual besides being the member of the formal organisation is also a member of informal organisation which is more near to him and which guides him. The Mayo, then, the concept of "social man"—motivated by social needs, wanting rewarding on-the-job relationships, and responding more to work-group pressures than to management control—was necessary to complement the old concept of "rational man" motivated by personal economic needs. All these findings might seem unremarkable today. But compare what Mayo and his associates considered relevant with what Ford and Weber found relevant, and you see what a change these ideas brought to management theory.[9]

Keith Devis has enumerated the following five practical benefits, which can be derived from informal organizations, which may be kept in mind by the management.

1. It blends with the formal organisation to make a workable system for getting the work done;
2. It lightens the workload of the formal manager and fills in some of the gaps in his abilities;
3. It gives suggestion and stability to work groups;
4. It is a very useful channel of communication in the organisation; and
5. Its presence encourages the manager to plan and act more carefully than he would otherwise do.[10]

(3) Understanding the Social Needs which are More Important for Organizations Development

Followers of the behavioural school view the important and focal point of managerial action to be the behaviour of the human being. What is achieved, how it is achieved, and why it is achieved are viewed in relation to their impact and influence on people, who are really the important component of management. Followers of this school say, "Management does not do; it gets others to do." Voluminous writings from this school show the need for the manager to use the best human relations practices. Among the more emphasized topics are human relations, motivation, leadership, training, and communication.[11]

The individual is viewed as a socio-phychological being, and the tasks facing the manager range from understanding and securing the best efforts from an employee by satisfying psychological needs, to comprehending the whole gamut of psychological behaviour of groups as representing the totality of management.[12]

Elton Mayo said:

(i) Man is basically motivated by social needs and obtains his basic sense of identity through relationships with others.

(ii) As a result of the industrial revolution and the

rationalization of work, meaning has gone out of work itself and must, therefore, be sought in the social relationships on the job.

(iii) Man is more responsive to the social forces of the peer group than to the incentives and controls of management.

(iv) Man is responsive to management to the extent that a supervisor can meet a subordinate's social needs and needs for acceptance.[13]

The Hawthorne studies were a turning point in the study of management. As the research became more widely known, managers and management experts began to recognize that human behaviour at work is a complex and powerful force. The human relations movement, inspired by this realization, emphasized that workers were not just given in the system, but had needs and desires that the organization and task had to accommodate.[14]

(4) Need of Understanding Psychological Impulses is to Promote Good Organisation

Elton Mayo observed: "What social and industrial research has not sufficiently realized as yet is that these minor irrationalities of the 'average normal' person are cumulative in their effect. They may not cause 'breakdown' in the individual but they do cause 'breakdown' in the industry . . . the non-logical response, that, which is in strict conformity with a social code, makes for social order and discipline, for effective collaboration in a restricted range of activity and for happiness and a sense of security in the individual."

(5) Disregard of Rabble Hypothesis

The word rabble means crowd or mob and Rabble hypothesis takes the view of men being a crowd of individuals interested in their individual interest. Such a negative view of man by Taylor's Scientific management was called rabble hypotheses Elton Mayo. Mayo puts the following points to refute the rabble theory.

(i) postulating that it was collaboration with others,

not competition among a disorganized horde, that was important:

(ii) stating that all individuals acted to protect their group status and not their self-interest; and

(iii) repeating the Hawthrone findings that thinking was guided more by sentiment than by logic.[15]

"We have learned how to destroy scores of thousands of human beings in a moment of time; we do not know how systematically to set about the task of inducing various groups and nations to collaborate in the tasks of civilization. It is not the atomic bomb that will destroy civilization. But civilized society can destroy itself . . . if it fails to understand intelligently and to control the aids and deterrents to cooperation."[16]

Thus, Elton Mayo, was the pioneer in building Human Relations theory.

If one walks through any factory and observes men at work, one finds that they generally work in small groups. We may call these groups primary working groups. While the work goes on, workers are found talking, to each other, gossiping, throwing paper balls, laughing or singing. In the process, the individual worker loses his identity and becomes a member of the group. The workers act and react to one another. Proper understanding of such working groups is important for organizational efficiency.[17]

CRITICISM

(I) Lack of Scientific Methodology

1. It lacks methodology—small sample size, limited organizations. It is based on a limited data, clinical bias, overlooked wider social context.
2. Limited to few countries
3. Clinical Bias
4. Pro-management bias
5. Anti-union
6. Lack of effective research design.

Indicating the significance of Mayo's studies and thoughts, Claude S. George writes: "As a result of Mayo's work, the industrial woods abound today with behavioural scientists, personnel counsellors, industrial chaplains, sensitivity trainers, group dynamicists, sociogram, analysts, non-directive interviewers, role-playing instructors, critical incident teachers, and industrial psychologists—each trying to satisfy management's demand for the creation of a work situation conducive to a maximum long-run productivity.[18]

Elton Mayo and his colleagues, who pioneered the 'Human Relations' school also recognized and emphasized the use of techniques as given in theory Y, the outline of *the* following principles, which may be followed by the Manager and other top personnel of an institution/organization to develop and maintain sound organizational health:

(i) The need for recognition of 'human' element and the well-being and motivation of the working teams.

(ii) Good 'supervision is exercised with proper understanding of the subordinates'.

(iii) It is important to have proper communication and consultation between the managers and the workers. This creates a sense of participation and involvement among the employees. There should be means of keeping the management informed of what the employees are thinking, fearing, hoping and equally of keeping the employees informed of what the management is thinking or proposing to do.

(iv) The Hawthorne experiments showed that economic incentive is far less powerful than the personal or social incentives.

(v) The flow of work and arrangements of operations should give full play to the informal organization of the workers.

Argyris feels that an organization following these principles would be able to achieve efficiency as well as keep their employees satisfied. He says: "every individual has 'psychological energy' to expend. Exerting that energy in a way that helps him fulfil his own social and egoistic needs is what motivates an individual therefore, provided a company is structured in such a way that an individual is able to meet their self-fulfilment needs. The psychological energy will be used in the company's interests. It the reverse is the case the psychological energy can easily be used to thwart the company; aims." [19]

Elton Mayo has been rightly called the father of industrial sociology as well as Human Relations Movement. Roethlisberger, while anaysing the contributions of Elton Mayo, has opined: "The manager is neither managing man nor managing work, he is administering a social system." For administering a social system, sophisticated social skills are needed. Elton Mayo emphasized social skills. He wrote, "If our social skills had advanced step by step with our technical skills, there would not have been another European War." Mayo's thoughts became a managerial ideology.

CONCLUSION

Elton Mayo has done pioneering work in revealing the need of encouraging informal groups for accelerating progress and satisfaction.

An individual human being is marvel of God's creation. He is unique in more than one sense. He is endowed with infinite potentialities, much of which remains untapped and unutilized. If these potentialities are harnessed and actualized properly, they are capable of bringing wonders. Human beings are like atoms containing tremendous energies. The physical law of 'fission' and 'fusion' operates on them also. If positively motivated they can bring prosperity to the humanity.

In addition, manager can generate among workers and employees enthusiasm through informal means. Leadership can achieve success provided workers are understood properly and channelised accordingly.

What is sadly missing today is an enthusiasm to get somewhere, to achieve something. Many people have the potential, they have youth, health, energy, education and training—everything with which to win the race—but they lack drive and determination. They cannot even start because they do not know where they are going. They need a goal, a spark, to set them afire so that they surge forward.

Human Relations Essential for Team Work

In today's environment human beings have to work among themselves to achieve the objectives of an organization whether industrial, commercial, bureaucratic. They can work together only provided there is good human relations. This will promote team work. For example, team nursing can promote good health care.

The trend today is to make use of authority in collaboration with colleagues—developing team work. Team nursing is a plan of nursing care which makes possible utilization of all levels of personnel to provide optimum patient care. The Nurse should be a team member. This means that the nurse is to be totally integrated into the function of the team. It means involvement of all nursing personnel in the planning and implementation of patient care. It implies, "expert planning and assigning of the duties to be performed by all those concerned with the care of the patient, so that nursing will be improved and the entire staff will function smoothly, efficiently and happily.[20]

The emphasis in team building is on improving the effectiveness and efficiency of the group and not of the individuals alone, as is the case in T-group. It is a set of techniques by which personnel in an organizational group diagnose as to how they work together and plan the needed changes that will improve their performance and ultimately organizational efficiency.

Organizations produce very little solely from individual effort. According to Margulies and Raja, "most effective team action is not easy to achieve in which Tom, Dick and Harry are trained independently or separately . . ."

Its design provides data for diagnosis and unfreezing, incorporate experimental learning, and provides the means for refreezing new behaviour. Furthermore, the process of team development is likely to change organizational inputs (needs, values and skills) and a wide variety of group (cohesiveness, communication, planning). Through problems identification, it can also effect immediate change in organizational output."[21]

Arthur C. Bech (Jr.) and Ellis D. Hillmar have rightly mentioned the following ingredients for developing team approach:

(a) High Expectations—Always expect a lot from people. They will not disappoint you very often.
(b) Respect for the individual—Ask for his ideas and use them where they are better or good as yours. If you do not use his ideas, tell him why. Requesting his help is a high compliment.
(c) Honest relationship—Play it straight. Scott Myers said, "when in doubt, be honest."
(d) Freedom to act—Within the framework and limitations set-up in objectives mutually agreed upon between boss and subordinate, give the employees freedom to achieve results.
(e) Team-orientation—Through objective-setting or problem-solving sessions develop teamwork and commitment to objectives and solutions.

The emphasis in team building is on improving the effectiveness and efficiency of the group and not of the individuals alone, as is the case in T-group. It is a set of techniques by which personnel in an organisational group diagnose as to how they work together and plan the needed changes that will improve their performance and ultimately organizational efficiency.

Elton Mayo and his team concluded that management had tasks: "The function of securing the common economic purpose of the total emterprise and the function of maintaining the equilibrium of the social organisation so that the individuals through contributing their services to the common purpose obtain personal satisfaction that makes them willing to co-operate."[22]

The major findings of the Hawthorne studies are that workers act not as isolated individuals but as members of the group and it is non-economic rewards and sanctions which affect employees behaviour and limit the efficiency of economic incentives.

Relevance

Elton Mayo research is outstanding and would be of great use in increasing productivity and good relations based upon his emphasis on informal groups in new millennium. Social needs of human beings are more important than economic. The individual wants recognition, colleagues to share their views, etc. which is possible only in informal groups.

In addition, managers can generate enthusiasm, dynamism and a sense of belongingness among workers through informal means. Leadership can achieve success provided social and informal needs of workers are understood properly and channelised accordingly otherwise leaders would embrace tensions, emotional pressures as they are not internally sound.

The greatest efficiency and productivity will flow from the efforts of those workers who find satisfaction (both at formal and informal level) in their work and conditions of service, who sense an awareness of usefulness of their functions, who feel encouraged to move ahead and to meet new challenge, who perceive their working environment as one in which high standards of performance are appreciated and encouraged both at formal and informal levels.

Elton Mayo would remain relevant in times to come as his theory of Human Relations and Industrial psychology can help industry, business and even non business institutions like Universities, hospitals, etc. to promote efficiency.

The new millennium would use the theories and ideas of scholars and thinkers like Elton Mayo to make future leaders dynamic. These leaders trained in philosophies of Elton Mayo can understand and redirect the change into fruitful results. Leaders are responsible for moral climate of industrial or other organizations. Thus there is an imperative need for a leader to have a clear vision of his organization. The Ideas of Elton Mayo are certainly going to help enterprises in their endeavour to promote excellence.

Notes and References

1. Noel Tichy and Ram Charan, "The CEO as Coach: An Interview with Allied-Signal's Lawrence A. Bossidy", *Harvard Business Review*, March-April, 1995, pp. 69-78.
2. Elton Mayo, "The Human Problem of Industrial Civilisation, The Viking Press, Inc. N.Y., 1960, pp. 157-58.
3. J.A.C. Brown Organizational Performance, *op. cit.*, p. 85.
4. Peter F. Drucker, The Practice of Management, London, Mercury Books, 1961, pp. 268-69.
5. D.S. Pugh *et al.*, Writers on Organizations, Penguin Books, 1971, p. 129.
6. Mayo Elton, The Social Problems of an Industrial Civilization, Graduate School of Business Administration, Boston, 1945, p. 3
7. *Ibid.*, p. 33.
8. James A.F. Stoner, Management (Sixth Edition), New Delhi, Prentice Hall of India, 1998, p. 42.
9. *Ibid.*
10. Keith Davis, Human Behaviour at Work, 4th Edition, Mc-Graw Hill, New York, 1972, pp. 257-59.
11. *Ibid.*, p. 24.
12. Terry and Franklin, *op. cit.*, pp. 23-24.
13. Edgar H. Schun, Organizational Psychology (New Delhi, Prentice Hall, 1969, p. 51.
14. Gary Dessler, *op. cit.*, p. 34.
15. Daniel A. Warden, *op. cit.*, p. 317.
16. Mayo, Human Problems, p. xvi, quoted by Wren, op. cit., p. 316.
17. C. Northcote Parkinson *et. al.*, Great Ideas, New Delhi, Vision Books, 1999, p. 25.
18. Claude S. George, *op. cit.*, p. 137.
19. Chris Argyris, International Management, McGraw Hill, 1976.
20. Elizabeth Jones and Joan Grube Ellsworth, "An Experiment in team assignment", *The American Journal of Nursing*, 49, 146, (March), p. 34.
21. Michael Beer, "The Technology of Organisational Development", Marwin D. Dunnete (ed.) Handbook of Industrial and Organisational Psychology, Chicago, Rand, IMC, Nally, 1979, p. 960.
22. Roethlisberger *et. al.*, Management and the Worker, Harvard University Press, Cambridge, 1939.

18

Abraham Maslow
(1908-1970)

Maslow is known because of his theory of motivation which throws light on human dynamics and human resource development. He developed the theory of hierarchy of needs in 1940's. (See Chart 18.1)

He opined that "The human acts as an integrated whole—motivation has to appeal to the whole and is, as a result, complex, continuous and fluctuating.

As Maslow himself said, "Motivation theory is not synonymous with behaviour theory. The motivators are only one class of determinants of behaviour. While behaviour is almost always motivated, it is also almost always biologically, culturally and situationally determined as well."[1]

Background

Abraham Maslow, son of a Russian immigrant couple, was born in 1908 in New York. He did not have a very happy childhood and lived in a Jewish ghetto. Later, the condition of his parents improved and they moved on to better middle-class neighbourhood. Here again he was maltreated and abused by Irish and Italian children. He majored in Psychology at the University of Wisconsin and did his post graduation also from the same University.

CHART 18.1

Hierarchy of Needs Theory of Maslow

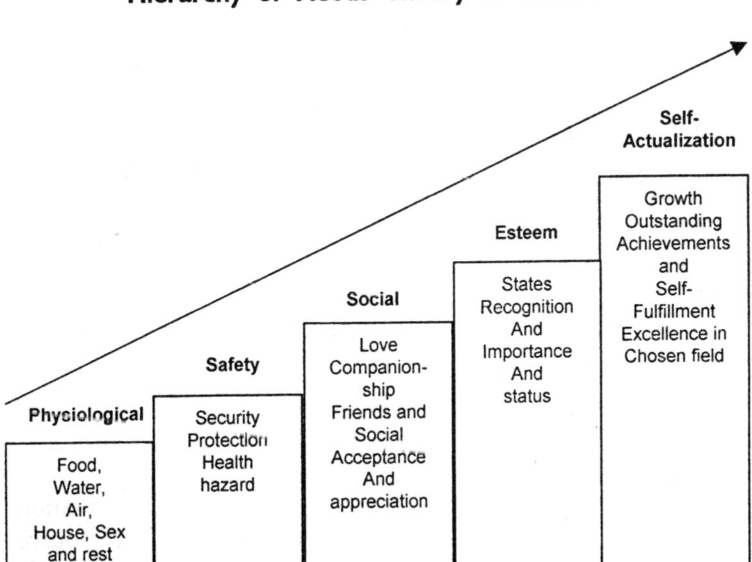

The major conclusion of his thesis that "some animals maintained customary social and sexual dominance through a feeling of self-confidence which the dominant animal was able to communicate (and not by means of physical aggression). He extended his concept of 'dominant feeling' to human beings. He concluded that highly dominant people have strong feelings of self-esteem and confidence

After a postdoctoral research position at Columbia University, he moved across town to Brooklyn College, where he spent 14 years teaching and doing research. His early publications were in comparative psychology and came increasingly to deal with dominance behaviour in primates. During the latter 1930s, he transferred this interest in dominance to the human level and extended it to human sexuality. Before long, he has shifted to personality theory almost entirely, using his research to legitimize his new role. He became interested in psychoanalysis during this period and established a clinical practice.

Books

Abraham Maslow wrote the following books:

1. Motivation and Personality, 1954
2. New Knowledge in Human Values, 1959
3. Towards a Psychology of Being, 1962
4. Eupsychian Management, 1965
5. Principles of Abnormal Psychology, (Published after death)
6. The Farther Reaches of Human Nature, (Pub. after death, 1978).

In 1981 Maslow moved to the Boston area to chair the psychology department at the newly established Brandeis University. He remained there until shortly before his death at the age of 62 in 1970.

Research

His researches are the result of his "own curiosity and pointed toward the solution of various personal, moral, ethical and scientific problems rather than to prove or demonstrate to others."

Maslow published his basic findings and conclusions of his researches and his experiences in his clinic for the first time in 1943. His papers were as follows:

1. "A Preface to Motivation Theory" published in *Psy-chosomatic Medicine*, Vol. 5, 1943.
2. "A Theory of Human Motivation," published in the *Psychological Review*, Vol. 50, 1943.

Later, his findings were published in the form of a comprehensive book, 'Motivation and Personality' in 1954. His first paper is concerned with the theory of human motivation, whereas in his second paper he has attempted to formulate a positive theory of motivation which, according to him, satisfies the theoretical demands presented in his first paper. A summary of the conclusions of his first paper are reproduced below:

1. The integrated wholeness of the organism must be one of the foundation-stones of motivation theory.
2. The hunger drive (or any other physiological drive) was rejected as a centering point or model for a definitive theory of motivation. Any drive that is somatically based and localisable was shown to be a typical rather than typical in human motivation.
3. Such a theory should stress and centre itself upon ultimate or basic goals rather than partial or superficial ones, upon ends rather than means to these ends. Such a stress would imply a more central place for unconscious than for conscious motivations.
4. There are usually available various cultural paths to the same goal. Therefore, conscious, specific local-cultural desires are not as fundamental in motivation theory as the more basic, unconscious goals.
5. Any motivated behaviour, either preparatory or consummatory, must be understood to be a channel through which many basic needs may be simultaneously expressed or satisfied. Typically an act has more than one motivation.
6. Practically all organismic states are to be understood as motivated and as motivating.
7. Human needs arrange themselves in hierarchies of prepotency. That is to say, the appearance of one need usually rests on the prior satisfaction of another, more proponent need. Man is a perpetually wanting animal. Also no need or drive can be treated as if it were isolated or discrete; every drive is related to the state of satisfaction or dissatisfaction of other drives.
8. Lists of drives will get us nowhere for various theoretical and practical reasons. Furthermore, any classification of motivations must deal with the problems of levels of specificity or generalizations of the motives to be classified.

9. Classification of motivations must be based upon goals rather than upon instigating drives or motivated behaviour.
10. Motivation theory should be human-centered rather than animal-centered.
11. The situation or the field in which the organism reacts must be taken into account but the field alone can rarely serve as an exclusive explanation for behaviour. Furthermore, the field itself must be interpreted in terms of the organism. Field theory cannot be a substitute for motivation theory.
12. Not only the integration or the organism must be taken into account, but also the possibility of isolated, specific, particular segmental reactions. It has since become necessary to add to these another affirmation.
13. Motivation theory is not synonymous with behaviour theory. The motivators are only one class of determinants of behaviour. While behaviour is almost always motivated, it is also almost always biologically, culturally and situationally determined as well.[2]

MASLOW'S HIERARCHY OF NEEDS

People are driven into action to fulfil their needs. A number of drives or needs play a crucial role in motivating human beings. All their actions are outcomes of several unfulfilled needs and motives. These needs operate in an order of hierarchy. A need once satisfied gives place to another unsatistied need and this process goes on endlessly because a man keeps on desiring something or the other. Or in other words, Maslow saw human needs in the form of a hierarchy, starting in an ascending order from the lowest to the highest needs, and concluded that when one set of needs was satisfied, this kind of need ceased to be a motivator.

Maslow arranges these needs in ascending order. Maslow arranged human needs in a hierarchy. The lowest needs in the hierarchy are the physiological and security needs, and the higher order need is the self-actualization need. In between there are social and self esteem needs which may be called middle order needs. The fulfilment of a lower order need is a precondition for a higher order need to surface into open. Unless the lower order needs are fulfilled, it is not possible for the higher order needs to show their strength on the human mind. The meaning and connotation of each of the five needs in the hierarchy, viz., physiological, security, social, esteem and self-actualisation are discussed below.

Physiological Needs

(I) The Physiological Needs

Physiological needs may be same as the biological needs of the human beings like food, water, hunger, thirst, sex, etc. The grip of it is so strong that unless these needs are met there is no place for other needs. A hungry person thinks not only about his food but also for some comfort to body and mind which can be fulfilled by eating food. For a person who has missed most of the needs in his life. Physiological needs are the main motivating forces. Once a physiological need is satisfied, the human organism looks. "If hunger is satisfied, it becomes unimportant in the current dynamics of the individual."

(2) The Security Needs

People look for security and safety from natural calamities, dangers and deprivations. For a person whose physiological needs are satisfied, his next goal is security. The need for safety can be better observed in infants and children. It is not very manifest in adults because they are taught to inhabit it. Among infants and children we can clearly see the reaction to bodily illness and injury. A child who is sick, has a need of reassurance from his parents that the sickness will be cured and will never repeat. Another feature of the need for security, very clearly seen in children, is their preference for a rhythm and routine in daily life. Even, for that matter, adults are also normally against any disturbing changes in their life. In an orderly peaceful and civilized society the safety and security is taken care of, to the most exterior by the government. In such societies safety need is no longer a motivator. We can see the expression of safety and security is taken care the most extensively the needs in people's preferences for a job with tenure and protection, the desire for a savings bank account, insurance. In Indian society, the need to have a male child in family is an expression of security need.

(3) The Social Needs

These are also called the belongingness and love needs. Man is a social animal. Once his physiological and safety needs are fulfilled, he seeks affection, love and belongingness from other human beings and the society around him. A person with social needs severely feels the absence of his friends, family, wife and children. He craves for affectionate relationship and a place of belongingness with his people. Children who are products of broken homes or those who are neglected by their parents in their childhood develop a strong desire for love and affection. These desires motivate their behaviour consciously and unconsciously.

(4) The Esteem Needs

People have a desire for respect and recognition from society, work place, family and friendship circles. People normally have a high evaluation of themselves. They have a need for self respect and Self-esteem. Self-esteem needs can be broadly divided into groups, viz., Achievement needs and Recognition needs. Achievement needs are expressed in the form of desire to be with self-confidence, desire to posses strength and assertiveness and desire to be free from depending on others. Recognition needs are expressed in the form of aspiring respect form others, recognition in society, attracting attention and the desire to become an important person. Satisfaction of esteem needs makes a person confident, self-sufficient and useful. Non-fulfilment of these needs makes one feel inferior, weak and helpless. This need plays an important role in moulding the personality of human beings.

(5) The Need for Self-Actualisation

Self-actualisation (the term was first coined by Kurt Goldstein) is considered to be the highest need in the hierarchy of needs and as such it is directed towards searching the meaning and purpose in life. Even if all other needs are satisfied, a human being feels restless and tries to achieve excellence in fields dearer to him. The desire for Self-fulfilment, actualisation and living a meaningful life is reflected in this need. The specific form this need takes varies from person to person. For example, one person haying desire to become an ideal mother, another one having a desire to become an ideal-teacher and so on. At the same time this need, need not necessarily be a need for creativity. After describing these five classes, Maslow separated these five needs into higher and lower levels. Physiological and safety needs were described as lower-order needs and social esteem, and self-actualization needs were called as higher-order needs. The difference was made to emphasize that the high-order needs are satisfied internally, whereas lower-order needs are mainly satisfied externally.

It refers to man's desire for excellence in his field by maximizing his potential; very few individuals try to achieve these needs. Only such individuals who aspire to fulfil their self-actualization needs can bring about creativity, innovation and development in the structure and functioning of the organization. The administration must provide congenial and creative environment for them as they are the builders of the organization. Such individuals may appear to be hostile but they can really contribute to generate social change and modernization

CRITICAL APPRAISAL

Fred Ludhans Feels that Maslow's contribution is a landmark in social-psychological research and he was a forerunner to many like Herzberg and Vroom. His theory of need hierarchy has had tremendous impact on modern management approach to motivation.[3]

Wabha and Birdwell noted that "there is no clear evidence that human needs are classified in five distinct categories, or that these categories are structured in a special hierarchy. There is some evidence for the existence of possibly two types of needs, deficiency and growth needs, although this categorization is not always operative."[4]

"In spite of the tremendous amount of research generated by Maslow's theory, it has never been tested adequately as a complete theory for a number of methodological reasons."

John B. Miner writes, "There certainly are some logical inconsistencies in the theory, especially in relation to the deficiency-growth formulation. Furthermore, Maslow's treatment of self-actualization does move into a mystical-religious arena where empirical tests of his propositions are almost impossible. There is a question whether the theory has been put forth in a manner that permits scientific confirmation or rejection."

Maslow himself noted that "We have spoken so far as if this hierarchy were a fixed order, but actually it is not nearly so rigid as we may have implied. It is true that most of the people with whom we have worked have seemed to have these basic needs in about the order that has been indicated. However, there have been a number of exceptions. . . . There are other apparently innately creative people in whom the drive to creativeness seems to be more important than any other counter-determinant. Their creativeness might appear not as self-actualization released by basic satisfaction, but in spite of lack of basic satisfaction."[5]

Some later behavioural scientists feel that even this model cannot explain all the factors that may motivate people in the workplace. They argue that not everyone goes predictably from one level of need to the next. For some people, work is only a means for meeting lower-level needs. Others are satisfied with nothing less than the fulfilment of their highest-level needs. they may even choose to work in jobs that threaten their safety if by doing so they can attain uniquely personal goals. The more realistic model of human motivation, these behavioural scientists argue, is "complex person." Using this model, the effective manager is aware that no two people are exactly alike and tailor motivational approaches according to individual needs.

Ancient Sanskrit Literature provides a higher level of motivation.

Maslow's theory of needs is limited to the height of self-actualization (Refer Chart 18.2). Indian Sanskrit literature goes a step higher and professes that individuals should try to reach to the level of Moksa and not waste life in petty needs.

CHART 18.2

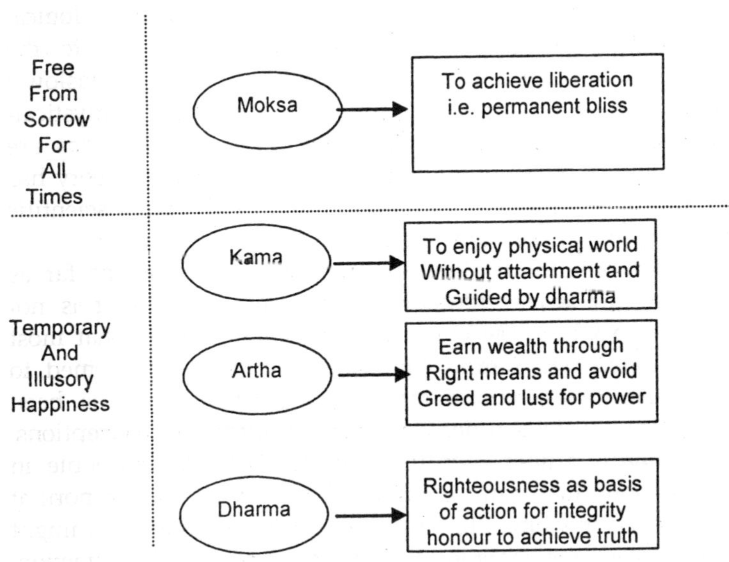

Swami Nikhilananda in his book "Self-Knowledge", Madras, Sri Ramkrishna Math explains the stages to achieve moksha. We have already spoken of the division of the Vedas into Karmakanda and Jananakanda, dealing with man's natural desire for enjoyment of material happiness and the attainment of the Highest Good. The Vedic seers also speak of the four ideals which serve the ends of human pursuit (purusartha). They are the springs of man's action and are known as Dharma, Artha, Kama, and Moksha. Dharma is righteousness; it is the law of inner growth and the basis of man's actions. It is in harmony with a man's spiritual evolution. Therefore, by following dharna one attains success in all actions. By negating dharma one brings confusion into one's life and retards the clock of progress. Dharma is not s sort of duty imposed from outside, but a sense of righteousness, integrity, and honour with which one is born as a result of past actions. So every man has his own dharma, in consequence of which he reacts in his own unique way to the outside world. His educational environment gives to this basic life-form only an outer shape. By fulfilling his dharma a man marches along the path of progress until he attains supreme dharma of all beings, namely, the realizing Truth.

Artha, or wealth, is a legitimate goal of pursuit at a certain stage of man's life. It is with most people, an effective mode of self-expression and an important means of establishing fellowship with others. But wealth must be acquired according to dharma, righteousness; otherwise, instead of serving a spiritual purpose, it will aggravate greed and lust for power and ultimately be a cause of misery.

Kama is the fulfilment of sensuous and aesthetic desire. Craving for sense pleasure is present in many sensitive persons to whom the enjoyment of wealth appears gross and inadequate. But Kama, too, must be guided by dharma; otherwise it degenerates into voluptuousness.

The satisfaction derived from the pursuit of dharma, artha and kama is neither deep nor abiding. There remains a hunger of the soul that can be fulfilled only by the attainment of moksha, or freedom. The first three ideals belong to the material world, and the happiness derived from them is therefore ephemeral and illusory. But the ideal of Freedom can be realized only in the realm of spirit, and the bliss that follows is essence of human life; and the pursuit of righteousness, wealth, and aesthetic satisfaction only support it.

In ancient Sanskrit literature, motivation is not to provide temporary inducements to fulfil material needs but it is a great struggle to achieve highest goals of life, i.e. spiritualism. Swami Yatiswarananda spells out this struggle.

Whereas in the case of worldly things and worldly relations you can never get any ultimate satisfaction, in the case of spirituality and spiritual life you can get that perfect satisfaction which is not dependent upon anything external. So the great sage Narada says, 'realizing that (divine love) a man attains perfection, immortality and ultimate fulfilment."

Relevance

Abraham Maslow's motivation theory holds good in the present context as motivation can energize people who can be effective in accelerating development. A huge bureaucracy in Government has become a dead wood which need motivation. While right motivation can help while wrong motivation can demoralize the entire administrative set-up. What is happening today in developing countries? Those who do not deserve motivation, i.e. are not fit are given motivation through promotion, honours in the form of awards, etc. resulting into demotivation of deserving candidates.

For example in India, we need highly qualified and talented people to occupy top positions in all areas of development? But actually who occupies them? The candidates who are not deserving but are known to persons who matter in appointing at these levels. What is the impact? All such institutions have become second rate. How can you expect a first rate excellent institution from a person who is mediocre? Maslow has rightly mentioned that those persons who have reached to the level of self actualization should be entrusted top position to achieve excellence but we give these positions to the persons who are merely on physiological needs. They have no interest in the oraganisation but feel happy in amassing wealth through corruption. It is strange that lower level persons in the ladder of motivation are being given top positions with disastrous consequences, Government should prepare roasters of persons who have reached high level, they only should be considered for strategic appointment.

Maslow would remain always relevant in the art and science of administration, business, industry. We can put his ideas into practice for accelerating progress, dynamism and development.

Larsen and Toubro in its Annual Report, 2006-07 (p. 10) has realized that the importance of the ideas of Maslow and is in the process of adopting them to meet the challenges of 21st century. A company wide endeavour covering over four thousand managers has been launched to enable them to sharpen their abilities in people management, and translate those skills into effective leadership and motivation. Team building and team maintenance can be sustained as an effective management practice only if it is supported by strong relationships between the members of the teams. The process of cascading the program to various levels has begun and is expected to bring significant change in the people management skills of the managers.

Notes and References

1. A.H. Maslow, "A theory of Human Motivation" in S.G. Humeryager and I.L. Heckmann, *Human Relations in Management*, Bombay, Taraporwale & Co., 1972, p. 334.
2. S.G. Hungeryages and I.L. Heckmann, Human Relations in Management, South Western Publishing Books Co., Ohio, 1967.
3. Fred Ludhans, Organizational Behaviour, New York, Mc-Graw Hill, 1977, p. 408
4. Randell B. Dunham, Organizational Beheaviour, Homewood, Richard D. Illwin, No. 1984, p.108.
5. A.H. Maslow, Motivation and Personality, *op. cit.*, p. 98.

19

Douglas McGregor (1906-1964)

Douglas McGregor was an eminent psychologist who worked in depth on Motivation. His books created a great impact on the development of the theory and practice of Management.

He received his doctoral degree from Harvard University in 1935 and taught social psychology at Harvard from 1935 to 1937. He became an assistant professor of psychology at the Massachusetts Institute of Technology in 1937 and served that institution for eleven years. He was president of Antioch College (1948-54) and between 1954 and 1964, he became professor of management at M.I.T. As a Professor of Management at MIT, McGregor concluded that reliance on authority as the primary means of control in business and industry leads to resistance and acts as a negative to motivation thus affecting output and efficiency.

His writing include the following:

1960 The Human Side of Enterprise.
1966 Leadership and Motivation: Essays of Douglas McGregor (Edited by Bennis and Schein).
1967 The Professional Manager (Edited by Bennis and McGregor).

Chart 19.1

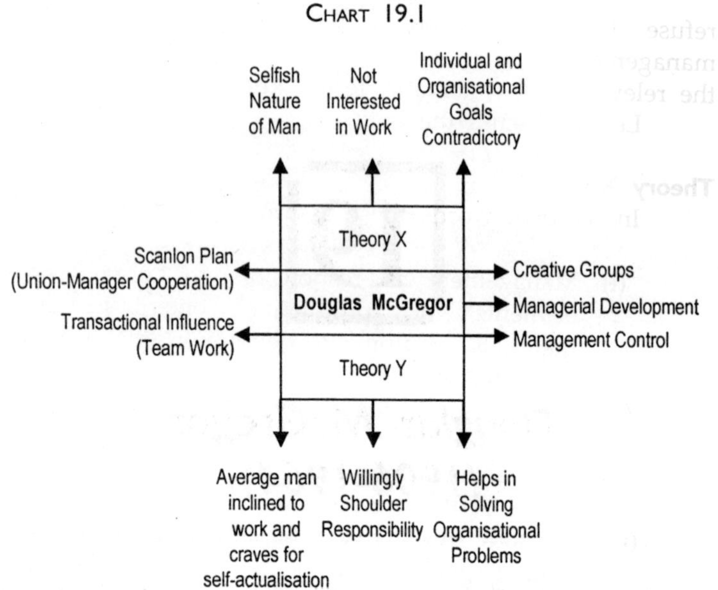

He propounded two contrasting theories—One is negative called Theory X and another positive called Theory Y.

The social sciences are a rich source, today for management even though they have not reached full maturity. He believes that management functions are based on some theory. To quote him: "The generalizations are derived from assumptions beliefs, opinions and convictions. Hence every managerial act, rests on a certain theory. A manager who says that he is being merely practical also, in reality, depends upon certain theoretical assumptions. The more correct the theory which he uses, the better will be the results. Hence management can be improved by utilizing the findings of the social sciences. McGregor maintains that to insist that management is an art is a common way of denying the importance of scientific theory. When a manager's cherished illusions are contradicted by scientific theory, he tends to reject it. The reason often given for rejection is that scientific knowledge has inadequacies and cannot provide a base for management, hence management remains an art. However, scientific knowledge is continually developing and so its inadequacies are being reduced. It is a mistake to refuse to utilize scientific knowledge. "To insist that management is an art is frequently no more than a denial of the relevance of systematic, tested knowledge to practice."

Let us discuss the two:

Theory X

In his own words these assumptions are as follows:

(i) Management is responsible for organizing the elements of productive enterprises—money, materials, equipment, people—in the interest of economic ends.

(ii) With respect to people, this is a process of directing their efforts, motivating them, controlling their actions, modifying their behaviour to fit the needs of the organization.

(iii) Without this active intervention by management, people would be passive—even resistant—to organizational needs. They must be persuaded, rewarded, punished, controlled, and their activities must be directed. This is management's task. We often sum it up by saying that management consists of getting things done through other people.

(iv) The average man is by nature indolent—he works as little as possible.

(v) He lacks ambition, dislikes responsibility, prefers to be led.

(vi) He is inherently self-centred, indifferent to organizational needs.

(vii) He is, by nature, resistant to change.

(viii) He is gullible, not very bright, the ready dupe of charlatan and the demagogue.

Executives believing in above mentioned characteristics of human nature believe in control, close supervision of their employees.

Theory Y

McGregor, however, points out that man's motivation

is far too complex and varied to be explained away wholly by the aforementioned assumptions. In line with other thinkers of social psychology school, McGregor describes his alternative model of motivation as theory Y. The assumptions of theory Y are described by McGragor's in the following words:

(i) The expenditure of physical and mental effort in work is natural as play or rest. The average human being does not inherently dislike work. Depending upon controllable conditions, work may be a source of satisfaction or a source of punishment.

(ii) External control and the threat of punishment are not the only means for bringing about effort towards organizational objectives. Man will exercise self-direction and self-control in the service of objectives to which he is committed.

(iii) Commitment to objectives is a function of the reward associated with their achievement. The most significant of such awards, e.g. the satisfaction of ego and self-actualisation needs, can be direct product of effort directed towards organizational objectives.

(iv) The average human being learns under proper conditions not only to accept, but to seek responsibility. Avoidance of responsibility, lack of ambition, an emphasis on security are generally consequences of experiences, not inherent human characteristics.

(v) The capacity to exercise a relatively high degree of imagination, ingenuity, and creativity in the solution of organizational problems is widely, not narrowly, distributed in the population.

(vi) Under the conditions of modern industrial life, the intellectual potentialities of the average human being are only partially utilized.

McGregor's assumptions in Theory Y roughly corresponds to what Maslow and Argyris have stated about human motivation. The running theme of all these thinkers has been to show that adequate attention has not been paid, so far, to the actual potentialities, creativity and responsible behaviour with which the ordinary man is endowed. That way, McGreger has successfully discarded the assumptions of classical school of thoughts. Douglas McGreger has rightly given his preference for Theory Y, which helps in true organizational building and development. He states:

"Theory X leads naturally to an emphasis on the tactics of control procedures and techniques for telling people what they need to do, for determining whether they are doing it, and for administering rewards and punishments. Since an underlying assumption is that people must be made to do what is necessary for the success of the enterprise, attention is naturally directed to the techniques of direction and control. Theory Y, on the other hand, leads to a pre-occupation with the nature of relationships, with creating an environment which will encourage commitment to organizational objectives and which will provide opportunities for the maximum exercise of initiative, ingenuity, and self direction in achieving them."[1]

A so-called human resources model is often associated with Douglas McGregor. McGregor and other theorists criticized the human relations model as simply a more sophisticated approach to the manipulation of employees. They also charged that, like the traditional model, the human relations model oversimplified motivation by focusing on just one factor, such as money or social relations.

McGregor identified two different sets of assumptions about employees. The traditional view, known as Theory X, holds that people have an inherent dislike of work. Although workers may view it as a necessity, they will avoid it whenever possible. In this view, most people prefer to be directed and to avoid responsibility. As a result, the work is of secondary importance, and managers must push employees to work.

Theory Y is more optimistic. It assumes that work is as natural as play or rest. In Theory Y, People want to and can derive a great deal of satisfaction from work. In this view, people have the capacity to accept-even seek-responsibility and to apply imagination, ingenuity, and creativity to organizational problems.[2]

The problem, according to Theory Y, is that modern industrial life does not fully tap the potential human beings. To take advantage of their employees' innate willingness and ability to work, managers using Theory Y should provide a climate that gives employees scope for personal improvement. Participative management is one way to do this.[3]

It is easy to see how the predominance of an X or Y assumption about people in general will affect one's attitude, behaviour, and "leading" of individuals. Numerous authors have conceptualized Theory Z, which suggests that both assumptions are correct at different times with different people—thus mandating different leadership approaches depending on certain variables in the organization. In Theory Z employees belong to the organisation and are a part and parcel of the organisation. It is being proacted in companies in Japan.

Whatever assumption is correct, X, Y, or Z. It is imperative that a manager be very conscious of his or her basic assumptions about subordinates and understanding these assumptions can have a dramatic impact on shaping a personal leadership style.[4]

Creative Groups

McGregor in his book, "The Human Side of Enterprise" discusses the characteristics of successful and creative groups which can promote changes in the organisation—

(a) The atmosphere tends to be informal, comfortable and relaxed.

(b) There is a lot of discussion in which virtually everyone participates but it remains pertinent to the task of the group.

(c) The task or objective of the group is well understood and accepted by the members.

(d) The members listen to each other. Every idea is given a hearing, people do not appear to be afraid of being foolish by putting forth a creative thought even if it seems fairly extreme.

(e) There is disagreement, disagreements are not suppressed or overridden by premature group action.
(f) Most decisions are reached by kind of consensus in which it is clear that everyone is in general agreement and willing to go along.
(g) Criticism is frequent, frank and relatively comfortable. There is little evidence of personal attack, either openly or in a hidden fashion.
(h) People are free in expressing their feelings as well as their ideas both on the problem and on the group's operation.
(i) When action is taken, clear assignments are made and accepted.
(j) The chair of the group does not dominate it, nor on the contrary does the group defer unduly to the leader. In fact, the leadership shifts from time to time depending upon the circumstances.
(k) The group is self-conscious of its own operation.[5]

Managerial Development

It depends upon how the organisation is made functional. McGregor wrote: It seems clear to me that the making of managers, in so far as they are made, is only to a rather small degree the results of management's formal efforts in management development. It is to a much greater degree the result of management's conception of the nature of its task and of all the policies and practices which are constructed to implement this conception. The way a business is managed determines to a very large extent what people are perceived to have 'potential' and how they develop. We go off on the wrong track when we seek to study management development in terms of the formal machinery of programmes carrying this label.[6]

Management Control

We should not use control as we think but rather should be done as per the need of the organization. To quote McGregor:

Human behaviour is predictable but as in physical science accurate prediction hinges on the correctness of underlying theoretical assumptions. . . . We can improve our ability to control only if we recognize that control consists in selective adaptation to human nature rather than in attempting to make human nature conform to our wishes. If our attempts to control is unsuccessful the cause generally lies in one choice of inappropriate means. We will be unlikely to improve our managerial competence by blaming people for falling to behave according to our predictions.[7]

The Scanlon Plan

Douglas McGregor in collaboration with Frederick Lesiaur developed the idea of union-management cooperation which is popularly known as Scanlon Plan. The Scalon Plan was not a formula or a set of procedures but a philosophy of management based on the assumptions of Theory Y. It has two central features[8]: (a) Cost Reduction Sharing—It involves sharing the economic gains resulting from cost reduction and improvements in organizational performance, and (b) Effective Participation—Participation is a means of ego satisfaction of the workers and subordinates and it motivates employees towards organizational objectives. McGregor says, 'Used wisely and with understanding participation is a natural commitment of management by integration and self-control.'[9]

Clinton Golden once remarked that, "by and large and over the long-run, management gets the kind of labour relation it deserves."

The Concept of Transactional Influence

Building of a team or to avoid differences is not a simple thing but is a challenge of organisation of managerial work

To develop team-work and to remove tensions in the management of differences, McGregor discusses three strategies namely: (i) divide and rule, (ii) the suppression of differences, and (iii) working through the differences. In fact, he should steer through the differences so that members may yield to innovation, commitment to decisions and sound relationships within the group.

CONCLUSION

Douglas McGregor Affirmed

"Fads will come and go. The fundamental fact of man's capacity to collaborate with his fellows in the face-to-face group will survive the fads and one day be recognized. Then, and only then, will management discover how seriously it has underestimated the true potential of its human resources."

Harold Geneen in his book "managing" asserts that Theories X and Y cannot be applied in pure form and their application is also not incident. He states:

"The beauty of Theory X and Theory Y was that they so neatly encompassed all of business management. But the trouble with these neat theories, however, is that no company that I know of is run in strict accordance with either Theory Y or Theory X. Not even the Army."

- Commitment objectives is a function of the rewards associated with their achievement.
- The average human being learns, under proper conditions, not only to accept but to seek responsibility.
- The capacity to exercise a relatively high degree of imagination, ingenuity, and creativity in the solution of organizational problems is widely, not narrowly, distributed in the population.

Another important research finding according to McGregor is that leadership is a relationship. "It means that leadership is not a property of the individual, but a complex relationship" among the variables relating to the characteristics of the leaders, the followers, the organization and the social economic and political milieu. It means functioning according to Theory Y, but also that supervisors should create the essential conditions in their individual ways and with due regard for their own particular situations.

Elton Mayo and his colleagues, who pioneered the 'Human Relations' school also recognized and emphasized the use of techniques as given in theory Y, the outline of the following principles which may be followed by the Manager and other top personnel of an institution/organization to develop and maintain sound organizational health:

(i) The need for recognition of 'Human' element and the well-being and motivation of the working teams.

(ii) Good supervision is exercised with proper understanding of the subordinates.

(iii) It is important to have proper communication and consultation between the managers and the workers. This creates sense of participation and involvement among the employees. There should be means of keeping the management informed of what the employees are thinking, fearing, hoping and equally of keeping the employees informed of what the management is thinking or proposing to do.

(iv) The Hawthorne experiments showed that economic incentive is far less powerful than the personal or social incentives.

(v) The flow of work and arrangements of operations should give full play to the informal organization of the workers.

He prefers Theory Y as compared to Theory X.

Relevance

Douglas McGregor has propounded X and Y theories to deal with personnel in organizations. In Theory X he has poor estimate of personnel as given by Hobbes while in Theory Y he gives an excellent picture of personnel. However in practice, it is not possible. The application of the X and Y theory must be judged based upon the organization you are dealing with. Douglas McGregor has also not given the methods to change the characteristics of Theory X. However, McGregor's theories would help managers to understand X and Y theories and choose a mixture of the two.

Swami Chinmaynanda beautifully sumps up the Ingredients of Commitment in the following words: The highest and the noblest type of an individual working in the world is known as the "man of achievement" (Yogi). Such men work, neither for the sake of wages, nor for success; they are not after mere sensual pleasures, nor do they aspire to reform the world; they dedicatedly perform their obligatory duties finding peace and fulfilment in their very activity. Their fulfilment consists in doing their duties to the best of their ability without claiming any rights and they are totally unmindful of whether the society commends or condemns their actions.[10]

The future of the public services is in the hands of its members who strive for creativity, academic excellence, and the pursuit of excellence of service in their professional activities. If the top administrators have faith in their subordinates, it would generate sufficient energy and enthusiasm to get the co-operation of the entire staff in an organization as faith is contagious. Staff members would try to make usc of the energy to promote efficiency in such a congenial environment. Such a situation would generate a chain effect of optimum performance and creativity. For the use of appropriate management task, we will have to train the personnel in these tasks, so that they can use them and make a definite impact on productivity.

Robert M. Hutchines writes in "The Administrator": "The rewards of the administrator may not be public memorials, religious rites and a pleasant journey to the Islands of the Blest for those things he should care not at all. His satisfaction will come, even if he fails, from having seen and attempted one of the most difficult works of the mind and one of the most challenging human tasks."[11]

We may suggest the corrective measures for personnel in Theory Y.

The HRD represents an intervention strategy with, *inter alia* the following overall objectives, namely:

1. Arresting obsolescence, both individual and organizational (preventive);
2. Bridging pre-active insufficiencies of knowledge and professional skills (curative);
3. Shaping adjustments with socio-technological, environmental changes (adaptive);

4. Developing new outlook, an ethological version of quality excellence and accomplishment (promotive); and
5. Making a total man with new cultural attributes (Transformative).[12]

Larsen and Toubro in its Annual Report 2006-07 (p. 12) has followed the ideas of McGregor. To quote the report: "Every great advance in science has emerged from a new audacity of imagination." Technology is the springboard to the future. It is the bridge between aspiration and accomplishment. Every technological achievement is both destination and point of depature for one breakthrough leads to another. . . . and another. If technology drives industry, what drives technology? The answer lies in the human mind, in a spirit that is impatient with the status quo and in the soaring flight of the imagination. It is an answer that is well known to L & T, and is indeed reflected in its tagine - it's all about imaginnering." "Strive for perfection in everything you do. Take the best that exists and make it better. When it does not exist, design it."

Notes and References

1. Douglas, *op. cit.*, p. 132.
2. Landy and Becku, Motivation theory Reconsidered, pp. 7-8. These processes are commonly called congnitive process.
3. James A.F. Stoner, Management, Sixth Edition, New Delhi, Prentice Hall of India, 1998, p. 447.
4. Terry and Franklin, Principles of Management, Eighth Edition, New Delhi, A.I.T.B.S., 2003, pp. 328-29.
5. McGregor, "The Human Side of Enterprise", p. 94.
6. *Ibid., op. cit.*, Preface (iv).
7. *Ibid.*, p. 11.
8. *Ibid.*, p. 111-14.
9. *Ibid.*, p. 131.
10. Swami Chinmayananda, Talks on Sankara, Viveka Choodamani, CCMT, 2001, pp. 61-62.
11. Swami Tejomayananda, Yoga Vasistha Sara Sangrahah, CCMT, Mumbai, 2001, pp. 25-27.
12. O.P. Dwivedi, Administration Theology, in *IJPA*, July-Sept. 1990, pp. 408-09.

20

Chris Argyris (1923-)

INTRODUCTION

One of the highly respected behavioural scientists, Chris Argyris is known the world over as a great psychologist and management thinker. He has a brilliant academic record. He holds a Master's degree in Economics, and a doctorate in Organizational Behaviour. The National Industrial Conference Board in the United States conducted a survey to find out as to which behavioural scientists have greatest impact on corporate management. 241 US companies responded and Argyris was placed fourth in the ranking. Further, he served, as Head of the Department of Administrative sciences at Yale University since 1971. His last assignment, was Professor of "Education and Organizational Behaviour at Graduate School of Education and Business at Harvard University. With a brilliant academic record, he devoted his life to academics and consulting career and worked in search of ways to match corporate needs with those of the individual.

Argyris a world class consultant with rich experience, is a well known authority on executive development and productivity, he advised several governments, viz. the USA,

CHART 20.1

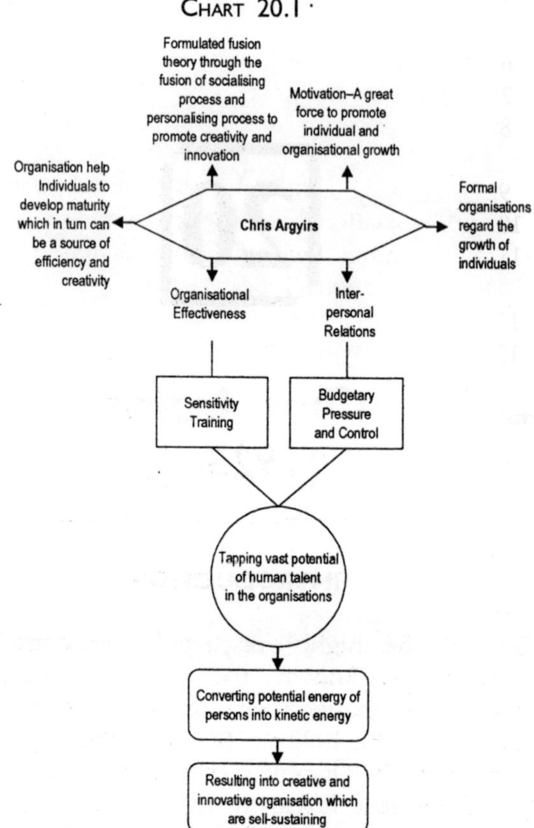

France, the Netherland, Germany, Sweden and Italy. He had been consultant to prestigious organisations like the international Business Machines, Du Pont and Shell Oil.

Argyris has written more than 15 books and over 100 research papers.

Some important books written by Chris Argyris are as follows:

1. Executive Leadership (1953)
2. Personality and Organization (1957)
3. Understanding Organisational Behaviour (1960)
4. Interpersonal Competence and Organisation Effectiveness (1962)

5. Integrating the Individual and the Organisation (1964)
6. Organisation and Innovation (1965)
7. Intervention Theory and Method (1970)
8. Management and Organisation Development (1971)
9. Increasing Leadership Effectiveness (1976)
10. Organisational Learning (1978)
11. Reasoning, Learning and Action: Individual and Organisation (1982)
12. Action Science (1985 co-auth.)
13. Strategy, Change and Defensive Routines (1985)

Important Articles

1. "Diagnosing Human Relations in Organisations", *Labour & Management Centre,* Yale University, Studies in Organisational behaviour, No. 2, New Haven, Conn. 1956.
2. "The Organisation: What makes it Healthy", *Harvard Business Review,* November-December 1958.
3. "Organisational Effectiveness under Stress", *Harvard Business Review,* May-June 1960.
4. "T-Groups for Organisational Effectiveness", *Hardvard Business Review,* March-April 1964.

CONTRIBUTION TO MANAGEMENT THOUGHT

I. Critical of Traditional Organizations

Argyris was not satisfied with the way organizations are traditionally run. In his opinion such organizations thwarted the development of individuals. Work is divided and sub-divided so minutely that it ceases to be interesting. It becomes monotonous and boring. The individual often cannot see the whole product and cannot identify himself with the work of his firm. A dichotomy develops between the individual and the organization and he feels alienated, frustrated and uninterested. How such individuals would contribute to organization. Similarly, the hierarchical pattern of organizations curbs his enthusiasm and initiative. The individual gradually loses interest in his work. He loses his self-respect. His psychological energy is wasted, its flow is diminished. Both the individual and the organization suffer as a result.[1]

He concludes that "the formal organisational principles make demands of relatively healthy individuals that are incongruent with their needs. Frustration, conflict, failure, and short-time perspective are predicted as resultant of this basic in congruency.[2]

2. Channelising Motivation to Meet Individual and Organizational Needs

His advice was sought by several governments, viz., the U.S.A., France, the Netherlands, Germany, Sweden and Italy on many issues facing the governments. He has rendered consultancy to well-known organiszations like International Business Machines, Du Pont and Shell Oil to solve their existing and emerging problems.

In his view, "every individual has 'psychological energy' to expend. Exerting that energy in a way that helps him fulfil his own social and egoistic needs is what motivates an individual. Therefore, provided a company is structured in such a way that an individual is able to meet these self-fulfilment needs, the psychological energy will be used in the company's interests. If the reverse is the case, the psychological energy can easily be used to thwart the company's aims."[3]

Thus Chris advised governments and companies to take meticulous care of the individuals working in governments and companies through providing all facilities to make them at ease on the job. Such individuals would put their best to accelerate the progress in their area of work.

3. Fusion Process Theory

This process is based on the combined benefits of individuals and organization.

In socializing process, organisation encourages individuals to develop fully and make use of the energies of individual while in Personalising process, individuals are

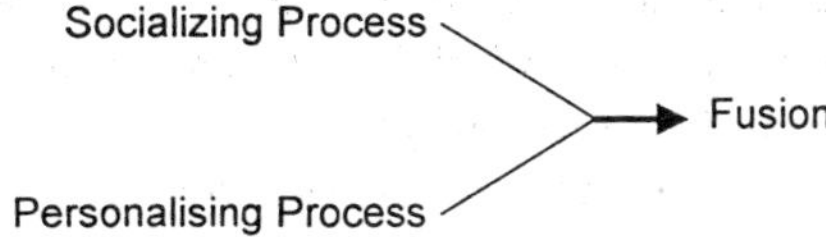

encouraged to contribute to the development of the organisation. The process is both formal and informal and the resultant process of fusion takes out of the individual potentialities to ensure organizational effectiveness to promote creative and innovative organizations.

The fusion process was developed over a period of more than twenty years of intensive research in different types of organizations by Argyris.

Professor Argyris later tested this theory. He undertook to study the operation of a bank. The results of this study were published in 1954. This study is significant, as for the first time the functioning of an organisation was examined in a systematic way.

The organisation, in order to be successful, should strive to meet its own needs as well as the needs of the individuals serving within the organisation. Argyris' fusion model depicts the real situation in the organisation.

The personality factors which were taken into account for the personalizing process are: Passive, Recluse, self-responsible variety seeking, mathematically minded, security conscious, directive, sociable, upward mobile, Challenge Accepting or rejecting, industrious, mechanical minded, detail minded and short hour minded.

Organisational factors taken into account were passive work, isolated work, self guided work, varied work, low wage work, security, directive works, diplomatic employee work, increasingly responsible work, continuous work, Free time Advantages work, Blind Alley work, Multi-Detailed work, Diplomatic customer work, accurate work, hostility accepting work. Based upon these factors fusion model was listed which gave interesting results.

He helped in designing creative and innovative organizations based upon his research. It is easy to understand that all problems would be solved automatically in an enlightened organization based on creativity and innovation.

4. The Immaturity-Maturity Model of Personality—The Immaturity-Maturity Model is Considered to be a Great Contribution of Chris Argyris

The following table shows the immaturity-maturity continuum developed by Argyris:

Immaturity	*Maturity*
Passivity	Activity
Dependence	Independence
Few ways of behaving	Diverse behaviour
Shallow interest	Deep interest
Short-term perspective	Long-term perspective
Subordinate position	Superordinate position
Lack of self-awareness	Self-awareness and control

Source: Adapted from Chris Argyris, Personality and Organisation, Harper & Bros., New York, 1957, p. 50.

Argyris feels that all persons reach the maturity end of the continuum and they do not move as per the stages given in the table. He feels that formal organizations treat individuals as passive, dependence, etc. and never allow them to function at mature level based on self awareness and control. He wants formal organisation to play a positive role and encourage individuals to develop maturity and in return, they would promote efficiency, effectiveness and productivity. It will also create formal organizations which are enlightened. He wanted formal organizations to create an healthy environment in which individuals can achieve maturity.

He mentioned the following about the above mentioned model:

1. The seven dimensions listed earlier represent only one aspect of the total personality. Much also depends upon the individual's perception, self-concept, adaptation and adjustment.
2. The seven dimensions continually change in degree from the infant to the adult end of the continuum.
3. The model, being only a construct, cannot predict

specific behaviour. However, it does provide a method of describing and measuring the growth of any individual in the culture.

4. The seven dimensions are based upon latent characteristics of the personality which may be quite different from the observable behaviour.[4]

Argyris argued that healthy people go through a maturation process. As they approach adulthood, they move to a state of increased activity, greater independence, and stronger interests, and they pass from the subordinate position of a child to an equal or super ordinate position as an adult. Gaining employees' compliance by assigning them to highly specialized jobs with no decision-making power and then closely supervising them inhibits normal maturation by encouraging workers to be dependent, passive, and subordinate. It would be better to give workers more responsibility and broader jobs.[5]

5. Inter-Personal Relations

Organizations consist of individuals, who work in relation to one another in different capacities, to produce results. Only a coordinated effort among individuals can sustain the efficiency of an organization. Else a major effort would be wasted in misunderstandings, jealousies, etc. Today, most of the organiations are plagued by poor interpersonal relations, resulting in lack of interactions, team work, harmony and resultant low output. Only effective interpersonal relations can lay the foundation of a sound organization, otherwise it would lead to desperate elements working in different directions, causing great harm to the efficiency of the organization.

Managers of today need to be trained in understanding the inter-personal relationships and their management to insulate the organization from internal behavioural disturbances. There are three inter-personal needs, (i) inclusion need for interaction and association, (ii) control—the need for authority and . power, and (iii) affection—the need for being loved and cared. Developing a successful inter-personal relation, conducive to achievement of organizational goals, is a challenging task and a slow process. It requires a deep psychological understanding of oneself as well as of others, with whom one comes in contact in various organizational capacities.

Argyris is a strong advocate of Inter-Personal relationship for which he lays down three conditions:

1. Self-acceptance: This refers to the degree to which the person values himself in a positive fashion.
2. Confirmation: By confirmation, Argyris means the reality-testing of one's own self-image.
3. Essentiality: This third condition for interpersonal competence is defined by Argyris as one's opportunity to 'utilise the central abilities and express his central needs'.

Argyris based upon his research mentioned four types of behaviour which can help in increasing competence of organizations:

1. Owning upto, or accepting responsibility for one's ideas and feelings.
2. Being open to ideas and feelings of others and those from within one's self.
3. Experimenting with new ideas and feelings.
4. Helping others to owe upto, be open to, and to experiment with their ideas and feelings.[6]

Agryris research findings on inter-personnel relations if applied can save the organization from a large number of problems occurring at informal as well as formal level. Team work is essential to avoid wastage on conflicts.

6. Budgetary Pressures and Control

Argyris based upon his researches feels that budgetary pressures put stresses and strains on supervisory personnel and top managers and these can create the following Problems:

1. Budget pressure tends to unite the employees against management, and tends to place the

factory supervisor under tension. This tension may lead to inefficiency, aggression and perhaps a complete breakdown on the part of the supervisor.

2. The finance staff can obtain feelings of success only by finding fault with factory people. These feelings of failure among factory supervisors lead to many human relations problems.
3. The use of budgets as "needlers" by top management tends to make each factory supervisor see only to the problems of his own department.
4. Supervisors use budgets as a way of expressing their own patterns of leadership. When this results in people getting hurt, the budget, in itself a neutral thing, often gets blamed.[7]

On the other hand the budgetary pressure can create the following changes among the employees who form groups which run counter to the organization:

1. First, the individuals sense an increase in pressure.
2. Then, they begin to see definite evidence of the pressure. They not only feel it; they can point to it.
3. Since they feel this pressure is on them personally, they begin to experience tension and general uneasiness.
4. Next, they usually "feel out" their fellow workers to see if they too sense the pressure.
5. Finding out that others have noted the pressure, they begin to feel more at ease. It helps to be able to say, "I'm not the only one."

Finally, they realize that they can acquire emotional support from each other by becoming a group. Furthermore, they can "blow their top" about this pressure in front of their group.[8]

Budgetary controlling handled in light of today's management knowledge should not lead to conflict. Certain beliefs about employees are necessary to achieve the most from budgetary controlling. Most managers and non-managers can relate their activities to company goals if they are told what the company goals are. Both top and lower-level managers can be satisfied it both participate in formulating the controlling by which they will be managed. Budgetary controlling is not a one-person operation, with a manager issuing orders and insisting that certain steps be followed. Effective budgetary controlling helps all members of a company to do their jobs better. Everyone in the enterprise should participate and feel that the budgeting practices are assisting him or her and making the enterprise a better place in which to work.[9]

7. Climate of Creativity

Argyris suggested for job enlargement and job enrichment to come over such budgetary pressure.

A climate of creativity must be developed and maintained by management. Maier and Hyes say that 'the optimal climate for creativity. . . is whatever human conditions is optimal for individual freedom and self-expression in social setting'. It is the duty of the officers of such units to make the employees feel that their work and their association with a given organization represent a vehicle which will accelerate the achievement of personal as well as the achievement of goals of the organization. It means to make the jobs interesting, challenging and meaningful. Koontz and O'Donnell have suggested the following to ensure job enrichment:

(a) giving workers more latitude in deciding about such things as work methods, sequence, and place or by letting them make decisions about accepting or rejecting materials;
(b) encouraging participation of subordinates and interaction between workers;
(c) giving workers a feeling of personal responsibility for their tasks;
(d) taking steps to make sure that people can see how their tasks contribute to a finished product and the welfare of the enterprise;

(e) giving people feedback on their job performance preferably before their supervisors get in; and
(f) involving workers in analysis and change of physical aspects of the work environment such as layout of office or plan, temperature, lighting and cleanliness.

Beside job enrichment, we must inculcate pride in the job among the staff members of an organization, i.e., doing job with their best ability to achieve excellence in their own fields. The Advertising Council of America once started a campaign which stated: "Are you doing the work you would be proud to sign with your own autograph?" It applied to all persons irrespective of the office they occupy in government. The pursuit of excellence would depend on development of this identity.

8. Organisational Effectiveness

According to Argyris, there are five basic characteristics of an organization which are as follows:

(i) Plurality of parts.
(ii) Inter-relatedness of parts by which they maintain each other.
(iii) Specific objectives to be achieved.
(iv) Adapting to the environment.
(v) Maintaining the inter-relatedness.

These properties of organization which lead to ineffectiveness and effectiveness are given in the Table 20.1.

9. Sensitivity Training

He states that the T-Group is ". . . A group experience designed to provide maximum possible opportunity to the individuals to expose their behaviour, give and receive feedback, experiment with new behaviour and develop an everlasting awareness and acceptance of self and others."

It is a method of changing behaviour of the personnel in the organisation, relying on unstructured group interaction to smoothen inter-personal relationships. In this process, the

TABLE 20.1

Properties of Effectiveness and Ineffectiveness in an Organisation

Sl. No.	*Properties Leading to ineffectiveness*	*Sl. No.*	*Properties leading to effectiveness*
1.	One part of the sub-set of parts controls the whole	1.	The whole is created and controlled through the inter-relationship of the parts.
2.	Awareness only of random plurality of parts.	2.	Awareness of pattern among parts.
3.	Objectives related only or mainly to parts.	3.	Objectives related to the whole.
4.	Inability to influence core activities whether they are internally or externally oriented	4.	Ability to influence core activities whether they are internally or externally oriented.
5.	Core activities only influenced by the immediate present	5.	Core activities influenced by past present and future.

Source: Chris Argyris.

actual technique employed is termed as T-group 'Sensitivity' in this context means sensitivity to self and self-other relationships. In this training, 10-12 persons are involved, who are assisted by a professional behavioural scientist, who acts as a catalyst. It provides a free atmosphere, which breaks through the barrier of intellectualization and verbalization. It emphasizes "open your eyes, look at yourself, see how you look to others. Then decide that changes if any, you want to make and in which direction you want to do." Thus, the emphasis of T-group is on self-improvement based on the analysis of one's behaviour *vis-a-vis* the other members of the organisation to ensure individual and organisational goal achievement.

Leyland Bradford, Jack-R. Gille and Kemeth Benne have mentioned the following objectives of Sensitivity Training:

(a) To make trainees sensitive to emotional reactions and expressions in themselves and others.

(b) The participants sharpen their ability to perceive and to learn the implications of their actions in the process of drawing their attention to their own or other's feelings.

(c) To stimulate and develop personal value and goals which are commensurate to social goals and scientific methods of personal decision-making.

(d) To develop a scientific attitude to tackling future situations.

(e) To help achieving behavioural effectiveness in transactions in environments obtained around the participants.

Argyris, in order to clarify the misconceptions, has specifically mentioned the following about sensitivity training.

1. Sensitivity training is not a set of hidden, manipulative processes by which individuals can be brainwashed into thinking, believing, and feeling the way someone might want them to without realizing what is happening to them.
2. Sensitivity training is not an educational process guided by a staff leader who is covertly in control and who by some magic hides this fact from the participants.
3. The objective of sensitivity training is not to suppress a conflict or to get everyone to like one another.
4. Senility training does not attempt to teach people to be callous or disrespectful to society and to dislike those who live a less open life.
5. Sensitivity training is neither psychoanalysis nor intensive group therapy.
6. Sensitivity training is not necessarily dangerous, but it must focus on feelings.
7. Sensitivity training is not education for authorization leadership. Its objective is to develop effective, reality-centered leaders. The most sensitivity training can do is to help the individual to see certain unintended consequences and costs

of his leadership and to develop other leadership styles if he wishes.

8. Sensitivity training does not guarantee change as a result of attendance at the training sessions.

CONCLUSION

According to Chris Argyris organizations very often keep their members passive and thus stunt their psychological growth. He stressed that individuals and organizations must adapt to the need of each other.

He suggests the following:

The objectives of a typical organization development programme are:

(i) to increase the level of the trust and support among individuals and groups throughout the organizations;

(ii) to create an open, problem-solving climate throughout the organization—where problem are confronted and differences are clarified, both within group and between groups in contrast to "sweeping problems under the rug";

(iii) to increase the level of personal enthusiasm and satisfaction in the organizations.

(iv) to attain better collaboration and cooperation between inter-department persons and/or groups;

(v) to increase the openness of communication laterally, vertically and diagonally;

(vi) to increase the level of self and group responsibility in planning and achievements of goals through optimum resource utilization; and

(vii) a shift in values so that human factors and feelings come to be considered as legitimate.[10]

He has been mainly criticized, because he de-emphasized authority in organization but, nevertheless his researchers and thought provoking concepts will continue to guide researches, students, academicians and managers in year to come.

There is a vast untapped reservoir of human talent in every organization. Jobs will therefore have to be enlarged so that they become meaningful and challenging. Work will have to be so restructured that every one has scope to develop himself and attain maturity to the best of his potential capacity. This is the way to use human energy in the best possible manner.

Relevance

Chris Argyris work is of high quality. He has written extensively. His ideas can change the culture of the organization. He does not believe in traditional formal organization which have been the cause of inefficiency, red-tapism, routine and dull. Those who work in these organizations feel frustrated. Those for whom such organizations work feel frustrated. In the 21st century, organizations are becoming complex. Machinery of Government is going out of control. The ideas based on research and experimentation of Chris Argyris can be applied and experimented. These will come out with good results. However, before we introduce his ideas, we have to change the culture of the organization. The ultimate purpose which Chris Argyris wanted is to tap the unlimited potentialities of individuals through making them comfortable and free from all misconceptions. Thus unlimited energy of individuals used by Innovative and creative organization can produce excellent results both in quantity and quality. Hence Chris Argyris is relevant for today but his ideas are so advanced that these can take care of the future as well.

Chris Argyris has emphatically said that, "Human Resource Development has become key functional area in Public Administration and management generally, since technology *per se* no longer grants sufficient competitive advantage in today's global world of accelerated dissemination of information and knowledge. People resources are therefore, to be optimally tapped for organization excellence, and here again the over emphasized left brain skills and analysis and logical manipulation are being found to be insufficient to meet the transformational needs generated by quickening change."

Notes and References

1. C. Northcole Parkinson, *et. al.*, Great Ideas in Management, *op. cit.*, p. 171.
2. Chris Argyris, Personality and Organization, Harper and Row, New York, 1957, p. 74.
3. Chris Argyris, International Management, McGraw Hills, 1976.
4. Chris Argyris, *op. cit.*, pp. 57-53.
5. Gary Dessber, Management: Leading People and Organizations in the 21st Century, New Jersy, Prentice Hall, 2nd Edition, p. 36.
6. Chris Argyris, Interventions Theory and Method, *A Behavioural Science View*, Reading (men) Addison, Wesley, 1970, p. 40.
7. Chris Argyris, Human Problems with budgets, *Harvard Business Review*, Jan.-Feb., p. 108.
8. Chris Argyris, *Ibid.*, p. 100.
9. M.Levine, "Participative Budgeting—Reviewing the Literature", *Business*, March 1979, pp. 49-52.
10. S.K. Bhatia and Nirmal Singh, Principles and Techniques of Personnel Management/Human Resource Management, Deep and Deep, New Delhi, (2nd ed. 2000), p. 106.

21

Rensis Likert

He was born in 1903 and obtained his Ph.D. in 1932 from Columbia University. Rensis Likert, a genius and an eminent social psychologist from USA who established the institute of Social Research in 1949 at the University of Michigan. He remained its Director until 1970. As a behavioural scientists, he examined the concepts of management, i.e. leadership, motivation, communication, supervision, etc. from the behavioural approach perspective. Likert and his associates conducted extensive organization researches on American Business and Government for a period of 25 years. Likert identified the factors which are responsible for good performance in an organization.

Likert claims to present 'a newer theory of organization based on the management principles and practices of the managers who are achieving the best results in American business and government." He suggests the setting up of foundations for the art of management. He says, "Of all the tasks of management, management of human component is the central and most important task, because all else depends on how well it is done." All now agree that human rather than capital is the key to development.

Likert treats the organization as a complex system based on the principle of supporting relationships, in which

FIG. 21.1

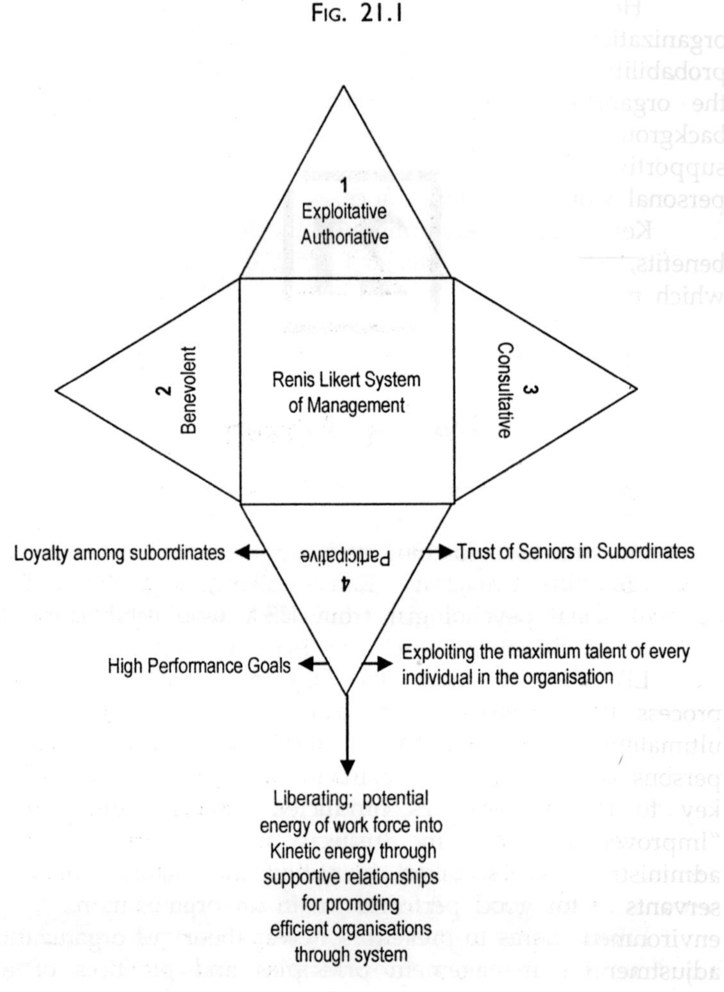

decisions-making, leadership, motivation, communication and control move together.[1] For achieving organisational objectives; he emphasizes participation in such a fashion that "a satisfactory integration of the needs and desires of all members of the organization and of persons are functionally related to it."

He states, "The leadership and other processes of the organization must be such as to assume a maximum probability that in all interactions and all relationships within the organization, each member will, in the light of his background values, and expectations, view the experience as supportive and one which builds and maintains his sense of personal worth and importance.[2]

Keith Devis has enumerated the following five practical benefits, which can be derived from informal organizations, which may be kept in mind by the management.

1. It blends with the formal organisation to make a workable system for getting the work done;
2. It lightens the workload of the formal manager and fills in some of the gaps in his abilities;
3. It gives suggestion and stability to work groups;
4. It is a very useful channel of communication in the organisation; and
5. Its presence encourages the manager to plan and act more carefully than he would otherwise do.[3]

Likert feels that Development is not mechanical process. It is a human enterprise and its success will depend ultimately on the skill, the quality and motivation of the persons associated with it Human rather than capital is the key to development. According to Prof. Merle Fainsod: "Improvements in the effectiveness of development administration depends on the quality and training of public servants who man it and on a social and political environment which liberates their energies. Structural adjustments can work no development miracles where administrative manpower is inadequate or the will to develop is lacking. The secret of development is not concealed in the interstices of governmental or administrative structure development takes place where skill is supported by commitment and the human material resources exist to translate dreams into actualities.[4]

"The performance and output of any enterprise depend entirely upon the quality of the human organization and its capacity to function as a tightly knit, highly motivated, ethically competent entity, i.e., as a highly effective interaction-influence system. High productivity, High quality products, high earnings, and successful use of research and development are not accomplished by impersonal equipment or computers. These goals are achieved by human beings. Successful organizations are those making the best use of competent personnel to perform efficiently all the tasks required by the enterprise."[5]

Books

Rensis Likert wrote the following books:

1961 New Patterns of Management, McGraw Hill, Kogokushha Ltd.
1967 The Human Organisation: Its Management and Value, New York, McGraw Hill Book Co.
1976 New Ways of Managing Conflict, New York, McGraw Hill Book Co., 1976, Co-author Likert J.G.

His other publications include:

1. An Improvement Cycle for Resource Development
2. Organizational Aspects of Human Behaviour and Human Beings in an Automatized World
3. Past and Future Perspectives on System IV
4. Profiles of Organisation Characteristics
5. Technique for the Management of Attitudes

These were supplemented by a number of journal articles.

CONTRIBUTION TO MANAGEMENT THOUGHT

1. Theory of Management Systems

Rensis Likert studied leadership style from an employee-centered and a job-centered perspective and concluded: "Supervisors with the best records of performance focus their primary attention on the human aspects of their subordinates problems and on endeavoring to build effective work groups with high performance goals."[6] Likert studied thousands of leaders and employees from business, government, and medical organizations to reach his conclusions. He categorized four styles or "systems" of leadership that exemplify different behavioural aspects of leaders. Each leadership style or system is defined by at least seven operating characteristics, which include:

1. Character of motivational forces.
2. Character of communication process.
3. Character of interaction-influence process.
4. Character of decision-making process.
5. Character of goal-setting or ordering
6. Character of control processes.[7]

The most important contribution of Rensis Likert lies in developing different systems of management along a continuum. He devised a four-level model of organization effectiveness incorporating the basic categories of task orientation and people-orientation. Likert feels that personnel are the precious assets and therefore must be treated and managed carefully. Likert classifies management philosophies into four convenient systems. 1. Exploitative authoritative, 2. Benevolent authoritative, 3. Consultative, 4. Participative.

In first approach, authority is centralised at the top and the subordinates are asked merely to obey under the threats of punishment. In system two, the leader is benevolent and autocratic. He allows the people to express themselves, but by and large, he behaves like a dictator. These managers have "Condescending Confidence" in employees. The system three refers to consultative management, wherein managers have substantial, but not complete confidence in employees abilities. The leader invites suggestions and ideas, shows his willingness to listen to his subordinates and may consider their views. He may, however keep control over decisions. In system four, "Participative" the manager runs the administration with the full consent and co-operation of the employees. Decision-making is highly decentralized and the subordinates are delegated authority to a great extent. Likert's conclusion is that most efficient organizations have system 4 characteristics and therefore organizations should move to system 4. Since the employees feel belongingness to the organization in system 4, it can yield positive results. After considerable study, Likert proposed that in contemporary society, System-4, organizations utilize human and technical resources more fully than System-1. The System-4 design emphasizes the importance of decentralized authority and non-directive, participative management behaviour. Relatively wide spans and control and heterogeneous departments facilitate the interaction of multiple and diverse points of view. Consequently, as circumstances and technology change, the organization is able to respond because of the diverse perspectives that can be brought to bear on any issue or problem that it confronts. Thus, advocates of System-4 organization design believe that it is universally applicable. But more important, they believe that it is the best way to organize in modern society. Likert argues that all managers should strive toward a system 4 participative style if they wish to maximize the quantity and quality of performance from employees. System-4 which is seen as the superior alternative in comparison to System-1,2 and 3.[8]

CHART 21.1

System-1 and System-4 Organizational Design

	System-1 Design	System-4 Design
Alternative terms often used to describe the design	Bureaucratic Classical Formalistic Mechanistic	Non-bureaucratic Neoclassical Informalistic Organic
Defining characteristics	High specialization of labour Homogeneous departments Narrow spans of control Centralized authority	Low specialization of labour Heterogeneous departments Wide spans of control Decentralized authority

2. Leadership Style

Likert carried out research studies at the University of Michigan Survey Research Centre on finding the best leader, i.e. whether job centred leaders or employee centred leaders. The experiments proved that employee centred leaders performance is better

Likert stated this principle as: "The leadership and other processes of the organization must be such as to ensure a maximum probability that in all interactions and all relationships with the organization each member will, in light of his background, values and expectation, view the experience as supportive and one which builds and maintains his sense of personal worth and importance."[9]

According to Likert, an organisation operating on an ideal interaction influence system will reveal some of the following characteristics:[10]

(1) Each member will find his personal values, needs and goals reflected in those of the workgroups and organisation as a whole.

(2) Every member of the organisation would be identified with the objectives of organisation and the goals of his workgroup and see the accomplishment of them as the best way to meet his own needs and personal goals.

(3) Pressure for high performance goals, efficient methods, and skill development come from the members themselves. The anxieties associated with hierarchical pressures in traditional organisations will be conspicuous by their absence.

(4) Authentic and sensitive communication processes within and between workgroups would ensure spontaneous and accurate information flows to providing rational basis for individual and group decisions and actions at all points in the organisation.

(5) Every member of the organisation will be able to exert his influence on decisions and actions of the organisation. The amount of influence exerted by any individual will be proportionate to the

significance of his ideas and contribution and not necessarily related to his position in the formal organisation.

(6) Cooperative motivation, communication and decision processes will enable each member in any part of the organisation to exert his influence, contribute his ideas, skills, resources and improve the total capacity of the organisation for problem-solving and goal-fulfilment.

In the modern context, individuals want greater freedom and initiative. They are not willing to accept pressure and close supervision.

In Likert's own words: "Managers who achieve high performance in their units accompanied by a sense of freedom, supervise by setting general goals and objectives and providing less specific direction than do the managers of low-producing units. . . . They use more participation and achieve higher involvement, greater interest in the work, and more responsibility for doing it than the low-producing managers."

Likert emphasized leadership style and group processes. "The low-producing managers, in keeping with the traditional practice, feel that the way to motivate and direct behaviour is to exercise control through autority."[11] In contrast, "the highest-producing managers feel, generally, that this manner of functioning does not produce the best results, that the resentment created by direct exercise of authority tends to limit its effectiveness." Therefore, said Likert, "widespread use of participation is one of the more important approaches employed by the high-producing managers."[12] He found that the value of participation applied to all aspects of the job and to work, "as, for example, in setting work goals and budgets, controlling costs, organizing the work, etc."[13]

What new management procedures are called for? Researcher Rensis Likert's work is an example of trends in management theory during the post-war years. Likert concluded that effective organizations differ from ineffective ones in several ways. Less effective job-centered companies focus on specialized jobs, efficiency, and close supervision of workers. More effective organizations, on the other hand, "focus their primary attention on endeavoring to build effective work groups with high performance goals."[14] As Likert noted, in these employee-centered companies the leadership and other processes of the organizations must be such as to insure a maximum probability that in all interactions and all relationships with the organization, each member will, in the light of his background, values and expectations, view the experience as supportive and one which builds and maintains his sense of personal worth and importance.[15]

3. Factors Responsible for Effective Performance of an Organisation

Likert has suggested that following factors should be taken into account while measuring the performance of a corporation, a division or a small group—

(i) Extent of loyalty to the institution and identification with it and its objectives.
(ii) Extent to which the goals of units and individuals facilitate the achievement of the organisation's objectives.
(iii) Level of motivation among members of the organisation with regard to such variables as:
    (a) performance including both quality and quantity of work done.
    (b) Concern for elimination of waste and reduction of costs.
    (c) Concern for improving the product.
    (d) Concern for improving processes.
(iv) Degree of confidence and trust among members of the organisation in each other and in the different hierarchical levels.
(v) Amount and quality of the teamwork in units and between units of the organisation.
(viii) Upward, downward, and sideward efficiency and adequacy of the communication process.
(ix) Leadership skills and abilities of supervisors and

managers, including their basic philosophies of management and orientation towards leadership processes.[16]

4. Conflict

Likert observes that conflict can be of both positive and negative value in calculating the worth of human assets. He says, "If bickering, distrust and irreconcilable conflict become greater, the human enterprise is worthless; if the capacity to use differences constructively and engage in cooperative teamwork improves, the human organization is a more valuable assets."

Rensis Likert in his book, "New Patterns of Management", has rightly said that conflict and differences of opinion always exist in a healthy organisation, for it is usually from such differences that new and better objectives and methods emerge. Differences are essential for program, but better unresolved differences can immobilize an organization. The central problem, consequently becomes not how to reduce or eliminate conflict but how to deal constructively with it. Effective Organizations have extra-ordinary capacity to handle conflict.

6. The Linking Pin Model

The linking Pin Model is based on the idea that every individual in the organisation is an important member of two groups i.e. linking pin for the units in the organisation above and below him. The individual is a group leader of the lower unit and a group member of the upper unit. In this model instead of man-to-man relationship, a group-to-group relationship exists. In this model the focus is upward. This upward orientation to the organization is found in the achievement of goals, communication, supervisory influence, and so on. This model is in sharp contrast to the classical hierarchical structure which has downward orientation. Likert developed this model further and added laterial (horizontal) linkage to the Model. His model emphasises upward orientation with added horizontal dimensions. This idea he has developed in his famous book, 'The Human Organisation', published in 1967.

Likert's Linking Pin Model has been criticized on the ground that it is just drawing triangles around the traditional hierarchical structure. Moreover, it slows down the process of decision-making. However, the Linking Pin Model does promote greater participation of individuals in decision-making. The emphasis on upward orientation in the organisation is certainly a novel idea. The linking pin arrangement with lateral linkages is definitely better than the traditional hierarchical arrangement.[17]

Organizational Improvement

Likert lays down the following guidelines for using the proposed organisational improvement cycle:[18]

(1) Focus the action efforts on the casual variables, such as leadership behaviour and structure. Do not try to change by direct action the intervening variables such as motivation and control. If the causal variables are improved, there will be subsequent improvements in the intervening variables;

(2) Move from system 1 to 4 gradually. Do not attempt one big jump from System 1 to 4. Both leaders and members of the organisation lack the skills for interaction and adaptation and many find it difficult to make a sudden, sizeable shift from System 1 to 4;

(3) Involve those whose behaviour has to be changed to bring the desired improvement, in planning the action to be taken. Involve all the persons affected in all the steps of the improvement cycle;

(4) Use objective, impersonal evidence as much as possible in the action planning process;

(5) As far as possible, ensure the initiative and active participation of those in the most powerful and influential position in the improvement programme; and

(6) Conduct the action planning in a supportive, helpful atmosphere.

TABLE 21.1

Likert's System of Management Leadership

Organisational Variable	*System 1 Exploitative*	*System 2 Benevolent*	*System 3 Consultative*	*System 4 Participative*
1. Extent to which superiors have confidence and trust in subordinates	Have no trust and confidence in subordinates	Have condenceding confidence and trust such as master has to servant	Substantial but not complete confidence and trust, still wishes to keep control of decisions.	Complete confidence and trust in all matters
2. Extent to which superiors behave so that subordi nates feel free to discuss important things about their jobs with their immediate superiors	Subordinates do not feel free at all to discuss things about the job with their superiors	Subordinates do not feel very free to discuss things about the job with their superiors	Subordinates feel rather free to discuss things about the job with their superiors.	Subordinate feel completely free to discuss things about the job with their superiors.
3. Extent to which immediate superior in solving job problems generally tries to get subordinates ideas and makes constructive use of them	Seldom gets ideas and opinions of subordinates in solving job problems	Sometimes gets ideas and opinions of subordinates in solving job problems	Usually gets ideas and opinions and usually tries to make constructive use of them.	Always gets ideas and opinions and always tries to make constructive use of them

Source: Rensis Likert: The Human Organizations, McGraw Hill Book Company, New York, 1967, p. 4.

CONCLUSION

"Henry B. Schacht, commenting on the changing trend in Organizational design and the use of human resources, has stressed that managers must learn to handle both the under-privileged and the bright young people, especially those who were calling for change. He states: "What this means is shorter, flatter Organizations; it means responsive management; it means a true willingness to allow people to participate in setting their own destiny; it means that militaristically-oriented hierarchy that has characterized societies and most business enterprises is a thing of the past, and the quicker we recognize it the better . . . all organizations will have to think of their key assets in terms of people and knowledge. People can be the most flexible of all assets; knowledge is the one thing that will give us insight into change and the consequences of change."

He stressed on the importance of individuals in an organization. Consistently, in study after study, the data show that treating people as 'human beings' rather than as 'cogs in a machine' is a variable related to the attitudes and motivation of the subordinate at every level in the organization."[19]

To conclude this portrayal of Professor Likert's model, in his own words:

"The performance and output of any enterprise depends entirely upon the quality of the human organization and its capacity to function as a tightly knit, highly motivated, technically competent entity, i.e. as a highly effective interaction influence system. High productivity, high quality products, high earnings and successful use of research and development are not accomplished by inter-personal equipment or computers. These goals are achieved by human beings. Successful organizations are those making the best use of competent personnel to perform well and efficient all the tasks required by the enterprise.[20]

Relevance for Future

Quality performance and desired organizational objectives can be attained only with excellent, dedicated, professionally sound and motivated personnel at all levels. This thinking has intensified more in recent times as the expenditure on personnel is spiraling and the civil services are beset with problems like corruption, unionism, apathy and indifference to work, disobedience, lack of punctuality, insubordination, complicated procedures, unwillingness to solve problems, unnecessary litigation, declining performance both in quantity and quality, lack of depth, mutual trust, dishonesty, etc.

The Likert's participative model can be extended to improve efficiency through Unfoldment of mind through creativity, which should be an integral part of HRD, HRD should promote pure thoughts, pure feelings and pure actions. When the energy of thought and action is stable, the individual is at peace with the self, in relationship with people and colleagues. This would increase the quality and output as there would be no wastage of energy in resolving conflicts. Peace must begin within each one of us. The most powerful organ of human body is the mind of man, which is endowed with unlimited potentialities that can be harnessed for the welfare of the people.

Good Governance and management is impossible without leaders who function according to Dharma and Spirituality. They only can set standards, e.g. Ram Rajya. Vedic Age was the golden period when leaders ruled according to Dharma and people enjoyed a contented life. Leaders emulated the qualities of great persons (Manur Bhava). Perseverance is what moulds a leader. While the others give up, the leader goes on, learning from every small failure on the way. And he takes responsibility by standing up. Compromise is no word in his vocabulary. He knows his strong and weak points, he doesn't believe in preventing and he knows the meaning of organization and the value of team work. In order to achieve the highest good, the leader has to be a disciplined person. His life has to be concentrated to studying and teaching the highest wisdom.

Eminent Industrialist, Mr. Rahul Bajaj, observes, "To realize our goals and aspirations, we need outstanding leadership in every field and .at every level. Leadership means that there is no substitute for excellence, no tolerance of mediocrity and no compromise with integrity. Leadership is not just charisma, not public relations, not showmanship. Leadership is performance, consistent behaviour and trust worthiness."[21]

Likert ideas if practiced in true spirit can generate, dynamisms and development in all organizations through his system 4 approach.

An individual human being is marvel of God's creation. He is unique in more than one sense. He is endowed with infinite potentialities, most of which remains untapped and unutilized. If these potentialities are harnessed and actualized properly, they are capable of bringing wonders. Human beings are like atoms containing tremendous energies. The physical law of 'fission' and 'fusion' operates on them also. If positively motivated they can bring prosperity to the humanity but if motivated negatively they can spell disaster.

Leader must create work culture and not psycho-fancy. Work culture is at the lowest ebbs. Bata K. Dey in his Article, Work Culture in India: Achievements and Failure rightly says that culture is not something which can be imported or transplanted; it must grow from within; it grows, and it does, in fertile soil and congenial climate. Gap in capital equipment or technology can be filled by import. You can even buy management, but not dedication commitment, culture. How to create that is a million dollar question.

Likert has tried to suggest such leadership based on participation. Likert system 4 organisation should be used in our present day malfunctioning organizations. Every member of the organization has high performance aspirations and by means of group interaction process, the precise goals that are set represent an optimum integration of the needs and desires of the organization members the financiers, the customers, the suppliers, others who are interested in the enterprises and the members, of the citizenary substantively affect by its operatives. In order to remove dead wood from Indian Administrative System, we must inject in them System 4 management through system 2 and 3. The research for future leadership also supports Likerts ideas.

Bass's Theory of Transformational Leadership

In his explorations of the concept of transformational leadership, Bernard M. Bass has contrasted two types of leadership behaviours: transactional and transformational. Transactional leaders determine what employees need to do to achieve their own and organizational objectives, classify those requirements, and help employees become confident and they can reach their objectives by expending the necessary efforts. In contrast, transformational leaders "motivate us to do more than we originally expected to do" by raising our sense of the importance and value of our tasks, by "getting us to transcend our own self-interests for the sake of the team, organization, or larger policy," and by raising our need level to the higher-order needs, such as self-actualization.[22]

Notes and References

1. Rensis Likert, New Patterns of Management, 1961.
2. Earnest Dale, Management: Theory and Practice, 1973, Tokyo Mc-Graw Hill, p. 149.
3. Keith Davis, Human Behaviour at Work, 4th Edition, Mc-Graw Hill, New York, 1972, pp. 257-59.
4. Merele Fainsode in Irwing Swerdlous (ed.), Development Administration, Concepts and Problems, Syracuse, 1963, p. 23.
5. Rensis Likert, The Human Organization: Its Management and Values, New York, McGraw Hill, 1967, International Students Edition Kogokurha Company, Tokyo, p. 134.
6. Rensis Likert, New Patterns of Management, New York, Mc-Graw Hill, 1961, p. 7.
7. Terry and Franklin, Principles of Management, Eighth Edition, Delhi, A.I.T.B.S., 2003, p. 336.
8. *Ibid.*, p. 337.
9. Rensis Likert, "The New Human Organization: Its Management and Value, New York, McGraw Hill 1967, International Students Edition, Kogakusha Company, Tokyo, p. 47.
10. *Ibid.*, pp. 181-83.
11. Sumatra Ghoshal and Christopher Bartlett, "Changing the Role of Top Management: Beyond Structure to Processes", *Harvard Business Review*, Jan.-Feb., 1995, pp. 86-96.
12. *Ibid.*, p. 91.
13. *Ibid.*, p. 94

14. Noel Tichy and Ram Charan, "The CEO as Coach: An Interview with Allied-Signal's Lawrence, A. Bossidy", *Harvard Business Review*, March-April, 1995, pp. 69-78.
15. *Ibid.*, p. 76.
16. Rensis Likert, Motivational Approach to Management Development, *Harvard Business Review*, July-Aug., 1959, pp. 27-77.
17. R.N. Singh, Management Thought and Timbers, Sultans Chand; New Delhi, 2002, p. 356.
18. R. Likert, An Implementation Cycle for Resource Development, *op. cit.*, pp. 56-59.
19. Dalton, E. McFarland, Management, Principles and Practices, 1970, pp. 551-52.
20. Rensis Likert, *op. cit.*, p. 134.
21. AIU, *University News*, March 13, 2000.
22. Bass, "Leadership: Good, Better, Best", pp. 27-31.

22

Fred W. Riggs

Fred W. Riggs, an eminent scholar is one of the few theorist who concentrated his work on comparative and Development administration. He concentrated on the Ecology of Public Administration. He developed models in the context of developing countries generally called Prismatic Society. He used interdisciplinary approach.

Fred W. Riggs, born in Kuling, China, in 1917, received his doctorate in Political Science from Columbia University in 1948. He served as a research associate of the Foreign Policy Association during 1948-51, as assistant to the Director of the Public Administration Clearing House in New York between 1951-55, and as a member of the Department of Government Indiana University, from 1956 through 1967. Fred W. Riggs is among the most innovative scholars in the discipline of Political Science and Public Administration. Since 1967 he has been a Professor of Political Science at the University of Hawaii. He has also been a senior specialist at the East-West Center, University of Hawaii, and a fellow of the Center for Advanced Study in the Behavioural Sciences, Stanford. In 1963 when the Comparative Administration Group (CAG) was set-up as a Committee of the American Society, F.W. Riggs was made the first Chairman of Comparative Administration Group a position that he held in 1970. The

CHART 22.1

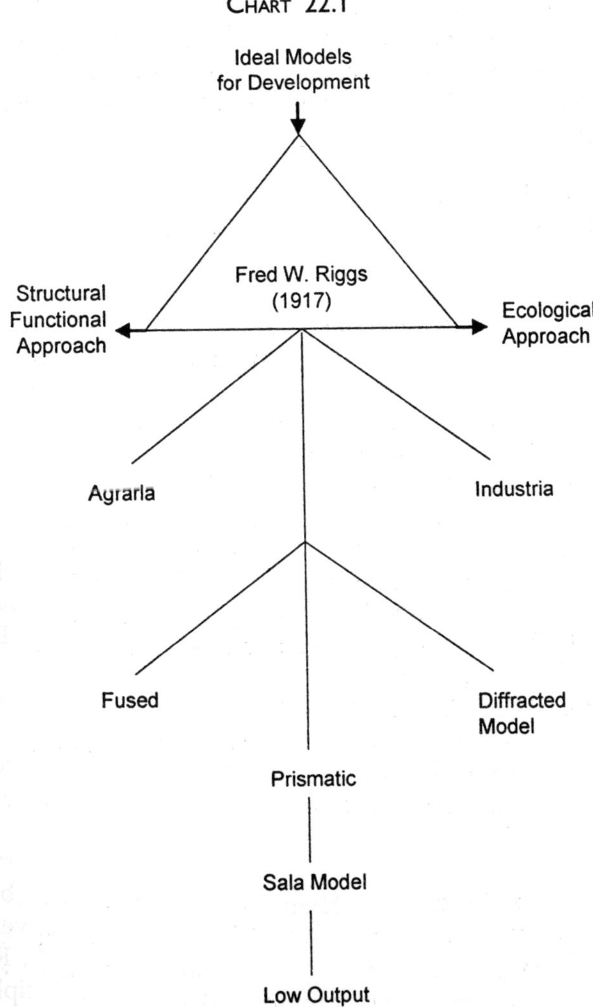

CAG was engaged in conducting cross cultural studies on the multi-dimensional administrative problems of the emerged nations. In Political Science and Public Administration, more specifically in comparative administration and development administration. Ferrel Heady is of the view that Rigg's Administration in Developing Countries: The Theory of Prismatic Society continues to be probably the most notable single contribution in comparative Public Administration.[1] Riggs has published a number of books and papers. As Heady has observed 'mere acquaintance with all his writings on comparative theory is in itself not an insignificant accomplishment.'[2]

Books and Papers

Riggs is a prolific author. He has written the following books:

1. Frontiers of Public Administration (edited)
2. Thailand: The Modernisation of a Bureaucratic Polity
3. Ecology of Public Administration, 1961
4. Prismatic Society Revisited, 1964
5. Applied Prismatics
6. Development Debate (in joint authorship)
7. Administration in Developing Countries, 1964
8. Agraria and Industria: Towards a Typology of Comparative Public Administration (Edited), 1957
9. Trends in the Comparative Study of Public Administration, 1962
10. The Sala Model, 1962
11. Further Considerations on Development: Administrative Change, 1976
12. Prismatic Societies and Public Administration, 1974.

The administrative theories and models which were developed before the Second World War, were not applicable for developing nations since the structure and functions of these countries underwent profound changes. These failed to understand the structure and functions, administrative systems in developing countries. It is in this context that Riggs developed entirely new models which emphasized cross-cultural and cross-national administrative needs and systems. Riggs borrowed concepts from sociology, physics and biology to propose new theories in public administration.

The three tools which he has employed to describe his analytical models are the ecological approach, structural functional approach and 'ideal' model building. Each of these needs elaboration.

Ecological Approach

Administration and its environment impact each other as well as influence the functioning of administration continuously. This approach is known as ecological approach.

Ecology is a term borrowed from biology. It deals with the science concerned with interrelationship of organisms and their environment. It is concerned with the interplay of living organisms and their physical and social environment and how organisms and environment are kept in balance for survival and other important objectives. In order to comprehend administrative system, we have to understand in depth the environment or ecology in which the administrative system is operating as the environment has profound influence on all components of administrative system. For example, plants where rainfall is limited had small leaves.

STRUCTURAL FUNCTIONAL APPROACH

Riggs holds the view that each system is made up of various structures which perform specific functions. A structure can be defined as a pattern of behaviour which has become a standard feature of the system, and its functions can be related to the role of the structure plays in a system. Structures can be concrete or analytic.

F.W. Riggs studied the relationship between the administration and economic, social, technological, political psychological, anthropological and communication factors in a larger perspective. He explained as to how environmental factors influence administrative system, in the context of his studies in Thailand and Phillipines. Thus, the structural-functional approach is a method of narrating the functions that are carried out in a society, the structures that are responsible to discharge the functions, and the methods that are adopted in undertaking the functions. According to Riggs, in every society five important types of functions are discharged viz., economic, social, communication, symbolic and political functions.

Ideal Models

Models are highly useful in the development of public administration as a subject from the normative to an empirical study. Models can explain the nature of functioning of a particular structure. Riggs first used his much published models in 1956, by classifying the societies into Agraria and Industria, i.e, agricultural and industrial societies. In this model Riggs differentiated between two types of societies where agricultural institutions dominated and societies where industrial institutions dominated. An example of the former was Imperial China and of the latter, contemporary America. Riggs models of Agrarian-Industries recompiles to a great extent Weber's traditional and legal rational authority system respectively. According to him all societies transform from Agraria to Industria at a given point. Riggs identified the following as the structural features of Agraria and Industria:

Agraria	*Industria*
1. Dominance Ascriptive values, Particularistic and diffuse pattern	1. Dominance of Universal, Specific and achievement norms
2. Local Groups are stable and there is limited social and spatial mobility	2. Degree of social and spatial mobility
3. Occupational differences are very simple and stable	3. Occupational system is well developed and cut-off from other social structures
4. A differential stratification of difference of impact	4. Existence of egalitarian class system based on generalized patterns of occupational achievement

Source: Fred W. Riggs.

Agraria Industria

Rigg's felt that transitional societies which do not fit in his model go out of the purview of the model . Later in 1957, he developed an equilibrium model named 'transitia' which represents to the transforming societies.

Soon after the typology was formulated Riggs realized that there were many limitations. These limitations are briefly summarized as follows:

(1) 'Agraria-Industria' typology is not of great use in studying the transitional societies, i.e., those societies which are moving from the agrarian stage towards the industrial stage;
(2) The system does not provide sufficient mechanisms to analyses mixed societies, since modern societies always have some agrarian featuers;
(3) The typology assumes a unidirectional movement from the agraria to the industria; and
(4) The models give very little emphasis to the analysis of the administrative system *per se*. The major stress is on the environment of the administrative system.

Fred W. Riggs himself abandoned looking to the limitations of the typology and its critiques this model and came out with another set of models "Faused-Prismatic-diffracted societies which is a improvement over the first typology.

Fused-Prismatic-Diffracted Model

Faced by above mentioned issues, difficulties, limitations and viability, the Riggs developed another model to study developing countries known as Fused, Prismatic and diffracted model. The typology of "fused" Prismatic and "diffracted" societies is based on the premise of structural functional approach which studies societies on the basis of functional differentiation of various social structures.

Riggs says: "if we could average the characteristics of real societies, we might be able to place them on the same scale, and I would suggest that traditional Siam might be put where I have placed the letter S, modern Thailand near T.P. would represent the Phillipines and A. America. Of course, these are speculative guesses and not the result of any exact measurement, but I believe that his method lends itself to quantification."[3] The following table indicates the broad characteristics of fused, prismatic and diffracted societies.

TABLE 22.1

Fused	Prismatic	Diffracted
Particularism	Selectivism	Universalism
Ascriptive values	Attainment	Achievement
Functionally diffuse	Poly-functionalism	Functional specificity

Riggs in his wide ranging analysis touched on various social, cultural and political sub-systems with a detailed examination of various connected issues and problems using a number of models. However, it is not possible exactly to quantify these environmental factors. But his primary interest has been to illuminate administrative problems in transitional or developing societies.[4] In his entire analysis, he made use of the fused and diffracted models as tools to explain the prismatic phenomenon of developing countries. However, it is difficult to explain the impact of all variables affect on administrative system.

Fused Society Model

These fused societies are structurally undifferentiated and multi-functional in character. The prevailing outlook in the society is traditional. The ruler performs in reality all the functions, i.e. legislative, executive and judiciary. There is no differentiation of functions, i.e. communications are not effective. These societies heavily depend upon agriculture with no industrialization. Their economic system is based on law of exchange and barter system which Riggs calls as 'redistributive model.' A fused society is undifferentiated. It is very difficult to separate the functions as these are done by the same agency.

These societies do not differentiate between justice and injustice, formal and informal, moral-immoral, Right-wrong, set-ups and governmental and non-governmental activities. Modern development in developed countries have not impacted them much. Ascriptive values play a predominant role in the society, and the behaviour of the people would be highly traditional. Age-old customs, beliefs, values, faith and traditional ways of living enable the people to live together and control their behaviour. People also do not want change. Elders have a predominant role in such societies. No body can deviate from standard behaviour.

Diffracted Model

A diffracted society can be defined as a highly differentiated one where there is a high level specialization and division of work leading to excellent performance of functions. Functions in such a society are very specific and the level of integration and differentiation is very high. Fred W. Riggs says: "If a society is highly differentiated and well integrated then it is diffracted, then if it is differentiated and partly integrated, or malintegrated, thus being an ideal type."

The society would be highly dynamic and has various associations and social groups. The economic system is based on market mechanism. Riggs called it 'marketised society'. The society is highly specialized as in USA. There is high level of integration and differentiation. Technology is highly developed. The government maintains public relations and remains responsive to the needs of the people. It protects human rights. Government officials have no coercive and absolute powers. Public obey the laws of the nation. Basic aspects of social life remain intact.

Prismatic Society Model

A society which is in between these two types is known as prismatic society. According to Riggs, the prismatic society is one which has achieved a certain level of differentiation; specialization of roles that is necessary for dealing with modern technology, but has failed to integrate these roles. Prismatic society shares the value-patterns of both fused and diffracted societies. It has moved away from the fused society but not reached differentiated society. According to Riggs prismatic society has three important characteristic features viz., (1) heterogeneity, (2) formalism, and (3) overlapping Riggs has coined the term chamber for the administrative sub-system, sala for a prismatic society and office for a diffracted society.

Such societies do not depend much on Government. There is private sector which has to compete with each other to provide excellent services to the people. The interference of the Government is minimum. Government only regulates the private sector to avoid exploitation.

Heterogeneity

Heterogeneity refers to 'the simultaneous existence, side by side, of quite different kinds of systems, practices and view points'.

They have extreme variations which is reflected in wide disparities in society in social, religious, economic areas. There are in a prismatic society, urban areas with 'sophisticated' intellectual class, western style offices and the modern gadgets of administration. However, there are small and medium towns who do not enjoy these facilities as there are more agrarian features than urban. There also exist a well developed communications system, skyscrapers, air conditioners, the existence of specialized agencies to discharge various social, political, economic and technical services. On the other hand, in the rural areas, people lead a highly traditional life with no facilities of modern living like use of telephones, refrigerators, etc. The village 'elders' combine various political, administrative, social, economic and religious roles. However, things are changing fast.

All these disparities and differences in structures and functions not only influence the working of administrative system but also create a number of problems to the administration which is very difficult to change as the administrative system lack these competencies. The government generally protects the interests of 'haves' and ignores the interests of 'have nots'. Riggs says that this creates a revolutionary climate in society. Thus, a revolutionary tug of war of have's and have not is created without any solutions.

Recently the Government of India created Sezs by acquiring lands of the people living in rural areas which was resisted by rural people. There was a crisis in which many people died and got injured. The Government of India intentionally or unintentionally helped the rich people at the cost of rural poor. A bad policy on Special Economic Zone have been made worse by a mid-course correction. The rules ensure that worst sort of zones will come up while the best sort will be killed off. This will strain existing infrastructure instead of improving it. The new rules muddle the problem.[5]

Formalism

According to Riggs, formalism refers to "the extent to which a discrepancy exists between the prescriptive and descriptive, between formal and effective power, between the impression given by the Constitution, laws and regulations, organization and charts and statistics and actual practices and facts of government and society."[6] In other words, it means the degree of variation occurring between theory and practices. That is why we say that the system of public administration in such societies like India differ in theory and practice.

Riggs points out that this "formalistic behaviour is caused by the lack of pressure by pressure groups and interest groups on the government towards the programme objectives, the weakness of the social power to influence the bureaucratic performance and a great permissiveness for arbitrary administration." Bureaucracy rules the country without caring for the needs of the people.

Though the laws, rules and regulations prescribe the style of functioning of the government officials, there are wide deviations in their actual behaviour as the people are not vocal and effective in getting their problems solved. The officers sometimes stick to the rules and sometimes overlook and even violate them depending upon their will. This formalistic behaviour is caused by the lack of pressure on the government towards the programme objectives, the weakness of the social power to influence the bureaucratic performance and a great permissiveness for arbitrary administration, people are not effective in controlled affairs.

While explaining the dimensions of formalism, Riggs also mentioned about the constitutional formalism. Constitutional formalism refers to the gap between the constitutional principles and their actual implementations. In all the developing countries like India, there is no adherence to constitutional provisions which are frequently violated. People in government say one thing but in practice do something different.

Overlapping

According to Riggs, overlapping refers to "the extent to which formally differentiated structures of a diffracted society co-exists with undifferentiated structures of a fused type."[7] That is how a great wastage of resources are done. Riggs further writes that in administrative systems what is described as administrative behaviour is actually determined by non-administrative criteria, i.e., by political, social, religious or other factors.[8] In a prismatic society, although 'modern' social structures are created, the old structures also continue to dominate the social system. Functions are carried out by old structures as well as by modern ones. This creates confusion and irregularity. Overlapping is responsible for great number of problems faced by the people.

Overlapping in a prismatic society manifests in several forms in various areas and these are termed as nepotism, favouratism, communalism.

It has five different aspects:

(a) Polycommunalism
(b) Polynormativism
(c) Nepotism
(d) Bazar-Canteen Model
(e) Authority versus Control

Sala Model—Administrative Sub-System of a Prismatic Society

Prismatic society is characterized by various economic, social, political and administrative sub-systems. Riggs termed the administrative sub-systems as 'Sala Model'. In a diffracted society its counterpart is called 'Bureau' or 'Office' and in a fused society it is termed 'Chamber'. These three have different features of their own. The Spanish word Sala has different connotations, e.g. office, religious conference, etc.

The main feature of sala model are mentioned below:

Lack of Rationality

The administrative efficiency available and rationality found in a bureau are absent here. The machinery of government run on hunches rather than facts.

Favoritisms

Favoritism, Nepotism and family rule are common in sala model. Decisions are not based on rules but personal relationships.

Low Administrative Output

Riggs pointed out that since the performance of the government depends on the efficiency of the Sala officials, there 'is a close link between bureaucratic behaviour and administrative output'. Administration gives more weightage to files rather than performance. There exists a dichotomy between administration and people as the former enjoy vast powers both in theory and practice. This implies that "the more powerful a bureaucrat, is the less effective he is as administrator." Consequently, it creates many problems like nepotism, institutionalised corruption, inefficiency, poor administration of laws, protection of self-interests, etc."

Concept and Nature of Development

F.W. Riggs views development and development administration in terms of his models.

Riggs defined development as 'a process of increasing autonomy (discretion) of social systems, made possible, by rising level of diffraction'. 'Discretion', he observes, is the 'ability to choose among alternatives' while diffraction refers to the degree of differentiation and integration in a social system. Ecologically development is increasing ability to make and carry out collective decisions affecting the environment.[9] He suggests the countries falling in Sala model should get rid of the administrative feature earlier mentioned and inject new variable as in a differentiated society.

Riggs considered differentiation and integration as the two key elements in the process of development. Differentiation means existence of a situation in which every function has a corresponding specialized structure for its performance. For example, Govt. of India has created the Ministry of Health and Family Welfare to promote health of the people, i.e. Physical, mental, social well-being. Integration means a mechanism to assimilate various kinds of specialized roles. There are large number of institutions under Ministry of Health taking care of different aspects of health. The need is to co-ordinate.

The level of differentiation in any country depends upon the technological and non-technological factors. The more the development of technology, the higher the level of differentiation. The integration depends on the important factors: (i) penetration, and (ii) participation. Penetration is the ability of a government to make and carry out decisions throughout the country. Participation is the receptivity of the people to law and the willingness to help carry out the laws and the policies which government has formulated.

CONCLUSION

Riggs concludes, "Suffice it to say that one way of judging the level of development of a society or social system may be the degree to which it exhibits the characteristics of balanced polity, organizational maturity, and the prevalence of a salary system in its bureaucracies."

He argued that "the human acts as an integrated whole—motivation has to appeal to the whole and is, as a result, complex, continuous and fluctuating."

Riggs models are not something new. We are already aware of them. It is very difficult to make administrative models as the culture even in a developing country differs in its different areas. For example in India, the same model of development cannot be applied to different states, as the values and customs differ in each state and within each state, there are differences from area to area. For example, in UP in India, there are lot of differences between East and North of UP. Thus, it is very difficult to make it so simplistic. The models of F.W. Riggs, do not reveal and fit into the system.

It is suggested that each government must develop its own indigenous model as they are able to understand the problems affecting the indigeneous model since they are embedded into it. For example, in India, we have more than 300 universities where eminent people are working. We must make use of their intelligence and come out with models along with steps which can be taken to make India a diffracted society or developed society. Scholars rather than simply study F.W. Riggs and teaching year after year to students, need to develop creativity and come out with models of development based on indigenous ecology. Our ancient models of development "Ram Rajya" has been there where all people enjoyed life and the king was bound to serve the people. The need is to locate those models which work for India.

We must read and teach great administrative thinkers but we should also teach about the relevance of F.W. Riggs thoughts to India. Our teachers and students must come out with models for making India a developed nation based upon its ancient ideology of renunciation, righteousness (Dharma) as laid down in our scriptures. Until and unless our academia would be enamored by reading and teaching foreign scholars works without actions, this would be futile exercise. Words, written or spoken are of no use unless put to action.

CRITICAL APPRAISAL

Riggs liberally coined new words to explain his concepts. In addition he also gave different meanings to a number of words already in use. There is no harm in coining new words when the existing vocabulary fails to convey the meaning and clarify the concepts.[10] There is also nothing wrong if one gives his own meaning for the effective expression of his views. But free use of new words, and words used with different meanings may create confusion instead of clarifying the concepts. Riggs in his enthusiasm to give a scientific temper to his models, borrowed most of his terminology from physical sciences. But by mere use of certain new words borrowed from physical sciences, administration cannot become a science.[11]

As Chapman has correctly observed that, in spite of many limitations, Riggs models may deepen our insight into some of the underlying problems of public administration in transitional societies. In some ways the prismatic model may be analogous to principles in administration. 'Principles may not be universal truths and they may have the defect of proverbs, that they occur in contradictory Pairs, but this does not mean that principles are worthless; indeed they may be particularly useful as criteria for describing and diagnosing administrative situations. In a similar way Riggs' approach and models may be considered as more sophisticated tools for describing and diagnosing administrative situations'.[12]

Relevance

Fred W. Riggs is relevant as he has given some models based on Ecology. His purpose is to study the administrative system of a country and its ecology . Most of the developing countries come under prismatic society for whom he develop sala model. The purpose of understanding the ecology and functioning of administration is to promote development. Development is nothing but changing prismatic societies into diffracted models that is introducing sophisticated system of administration. So, Prof. Fred W. Riggs would always be relevant for his relationship between ecology and actual functioning of administration.

However, he has made it so simple that in reality it is difficult to experiment this. All the developing countries have their cultural, social and anthropological issues which came to be clubbed in any particular model. What is needed is that the scholars and academia in Indian Universities and Higher Education System should work out the model in their country which would be based on reality. Thus, we should design our own models and inject development rather than simply study and teach Riggs. The Value of Work would be assessed by the models made by every country. F.W. Riggs has given a new thrust to promote development which would be useful for developing countries.

Notes and References

1. Ferrel Heady Public Administration: A Comparative Perspective, Second Edition, Mueel Dekker, New York, 1979, p. 13.
2. Ferrel Heady and Sybil Stokes, Papers in Comparative Public Administrative, University of Michigan, Ann Arbor, 1962.
3. Quoted in Ramesh K. Arora, Comparative Public Administration: An Ecological Perspective, New Delhi, Associated Publishing House, p. 10.
4. *Ibid.*

5. S. Swaninathan and Anklesaria Aiyar, Killing the Best, Adding the Worst SEZ, in *Economic Times,* 11th March, 2007.
6. F.W. Riggs, The Ecology of Public Administration, *op. cit.,* pp. 91-92.
7. F.W. Riggs, The Sala Model, An Ecological Approach to the Study of Comparative Public Administration, *op. cit.,* p. 6.
8. F.W. Riggs, The Ecology of Public Administration, *op. cit.,* p. 92.
9. F.W. Riggs, "Further Consideration on Development", *Administrative Changes,* Vol. 4, No. 1, July-Dec. 1976, p. 2.
10. Richard, A. Chapman, "Prismatic Theory in Public Administration: A Review of Theories of Fred W. Riggs," *Public Administration,* Vol. 44, Winter, 1966, p. 418.
11. Kishan Khanna, "Contemporary Models of Public Administration: An Assessment of their Utility and Exposition of Inherent Fallacies", *Philippines Journal of Public Administration,* Vol. XVIII, No. 2, April, 1974, p. 103.
12. Richard A. Chapman, *op. cit.,* p. 427.

23

Peter F. Drucker

He was Born in Austria in 1909. He qualified in law and worked as a journalist in Germany. His major contribution is in providing excellent literature in management and administration serving as a reputed journalist, consultant and an eminent scholar and teacher. He has been awarded with national and international awards.

Important Books

He has written a large number of books. Some of which are.

1. The End of Economic Man (1939)
2. The Future of Industrial Man (1942)
3. Concept of the Corporation (1946)
4. The New Society (1950)
5. The Practice of Management (1954)
6. America's Next Twenty Years (1957)
7. The Landmarks of Tomorrow (1959)
8. Managing for Results (1964)
9. The Effective Executive (1966)
10. The Age of Discontinuity (1969)
11. Technology, Management and Society (1970)
12. Men, Ideas and Politics (1971)

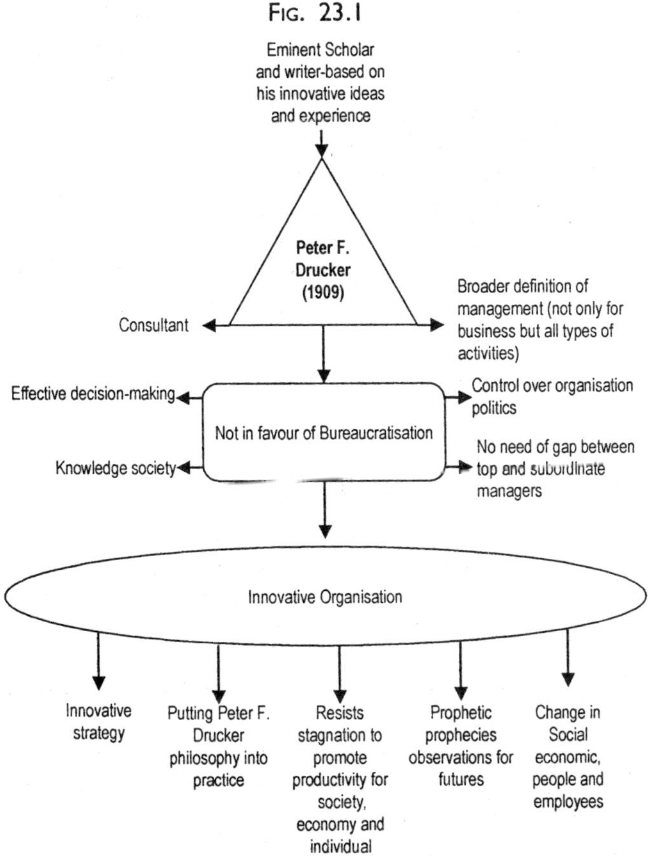

FIG. 23.1

13. The New Markets and Other Essays (1971)
14. Management, Tasks, Responsibilities, Practices (1974)
15. The Unseen Revolution: How Pension Fund Socialism came to America (1976)
16. Management Cases (1977)
17. People and Performance (1977)
18. An Introductory View of Management (1978)
19. Adventures of a Bystander (1979)
20. Managing in Turbulent Times (1980)
21. Towards the Next Economics and Other Essays (1981)
22. The changing World of the Executives (1982)

23. The Last of all Possible Worlds (Fiction) (1982)
24. The Temptation to do Good (Fiction) (1984)
25. Innovation and Entrepreneurship (1985)
26. Frontiers of Management (1987)
27. The New Realities (1989)
28. Managing the Non-profit Organisation, (1990)
29. Managing for the Future
30. Managing in a Time of Great Change
31. Management Challenges for the 21st Century
32. Managing in the Next Society

Major Articles (Papers)

"Meaning and Function of Economic Policy Today", *Review of Politics* (April, 1943).

"Way to Industrial Peace", *Harper's* (1946).

"Frontier for this Century", *Harper's* (March, 1952).

"How to Be an Employee", *Fortune* (May, 1952).

"The American Genius is Politics", *Perspectives U.S.A.* (1953).

"Business Objectives and Survival Needs", *Journal of Business* (April, 1958).

"Potentials of Management Science", *Harvard Business Review* (January, 1959).

"The Technological Revolution; Notes on the Relationship of Technology, Science and Culture", *Technology and Culture* (Fall, 1961).

"Japan Tries for a Second Miracle", *Harper's* (March, 1963),

"Care and Feeding of the Profitable Product", *Fortune* (March, 1964).

"If I Were a Company President", *Harper's* (April, 1964).

"Automation Is Not the Villain", *New York Times Magazine* (January 10, 1965).

"On the Economic Basis of American Politics", *The Public Interest* (Winter, 1968).

"The Surprising Seventies", *Harper's* (July and Sept., 1971).

"What We can Learn from Japanese Management", *Harvard Business Review* (March. 1971).

"Six Durable Economic Myths", *Wall Street Journal* (Sept. 6, 1975).

"Managing the Knowledge Worker", *Wall Street Journal* (Nov. 7, 1975)

CONTRIBUTION TO MANAGEMENT THOUGHT

His contributions is immense and everlasting. His ideas have inspired large number of students, Manager, Business Organizations and teachers. He is a prolific writer

(I) Role and Significance of Management (Drucker)

Management is work, and as such it has its own skills, its own tools, its own techniques. For Management is the organ, the life-giving, acting, dynamic organ of the institution it manages. Without the institution, e.g., the business enterprise, there would be no management. But without management there would also be only a mob rather than an institution. The institution, in turn, is in itself an organ of society and exists only to contribute a needed result to society, the economy, and the individual. Organs, however, are never defined by what they do, let alone by how they do it. They are defined by their contribution.

Management, the Drucker maintains throughout, is a discipline, or at least is capable of becoming one. It is not just common sense. It is not just codified experience. It is at least potentially an organized body of knowledge.

The emergence of management in this century may have been a pivotal event of history. It signaled a major transformation of society into a pluralist society of institutions of which management is the effective organ. Management, after more than a century of development as a practice and as a discipline, burst into public consciousness in the management boom that began after World War II and lasted through the 1960s. What has the boom accomplished? What have we learned? and what are the new knowledge we need, the new challenges we face, the new tasks ahead, now that the management boom is over?

"The manager is the dynamic, life-giving element in every business. Without his leadership the 'resources of production' remain resources and never become production."

Peter F. Drucker has rightly pointed out that "Management is the crucial factor in economic and social development. It was obvious that the economists' traditional view of development as a function of savings and capital investment do not produce management and economic development. On the contrary, management produces economic and social development and with its savings and capital investment. It becomes apparent that the developing countries are not underdeveloped, they are under managed.

(2) Top Management—Need of Team Structure

Top-management work is work for a team rather than for one man. It is quite unlikely that any one man will, in his own person, unite the divergent temperaments which the job requires. Moreover, it will be found, when the top-management tasks are analyzed, that there is more work to be done than any one man can do. The tasks require, except in the smallest business, at least one full-time man who does nothing else, and then one or two, at least for a major part of their time, who take on part of the task in which they are then the "leaders" and have primary responsibility.

There are additional reasons why the one-man top management tends to malfunction. Every top-management succession in a one-man top management is a "crisis" and a desperate gamble. No one in the business except the former top man has really done the top-management work and proven himself in it.

To recognize the team nature of the top-management job is particularly important in the small business. the one-man top management is a major reason why business fail to grow.

But the job itself is a team job to begin with. Whatever the titles on the organization chart, the top-management job in a healthy company is almost always actually done by a team.

We can now summarize the basic specifications for a functioning top-management structure: The starting point is an analysis of the top-management tasks.

Each top-management task must be clearly assigned to someone who has direct and full responsibility for it.

This requires a top-management team, with responsibility assigned to fit the personalities, qualifications, and temperaments of the members.

Whoever has assigned responsibility for a top-management activity is "top management" whatever his title.

Except in the small and simple business no one who has top management responsibilities does any but top-management work.

The complex business requires more than one top-management team, each structured according to these rules.

No business can do better than its top management will permit; the " bottleneck" is, after all, always "at the head of the bottle." Of all the jobs in the enterprise the top-management job is the most difficult one to organize. But it is also the most important one to organize.

(3) Need of Attending on Priority Top Managerial Challenges and Opportunities

The job, task, and responsibilities of worker and foreman in the plant, key-punch operator and secretary in the office, metallurgist in the engineering lab, field salesman and branch manager of a bank or insurance company are little affected by size, complexity, growth, or diversity. Even innovation has an effect on most people in an organization only after it has become an accomplished fact. But the structure, the behaviour, the tasks, and the strategies of top management are profoundly molded by changes in size and complexity, by diversification, growth, and innovation. And, in turn, top management—and only top management—can make the strategic decisions that lead to growth, diversification, or innovation. The managerial strategies that relate to a company's basic structure have received almost no attention. They may, however, be of greater importance than strategies with respect to finances, product-development, or marketing on which the discussion has focused. Size, diversity, complexity, growth, and innovation are, above all, managerial challenges and opportunities to top management and make managerial demands on it.

Specifically, there are five major areas to be considered:

1. Managing smallness and bigness—that is, the management requirements of size by itself. "How big is big?" "What are 'right' sizes and what are

'wrong' sizes?" What are the limits beyond which further growth is degenerative?" And, "What are the implications of size for business strategy?"

2. The second major area is the management of complexity and diversity. "How complex is complex?" "How complex is too complex?" And, "What requirements does complexity make?" A separate problem in complexity that deserves some discussion is that of the limits on the family-owned business. "Can it perpetuate itself", "Can it grow beyond small size?" And, "What are its limits in time and size?"
3. A special case of complexity, so important as to deserve a separate chapter, is the most complex of business organizations, the multinational corporation. For here is added to complexities of size, markets, products, and technologies, the complexities of cultures and the complexities of multiple political and governmental relationships and restraints.
4. Managing change and growth is the next major topic. "At what point in change and growth does management have to change its characteristics, its structure, its behaviour?" And, "How can it prepare itself so that it is ready for change and for growth without, at the same time, overloading the company with functions and complexities which, at the present state of the business, it does so require and can ill afford?"
5. Managing innovation is a topic in itself.

"Man is the only animal capable of purposeful evolution; he makes tools." This insight of Alfred Russel Wallace, co-discoverer with Darwin of the principle of evolution, means that man and his social organizations can innovate. They can create, so to speak, a different animal. Indeed, in a changing environment their survival depends on their capacity to innovate. What does an innovative organization have to be and how does it have to be structured and managed?

4. Not in Favour of Bureaucratic Management

Peter F. Drucker is against bureaucratic management. He emphasises creative management, i.e., the manager should be an innovator. In his book, 'The Practice of Management' he wrote, "Managing a business cannot be a bureaucratic, an administrative, or even a policy-making job. . . (it) must be a creative rather an adaptive task."

In his words, "in the last analysis, management is practice, its essence is not knowing but doing. Its test is not logic but results. Its only authority is performance."

5. Planning

There has been a tremendous upsurge in long-range planning these last twenty years. The very idea was practically unknown a few decades ago. Now it is the rare large company (at least in the U.S. and in Japan) that does not have a long-range planning staff and elaborate long-range plans.

It is true that practically every basic management decision is a long-range decision—ten years is a rather short time span these days. Whether concerned with research or with building a new plant, designing a new marketing organization or a new product, every major management decision takes years before it is really effective. And it has to be productive for years thereafter to pay-off the investment of men and money. Managers, therefore, need to be skilled in making decisions with long futurity on a systematic basis.

Management has no choice but to anticipate the future, to attempt to mold it, and to balance short-range and long-range goals. It is not given to mortals to do well any of these things. But lacking divine guidance, management must make sure that these difficult responsibilities are not overlooked or neglected but taken care of as well as is humanly possible.

"To plan is to produce a scheme for future action, to bring about specified results, at specified cost, in a specified period of time. It is a deliberate attempt to influence, exploit, bring about, and control the nature, direction, extent, speed and effects of change. It may even attempt deliberately to create change. It is a carefully controlled and co-ordinated activity."

Strategic planning does not substitute facts for judgement, does not substitute science for the manager. It does not even lessen the importance and role of managerial ability, courage, experience, intuition, or even hunch-just as scientific biology and systematic medicine have not lessened the importance of these qualities in the individual physician. On the contrary, the systematic organization of the planning job and the supply of knowledge to it strengthen the manager's judgement, leadership, and vision.

6. Decisions Need be Based on Developing Alternatives

Decisions made without considering alternatives may have unfortunate consequences. Druker makes this point succinctly in the following passage: "Whenever one has to judge, one must have alternatives among which one can choose. A judgement in which one can only say 'yes' or 'no' is no judgement at all. Only, if there are alternatives one can hope to get insight into what is truly at stake. A decision without an alternative is a desperate gambler's throw, no matter, how carefully thought it might be. If one has thought through, alternatives during the decision-making process, one has something to fall back on, something that has already been thought through, that has been studied, that is understood. Without such an alternative, one is likely to flounder dismally when reality proves a decision to be inoperative."

7. Decentralized Model

In simple words, an organization is said to be Centralised, if most of the powers of decisions are vested in the top level. A decentralized organization, on the other hand, is the one, in which the lower level managers are allowed to decide. Simply stated, Sloan's General Motors Model utilizes centralized control of decentralized operations. Many large industrial organizations have designed themselves, after the Sloan Model. One important way, these complex organizations in USA have overcome breakdowns in communication, control and managerial effectiveness is through centralized control of decentralized operations.

Peter Drucker interviewed several GM executives who

had worked under the Sloan type of structure. He found that some practical and day-to-day benefits have resulted from this model. These advantages are summarized by Peter Drucker:

(1) The speed and lack of confusion with which a decision can be made.
(2) The absence of conflict of interest between corporate management and the divisions.
(3) The sense of fairness, appreciation, confidence, and security that comes when organizational 'politics' are kept under control.
(4) The democracy and informality in management where everyone is free to criticize but no one tries to sabotage.
(5) The absence of gap between "the privileged few" top managers and the "great many" subordinate managers in the organization.
(6) The availability of large supply of goods, experienced leaders capable to take top responsibility.

8. Need of Good Organisation

Organizational analysis is a technique to ensure the achievement of maximum results with minimum costs, in terms of human and material resources of the organizations. The objective of organizational analysis is to improve pattern of relationships between persons in an organization and to create harmonious arrangement of work with reference to its main objectives. The need for the design of sound organizational structures for an enterprise and their continual evaluation in terms of suitability through organizational analysis has been recognized as an effective means to promote improvement in corporate performance. Peter F. Drucker has rightly observed: "Good organization structure does not by itself produce good performance—just as good constitution does not guarantee great Presidents, or good laws and a moral society. But a poor organization structure makes good performance impossible, no matter how good the individuals may be.

He states, "the alternative to autonomous institutions that function and perform is not freedom. It is totalitarian tyranny. The large organisation makes a living possible through knowledge. Knowledge is the very foundation of the modern organisation.

9. Management by Objectives can Promote Efficiency

For organizational success work activities should be so designed and directed as to support each other towards the achievement of objectives. It also implies that working relations should contribute to the success of each activity and thus to general effectiveness. The working relations between people are usually described as functional and structural. Functional relations are derived from the technical nature of the work and where, when and in which sequence it takes place. Structural relations pertain to administrative rules and standards and in particular to the authority and responsibility assigned to individuals. This is known as convergence of work.

Management by objectives is one of the techniques by which executives can improve organizational performance and effectiveness.

According to George Odiorne, "MBO (Management By Objectives) is a system wherein the superior and the subordinate managers of an organization jointly define its common goals, define each individual's major areas of responsibility in terms of the results expected of him and use these measures as guides for operating the unit and assessing the contribution of each of its members.

Peter Drucker defines the Philosophy of MBO thus: "What the Business enterprise needs is a principle of management that will give full scope to individual strength and responsibility, and at the same time give common direction of vision and effort, establish team work and harmonize the goal of the individual with the common weal. The only principle that can do this is management by objectives and self-control. It makes the common weal the aim of every manager. It substitutes control from outside by control from within. It motivates the manager to action, not because somebody tells him to do something or takes him into doing it, but because the objective needs of his task demand it. He acts not because somebody wants him to but because he himself decides that he has to—he acts, in other words, as a free man."

Drucker's MBO, in his opinion, is a philosophy. "It rests on a concept of human action, human behaviour and human motivation. Finally, it applies to every manager, whatever his level of function, and to any business enterprise whether large or small. It ensures performance by converting objective needs into personal goals."

10. Business Mission—Customer Satisfaction

An essential step in deciding what our business is, what it will be, and what it should be is, therefore, systematic analysis of all existing products, services, processes, markets, end uses, and distribution channels. Are they still viable? And are they likely to remain viable? Do they still give value to the customer? And are they likely to do so tomorrow? Do they still fit the realities of population and markets, of technology and economy? And if not, how can we best abandon them—or at least stop pouring in further resources and efforts? Unless these questions are being asked seriously and systematically, and unless managements are willing to act on the answers to them, the best definition of "What our business is, will be, and should be" will remain a pious platitude. Energy will be used up in defending yesterday. Not one will have the time, resources, or will to work on exploiting today, let alone to work on making tomorrow.

'Planned abandonment was first discussed and advocated in Peter's book "Managing for Results." It first was adopted as a systematic policy a few years later by the General Electric Company. Most long-range planning in large companies, like Unilever, focuses on the question "What will our business be?" GE's strategic business planning developed in the late sixties is an exception. Its aim is to answer "What should our business be?" Yet GE's planning does not start out with "What existing product lines and business should we abandon?" and "Which ones should we cut back and deemphasize?"

Defining the purpose and mission of the business is difficult, painful, and risky. But it alone enables a business to set objectives, to develop strategies, to concentrate its resources and to go to work. It alone enables a business to be managed for performance.

11. Poor Performance of Services Institution: Need of Research and Consultancy

Yet the evidence for performance in the service institutions is not impressive, let alone overwhelming. Schools, hospitals, and universities are all big today beyond the imagination of an earlier generation. Their budgets have grown even faster. Yet everywhere they are in crisis. A generation or two ago their performance was taken for granted. Today they are being attacked on all sides for lack of performance. Services which the nineteenth century managed with aplomb and apparently with little effort—the postal service, for instance, or the railroads—are deeply in the red, require enormous and growing subsidies and give poorer service everywhere. Government agencies, both in national and in local governments, are constantly being reorganized so as to be more efficient. Yet in every country the citizen complains ever more loudly of bureaucracy in government. What he means by this complaint is that the government agency is being run for the convenience of its employees rather than for contribution and performance. This is mismanagement.

The most persistent critics of bureaucracy in government and in the public service institutions tend to be business executives. But it is by no means certain that business's own service institutions are any more effective than the public-service bureaucracies.

The service institutions themselves have become "management conscious." Service institutions increasingly turn to business to learn management. In all service institutions, manager development, management by objectives, and many other concepts and tools of business management are now common.

This is a healthy sign but it does not mean that the service institutions understand the problems of managing themselves. It only means that they begin to realize that at present they are not being managed.

But the service institution is different fundamentally from business in its "business." It is different in its purpose. It has different values. It needs different objectives, and it makes a different contribution to society. Performance and results are quite different in a service institution from what they are in a business. Managing for performance is the one area in which the service institution differs significantly from a business.

We have no coherent theory of institutions and their management that would encompass the service institution. Compared to the work done in business management over the last seventy years, little has been done on the management of the service institution. All we can attempt so far is a first sketch.

We do understand why the service institution has difficulty in performing. And we can define what is needed to offset the built-in obstacles in the service institution to performance and results.

There are three popular explanations for the common failure of service institutions to perform:

- their managers aren't businesslike;
- they need better men; and
- their objectives and results are intangible.

All service institutions are threatened by the tendencies to cling to yesterday rather than to slough it off, and to put their best and ablest people on defending what no longer makes sense or serves a purpose. Government is particularly prone to this disease.

Underlying traditional political theory is the axiom that the functions of government are eternal. There is an implicit belief, held almost with the strength of dogma, that whatever government does is for all times. Yet government is a human activity. Everything human beings do, except their biological and spiritual functions, obsoletes sooner or later. The proper rule for government today, as for all other institutions, is not, "Whatever we do we'll do forever"; the proper rule is,

"Whatever we do today will in all likelihood be a candidate for abandonment within a fairly short period of years."

CONCLUSION

Drucker writes, "Rarely in human history has any institution emerged as quickly as management or had as great an impact so fast. In less than one hundred fifty years, management has transformed the social and economic fabric of the world's developed countries. It has created a global economy. The fundamental task of management remains the same: to make people capable of joint performance through common goals, common values, the right structure, and the training and development they need to perform and to respond to change. But the very meaning of this task has changed, if only because the performance of management has converted the workforce from one composed largely of unskilled labourers to one of highly educated knowledge workers. After World War II we began to see that management is not business management. It pertains to every human effort that brings together in one organizations people of diverse knowledge and skills."

He is rightly called 'the man who invented the corporate society. He is recognized management thinker even in the USSR. D. Gvishiani, the Soviet author in his book, "Organisation and Management: A Sociological Analysis of Western Theories", has mentioned the contributions of Peter Drucker very prominently.

He says, "Drucker shows a certain farsightedness and understanding of the development prospects of modern production when he opposes the view that the worker is no more than an appendage of the machine. Moved by the desire to strengthen the position of capitalism he endeavours at the same time to give due consideration also to some objective trends in production management. Drucker, therefore, tells the industrialists not to fear a limited participation of the workers in the management of production processes. . . He warns them that if they do not abandon that fear, the consequences may be fatal to them. Drucker realizes that the progress of industrial production demands that the sphere of management be extended and that it should enlist the help of more people at present engaged in the process of production, since isolated individuals are unable to carry out the complex state of operations linked with the management of modern industry. Drucker fails to see, however, that the capitalist mode of production is organically hostile to this objectively developing tendency. On the contrary, he endeavours to prove that the capitalist system of management promotes a democratization of management.

"He is certainly the greatest management philosopher of any time. He has had extraordinarily perceptive insights . . . 'management by objectives', 'control by self-control', 'federal decentralization' and many others. These insights have had great impact on practice and on management thinking."

— *Harold Koontz*

Relevance

Peter F. Drucker has all along been concerned with the 'futurity'. He bases his forecasts on the present actions and decisions. He is not concerned with predictions, though he extrapolates from past and present situations. He identifies the major trends by which the society can find ways and means for better survival. He is obsessed by the rapid pace of the development of technology and its effect on society. He does not profess resistance to change. In his opinion change is inevitable. How we live with it and what we do with it is the measure of us as civilized people. His books, 'The New Society' and the 'Age of Discontinuity' reflect his thinking on the technological developments and its likely impact on society. The explosion of knowledge in behavioural and physical sciences and technology, in Drucker's view, make projection much less prediction impossible. It is almost impossible to foresee the shape of things to come in view of the complexity and profoundness of the revolutionary changes occurring in the society at a terrific pace. In his view, we can only try to understand the nature of discontinuities in historical perspective and develop a philosophy of life which can cope with the changes, nay build up a better society. Mankind should take change as a challenge and try to cope with it.

Peter Drucker is famous for his prophetic prophecies and startling observations. His remarks and utterances sometimes are very pungent. His following observations and cryptic remarks amply bear this out:

"If you have too many problems, may be you should go out of business. There is no law that says a company must last forever."

"For twenty-five years the bona-fide liberal has been screaming for true internationalism. He got it—the multinational corporation—in a form he didn't like."

To Drucker, management is a universal force. Good management is our best hope for world peace. He says that quality of life, technological progress, and world peace are all the products of good management. Drucker feels that 'management plays such a central role in our lives Assessing Drucker's contribution to management thought, Tom Peters has said: "Knowledge is cumulative. Our debt to Peter Drucker knows no limit." Another critic expresses his viewpoint. "Drucker has done for several generations of managers. He taught the care and feelings of the enterprise. And, most important, managers listened and learned." Peter Drucker is no doubt the first philosopher to present in an organized way the role, nature and functions of management. He made the management 'a dynamic and life-giving elements in every business' Drucker will be remembered for centuries for his unique and creative contribution to management thinking.

His writings would always remain relevant for all times to come. He directed the whole of his life to research, teaching and consultancy of management which he uses in wider sense and not merely business enterprizes. His main emphasis in innovation deserves appreciation.

In sharp contrast to the nineteenth century, however, innovation from now on will have to be built into existing organizations. Large businesses—and equally large public-service institutions—will have to become increasingly capable of organizing themselves for innovation as well as for administration.

Innovation is not a technical term. It is an economic and social term. Its criterion is not science or technology, but a change in the economic or social environment, a change in the behaviour of people as consumers or producers, as citizens, as students or as teachers, and so on. Innovation creates new wealth or new potential of action rather than new knowledge. This means that the bulk of innovative efforts will have to come from the places that control the manpower and the money needed for development and marketing, that is, from the existing large aggregation of trained manpower and disposable money-existing businesses and existing public-service institutions.

These various innovative organizations are very different indeed in their structures, their businesses, their characteristics, and even their organizations and management philosophies. But they do have certain characteristics in common—

1. Innovating organizations know what "innovation" means.
2. Innovative organizations understand the dynamics of innovation.
3. They have an innovative strategy.
4. They know that innovation requires objectives, goals, and measurements that are different from the objectives, goals, and measurements of a managerial organization, and appropriate to the dynamics of innovation.
5. Management, especially top management, plays a different role and has a different attitude in an innovative organization.
6. The innovative organization is structured differently and set-up differently from the managerial organization.

The innovative organization, the organization that resists stagnation rather than change, is a major challenge to management, private and public. That such organizations are possible, we can assert with confidence; there are enough of them around. But how to make such organizations general, how to make them productive for society, economy, and individual alike, is still largely an unsolved task. There is every indication that the period ahead will be an innovative one, one of rapid change in technology, society economy, and institutions. There is every indication, therefore, that the innovative organization will have to be developed into a central institution for the last quarter of the twentieth century.

What is needed to break out of the straitjacket of old slogans and old issues is management performance. This first requires performance as a technocrat. It requires performance that makes the manager's organization capable of supplying to society and economy the contribution for the sake of which it exists, such as economic goods and services and the capital fund for tomorrow. But it also requires performance beyond the immediate mission, beyond technocracy: performance in making work productive and the worker achieving and performance with respect to the quality of life. But above all, it has to be performance with respect to the quality of life. But above all, it has to be performance with respect to the role and function of the manager. If he is to remain—as he should—the manager of an autonomous institution, he must accept that he is a public man. He must accept the moral responsibility of organization, the responsibility of making individual strengths productive and achieving.

Bibliography

A.H. Maslow, Motivation and Personality, Harper & Row, New York, 1954.

Adam Smith, An Equiry into the Nature and Causes of the Wealth of Nations, (London, A. Strahan, & T. Cadell, 1793.

Administration Review, "Time and Public Administration", *Public Administration Review,* 41(1), 1981, pp. 115-19.

Administration Review, Nov.-Dec., 1911, Vol. 31, No. 6, pp. 106-111.

Al-Koubaisy, Amer, "The Classical *vs.* Modern Organization Theories in Developing Countries," *Development Policy and Administration Review,* 4(1) Jan.-June, 78, pp. 50-64.

Aiyar, S.P. and Marina Pinto, "Humanistic ethics in the writings of Chester Barnard", *Administrative Change,* Vol. 12, Jan. 1985, No. 2, pp. 182-93.

Albrow, Manin, Bureaucracy, London, Macmillan, 1970.

Allen, L.A., Management and Organisation, New York: McGraw-Hill Book Company, 1958.

American Academy of Political and Social Science, 1968, pp. 128-39.

Argyris, Chris, "Double Loop Learning in Organizations", *Harvard Business Review,* Vol. 55, No. 5, 1977, pp. 115-25.

Argyris, Chris, "Interpersonal Barriers to Decision-Making", *Harvard Business Review,* Vol. 22, No. 2, pp. 84-97.

Argyris, Chris, "Making the Undiscussable and its Undiscussability Discussable," *Public Administration Review,* Vol. 40, May-June, 1980, p. 205.

Argyris, Chris, "Organisational Effectiveness Under Stress," *Harvard Business Review,* Vol. 38, No. 3, 1960, pp. 137-46.

Argyris, Chris, "Personality *vs.* Organization", *Organizational Dynamics,* Vol. 3, No. 2, 1974, pp. 3-17.

Argyris, Chris, "The Fusion of an Individual with the Organization", *American Sociological Review,* Vol. 19, No. 3, June-July, 1954, pp. 267-72.

Argyris, Chris, "The Individual and Organization: Some Problems of Mutual Adjustment", *Administrative Science Quarterly,* Vol. 2, No. 1, June, 1957, pp. 1-22.

Argyris, Chris, "The Organization: What Makes It Heathy", *Harvard Business Review,* Vol. 36, No. 6, 1958, pp. 107-16.

Argyris, Chris, "Understanding Human Behaviour in Organizations: One Viewpoint." In Manson Haire, (Eds.), Modern Organization Theory, New York: Wiley, 1959, pp. 115-54.

Argyris, Chris, Executive Leadership, New York, Harper, 1953.

Argyris, Chris, Integrating the Individual and the Organisation, New York, Wiley, 1964.

Argyris, Chris, Interpersonal Competence and Organization Behaviour, London, Tavistock Publication, Dorsey Press, 1962.

Argyris, Chris, Intervention Theory and Method: A Behavioural Science View, Reading (Mass), Addison-Wesley, 1970.

Argyris, Chris, Management and Organizational Development: The Path From XA to YB, New York, McGraw-Hill Book Company, 1971.

Argyris, Chris, Organization and Innovation, Homewood III, R.D. Irwin, 1965.

Argyris, Chris, "Some Limits to Ralional Man Organization Theory", *Public Administration Review,* Vol. 33, No. 3, (May-June, 1973), pp. 253-67.

Argyris, Chris, Understanding Organisational Behaviour, Homewood III, Dorsey, 1960.

Argyris, Chris, and Donald A. Schon, Theory in Practice: Increasing Professional Effectiveness, London, Jossey Bass Publishers, 1974.

Argyris, Chris, Integrating the Individual and the Organization, New York: Wiley, 1964.

Argyris, Chris, Management and Organizational Development: The Path from XA to YB. New York. McGraw-Hill, 1971.

Argyris, Chris, Personality and Organization, New York. Harper and Row, 1957.

Argyris, Chris and Donald A. Schon, Organizational Learning: A Theory of Action Perspectiveness, Reading. Mass: Addison-Wesley, 1978.

Arora, Ramesh K., (Ed) Administrative Theory, New Delhi, Indian Institute of Public Administration, 1984.

Arora, Ramesh K., (Ed.). Perspectives in Administration Theory, New Delhi, Associated Publishing House, 1979.

Arora, Ramesh K., Comparative Public Administration: An Ecological Approach, New Delhi, Associated Publishing House, 1972.

Bagozzi, Richard P. and Lynn W. Phillips, "Representing and Testing Organizational Theories: A Holistic Construal", *Administrative Science Quarterly*, Vol. 27, No. 3, Sept. 1982, pp. 459-89.

Bailey, Stephen K., "Objectives of the Theory of Public Administration" in Charlesworth, James C., (Eds.), Theory and Practice of Public Administration: Scope, Objectives and Methods, Philadelphia.

Baker, R.J.S., Administrative Theory and Public Administration, London, Hutchinson University Library, 1972.

Baker, R.J.S., Ray Standard and Dodd, William E., (Eds.), The Public Papers of Woodrow Wilson: "College and State," New York, Harper & Bros, 1925.

Barnard, Chester I., Organisation and Management, Cambridge, Massachusetts, Harvard University Press, 1948.

Barnard, Chester I., The Functions of the Executive, Cambridge, Mass, Harward University Press, 1938.

Barnard, The Functions of the Executive, Harvard Univ. Press Cambridge Mass, 1935,

Bedeian, Anhur G., The Administrative Writings of Henri Fayol: A Bibliographic Investigation, Monticello, III: Vane Bibliographies, 1979.

Bendics, Reinhard and Fisher, Lloyd H., "The Perspectives of Elton Mayo", *The Review of Economics and Statistics*, Vol. 31, No. 4, Nov., 1949, pp. 312-19.

Bendix, Reinhard, Maxweber, An Intellectual Portrait, Garden City, New York, Doubleday, 1960.

Bennis, Warren G., "Leadership Theory and Administrative Behaviour: The Problem of Authority", *Administrative Science Quarterly*, Vol. IV, No. 3, Dec., 1959, pp. 259-301.

Bhargava, B.S., "Riggs' Concept of Formalism", Prashasnika, Vol. VI, No. 4, Oct.-Dec., 1977, pp. 4-11.

Blake, Robert R. and Mouton, James S., The Management Grid: Key Orientations for Achieving Production through People, Houston, Gulf Publishing Company, 1946.

Blan, Peter, M., Bureaucracy in Modern Society, New York, Random House, 1962.

Blan, Peter, M., The Dynamics of Bureaucracy, Chicago, University of Chicago Press, 1955.

Blau, Peter M., "Critical Remarks on Weber's Theory of Authority", *American Political Science Review*, Vol. LVII, No. 2, 1963, pp. 305-16.

Boulding, Kenneth E., "Evidences for an Administrative Science", *Administrative Science Quarterly*, Vol. 3, No. I, June, 1958, pp. 1-22.

Bourgeois, V. Warren and Craig C. Pinder, "Contrasting Philosophical Perspectives in Administrative Science: A Reply to Morgan", *Administrative Science Quarterly*, Vol. 28. No. 4, Dec., 1983, pp. 608-13.

Bowers, D.G. and S.E., Seashore, "Predicting Organizational Effectiveness with a Four Factor Theory of Leadership", *Administrative Science Quarterly*, Vol. XI, No. 2, 1966, pp. 238-63.

Bowman, James S., "Managerial Theory and Practice: The Transfer of Knowledge in Public Administration", *Public Administration Review*, Vol. 38, No.6, Nov.-Dec. 1978, pp. 563-70.

Brady, James R., "Improving the Thing of Administration: Counsel and Confusion from the Literature", *Chinese Journal Administration*, May, 1981, pp. 1-8.

Bragden, Henry W., Woodrow Wilson: The Academic Years, Cambridge, Massachusetts, Harvard University Press, 1967.

Breeze, John D. and Frederick C. Miner, "Henri Fayol: A New Definition of Administration", Academy of Management Proceedings, 1980, pp. 110-13.

Brodie, M.B., "Henri Fayol: Administration Industrielle et Generale: A re-interpretation", *Public Administration*, 40, Autumn, 1962, pp. 311-317.

Brodie, M.B., Fayol on Administration, London, Lyon, Grant and Green, 1967.

Brooks, Stephell, "The Western Marxist Critique of Organisation Theory: Towards a Rebuttal", *The Indian Journal of Public Administration,* Vol. 28 (4), Oct.-Dec. pp. 767-82.

Brown, Douglas, J., The Human Nature of Organization, New York, Amacom, 135 W. 50th St., 1973.

Buchrig, Edward H., "Woodrow Wilson to 1902: A Review Essay", *The American Political Science Review,* Vol. 67, No. 2, June, 1973, pp. 589-91.

Butterfield, D. Anthony, and George F. Farris, "The Likert Organisational Profile: Methodological Analysis and Test of System 4 Theory in Brazil", *Journal of Applied Psychology,* Vol. 59, 1974, pp. 15-23.

Caiden, Gerald E., The Dynamics of Public Administration: Guidelines to Current Transformations in Theory and Practice, New York, Holt, Rinehart and Winston, Inc., 1971.

Caldwell, Lynton K., "Methodology in the Theory of Public Administration", in Charlesworth, James C., (Eds.), Theory and Practice of Public Administration Scope Objectives, and Methods, Philadelphia, *American Academy of Political and Social Sciences,* 1968, pp. 205-22.

Carey, Alex, "The Hawthorne Studies: A Radical Criticism", *American Sociological Review,* Vol. 32, No. 3, June, 1967, pp. 403-16.

Centinals, "Continuities and Culture", *Public Administration Review,* 43(2) March-April, 1983, pp. 99-107.

Chapman, Richard, A., "Prismatic Theory in Public Administration: A Review of Theories of Fed W.

Riggs", *Public Administration,* Vol. 44, Winter, 1966, pp. 415-33.

Chi-Yuen Wu, "Public Administrators and Public Policy-Making", *International Review Administrative Sciences,* 44(4), 1978, pp. 333-46.

Chitlallgi, B.M., A Study of Administration 1987: Centenary of Woodrow Wilson's Essay, *Indian Journal of Public Administration,* Vol. 33, No. 4, Oct.-Dec. 1987, pp. 913-917.

Chowdhury, Mustafa, "Weber's Ideal Type of Bureaucracy", *The Indian Journal of Public Administration,* 30(1) Jan.-March 1984, pp. 177-83.

Chris Argyris, Human Proclems with Budgets, *Harward Business Review,* January-February, 1953.

Copley, Frank, B., Fredric W. Taylor: Father of Scientific Management, 2 Vols., New York, Harpert Bros., 1923.

Crozier, Michel, The Bureaucratic Phenomenon, Chicago, The University of Chicago Press, 1964.

Dale, Ernest, Management: Theory and Practice, New York, McGraw-Hill Book Company, 1965.

Douglas McGregor, The Human Side of Enterprise, McGraw Hill Book Co., New York, 1960.

Downs, Anthony, Inside Bureaucracy, Boston, Little Brown, 1967.

Dror, Yehezkel, Design for Policy Sciences, New York, American Elsevier Publishing Company, Inc., 1971.

Dror, Yehezkel, Policy-making Under Adversity, New Brunswick, Transaction Books, 1985.

Dror, Yehezkel, Public Policy-making Re-examined, (New Edn.) New Brunswick, NJ, Transactions Books, 1983.

Dror, Yehezkel, Ventures in Policy Sciences: Concepts and Applications, New York, American Elsevier Publishing Company, Inc., 1971.

Drucker, Peter, F., Management: Tasks. Responsibilities, Practices, Bombay, Allied Publishers, 1975.

Drucker, Peter, F., The Practice of Management, London, Mercury Books, 1965.

Dubin, Robert, Human Relations in Administration, Englewood Cliffs, Prentice-Hall, 1951.

E.F.L. Brech: The Principles and Practice of Management, Longman, 1972.

Edward C. Banfield, "The Decision-Making Scheme," *Public Administrative Review*, Vol. XVII, No. 4, Autumn 1951, pp. 218- 285.

Edward S. Mason, The Corporation in Modern Society, Harvard University Press, Cambridge Mass, 1960.

Elton Mayo, The Social Problems of an Industrial Civilization, Boston, 1943.

Ernest Dale, The Great Orgaisers, New York, 1900.

Etizioni, Amitai, (Ed), Readings on Modern Organizations, Englewood Cliffs, Prentice-Hall, 1969.

Etizioni, Amitai, Creative Experience, London, Longmans Green, 1924.

Etizioni, Amitai, Modern Organizations, Englewood Cliffs, Prentice-Hall, 1964. Follett, Mary P., The New State, London: Langmans Green, 1918.

Etizioni, E., (ed). Complex Organizations, New York, Holt, Rinehart and Winston, 1962.

Fayol, Henri, "The Importance of the Administrative Factor." In Ernest Dale (Eds.), Readings in Management: landmarks and New Frontiers, New York: McGraw-Hill, 1910, pp. 148-49.

Fayol, Henri, The Administrative Theory in the State" in Gullick, L and Urwick, L., (Eds.), Papers on the Science of Administration, New York, Columbia University Press, 1931, pp. 99-114.

FinkJe, Arthur L., "A Discipline in search of Legitimacy," Bureaucrat, 13(2) Summer 1984, pp. 58-60.

Follett, Mary P., 'The Process of Control" in Luther Gulick and L. Urwick, (Eds.), Papers on the Science 01 Administration, New York. Columbia University, Institute of Public Administration 1931, pp. 159-69.

Fox, Douglas, M., "What's Public Administration," *Administrative Science Quarterly*, Vol. 21, June, 1916, pp. 346-52.

Fox, Elliot M., "Mary Parker Follett: The Enduring Contribution," *Public Administration Review*, Vol. XXVIII, No. 6, Nov.-Dec., 1968.

Franke, Richard H. and James, D. Kaul, "The Hawthorne Experiments: First Statistical Interpretation," *American Sociological Review*, Vol. 43, 1918, pp. 623-43.

Fred Harbinson and Charles A. Myers, Management in the Industrial World, New York, 1959.

Fredeick W. Taylor, Principles of Scientific Management, New York, Harper & Bros. 1911.

Freund, Julien, The Sociology of Max Weber, Hammondsworth: Penguin, 1968.

G.P. Asthana, The Groundwork of Management—Nature, Development and Trends, 1972.

Gaus, John Merriman, "Trends in the Theory of Public Administration," *Public Administration Review*, 10 Summer, 1950, pp. 163-68.

George Jr., Claude S., The History of Management Thought, 2nd ed., Prentice-Hall of India Private Limited, 1974.

Golcmbicwski, Robert T., Public Administration as a Developing Discipline, 2 Parts, New York, Marcel Dekker, Inc., 1977.

Gouldner, Alvin, Patterns of Industrial Bureaucracy, Glencoe, Free Press, 1954.

Griffiths, Daniel E., Administrative Theory, Bombay, D.B. Taraporevala Sons & Co. Pvt. Ltd., 1978.

Gruss, Bertram M., Organisations and Their Managing, New York, Free Press, 1968.

Gruss, Bertram M., The Managing of Organisations: The Administrative Struggle, 2 Vol., New York, The Free Press, 1964.

Gulick L. and Urwick, L. Eds. Papers, in the Science of Administration which includes Fayols paper, "The Administrative Theory of the State", Columbia Univ., 1937.

Gulick, Luther, "Democracy and Administration Face the Future", *Public Administration Review*.

Gulick, Luther, "The Dynamics of Public Administrative Today as a Guidelines for the Future," *Public Administration Review*, 43 (3) May-June, 1983, pp. 193-8.

Gvishiani, D., Organisation and Management: A Sociological Analysis of Western Theories, Moscow, Progress Publishers.

Haberman, John, "Discipline Without Punishment, "*Harward Business Review*, Vol. XXXVI, May, 1961, pp. 62-68.

Harold Koontz, The Management Theory of Jungle", in Readings in Management, ed. By Richards/Nilander.

Haynes, Warren W., and Massie, Joseph. L. Management: Analysis. Concepts and Cases, Englewood Cliffs, N.J., Prentice-Hall, Inc., 1961.

Heady, Ferrel, Public Administration: A Comparative Perspective, 2nd Ed., New York, Marcel Dejcker, Inc., 1984.

Henderson, Keilh M., Emerging Synlhuis in American Public Administration, Bombay, Asia Publishing House, 1970.

Henri, Fayol, General and Industrial Management, London, 1.saac Pitman, 1957.

Henry, H. Albers, Principles of Organisation and Management, New York, John Wiley, 1961.

Henry, Nicholas, Public Administration and Public Affairs, Englewood Cliffs, New Jersey, Prentice-Hall, Inc., 1975.

Herbert, A. Simon, Administrative Behaviour, New York, 1947.

Herbert, A. Simon, The New Science of Management Decision, Harper and Row Publishers Incorporated, New York, 1960.

Hersey, Paul and Blanchard, Kenneth, H., Management of Organisational Behaviour: Utilising Human Resources, New Delhi, Prentice-Hall of India Pvt. Ltd., 1974.

Huneryager, S.G. and Heckmann, I.L. (Eds.), Human Relations in Management Bombay, D.B. Taraporevala Sons & Co., 1972.

International Management, McGraw Hill, 1976.

J.B. Say, Criticism of Political Economy, 1817.

J.S. March & Herbert, A. Simon, Organisation, New York, 1958.

James Mill, Elements of Political Economy (3rd Ed.) London, Baldwin Cradock & Joy.

John F. Mee, Management Thought in a Dynamic Economy, New York, 1963.

John J. Tarrant, Drucker: The Man Who Invented the Corporate Society, Boston, 1976.

Joseph Massie, Essentials of Management, New Delhi, 1973.

Koontz, Harold (Eds.), Toward a Unified Theory of Management, New York, McGraw-Hill Book Co., 1964.

Kurt Lewin, Ronald Lippitt and Ralph K. White, "Patterns of Aggressive Behaviour in Experimentally Created Social Climate", *Journal of Social Psychology*, May 1939.

LaLham, Earl., (Eds.), The Philosophy and Politics of Woodrow Wilson, Chicago, University of Chicago Press, 1958.

Likert, R. and Likert, J.G., New Ways of Managing Conflict, New York, McGraw-Hill Book Co., 1976.

Likert, R., New Patterns of Management, New York, McGraw-Hill Book Co., 1961.

Likert, R., Pasl and Future Perspectives on System-4. Ann Arbor, Michigan, Rensis Likert Associates, 1977.

Likert, R., Profile of Organisational Characteristics: Forms, Ann Arbor, Michigan, Rensis Likert Associates, 1977.

Likert, R., The Human Organization, New York, McGraw-Hill Book Co., 1967.

Lyndall, Urwick, The Elements of Administration, New York.

Malick, Sidney and Vanness, Edward H., (Eds.), Concepts and Issues in Administrative Behaviour, Englewood Cliffs, N.J., Prentice Hall, Inc., 1962.

Malterson, Michael T. and Ivaneenich, John M., Management Classics, Santa Monica, Good Year Publishing Co., 1977.

March, James G. and Simon, Herbert A., Organisations, New York, Wiley, 1958.

Marini, Frank (Ed.), Toward a New Public Administration: The Minnowbrook Perspective, Scranton, Pa. Chandler Publishing Co., 1971.

Maslow, A., Motivation and Personality, New York, Harper &. Row, 1954.

Max Weber, The Protestant Ethic and the Spirit of Capitalism (Translation), New York, 1958.

Mayo, George Elton, The Human Problems of Industrial Civilization, Boston, Harvard Business School, 1946, 2nd Ed.

Mayo, George Elton, The Social Problems of Industrial Civilization, London, Routledge & Kegan Paul, 1945.

McGregor, Douglas, Leadership and Motivation, Boston, MIT Press, 1966.

McGregor, Douglas, The Human Side of Enterprise, New York, McGraw-Hill Book Co., 1960.

McGregor, Douglas, The Professional Manager, McGregor Caroline and Bennis, Warren G., (Eds.), New York, McGraw-Hill Book Co., 1967.

Merril, Harwood F., (Ed.), Classics in Management, New York, American Management Association, 1960.

Merton, Robert K., *et. al.*, (Ed.), Reader in Bureaucracy, Glencoe, Free Press, 1952.

Metcalf, Henry C., and Urwick, Lyndall, (Eds.), Dynamic Administration: The Collected Papers of Mary Parker Follett, New York, Harper & Row, 1940.

Miner, John B., Theories of Organisational Structure and Process. Chicago, The Dryden Press, 1982.

Mooney, James D. and Reilev, Alan C. The Principles of Organization, New York, Harper & Brothers, 1939.

Mosher, Frederick C., (Ed.), American Public Administration: Past, Present, Future, Alabama, The University of Alabama Press, 1975.

New Brunswick, Policy-making under Adversity, NJ: Transaction Books, 1985.

New Brunswick, Public Policy Re-examined, NJ: Transaction Books, 1983.

Notes on the Theory of Organisation, in Luther Gulick and Lyndall Urwick (eds.), "Papers on the Science of Administration" Institute of Public Administration, New York, 1937.

Ostrom, Vincent, The Intellectual Crisis in American Public Administration, Alabama, The University of Alabama Press, 1973.

Peter Drucker in *Harward Business Review*, Jan.-Feb. 1967.

Peter F. Drucker, The Practice of Management, New York, 1954.

Peter F. Drucker, Concept of the Corporation, New York, 1946.

Peter F. Drucker, Management: Tasks, Responsibilities Practices, Bombay, 1975.

Peter, F. Mee, "Scientific Management of Economic

Development" in Ettinger (ed.), International Management Handbook.

Public Administration and Development, 2(1), Jan.-Mar. 1982, pp. 59-61.

Rennis, Warren G., Beyond Bureaucracy: Essays on the Development and Evolution of Human Organizations, New York, McGraw-Hill Book Company, 1973.

Rennis, Warren G., Organization Development: Its Nature, Origins and Prospects, Reading, Mass, Addison-Wesley Publishing Company, 1969.

Rensis Likert, New Patterns of Managcment, 1961.

Rensis Likert, Developing Patterns in Management: I, American Management Association, General Management Series No. 178.

Rensis Likert, Motivational Approach to Management Development, *Harward Business Review*, July-August, 1959.

Sethi, Narendra, K., Managerial Dynamics: A Multi-dimensional View, New Delhi, Sterling Publishers Pvt. Ltd., 1978.

Shafritz, Jay M. and Hyde, Albert C., (Eds.) Classics of Public Administration, Oak Park, Illinois, Moore Publishing Company, 1978.

Simon, H.A., Administrative Behaviour: A Study of Decision-Making Processes in Administrative Organization, New York, The Free Press, 1957.

Simon, Herbet, A. in a Symposium in Los Angles, Nov. 8-9, 1962.

Simon, Herbert A., "Approaching the Theory of Management," In Harold Koontz (Eds.), Toward a Unified Theory of Management, New York: McGraw-Hill, 1964.

Simon, Herbert, Models of Man, New York, Wiley, 1957.

Simon, Herbert, Smilhsburg, Donald W. and Thompson, Victor A., Public Administration, New York, Knopf, 1950.

Simon, Herbert, The Shape of Automation, New York, Harper, and Row, 1965.

Simon, Herbert, TM New Science of Management Decision, New York, Harper and Row, 1960.

Simon, Herbert, TM Science of to Artificial, Mass, Mil Press, 1969.

Singh, R.N., Management Thought and Thinkers, Delhi, Sultan Chand & Sons, 1977.

Taylor, Fredrick W., Scientific Management, New York, Harper, 1947.

Tillett, T. Kempner and G. Wills (eds.): Management Thinkers, Penguin Books, 1970.

Ucrih, H.H. and Mills, C. Wright, (Ed.), From Max Weber: Essays in Sociology, New York, Oxford University Press, 1946.

Urwick, L. and Breck, E.F.L., TM Making of Scientific Management, 3 Vols., London, Management Publications Trust, 1949.

Urwick, Lyndall F., Notes on the Theory of Organization, New York, American Management Association, 1952.

Urwick, Lyndall F., The Elements of Administration, New York, Harper, 1943.

Urwick, Lyndall F., The Golden Book of Administration, London, Newsman Neame Ltd., 1956.

Urwick, Lyndall F., The Life and Work of Elton Mayo, London, Urwick, 1960.

Urwick, The Elements of Administration.

W.B. Wolf, How to Understand Management: An Introduction to Chester I. Barnard, Lucas Publishers, Los Angels 1968.

Waldo, Dwight, (Eds.), Public Administration in a Time of Turbulence, Scranton-Chandler, 1971.

Waldo, Dwight, The Administrative State, New York, The Ronald Press Company, 1948.

Waldo, Dwight, The Study of Public Administration, Gareten City, New York, Doubleday, 1955.

Weber, Marianne, Max Weber: A Biography, Translated and edited by Harry Zohn, New York: Wiley, 1975.

Weber, Max, Economy and Society, Vols. I-III, translated and edited by Guenther Roth and Claus Wittich, New York: Bedminster Press, 1968.

Weber, Max, The Theory of Social and Economic Organization, Glencoe III, Free Press, 1947,

Weber, Max, The Theory of Social and Economic

Organization, Trans., A.H. Henderson, and ed. Talcott Parsons, New York, Oxford University Press, 1946.

Whyte, William F., Man and Organization, Homewood III, Richard D. Irwin, Inc., 1959.

Whyte, William H., Jr., The Organization Man, New York, Simon & Schuster, 1956.

William Kemp, Economic Development & Economic Planning in India, Bombay, quoting D. Narayan.

Wolf, William B., How to Understand Management: An Introduction to Chester I. Barnard, Los Angeles, Lukas Publishers, 1968.

Wolf, William B., The Basic Barnard: An Introduction to Chester I. Barnard and his Theories of Organisation and Management, Ithaca. New York, Cornell University Press, 1974.

Wren, Daniel A., The Evolution of Management Thought, New York, The Ronald Press Company, 1972.

Index